EDUCATING WITH
THE INTERNET

Using Net Resources at School and Home

Second Edition

EDUCATING WITH THE INTERNET

Using Net Resources at School and Home

Second Edition

NANCY SKOMARS

CHARLES RIVER MEDIA, INC.
Rockland, Massachusetts

Executive Editor: Jenifer Niles
Interior Design/Comp.: Reuben Kantor & Lydia Zabarsky
Cover Design: Sherry Stinson
Printer: InterCity Press, Rockland, MA.

CHARLES RIVER MEDIA, INC.
P.O. Box 417
403 VFW Drive
Rockland, Massachusetts 02370
781-871-4184
781-871-4376 (FAX)
chrivmedia@aol.com
http://www.charlesriver.com

This book is printed on acid-free paper.

Nancy Skomars. *Educating with the Internet:
    Using Net Resources at School and Home. Second Edition*
ISBN: 1-886801-76-2

Printed in the United States of America
99 00 01 02 03 7 6 5 4 3 2 1

CHARLES RIVER MEDIA titles are available for site license or
bulk purchase by institutions, user groups, corporations, etc.
For additional information, please contact the Special Sales
Department at 781-871-4184.

For my Mom, Janice Connick Skomars

Your spirit lives on

CONTENTS

ACKNOWLEDGMENTS

My thanks to Karen Craig, Principal of SBHS, for asking me to come back and try new things. To Jenifer for keeping me on schedule long distance editing at its finest! To Janet Travis who is mastering all the new technology and helping bring the kids online. To the teachers and students at SBHS who are willing to give this new technology a try.

My gratitude, as always, to my family. You are the best. And for Jason, you make this all worthwhile.

PREFACE

"Content may be why people visit a site. But community is why they stay."
—Tom Rielly, CEO of "Planet Out" New Media, 1998

Night and day. That's the difference between my two schools this past year. One had more technology and connectivity than most schools will ever see, while the other falls in the category of a have-not school where most teachers have never had a computer in their classrooms, much less a computer connected with the Internet.

Both of these schools have a mandate that implies they will become "Digital High Schools." What that means in reality is often quite different than what was intended with the first designs on paper. The issues both schools face are the same, though perhaps in different degrees. The problems they face in becoming digital are different.

How close can your school or classroom come to being "digital?" How do you know when you've achieved the state of being digital? Is one computer in a classroom enough to achieve your goals? How do you parcel out technology that is limited by budget constraints? What do you buy? Where do you put it? How do you make the best use of the tools? What *are* the tools? How do you monitor the use of your technology to ensure that it's used appropriately and effectively? How do you know where to begin?

How do you take a school from a state of nonconnectivity to full connectivity? How do you assess students' work when the Internet becomes part of their tool chest? How do you adjust your time, your curriculum, your teaching style, and your attitudes?

One thing is certain: using the Internet in your classroom will bring about changes — in you, in your kids, and in what and how you teach.

How do you prepare? Adapt? Grow? How do nondigital teachers work with digital kids in their world? What can you expect when the Internet becomes part of your class?

These are some of the issues both schools face, and most are addressed in this book.

Wonderful advances are being made in so many aspects of the Internet. The new streaming audio and video present live concerts, live radio, talks with stars and experts, U.S. space shuttle transmissions as they happen, speeches, films, animations, and simulations. These are all in their infancy. Keep your eyes on this medium as it changes the way we communicate with one another and as it changes the way we, as educators, do business.

As we move into a time when the Internet is an integral part of students' private lives, when we see more and more students with e-mail and home pages, we must learn more about this world and what it is becoming.

If projections are true that in a short period of time, students will be able to talk to computers and have them type or speak what they say, or listen as a computer reads them a story, then there are some powerful issues to be addressed. If our reluctant learners can buy a machine that reads to them or writes for them, what will that do to their skills? And what do we want to do about it?

Issues abound with this new technology, and I urge you and your staff to discuss them as often as possible and in as many forms of communication as possible. And by all means, use e-mail!

For those of you just getting online, prepare to be amazed. Long-time users, I hope you've found new and exciting ways to use this tool and are looking to expand.

For all of you, I hope this book is of help.

Continue to give your kids the world . . . it's theirs, you know. If we're quick, they'll let us be part of it.

INTRODUCTION

After another full year of online use just past, new issues confront us as well as new challenges. This book has been updated to focus on some of those issues, to review the changes in Internet technology and computer hardware, and to showcase some of the wonderful new sites that have emerged to help us make this technology one more tool our students use efficiently and wisely. There is also a new chapter at the end on how to develop a vision for your school, and how to address the issues of integrating technology including taining, assessment, and changes in curriculum.

In this book, you will learn the following:

- **Getting connected.** What do you buy, how many computers do you need, where do you put them?
- **Developing a vision.** What does it mean to be a "Digital School?"
- **Training your staff and students.** How much time do you need, how do you train, what do you train them in?
- **Using your connectivity.** How do you incorporate the Net into your classroom?
- **E-mail and your students.** Do they all need it, and how can they use it effectively?
- **Avoiding the road kill on the highway.** How do you keep the kids away from inappropriate sites?
- **Browsing.** Which browser do you use, and how do you use it effectively?
- **Searching,** Which search tool is right for which kids and which needs?
- **Assessment.** How do you give kids a grade when it's not all cut and dried anymore?
- **Creating Web pages.** What do you use, and what do you create?

This book will also present:

- **Sample lesson ideas** for incorporating the Net in your class.
- An abundance of **sites** for all we teach to get you started.

Do I still feel that if you give your kids the Net, you give them the world? Absolutely, and so do they. Don't delay. The longer you and they are offline, the more out of touch your kids become with the emerging digital world. This is the world they will inherit, work in, and control. It's their world, just as the world of TV was ours and shaped us for generations to come. The Internet will do the same for them.

Adopt it. Adapt it. Become part of it. If you don't, your kids will be left behind.

Hardware

The first step to acquiring all this Net information is to get online using the right equipment. Although I can't tell you what computer to buy, I can make general recommendations to help you find the best machine. Just remember, hardware is constantly being improved in memory, as well as in speed of the processor, modem, and CD-ROM drive. Expect rapid changes, and make sure you can upgrade your computer with more memory over time.

I've noticed that since Windows 98 came out, the prices of PCs have dropped dramatically. Some computers that will make great starter machines, with Pentium processors, are selling for under $1000. Because educational budgets are so tight, try to find some of these bargains and upgrade them over time.

About the new Macs: One of my labs will have the new Mac G3s. iMacs might present a low-cost solution to getting computers into the classroom. I also think WebTV is worth looking into for another low-cost solution to connectivity.

Whatever you do, hang on to your Apple IIE, IIGS, 386, and 486 machines. They are great for software and especially for keyboarding and word processing. Keep track of Microsoft, which recently mentioned the possibility of turning 386 machines into Internet-ready machines.

This rule still applies to new hardware: Get the most memory, the fastest processor and CD-ROM drive, the largest monitor, and the fastest Internet connection you can.

The guidelines listed here are for bottom-line optimum use. Faster machines than those listed exist.

Essentials: Memory and Speed

Computer essentials are memory and speed. Get as much memory as you can already built into the machine. As for speed, Pentium II processors are the norm now for PCs and clones, but I understand that Intel has something faster in the works.

Computers used to be described as having bytes of memory, then kilobytes (thousands of bytes — a *byte* is eight bits, and it takes eight bits to define a single letter of the alphabet). Soon, they had *megabytes* (millions of bytes) of memory, and now computers, disk drives, and network servers have *gigabytes* (billions of bytes) of memory or storage capacity.

Buy a hard drive with a gigabyte of storage or more. Also, buy a computer with as much RAM (random access memory) as possible. RAM can be accessed instantly by your computer's CPU, or central processing unit — the main brain of the machine. RAM is measured in megabytes. Your computer should have anywhere from 8 (on the very low side) to 64 megabytes of RAM located on the motherboard. When you need more RAM, you can purchase plug-in modules that are easy to install.

Also, check the speed of your CPU. The more megahertz (MHz), the faster the computer. Make sure you buy a computer with at least a 166-MHz processor. Some of the newer ones come with better than 200-MHz processors, so watch for those.

With the advances being made online in streaming audio, *sound* is important on a computer, so purchase one with a sound card and external speakers. The industry standard for IBM and compatibles is a SoundBlaster 64. Get that or something comparable. Macs have their own built-in sound and speakers.

CD-ROM drives should also be as fast as possible. A 16x speed is the minimum to buy. Today's faster drives are 24x.

Suggested Minimum System

16MB SDRAM memory

2.1-GB hard drive

15-inch monitor

16x CD-ROM drive

33.6 data/fax modem

SoundBlaster 64 or equivalent

Modems

Modems allow one computer to connect with another so they can exchange information over telephone lines. They are either internal or external. The essentials are speed and "plug and play" capability. "Plug and play" is technology for newbies (people who are new to technology) making installation easier. A "plug and play" modem is usually smart enough to configure itself to your system.

It's probably worth the money to get the fastest modem possible. The current top speed is 56 kbps (kilobytes per second). However, modems operating at 33.6 and 28.8 kbps are satisfactory.

I have been online at home with a 14.4 and a 33.6. With a 14.4, you might as well forget loading Internet sites that are graphics intensive. Either that, or begin loading a page, mow your lawn, then come back and enjoy! The 33.6 was not bad at loading graphics pages, but the wait did exceed the usual 8 seconds most Net users will give a site to load!

Your computer retailer should be able to help you with any configuration problems you might encounter. If the modem is already part of the computer, you're one step closer to being connected. For years, Hayes modems have set industry standards, and many modems are advertised as being "Hayes-compatible," so look for either a Hayes or a Hayes-compatible modem.

Monitors

A good monitor can make the difference between enjoying and disliking the Net experience. Monitor screen sizes were a standard 13 diagonal inches for years. However, they've been growing to keep up with the new multimedia capabilities of CD-ROMS and streaming video on the Internet. Sizes vary from 12.1- to 31inch. A 17- or 21-inch monitor is a nice size for a good viewing experience. Also, look for monitors advertised as "low radiation" and "easy on your eyes."

Monitors at School

Student stations should have a monitor like those listed above. If at all possible, have at least one or two larger monitors, 31-inch or better, positioned in such a way that all your kids can see the screens and Internet or CD-ROM content. If you only have one computer, do what you can to add the largest viewing screen possible.

IBM or Mac?

In deciding which platform to buy, consider the factors of technical support and school support. At both my most recent schools, both platforms were being used. For graphics, both CAD (computer-assisted design) and graphics arts programs, Macs were used. Macintosh has always maintained strong support in the graphics areas. Macs were also the computer of choice of the core subjects, partly because they had already been using older Macs, Apple IIGSs, or IIEs, or because of software needs.

In our banking and finance, MIS, computer programming, and STS areas, PCs were used, and most had been upgraded to Windows 95.

To make student work available on either platform, we used Microsoft Office software for word processing, spreadsheets, and PowerPoint presentations. Data bases were created with Microsoft Access on the PCs and with ClarisWorks on the Macs.

SOFTWARE

Your decisions for software purchases might be determined by the number of connected computers you have. If you have one computer per student, or perhaps a 2-to-1 ratio, and money to spend on software, then purchase those products that either enhance your subject and are viewable by all students at once, or are so terrific that one or two kids at a time can benefit from them. With money and time in short supply, I tend to look at software and ask, "If I give up the same amount of time online as it takes to adequately use this software, will it be as valuable an experience for the kids?"

If you feel that time is better spent online than with a given piece of software, then look at other software.

Many of your computer systems will come with packages of software. These vary and can include an encyclopedia, word processing, Internet connection packages, or others. In some cases, you can specify which pieces of software you want, but don't sacrifice speed and memory for software.

If you have an internal modem, the software will come preloaded on your machine. If you buy an external modem, the software will be part of the package. Your *Internet Service Provider* (to be covered soon) will give you the software you need to connect to their service, and technical support should be available not only from the company that sold you the computer, but also from the company that built it, and from your Internet Service Provider.

Phone Lines

At Home

If you have one phone line with call waiting, be prepared to be bumped offline if someone calls when you're online. Modem software can block incoming calls while you're online if you program your modem or software to use the call blocking code *70. You can do this with most modem software with the click of a mouse button. However, a phone line dedicated to the Internet is the best way to go.

At School

A phone line can be one of the hardest things to get installed in a school. Some teachers have told me they believe they'll never see a phone line in their classroom. If this is your case, you must work to change this. A dedicated line in your classroom is essential if your entire school is not being wired. You can use a line that requires dialing 9 to get an outside line, but you might be bumped off by incoming calls. A special, high-speed T1 or T3 line is the fastest way for your students to access Internet information. Such a line is expensive, meaning you must have serious commitment from your school's administration — but it's absolutely the way you must ultimately head.

Options

You might consider new, less expensive systems that don't use a costly computer to get you online. Both Phillips Electronics and Sony have designed an Internet device that connects directly to a classroom TV.

The Internet Terminal from WebTV, newly purchased by Microsoft, sells for less than $300. Make sure you include the optional keyboard for direct access to all Web sites. WebTV comes bundled with 500 sites in memory, accessible by remote control. With the device, online access and an e-mail address costs the same $19.95 a month as most other providers. Although your kids won't be able to create Web pages, you can get them online and use sites in class or print what you need — and it's easier on your budget.

WebTV Specifications

33.6 kbps, V.34bis modem

112MHz, 64 bit, R4640 RISC processor

Custom WebTV graphics processor

16-bit stereo for CD-quality audio

WebTV browser compatible with HTTP, MIME, HTML

Auto-update keeps browser current

Supports MIDI embedded audio files

Telephone line (RJ-11)

Keyboard input

The WebTV Port connector can support printers and cable modems. The built-in "smart card" slot allows shopping and banking now, with other transactions possible in the future.

Sega Game Gear also has a device that connects between its Game Gear product and your TV to give you access. This device should sell for under $300.

Look for these alternatives to the cost of getting online, but first, get a phone line into your classroom.

Also consider looking into some of the new computers that sell for less than $600, with a monitor. These computers are designed for word processing, spreadsheet, and Internet use. Check these sites for more information

MICRO STORES SELLING THE POWER SPEC COMPUTER

```
http://www.microcenter.com/
http://www.powerspec.com/
```

EGGHEAD SOFTWARE SELLING THE PRECISIONTEC LLC—GAZELLE CYRIX

```
http://www.egghead.com/
```

Another possible computer to look at if you're on a tight budget is the new iMac. As of this writing, it's priced below $1300.

NetDay

Across the country, there are grassroots efforts to wire as many class-rooms as possible. Seek them out. Some states are wiring all their schools, while others are working a room or a school at a time, usually starting with the library.

The people from NetDay offer wiring kits. The cost of a kit to wire several rooms varies from $318 to $650 for schools that need special wiring to meet fire code regulations. A single wiring kit provides the equipment you need to run two Category 5 network cables to six classrooms.

Once you get online, go to this address to find out about NetDay:

http://www.explornet.org/netday/

According to the organizers, future plans include:

- Helping schools finish their installations by identifying support partners in your community
- Working with those schools, districts, or states that didn't participate in past NetDays to bring them online
- Looking for training materials and personnel to help teachers and students with their new tools

The NetDay organizers are committed to establishing partnerships between the private sector and the schools to increase classroom use of the Internet.

ABOUT THE LESSONS

THE LESSONS

The lessons you will find throughout this book were developed from my experiences using the Net in the classroom. Many of these lessons have worked well for other instructors, and many are brand new to this edition.

These lessons are intended to help students expand their frames of reference, broaden their knowledge, search for new information, or explore one subject in depth with special emphasis on the logical learning extensions that occur. Some of the sample lessons are designed merely for browsing through a site or subject, while others are designed to build on a concept or expand the use of Internet tools.

How can you make use of the lessons in this book? I know of one teacher, who has a computer in the library, who used the *Romeo and Juliet* lesson by printing out some of the pictures and showing his students the new information he had found on the Net.

Much of your use of the Net will depend on your Net access. Otherwise, all of the lessons serve two purposes:

1. To give you ready-made sets of practice lessons, extended searches, and projects so you and your students can learn the tools of the Web and practice infusing the Net into your classroom.
2. To serve as templates for you to use with your curriculum. Insert your vocabulary, concepts, and knowledge. Add sites you find, and go.

A Note about Grade Levels

I try to indicate the ages I feel are most appropriate for each lesson. I spend very little time with grades K–6, and those of you who do may find that I've estimated on the high or low side. With your guidance, even the youngest children can find their way online. Please adjust the lessons accordingly.

Computer Ratio

Not everyone has an ideal computer setup. As usual, do the best you can with what you have. I once taught computer literacy to 40 high school kids in a room that had once been an art display case. For us, it was a long, thin room with one Apple IIE, a 13-inch monitor, and lots of eye strain. Even if you only have one computer, the wonders of the Net need not be lost to your kids.

My old classroom, at Advanced Technologies Academy, was pretty close to ideal. While the rooms varied as to platform, I used both IBM and Mac, the teacher's stations were the same, and the student/computer ratio was almost always 1-to-1. The teacher's station surrounded the teacher with all the necessary tools to incorporate the Internet and other technologies into the curriculum.

An optimum class for some subjects is not, however, the same as for another. I like having a 1-to-1 ratio, large-screen monitors, VCR, laserdisc player, scanner, full Net access, and a LAN at my disposal. And that is what I had.

At my new school, San Bernardino High School, we're starting from the ground up, but with more students and a much smaller budget. My room will still have at least a 2-to-1 ratio of kids to computers, with Internet access through a firewall. That means some sites will be blocked to us. It remains to be seen how disrupting this may be when students start doing extensive research. I will also have a large monitor, scanner, laserdisc player, and VCR, if I need them.

The other classrooms, the majority of them, will have only one new computer. Either platform was available and departments decided which met their needs. So the question becomes one of what do you do with the lessons in this book and developing lessons of your own, if you have only one computer for your 25–40 kids, or if you have one for each, or if you perhaps have six. Our school is hoping that, ultimately, each classroom will have six Internet computers. So what do you do?

If your school has minimal computers online, using the lesson plans will be challenging, but here are some suggestions:

One computer and no large display capabilities: First use overheads to teach your kids how to type in URLs. Later, expand to teaching search tools, bookmarks, folders, copy and paste. Print out graphics and information and add to your lessons what you find on the Net. Beyond teaching the tools, if you cannot display, try putting together a PowerPoint presentation using Net resources to introduce new concepts and provide URLs for connected kids who can help print information and pictures. If you can't create a PowerPoint, make overheads (you will need a word processor for this).

My general rule is to present, in any way possible, as often as possible, all that I find to broaden the kids' understanding of each concept.

Also, connect by e-mail with students and staff and get help with the searching and with the output.

- One computer with display capabilities to full class: Teach by demonstration, but also display the results of typing in URLs, searching, and linking. Display those sites from the lessons that all can see and print what you need from others.
- One computer for every three or four students: Use overheads to instruct on the tools of the Net, then share time online and findings as you work toward a common goal. This is where you begin to divide the tasks of the exploration. With three kids on a computer, one can read the URL, one can type, and one can use the mouse. Rotate the duties and make sure they learn to scan text for pertinent information and find a way to communicate their findings.
- One computer for every two students: Once you've taught the basic Net skills, have one student type the URL while another proofreads. Both can read text and suggest links to follow. They should be given one piece of the exploration and a method of communicating their findings.
- One computer for every student: Everyone gets to participate in an exploration or lesson. Each student must know the browser and basic tools as well as the keyboard. Each student can be assigned one part of the lesson or exploration or work with others on the same aspect.

A great deal of collaboration begins when you take on a lesson or exploration. Expect it and use it.

- One printer: Be selective with output. If you can display graphics on a monitor, don't print them. If not, print the most useful. It's also wise sometimes to copy and paste Internet text into your word processor for faster and shorter printing. Much of your students' output will not be computer generated but on paper, and even then it can be exceptional.

- More than one printer: You can be more creative in your output, printing pages from online, creating brochures, posters, typed essays, newsletters, reports, etc.

Tasks You Will Practice Online

1. **Keyboarding:**	Typing URLs, responding to questions, e-mail
2. **Mouse:**	Using icons, pulldown menu items, links, scroll bars (arrows)
3. **Scanning:**	For keywords or information
4. **Skimming:**	For information or links
5. **Reading:**	For pleasure or information
6. **Copying and pasting:**	Information, graphics, Web design enhancements. This is a good opportunity to teach editing and paraphrasing skills.

How to Avoid Plagiarism

I've been asked several times, with so much information so readily available, what's to keep students from just copying Net information and calling it their own? If I ask a student to simply write a report about a topic, a factual account of something, the kind of thing that lends itself to copy and paste, then I cannot control the output as well.

You'll notice that the lessons I use require more gathering of information that will be synthesized later to solve a problem or answer a question. I want more than the facts. I want the kids to do something with the facts.

GUIDELINES FOR USING THE LESSONS

Each of these lessons can be extended beyond a simple browse or search into assignments with output. Following is a list of the lessons grouped by their activity type with a suggestion of appropriate age groups. You may find that your younger kids are capable of these lessons once they've mastered the tools of the Net. You may simply need to adjust the content for relevance or skill level.

Browsing Practice

To practice using the tools of your browser, learn some of the depth of the Net, and read for purpose.

Time on task: 10–20 minutes

Quick Searches

To practice using search tools, locate information, plan for an outcome.

Time on task: 10–90 minutes

Extended Searches

To build a frame of reference, locate information, cross-reference, practice Internet tools, plan for output.

Time on task: 30 minutes to 1 week with output

Extended Searches with Output

To synthesize information and generate output which displays understanding of concepts and information.

Time on task: 1–2 weeks

Packaged Deals

To add to present curriculum, extend beyond initial concepts, utilize Net resources more fully, and generate output.

Time on task: Some projects are ongoing, while others are standalone and take 1–3 weeks, depending on the type of output and the depth of the exploration.

Time online: 1–5 hours or more per lesson

A Typical Day in Our Internet Classroom

To give you some idea of how a lesson works:

6:30 A.M.	The usual group of three waiting at my door with more to follow in a few minutes.
6:35 A.M.	SRO. All 20 computers are going. Some kids are using Word, while others are on PowerPoint. A few are cruising the Net. The usual three are into the high-end stuff—streaming audio and video. I keep frustrating them by disconnecting external hardware and dumping plug-ins they deem necessary. Our computer memory is too valuable to give too much over to the scripting and streaming. But I do leave one with the plug-ins and memory they need.
7:10 A.M.	First period: Computer Fundamentals (4 periods, 22 kids each period, 45 minutes). These lessons are for kids new to the Net who have been online for just a couple of weeks.

Lesson 1

Objective: To practice a quick search. On the board, the kids find, "The Alvarez Impact Theory."

Assignment: "Quick, what fields of science am I studying if this is important to me?" While they are searching, I ask questions such as, "Who is Alvarez? What was impacted? How come it's still a theory?"

When they locate, very quickly, the fields of paleontology and geology, along the way, they find the answers to the questions and have their curiosity piqued.

Time on task: 10–15 minutes

Lesson 2

Objective: To use keywords to locate information and practice cross-referencing. On the board are:

The Sacred Turtles of Kadavu
The Tagimaucia Flower
Vitu Levi

Mount Uluiqalau
Archipelago
"Ni Sa Bula"
Captain William Bligh
Lovoni

Assignment: "If you go online, not only will you be able to pronounce the names and places on the board, but you will see some beautiful pictures of a very interesting place. Where are we?"

This is an easy one to locate, right off the bat, but along the way, I ask:

"Can you find a picture of the flower? The mountain? What's the weather like today? If I were graduating from high school, what's the nearest university? By the way, where is this place? What is its closest neighbor to the east? The west? Where could you stay if you visited? Did you find the pronunciations of the words? If I took $2000 of my money to this place, how much of their money would I get in exchange? (I direct them to http://xe.net/currency for a currency converter.)

"It's interesting," I tell them, "that the men live to an average age of 62, while the women live to 67. And that the men attain a higher literacy rate than the women.

"What might account for that? Can you find a picture of an old woman getting exercise doing something we use a labor-saving device for?"

They get so caught up in this, extending on their own to foods, an island they found for rent, a resort owned by the son of Jacques Cousteau, Jean-Michel. We locate the islands on our classroom map and place them in location to the Great Barrier Reef. This would be a nice side trip for some, but the bell rings.

Each of these lessons elicits verbal output. Lots of calling out of information, addresses, and links. More sharing of findings; pictures, maps, statistics, information. Noisy but productive and friendly. Camaraderie abounds. I'm out of my seat a lot, being called over to see something they've found while what I find is displayed on our overhead monitors.

Time on task: 25–30 minutes

Grading: Since these were just for practice, I don't assign a grade. (See the note at the end of the section on grading.)

Periods 5 and 7 (45 minutes) These kids have been on the Net steadily for several months. They've learned to use these software packages: Microsoft Word, PowerPoint, Access, Hypercard, Hyperstudio, and Works word processor and data base. They use Netscape Communicator as their browser.

Lesson 3

Objective: To practice using one of two software packages. To practice searching for purpose with directed output. To prepare their presentation for an audience of their peers who are just about to read *Great Expectations* and who have no visual frame of reference about the time period or the geographical location of the novel.

This is a lesson, extended from the Louisa May Alcott lesson (see Lesson section for full copy), which started with a quick search warm-up. Since the time periods are similar, one lesson links to the preparation for the next.

The kids have chosen one of the 14 side trips dealing with the setting of the novel: 1865 South of France, Europe, and England. They are to put together a pictorial tour with appropriate captions of the one aspect they've chosen. The software they can use is either PowerPoint or Hyperstudio.

Length: It's hard to say how many pictures they'll find online, so it's easier to direct them to creating a timed presentation as opposed to dictating a length. In this case, 2 minutes gives them time to include quite a few pictures, transitions, effects, and captions, as each slide will only be viewed for a few seconds.

As they begin searching for pictures and information, I direct them, on the board and verbally, to pay close attention to their captions. They should be descriptive and colorful, but precise. I also direct them online to a thesaurus, which they place in their bookmark folder, and remind them to use captions they find online as examples of word play and usage. I remind them they are building a frame of reference for someone who knows nothing about the time period, and they are to give them thorough but concise overviews.

When they've finished putting together their presentations, we will display them on the overhead monitors for the class to view, appreciate, and critique. Selected ones will be printed to showcase the best of the best.

As with the other lessons, there is a sharing of sites and findings. Some find that their search leads to sites that will help a neighbor. I give them starting points, if they need them from the sites in this book, my bookmarks, or from a new search I do along with them.

Time on task: Two weeks — with mandatory editing, a further requirement to focus attention on the visual impact of their presentation, and a final direction to use the thesaurus.

Grading

- Lessons 1 and 2: This type of assignment does give me an opportunity to see who is grasping the concepts of searching, using the browser, and mastering their computer as well. Students who don't hesitate, who know exactly where to go to start their search, focus well on keywords, scan text quickly, and draw conclusions from context clues will have the answer first and be headed off to answer some of the other questions I've asked along the way. Those less comfortable with the hardware and software will hesitate, trying to recall the name of the search engine they like best and start their search just a step behind — unless they are still reading the board. Most rise to the challenge, having a solid mastery of the hardware, software, and browser.

  For a grade, they all get an A in participation, while some would get a B or C in mastery of the hardware and software. It's very subjective on my part. Rubrics are being created that will help with this process, especially when you get to output, but in the meantime, I want the kids to relax, learn the tools, and enjoy the learning experience. I do expect to see a steady improvement in their skills online and off, working toward a level of mastery and comfort — no hesitation in use of hardware and software and, eventually, well-thought-out communication and output.

- *Grading their output:* It is when we come to the area of output that graded differentiations can made. I grade data bases, spreadsheets, posters, newsletters, visual presentations, essays — a variety of different outputs, many of which don't fit into any usual grading scale or pattern. Again, I am looking for mastery of certain skills that go with using computers and the Internet, along with esthetics in the writing and visual presentation. I grade, midway through the project, their time on task, their ability to locate information, and their mastery of the tools. When I have the output, I grade using a rubric with input from the kids as their view each other's presentations.

These are just a few examples of how I have used the Internet. You'll find a variety of these lessons throughout the book. Please refer to this section and the extensive chart that follows. It will assist you as you begin to integrate the Internet into your curriculum.

TABLE OF LESSONS

BR = Browsing   QS = Quick searches   ES = Extended searches   EO = Extended searches with output   PD = Packaged deals

BR = Browsing QS = Quick searches ES = Extended searches EO = Extended searches with output PD = Packaged deals

BR = Browsing QS = Quick searches ES = Extended searches EO = Extended searches with output PD = Packaged deals

BR = Browsing QS = Quick searches ES = Extended searches EO = Extended searches with output PD = Packaged deals

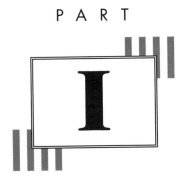

PART

I

USING THE NET IN YOUR CLASSROOM

PREVIEW

OKAY, NOW HOW DO I GET THERE?

GETTING CONNECTED TO AN ONLINE SERVICE

IN THIS CHAPTER

- Getting Connected to an Online Service
- Internet Service Providers (ISPs)

By now, you have purchased and set up your equipment. Your modem is plugged in, configured, and turned on — but nothing is happening. No wonders of the world pop up on your new monitor. You're not walking in Romeo's determined footsteps or casually strolling down the Champs Elysées. You can't read any online magazines; you're wondering what to do now.

A Quiz: Do You Need This Information?

Do you have your modem configured, your browser software installed? Are you familiar with your browser's tools, know what a URL is, and know where to type it? If you answer "yes," then go to the site listings, learn more about searching, or try some sample lessons. If you have no idea what all that means and have no Internet Service Provider, then follow along.

If your equipment is out of the box and up and running, all you need now is a way to connect the computer to the Internet. To do this, you need an *Internet Service Provider*. These are companies with the technology to connect your system to their hardware for routing onto the Information Highway.

3

Keywords You Will Learn in This Chapter

The Language of the Internet — for the Lay Person

Internet Service Provider (ISP): The company or service that connects you directly to the Internet via a phone line.

Commercial online services: Provide Internet access and special services for subscribers. These are companies such as America Online, Prodigy, and CompuServe.

Browser: The software used to get around (navigate) the Internet. It might be Netscape Navigator or Communicator, Microsoft Internet Explorer, America Online, or others.

Site: This is where your browser takes you. It is like the cover of a magazine. Someone has created a descriptive visual experience or text output which may consist of one page or several. This information resides on a computer somewhere that distributes the information over phone lines to you and, potentially, millions of other people.

URL: Uniform Resource Locator. This is the site address, such as `http://www.yahoo.com/`, which might be located on the World Wide Web, on a gopher server, or it might be an ftp (file transfer protocol) location. For now, begin with the Web, then move along later to the rest of the Internet. There are many layers to the Net. The World Wide Web is just one.

Home Page: Like the cover of a magazine, putting your best foot forward is your home page. This is the entry to a site, usually with information about what you will find in the site and buttons to help you find what you want.

Hyperlinks: Words highlighted in color that will take you to another section of a site or to another page entirely, when you click on them. When you move your mouse around on a Web page, the pointer will often change to a hand. When it is a hand, it is sitting on a link. Hyperlink words and phrases are usually written in blue text, but other colors can be used. Watch for the hand on text or on pictures. One click and away you go!

INTERNET SERVICE PROVIDERS (ISPS)

For a small fee, or sometimes for free, you can get connected to the Internet by a service provider. Once you are connected over normal phone lines, you will be expected to pay for your time online. As of this printing, most providers offered unlimited time online for about $20 a month. This means you can stay online, as long as you want, every day, all day, for $20 a month. Fee schedules may change in the future as more people use online time, creating a kind of Information Highway traffic jam. Rumors in industry magazines hint that the unlimited use fee may disappear as use increases.

While the industry has been making forward strides, especially in the area of accommodating new users online, ISPs are still plentiful and quite similar. Make sure that the ISP you choose is prepared to upgrade and stay with the latest technologies. You don't want to be stuck with a fast machine on a slow line.

Before you sign up, check these suggestions from:*

`http://www.longmont.com/mnc/classes/chamber/on101/15ques.htm`

1. What type of Internet access do you provide?
2. What is your installation fee?
3. What are your rates for each type of account?
4. Do you have any automatic cut-off features?
5. What modem types and modem speed connections do you support?
6. Is there a premium rate for high-speed (28,800 bps or above) access?
7. Do you charge for disk space?
8. Do you provide an 800 number dial-in capability? What are your local calling areas?
9. What are the chances of getting a busy signal when I dial in?
10. What Internet functions do you provide? Options include e-mail, World Wide Web, telnet, gopher, Internet relay chat.
11. What are the hours for your technical support and help desk?
12. How much help will you give me to configure my software?
13. Do you have any preconfigured software for your customers?
14. What kind of documentation do I get with my account?
15. Do you provide a method of keeping customers up to date?

---

* Source: Courtesy of AES Consulting and ISP subscribers. Courtesy of Colorado ComputerUser

Providers are available from one geographical location to another. Your phone book, local college, a school online, a friend online, or a computer magazine can give you the names of local providers. Many school districts that are online offer discounts for teachers who use the same provider, and many local colleges offer reduced rates for educators. Check around.

Some national ISPs are:

- Concentric Network http://www.concentric.net/ 1-800-939-4CNC
- Earthlink Network http://www.earthlink.net/ 1-800-395-8425
- Netcom NetCruiser http://www.net/com.com/ 1-800353-6600
- PSINet's Pipeline USA http://www.usa.pipeline.com/ 1-800-827-7482

Commercial online services:

- Microsoft Network http://www.msn.com/msn.htm 1-800-freemsn
- Prodigy 1-800-776-3449
- CompuServe 1-800-848-8990
- America Online 1-800-827-6364

What You Can Expect from a Provider

A *free guest account* will demonstrate the provider's services — what you can get, how easy it is to connect, and how easy or difficult it is to configure the software to your computer.

Software to Connect to the Internet

Ask if the provider offers a choice of browsers — software to get you around the Internet. The two most common from noncommercial providers are Netscape Communicator and Microsoft Internet Explorer (MSIE or IE). Most commercial services provide their own browser, but also let you use either of the other two.

Also check to see if the provider charges an activation fee. Some of the companies will get you online for free and then charge you for the first month. Others charge a one-time setup fee. Make sure they have local access numbers for your dialing area; otherwise, you'll have to pay long distance charges when you're online. Most providers will offer a local number so the call is free.

Technical Support

A good provider will not leave you hanging in the middle of the night with connectivity problems. Most offer 24-hour toll-free help lines.

Support for a Faster Modem

A slow modem is considered to be one with a 14.4-kbps baud rate (kilobits per second, or how fast the information can be sent over the phone line). With higher baud rates, the information gets to you faster. The newer modems operate at a fast 56 kbps, outpacing older models running at 33.6 or 28.8 kbps. You want to make sure that as you upgrade your speed, so does your provider. Many of them are switching their lines to accommodate modems faster than 56 kbps. Make sure yours has or is going to do so.

Full Access via TCP/IP

Transmission Control Protocol/Internet Protocol (TCP/IP) is a suite of networking protocols that help to access different parts of the Internet. This is important if you are using a dial-up line at home or school. I cannot imagine a provider who knows nothing of TCP/IP at this stage of development.

At Least One E-mail Address

Your provider should give you at least one e-mail address. Some will even give you addresses for your family. America Online offers up to five addresses at no extra charge. You can also find many places online where e-mail addresses are offered for free. Advantages of the free services will be discussed later.

Configuring Your Modem Software

How you set up your software (configure it) depends upon what kind of modem and computer you're using (Mac or PC). Most of the modems now are plug-and-play and require very little technical knowledge to get set up. They usually read your machine's specifications and walk you through a step-by-step process until your modem is ready to go.

Many companies that sell computers will set up and configure your software, free or for a small fee. Your ISP can also help with the configuration. When I moved back to California, I actually drove over to my ISP to get help configuring my modem and they set it up for free. Read the installation instructions that come with your modem, if it was not already part of your machine. If it was part of your system, it should be ready to play.

Sometimes, however, even a plug-and-play system can plug but not play. I got help with the configuration when mine wouldn't play. Don't be afraid to ask for help, but also try using Wizards on PCs for setup, or follow the configuration instructions. I ran into problems because my machine was originally set for a school Ethernet configuration and had to be reset.

If you are buying for home, you should have few problems setting up your modem. If your connection is at school, you can hope that connectivity is someone else's domain. Your job is to use the connection in your classes, not usually to set everything up. But then again, the number of people who can set up and run networked systems is small in light of the growing demand.

An Aside about Jobs

Setting up and running a network system is a growing job field for your kids. I know a 16-year-old junior in a Northern California high school who taught himself and is now the Network Specialist for his school. I have seen ads for Web designers who, with one year of experience, are starting at a salary of $35–40,000. Keep an eye on those of your kids who seem to get into any aspect of this technology and encourage them. Many of them will be employable before they leave high school.

WHERE YOU ARE NOW AND WHAT'S NEXT

IN THIS CHAPTER

- Browsers
  - Microsoft Internet Explorer
  - Netscape Navigator
- Icons/Buttons
- Pulldown Menu Items
- Reading a URL
- Bookmarks/Favorites
- Search Engines

Your hardware is ready; the computer is set up and running; your modem is configured and connected to a phone line; and your Internet Service Provider is a dial tone and a few numbers away. You will be ready see the wonders of the Internet as soon as you master one more thing.

Shortly after you dial up your provider a new piece of software will open up on your monitor's desktop called a *browser*. A browser is software that navigates around the Internet. Browsers take you to specific sites; allow you to go back to favorite sites using bookmarks; search the Net for more sites you may want to get to; and send and receive e-mail. It is *the* tool you rely on to navigate the Net.

Most Internet Service Providers will send you either Netscape Navigator or Microsoft Internet Explorer to use as your browser. If you are using a recently purchased PC, several browsers, including MSIE, will be available on your desktop. The new Apple iMac comes with MSIE installed. Customers of CompuServe, Prodigy, and America Online can use either one. America Online has its own browser, but allows users to download and use Netscape or MSIE instead.

Different browsers each have a unique desktop appearance. They all do, however, offer menus that are set up as buttons or links to enable you to get where you want to go.

9

Commercial services provide not only Internet access, but also a wealth of other informational services specific to the provider exclusively for their respective subscribers.

Both Netscape Communicator and Microsoft Internet Explorer (IE) have made some changes to improve your Net experience. They are offering quick links to popular sites, and most of the common plug-ins are already loaded. (More about new plug-ins later.)

I have used both browsers and like different aspects of them.

- **Bookmarks/Favorites:** Easy placement into folders with MSIE and Netscape.
- **Printing:** You can print at the touch of an icon with Netscape; MSIE requires one step more with a pulldown menu.
- **Web page creation:** Creation software is part of the Netscape browser, making for easy access; MSIE relies on using other software such as Word.

All things being equal, if I am creating Web pages, I prefer to use Navigator, but IE will work just as well. You won't be hindered by using either browser.

Teach your kids the icons and menu items they need to know, and then continue to add to their knowledge and use. Show them both browsers so they are able to move from one to the next with ease. But, since time is critical in online use, most of us use one or the other, usually because that's where our bookmarks are.

USING MICROSOFT INTERNET EXPLORER

As soon as the browser software begins to run, a colorful screen will appear on your monitor. The page you see is the service provider's *default home page,* automatically displayed each time the browser is run. A home page is the first one you see every time you load your browser. You can reset this page to be any page. Most schools set their school or district home page as the default home page on students' machines.

At the top of the screen is the menu, and the images you see are push buttons called icons. You place the mouse pointer on an icon and click the mouse button once.

Microsoft Explorer Home Page

Icons and Buttons You Will Use Often

BACK — Go back to the last screen you were viewing.

FORWARD — Go forward to the screen you just left using **Back**.

STOP — Stop incoming text and graphics from loading. Sometimes, a site loads very slowly, or you change your mind about seeing it and want to go to another site. **Stop** will interrupt the arriving flow of information and allow you to go on with your other choice.

REFRESH — Sometimes site graphics, which might be extensive, will not appear on the screen. This button will reload the site and usually give you full text and graphics.

HOME — Each browser will be set to a (default) home page. Usually it is the home page of the provider or browser. It is possible to set the home page to be any page you choose. In my classroom all computers automatically are set to load our school's home page. Every time we press "Home" we go directly to that page. Set this feature by going to **Options** in your browser menu.

SEARCH Each browser is set to go directly to a particular search engine when this button is pressed.

FAVORITES Some sites are so terrific, you want to remember where they are and go to them again and again — and you don't want to keep typing in their long and complicated addresses. **Favorites** is the icon you press to store the site's address.

HISTORY This is an important tool for educators monitoring student use of the Internet. Click on the icon and a weekly list of URLs is shown. The list extends back 3 weeks, and if you point at a URL, you can immediately connect to that site.

PRINT No longer a menu icon. You find **Print** under the **File** menu. You can print all the materials from the site you are on. Be careful — you cannot control how many pages you print from the Net, and some sites are lengthy. Check the length before you print.

EDIT No longer an icon. This function is now under the **Edit** pulldown menu. This allows editing of the HTML (the computer language the site uses to display page contents) of your home page.

OPTIONS This has been moved to the **View** pulldown menu. To change your settings for default home page, cache, mail address, etc., press here.

CHANNELS This new icon gives you a list of pre-selected sites in categories such as news, technology, sports, business, and entertainment.

Below the icons are a new set of items beside the word "links". These links are provided by the browser and connect to sites titled Best of the Web, Channel Guide, Customize Links, Internet Explorer News, and Internet Start.

Pulldown Menu Items

FILE Allows you to open a new file or a new window (which is a site), close windows or files, print, or go back to sites you've visited during this session.

EDIT

Helpful for copying and pasting pictures and text from the Internet to other software applications.

VIEW

Lets you turn on or off toolbars. You can also refresh from here. More importantly, you can access "Internet Options" at the bottom of the list. Here is where you change the default settings for things like your home page, history, or cleaning up the cache.

Click on "Content" and check out the content advisor. You must have already logged on to Windows 95 using User profiles and must have a password. When you have done this, in lieu of or in addition to safety software, you can adjust the levels of language and explicit content you want and password-protect the settings.

Also, if you are on a slower modem connection, go to "Advanced" and turn off some multimedia options such as animations that can slow down the load time of a site.

GO

Has been changed and offers back and forward as well as specific sites or areas where you can GO.

If you have visited several sites in one session and wish to go back to one you were viewing three, four, or more screens ago, just go to the **FILE** menu and a list of the sites you have visited will appear. Scroll down to the one you want, click, and immediately go there.

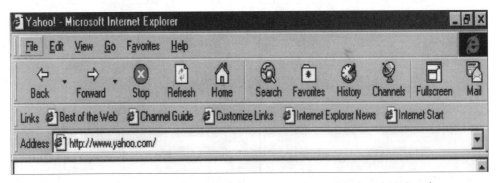

The pulldown menu items are **File**, **Edit**, **View**, **Go**, **Favorites**, and **Help**. If you use a word processor, these should be familiar. Just click on the pulldown menu item name to see what tools are available. Notice that most menu items have corresponding keyboard shortcut combinations that can be used instead of the mouse.

FAVORITES is a list of your preferred sites. As your list grows, so will this menu. Each site you have set as a favorite will appear with its name and a brief description. The descriptions and names can be changed to make them more meaningful to you. To get to any one site immediately, once you've marked it as a favorite, just scroll down and highlight the site name in the favorites list. Let go of your mouse button and the browser will take you to that site. (Netscape Navigator calls these preferred sites bookmarks.) You can organize your favorites by putting them into folders. Create the folders beforehand and then, as you save a site, indicate which folder to place it in.

HELP Takes you to a menu to provide you with guidance if you encounter any common problems.

Below the **Links** icon is the **Address Line**, where you type in any URL to go to any site listed in this book or from any other source. For more on URLs, read on.

Using Netscape Navigator

The browser used most often by Internet users is Netscape Navigator, part of the Communicator suite. When you open Navigator you will see a default home page similar to Explorer's, as well as menu items.

Icons and Buttons You Will Use Often

Some icons will serve the same function as in MS Explorer.

BACK Go back to the last screen you were viewing.

FORWARD Go forward to the screen you just left using **Back**.

HOME Each browser will be set to a (default) home page. Usually it is the home page of the provider or browser. It is possible to set the home page to be any page you choose. In my classroom all computers automatically are set to load our school's home

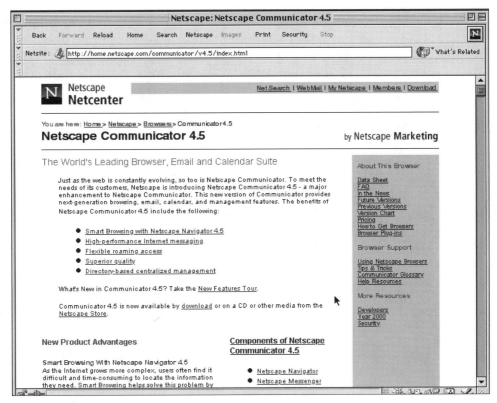

Netscape Communicator

page. Every time we press "Home" we go directly to that page. Set this feature by going to **Options** in your browser menu.

RELOAD
Sometimes site graphics, which might be extensive, will not appear on the screen. This button will reload the site and usually give you full text and graphics.

IMAGES
Similar to the RELOAD button, except that it reloads only the images from a site, rather than the entire site.

OPEN
Presents a small dialog box where you can type in the URL of a site you want to go to. You can use this instead of the location/address line. We tend to put all URLs in the location line.

PRINT
This is still an icon on Communicator.

FIND
Locates, in the text, the keywords you type in.

STOP   Stop incoming text and graphics from loading. Sometimes, a site loads very slowly, or you change your mind about seeing it and want to go to another site. **Stop** will interrupt the arriving flow of information and allow you to go on with your other choice.

Pulldown Menu Items

BOOKMARKS   This is the same as **Favorites** in Internet Explorer. In order to place your bookmarks into folders, you must edit your bookmarks and drag each selected one into the appropriate folder.

OPTIONS   This allows you to change some of the settings for Navigator. We access network preferences to empty the cache, the place where the pictures and information from each site visited that the browser are stored during your session. Locate the file cache on your hard drive to more thoroughly empty this memory. If you see a subdirectory called "cache" in your browser's main directory, the files you see there are the copies of Internet pages you have visited. If it gets too full, it will slow down your browser.

DIRECTORY   This gives you these choices: **Netscape's Home**, **What's New**, **What's Cool**, **Customer Showcase**, and **Netscape's Destinations**. (**What's New** and **What's Cool** are just what you might expect.)

The pulldown menu items are **File**, **Edit**, **View**, **Go**, **Bookmarks**, **Options**, **Directory**, and **Window**. Those which are the same as in MSIE are **File**, **Edit**, and **View**.

HANDBOOK	A handy guide to Netscape with a tutorial and information.
NET SEARCH	Connects you to Netscape's search engine.
NET DIRECTORY	Connects you to several search engines located all in one place.
SOFTWARE	A place to get more add-ons and plug-ins (more about these later).

Below the icons is the location line where we type in URLs.

To add bookmarks from your pulldown menu, point your mouse button at **Bookmarks**, scroll down to **Add Bookmarks**, then just let go of the mouse button. Now you will see, under the **Bookmark** menu, a short title for that site. (These can be edited to be more meaningful to you. Just locate the menu item **Window**. Go down to **Bookmarks**. Your pulldown menu will change. Go to **Item** to edit your bookmarks and insert folders for your needs.) To put your bookmark in your folder, drag the name up to your folder.

UNDERSTANDING URLS

So now you are connected to the Internet with your service provider. You have loaded your browser and checked out the icons and pulldown menu items. Now you need to learn to use URLs (Uniform Resource Locators).

What All Those Letters Mean

`http://`	means Hypertext Transfer Protocol. This creates a document with links and graphics.
`www`	indicates a site on the World Wide Web.
`.vacations`	is the name of the Internet Service Provider.
`.com`	means that this is a commercial site.
`/index`	is the name of the page you are loading.
`.html`	means HyperText Markup Language, the code or language that created the page.

To find a specific site on the World Wide Web or on other parts of the Internet, you need to type in a URL. A URL is the address of an Internet site, which will look something like this:

```
http://www.vacations.com/index.html
```

Other Types of Sites

`.com` is commercial; `.edu` means an educational institution; `.gov` means government; `.org` means an organization; and `.net` means a network.

Punctuation on the Net

Certain punctuation marks are used extensively in URLs or in other places on the Net. Watch for these:

What All Those Symbols Mean

@ the symbol for the word "at" is used in all e-mail addresses, as in
   `nskomars@hotmail.com/`

~ is a tilde (we call it a squiggle!) and is used in some URLs

// is used in URLs after `http`; it's always the front, or forward, slash

: is used in URLs after `http` and sometimes before a number, as in `:80`

. is called a "dot" and is used after parts of a URL, as in `http://www.msn.com/`

/ separates URL extensions, as in `http://www.intesys.it/Tour/`

Say It With Feeling

Once you have put all that punctuation together, an address looks like this:

```
http://www.pathfinder.com/index.html
```

and is pronounced like this: "http colon slash slash www dot pathfinder dot com slash index dot html."

Typing In An Address

Load up your browser and get your default homepage loaded.

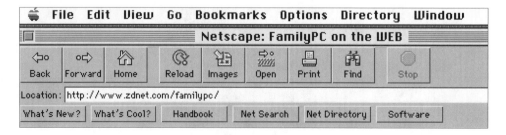

Then locate your *address/location* line.

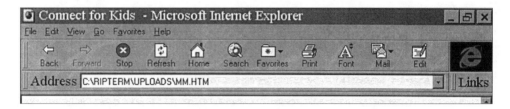

URLs (Addresses) In This Book

Much of this book consists of a list of URLs leading to Internet sites for every subject we teach, K–12.

Here's a sample:

> *Name:*   SCHOOL EXPRESS
>
> *URL:*   http://www.schoolexpress.com/
>
> *Annotation:*   Start here and find links for teachers and parents

In this book, the first line of each entry is usually the name of the site or a descriptor. The second line is the URL — the address you type on the address/location line. Once it is typed in, press **Return** or **Enter**, and you should go to that site. The third line is a brief annotation of what you'll find at the site.

Now that you know where to type in a URL, you're ready to browse the Internet.

LESSON 1

BROWSING

Browsing can be an enjoyable experience or time wasted. It can be enjoyable if you quickly find something worthwhile, and frustrating if you end up nowhere and feel your time online has been wasted. Browsing needs a starting point, perhaps a site address you found in a magazine, saw on TV, or were given by a friend. If you're looking for specific information, browsing is not a productive way to find it. Searching for specific sites will be covered in the next chapter. In the meantime, here are some great places to spend time just looking around.

1.1 *Not Looking for Anything in Particular*

BROWSING

BR   **Grade Level: All**

After you've logged on to the Internet, clear the address (URL) you see in the address/location line of your browser so you can type in a new address. Click on the right side of the address you see there. Hold down your mouse button and drag left to highlight the entire address. Press **Delete**, then type in this URL:

```
http://www.disney.com/dig/today
```

Be accurate.   URLs, like everything about a computer, are very specific. Miss a . or a ~ or a / and you'll get a polite message saying something or other about "DNS" entries, meaning, "Sorry, that site is closed to you," or, perhaps, "You type funny!" If it doesn't work check your typing and try again. You'll find yourself at Disney's search engine.

Hands and Pointers on Your Screen

Move your mouse around and notice that as you move your cursor it changes from a pointer to a hand. Each time you see a hand, you have found a *hyperlink*. These hyperlinks take you somewhere else. Maybe you'll find another article relating to the main page, or more often, you'll jump to a related site.

Click on some of the hyperlinks and *browse*, which is similar to leafing through a book. Using **Back** and **Forward** buttons, learn to move around from the home page and come back to it again. As in navigation on the earth, navigation on the

Internet is a matter of knowing where you are and how to get back to where you came from. Once you get the hang of it, it's easy.

Working with Long URLs

When you get a 404 up on your screen — Not Found Error (or any error indicating you cannot access a site), it's not the end of the world and most likely you didn't do anything seriously wrong.

Sometimes you might have trouble connecting to a site with lengthy or complicated extensions on its URL. Type it all in and see if it works. If not erase, from the right to left. Erase back to the last /, then press **Return (Enter)** and see if you get closer to the site. If not, erase again to the next /. Go all the way back to the .com/ or the .edu/ if you have to, to get to the home page of the site.

Some sites that are extensions are created by private individuals, brought to the Net through their provider. Often, these personal sites are not maintained and subsequently, eventually, they disappear.

As an example, this site's URL:

```
http://www.tc.cornell.edu:80/Edu/MathSciGateway/math.html
```

tells me I am looking for a math site (math.html) passing through something called the MathSciGateway (this you could search for as well — later) from possibly the Education Department (Edu) of Cornell University (cornell.edu).

If typing the entire address fails to get me to the site, I'll remove the math.html first, and if that doesn't work I'll remove MathSciGateway.

Remembering that my ultimate destination was a math program, I think it might be best to get there from the home page and then follow logical links.

In this instance, from the home page, I would look for the .Edu (probably the education department, but it may only indicate that the page was posted by an educational institution). Then I would look for MathSciGateway and so forth, until I get where I really want to be.

If all that fails to get you to the site, no problem — there are many more sites you can locate by searching later.

1.2 *A Little More Browsing*   **BROWSING**

BR   ### Grade Level: All

Now that you know where and how to type in a URL, try a few more sites for browsing. Remember to look for the hand to appear as you move your cursor over the screen, and try out links. If you get lost, just click **Home** or **Go** and take yourself someplace else.

Practice using these menu items: **Back**, **Forward**, **Go**, and **Bookmarks** or **Favorites**.

KNOWLEDGE ADVENTURE

http://www.adventure.com/

LOOKSMART

http://www.looksmart.com/

LONELY PLANET

http://www.lonelyplanet.com/

CDNOW

http://www.cdnow.com/

SITES THAT DO STUFF

http://www.amused.com/sites.html

DIGITAL LIBRARIAN

http://www.servtech.com/public/mvail/home.html

1.3 Practice Typing in URLs and Using Links

BROWSING

BR **Grade Level: 4th and Up**

Move your cursor back to the address/location line and erase all that you see there. Did the URL get longer as you checked out some links? Don't worry about such long addresses. If you bookmark a site, you only have to type in the URL once.

- Now that the old address is erased, type in

  http://www.seti.org/game/

- Once the screen changes, you are on the SETI Home Page.
- Scroll toward the bottom of the screen and click on "How Will You Search?"
- Make a choice from the two presented and move along.
- Your next move will depend upon the choices you make. Once you have finished exploring space, type in this URL:

  http://www.thinkquest.org/

Click on **Library of Entries**. Click on any year for the entries you want to see or check out the alphabetical listing.

1.4 *Browsing through the Subjects*

BROWSING

BR **Grade Level: 3rd and Up**

Here are some more sites to explore. Be creative and try new things.

Elementary Kids

ENCHANTED LEARNING: LITTLE EXPLORERS

> http://www.EnchantedLearning.com/

BERIT'S BEST SITES

> http://www.cochran.com/theosite/KSites.html

KIDS COM

> http://www.kidscom.com/

FUNK AND WAGNALLS KNOWLEDGE CENTER

> http://www.funkandwagnalls.com/

Literature

STORYTELLERS SOURCES ON THE NET

> http://members.aol.com/storypage/sources.html

CHILDREN'S LITERATURE

> http://www.ucalgary.ca/~dkbrown/

TALES TO TELL

> http://www.thekids.com/

STORY BROOK LANE

> http://www.geocities.com/Athens/Parthenon/2087/

With choices, kids can help determine the plot of these stories.

Writing Skills

PURDUE WRITING RESOURCES

http://owl.english.purdue.edu/

ST. CLOUD UNIVERSITY LITERACY ONLINE

http://leo.stcloud.msus.edu/

GUIDE TO GRAMMAR AND WRITING

http://webster.commnet.edu/HP/pages/darling/original.htm

More writing help.

The News

NEWSPAPERS AROUND THE WORLD

http://www.webwombat.com.au/

NEWS FROM ALL OVER

http://newo.com/news/

NEWSPAPERS ONLINE

http://www.hotcc.com/newspapr.html

TOMORROW'S MORNING

http://www.morning.com/

A newspaper for kids.

Math

MATH LINKS

http://www.npac.syr.edu:80/textbook/kidsweb/math.html

STREET CENTS

http://www.screen.com/streetsite/topics.html

FAMILY MATH

http://theory.lcs.mit.edu/~emjordan/famMath.html

A+ MATH

http://www.aplusmath.com/

Science

SCIENCE

ECOMALL

http://www.ecomall.com/

MIAMI MUSEUM OF SCIENCE

http://www.miamisci.org

SCIENCE SEARCH TOOL

http://www.fishered.com/v1/constr.html

WHAT'S IT LIKE WHERE YOU LIVE?

http://www.mobot.org/MGBnet/

From the desert to the rain forest, pictures and text tell you what it's like to live in different places.

History

THE MAYAS

http://www.indians.org/welker/mayamenu.htm

ANCIENT CIVILIZATIONS OF THE MIDDLE EAST

http://tqd.advanced.org/2840/

ELLIS ISLAND

http://www.i-channel.com/ellis

U.S. HISTORY

http://www.ushistory.org/

Another wonderful U.S. history site.

French

PARIS

http://paris.org/

THE VIRTUAL BAGUETTE

http://www.mmania.com/

TENNESSEE BOB'S AMAZING FRENCH LINKS

http://wnix1.utm.edu/departments/french/french.html

Language Experiences

http://www.geocities.com/Athens/Academy/7726/

A site designed for English speakers wanting to learn another language. With exercises, resources, and projects.

Spanish

Discover Spain

http://www.ozemail.com.au/~spain/overview.htm

Spanish Resources

http://www.santacruz.k12.ca.us/vft/spanre.html

Hispanic Online

http://www.hisp.com/

Voyages de Decouvertes

http://www.geocities.com/Paris/Bistro/7445/index.html

Plenty of practice for those learning French or Spanish.

Careers and College

Career Magazine

http://www.careermag.com/careermag/

CareerWeb

http://www.cweb.com/

The Student Survival Guide

http://www.luminet.net/~jackp/survive.html

Test Prep

http://www.testprep.com/

Help for those preparing for the SAT.

Law and Government

1000 Law Links

http://seamless.com/road.html

Teen Court

http://tqd.advanced.org/2640/

RATE YOUR RISK OF CRIME

http://www.nashville.net/~police/risk/

Health and PE

SPORTSLINE

http://www.sportsline.com/

PE CENTRAL

http://infoserver.etl.vt.edu/~/PE.Central/PEC2.html

WORLD HEALTH NET

http://www.who.ch/

BENNYGOODSPORT

http://www.bennygoodsport.com/

KIDS FOOD CYBERCLUB

http://www.kidsfood.org/

Business and Finance

ONLINE BANKING DEMO

http://www.edify.com/

FINANCIAL WEB

http://www.finweb.com/

WORLDCLASS

http://web.idirect.com/~tiger/

CONSUMER PRODUCT SAFETY COMMISSION

http://www.cpsc.gov/

Find information about various products here — download Adobe Acrobat to read some of the files.

Computer-Related

PLANET9

http://www.planet9.com/

COMPUTER LIFE

http://www.zdnet.com/complife/

THE BOSTON COMPUTER MUSEUM

http://www.tcm.org/

BRAINPAINT

http://www.brainpaint.com/

News and information about the World Wide Web.

Art and Computer Graphics

COMPUTER ART LINKS

http://www.nerdworld.com/nw1177.html

WORLDWIDE COMPUTER ART

http://www.uc.edu/~kidart/kidart.html

WORLD ART TREASURES

http://sgwww.epfl.ch/BERGER/

WEBSEEK

http://www.ctr.columbia.edu/webseek/

Find just the picture you need with this search tool

Interesting Sites

WHEEL OF FORTUNE

http://www.wheelfortune.com/

GREAT OUTDOOR RECREATION PAGES

http://www.gorp.com/

AVALON

http://www.avalon.co.uk/avalon/

ON-LION FOR KIDS

http://www.nypl.org/branch/kids/onlion.html

The New York Public Library provides plenty of links.

Cars

THE AUTO CHANNEL

http://www.theautochannel.com/

CAR AND DRIVER

http://www.caranddriver.com/

AUTO WEEK

http://www.autoweek.com/

KELLY BLUE BOOK

http://www.kbb.com/

What is your car worth? How much should you pay for a new car?

Music

BILLBOARD ONLINE

http://www.billboard-online.com/

LIBRARY OF MUSICAL LINKS

http://www-scf.usc.edu/~jrush/music/

MTV

http://www.mtv.com/

CHILDREN'S MUSIC WEB

http://www.childrensmusic.org/

Movies

BOXOFFICE ONLINE

http://boxoff.com/

INTERNET MOVIE DATA BASE

http://www.imdb.com/

CINEMANIA

http://www.msn.com/cinemania/

FILM FINDERS

http://www.filmfinders.com/

TV

TV PLEX

http://directnet.com/wow/tv/

TV TONIGHT

http://www.tvtonight.com/

TV SCHEDULES AROUND THE WORLD

http://www.buttle.com/tv/schedule.htm

TV GEN

http://www.tvgen.com/

Shopping

21ST CENTURY PLAZA

http://www.21stcenturyplaza.com/

BIGDEAL

http://www.bigdeal.com/

TOYTROPOLIS

http://www.toytropolis.com/

BOTTOM DOLLAR

http://www.bottomdollar.com/

Travel

VIRTUAL TOURIST

http://www.vtourist.com/

TRAVEL.ORG

http://www.travel.org

MICROSOFT EXPEDIA TRAVEL

http://www.expedia.msn.com/daily/home/default.hts

ALTAPEDIA

http://www.atlapedia.com/

Maps and statistics for many countries.

SEARCHING THE NET

AFTER BROWSING COMES SEARCHING

At this point, you have typed in several URLs, followed some links, and seen some of the wonders of the Web. Browsing, although enjoyable, is not the best way to find information you need; you'll have to search for it.

Searching is like going to the mall to locate a hard-to-find item. You may wander around and look in several places before you find just the right item.

Providing tools to find information easily on the Net is a competitive business. Search engines are like any other site on the Internet accessed by a browser. They are created and designed to do a lightning-fast sort through massive numbers of Internet sites, quickly locating sites containing keywords you type in.

Yahoo! (www.yahoo.com) was the first search engine to appear on the Net. Another is Lycos (www.lycos.com). Do a search on "search engines" to discover many other search engines. All search engines use keywords for searching. Subtle differences governing the format of keywords will be discussed as each search engine is profiled.

Other types of search engines that are appearing on the Net are those that offer the user access to Lycos, Altavista, and Yahoo! without actually having to go to their sites. For example, at Search.com you can elect to do a site search using Altavista's engine, the one from Lycos, or others.

Many of the Net sites you access will have internal search engines that help you navigate through just that one site. Look for search buttons while navigating a site.

IN THIS CHAPTER

- Search engines
- Keyword
- Altavista
- Lycos
- Yahoo!
- Search.com

Strengths of Search Tools

Before you begin your search, know the difference between a search directory, a search engine, and a metacrawler:

- *Search directories* are best used when looking for general categories, which makes them a good place for kids to start as they learn to narrow their topics. (Yahoo!)
- *Search engines* will look through descriptions of the sites, searching for your exact terms. Engines are good for more specific searches. (Excite, Lycos, Altavista)
- *Metacrawlers* search more than one engine at a time for you. This is good for cross-referencing. (Dogpile)

All search tools return *hits*, sites or pages that contain your keyword. These hits are listed by some engines with the most relevant being presented first. Except for Yahoo!, which is a search directory, the list of hits will also contain the name of the site, the URL, and a brief description of the contents.

For younger children, there are a growing number of search tools to use. One that is directly geared to children, Yahooligans, can be found from Yahoo!'s main menu or by going to http://www.yahooligans.com/. Yahooligans searches by keyword and presents categories from which the information may be found. Because this tool is aimed toward children, the search is limited to approved kids' sites.

An alternative for safe searching is to use *Looksmart*, a search directory, at http://www.looksmart.com/. Looksmart, prepared by *Reader's Digest*, searches through categories for sites that contain your keywords. Looksmart has a more limited search range, but the sites it finds are safe for kids. Another safe kids' search tool is *Lycos' Safety Net*. Use this one as a starter or to cross-reference.

For more advanced students and searches, there are many tools to choose from. I tend to use Yahoo! for a quick search, to get started. If I still have not found what I need, I usually go to Excite because of the "more like this" feature. Excite, a search engine, will list relevant sites and then link to other sites that appear to have similar information. Excite is very powerful and broad, searching almost 50 million pages.

Altavista and Lycos are two other popular search engines that I use for cross-referencing. Altavista searches about 35 million pages and is a good tool for searching for obscure terms because it looks at every word in each page of the sites it has catalogued.

Lycos, an additional search engine, works like Altavista and Excite with a fairly wide database of 50 million pages. Hits are listed by relevancy, and advanced search tools that narrow your search even more are available.

Your students have to learn how to use several of these search engines so they can quickly find the information they want and learn how to cross-reference. **Practice** searching by providing keywords to your students, and after the engine has performed its search, have them discuss which sites seem the most useful or relevant.

Later, **practice** deciding which keywords they would use to find the information they want. Provide them with a paragraph from their text and have them tell you which words they would use as keywords when looking for more information. Then use those choices as keyword searches and discuss the results.

Advanced searches include Boolean operators such as AND, OR, NOT, and NEAR. These are accepted by most search engines and can be used to help limit the number of hits returned. Words in quotes are treated as phrases and the entire set of words is searched for. Most of these search tools also allow the use of + to include a term and – to exclude it.

My Excite, My Yahoo!, and Setting Preferences

Within the past year, search engines have begun to do more than search. They are now set to offer more personalized information gathering and push to you just what you demand. For example, with Excite, you can tell the search engine which newspapers or magazines you want ready access to, and these will be available with the click of your mouse. You can also get free e-mail services from many of the search engines. Yahoo! and Excite both offer this service. Search engines also provide easy links to mapping capabilities like Mapquest, travel assistance, dictionaries, news, sports, weather, and more. It is in this area, of offering more services, that the search tools are getting more competitive.

Additional Features

Yahoo!, Excite, and Lycos have developed country- and city-specific collections of sites such as Yahoo! San Francisco, Global Excite, and Lycos Netherlands. If you are looking for information about one specific city or country, this feature can be most helpful and time saving. A challenge for many will be that the sites found are often in the language of the country, and it may take some assistance or deduction to find just the right site.

Four Search Engines — Four Ways to Find Sites

The following pages will provide an overview of four commonly used search engines. Using each engine, I typed in the keyword "Verona," looking for a tour or pictures of Verona, Italy.

Here are samples of what the searches provided.

Lycos

One of the more popular search engines, Lycos, searches by keyword, provides descriptions of the site as well as the URL, and gives a degree of relevancy to your search. Type in keywork *Verona* and you will get the results below.

Results of the Lycos Search

LYCOS

    http://www.bdp.it
        SCUOLE VERONA 18 S C U O L E V E R O N A 1 8 Italia , 37137 Verona ,
        Via S. Elisabetta 5 tel: +39-(0)45-953031 fax:+39-(0)45-8621819
        vr.dd18@iol.it vree0001

        http://www.bdp.it/~vree0001/conted1.html

    More Like This

    http://www.operabase.com/
        Verona(Arena), Ente Lirico Arena EN FR DE ES Verona(Arena), Ente Lirico Arena
        Indirizzo: Ente Lirico Arena Piazza Bra 28 Verona ITALY Sito Web: Prenotazi

        http://www.operabase.com/mkhouse.cgi?id=none&lang=it&ho

    More Like This

    http://www.univr.it
        Museo Civico di Scienze Naturali di Verona

Type the keyword   Press here.
in this space.

Museo Civico di Scienze Naturali di Verona
Attenzione! Le nostre pagine web ora si trovano
all'indirizzo: http://linus.univr.it/mcsn/ Se sta

```
http://www.univr.it/mcsn/
```

More Like This

Reading Lycos Search Information

The response to the keyword "Verona" brings this information:

Entry #1
The URL (`http://www.bdp.it`) tells you it's in Italy. The rest of the information is less helpful. But we would check this site.

Entry #2
From its URL, (`http://www.operabase.com/`)it seems to be a site about opera. We might visit this site for additional information but not use it as our primary site.

Entry #3
This one is also from Italy (`http://www.univr.it`) and would be one we would check out.

Because the keyword search asked only for sites with a reference to Verona and did not ask for pictures or a tour, the relevancy might be misleading. Adjusting your keywords will help narrow your search and shorten your search time.

Excite

Excite is an excellent search engine that accesses a large number of Internet sites. It returns your search with descriptions of the contents of the sites and a degree of relevancy to your search. In addition, the URL of each site is provided to give you some idea of where you might be going.

Excite searches by keywords as all search engines do. The keyword or words are typed into the space provided and then you click on **Search**. using the same keyword *Verona,* the following results are found with Excite.

EXCITE

65% Verona Area School District - Verona Area School District Welcome to The Verona Area School District's Web Site. From this main page, you will be able to access information about all of our schools as well as new and exciting technologies being offered from the Verona Area School District.

http://www.verona.k12.wi.us/

Search for more documents like this one

63% Walton-Verona District Home Page - The Walton-Verona Independent School District is located in Northern Kentucky in the southern most tip of Boone County and serves the residents of Walton &Verona, Ky. The Walton-Verona Schools enjoy a rich history dating back to 1880.

http://www.w-v.k12.ky.us/

Search for more documents like this one

62% The Verona Community and the Verona Community Association - This site is about Verona Ontario Canada, the sponsor the Verona Community Association and activities. The business and associations that make Verona what it is.

http://www.veronacommunity.on.ca/

Search for more documents like this one

62% Serie A 1996/97: Calendario della Stagione - Giornata n. 1 and. rit. 08/09 26/01 Bologna-Lazio 1-0 2-1 Cagliari-Atalanta 2-0 1-4 Fiorentina-Vicenza 2-4 2-3 Milan-Verona 4-1 1-3 Parma-Napoli 3-0 1-2 Perugia-

Sampdoria 1-0 2-5 Reggiana-Juventus 1-1 1-3 Roma-Piacenza 3-1 0-0
Udinese-Inter 0-1 1-1 ------ Totale Reti 25 33

`http://www.raisport.rai.it/mcalcio/967a/cld.htm`

Search for more documents like this one

Reading Excite Search Information

Entry #1 will not take us to Verona, Italy. It will take us to a school, and from the URL, it appears to be in Wisconsin (wi)

Entries #2 and 3 seem to be more Verona school or community sites. One takes you to Kentucky. (ky) while the other is in Canada.

Entry #4 has the most potential so far and should be explored. The URL indicates that it is in Italy (.it)

A better way to approach this search would be to indicate Verona, Italy, as the keywords.

Note that the same keyword brought totally different listings from these two engines. If you need more choices, cross-reference with Altavista.com, another good search tool.

Yahoo! Search

Yahoo! is one of the most famous and popular of the search engines. Yahoo! places search results into categories. Although no site descriptions or URLs are provided, it is still a comprehensive search engine.

A Word of Caution

When my students need to search, I send them to Altavista, Lycos, or Excite rather than Yahoo!. We try to keep kids away from inappropriate sites, and it is helpful to know where we might be going before we access a site. Our only indicators are the name of the site, a description, and its URL, and Yahoo! does not provide the last two. For those reasons, I do not have the kids search Yahoo! when they are doing an open keyword search.

Results of the Yahoo! Search Using Keyword Verona

Yahoo! Category Matches (1 - 9 of 9)

Regional: Countries: Italy: Regions: Veneto: Provinces: Verona

Regional: U.S. States: New Jersey: Cities: Verona

Yahoo! Site Matches (1 - 11 of 41)

Arts: Humanities: Literature: Genres: Drama: Playwrights: Shakespeare, William (1564-1616): Works: Romeo and Juliet

> Romeo & Juliet's Fair Verona write a letter to Romeo, or any other character residing in
> Verona, and thou will receive a response.

Entertainment: Movies and Film: Titles: Action and Adventure: Man in the Iron Mask

> Verona's Man In The Iron Mask Site

Business and Economy: Companies: Construction: Browse By Region: U.S. States: Texas: Complete Listing

> Verona Marble Company suppliers of marble, granite, agglomerates, and exterior pavers, in tile and slab format.

Reading a Yahoo! Search

Entry #1 will take us to links about Verona, Italy. We might find what we want here. Notice that Yahoo! offers sites by category.

Entry #2, a site from New Jersey, is not where we wanted to go.

> **Entry #3** pertains to the Shakespearean drama and may not be exactly what we want, but it is worth a look.

I would follow the first link and see what comes up. I still have not gotten a direct link to a site, but with Yahoo!, you must follow their chain.

One Final and Comprehensive Search Engine

Going to Search.com (`http://www.search.com/`) gives you the opportunity of searching with many of the most popular search engines all from one page. The second section of the Search.com home page, the Express Search, lets you choose which engine you want Search.com to use. From here, you can access Lycos, Altavista, Yahoo!, Infoseek, Magellan, and several others.

If you have tried Search.com or other multiple search engines, also try Dogpile (`http://www.dogpile.com/`) for a quick engine that searches all the others. Here are some other well-respected metacrawler:

METACRAWLER

`http://www.metacrawler.com/`

INFERENCE FIND

`http://www.inference.com/ifind.`

A Couple of New Tools to Try

STARTING POINT

`http://www.stpt.com/`

SNAP

`http://home.snap.com/`

Give your kids plenty of opportunities to search using your curriculum as the starting point.

> *Kids' Tips:* When doing extensive research, try cross-referencing with two or three search engines. Lycos, Altavista, and Excite all have proven to be comprehensive. Many of my kids are now relying on Excite at `http://www.excite.com/`. They like the "more like this" feature that directly links them to more sites in their search area.

LESSON

2   **SEARCHING**

To get this far, you must know how to open/load your browser, locate the location/address line, and type in a URL.

(The reason for the double words? IBM/Apple. You'll see: one uses *exit*, the other *quit*. Subtle differences. Some of you will be using a control key, while others will use an Apple command key. I use a Mac at school and an IBM at home. As long as the software I use is compatible, and I use MS Office created to be compatible with both platforms, I have no problem.)

2.1   *Practice Browsing and Searching*   SEARCHING

BR/QS   Grade Level: 4th and Up

Let's spend a few minutes *browsing* through a site. Then we'll *search* through it for more specific information.

1. Type in this URL:
   http://www.infoplease.com/

2. Go to the menu bar at the top of your browser.

3. Pull down the menu for favorites/bookmarks and follow the directions to bookmark or add a favorite.

4. When that's done, use the right vertical down arrow to scroll down through the site.

5. When your pointer changes to a hand, you are on a link. Click on a category that interests you.

6. Click on one of the links provided about that category. Wait for a new page to load.

7. Now click **Home** — go ahead, do it!

8. Now click **Back** — OK now? You should be back on InfoPlease.

9. Now, when you're ready, let's go back and search this site.

10. Scroll down to the bottom of the page (you should not be out of the InfoPlease site yet. If you are, click **Back** until you are at InfoPlease.)

11. At the bottom left of the screen, find the word Home and click on it.

12. Locate the box labeled **Search for**. In the box, type the descriptive word of something you are interested in knowing more about. Press **Go**. Wait for your screen to change.

13. You should see a descriptive list of sites that fit your keyword. Certain words are written in **blue.**

14. Click on a title or the blue name to try out a site. (Watch for the hand. Check out more links and bookmark what you want.)

15. Go back to the InfoPlease home page and search again.

Go ahead and bookmark everything you want to see again. Your browser can hold a lot of bookmarks, so don't be stingy. If you don't like where you end up, click **Home**, **Back**, or **Go**, or try another link. If you are using MSIE and want to GO back several sites without using the **Back** button, click on **File.** At the bottom of the list will be the names of the sites you have visited recently, in order of your visit.

Netscape users: Later, when your bookmarks grow, spend some time creating folders for different subjects and using your mouse, drag the appropriate bookmarked sites into the appropriate folder.

MSIE users: When you add favorites, you can automatically tell your browser which folder to put the favorite in. Set up folders in advance and save time.

For new sites, when this entire book is bookmarked, check out Yahoo!'s "What's New" feature or "What's New" at Yahooligans, or go to www.net/guide.com/ and check out the latest issue for more information and sites.

2.2 *Underwater Life*   **N E W   L E S S O N S**

EO/PD   Subjects: Marine Biology, Ecology, Geography, Technology
Grade Levels: 4th and Up

Humans have begun using new technologies to explore and protect our oceans and underwater worlds. An exploration online can show you not only what this undersea world looks like, but what we are doing to explore it, protect it, and inhabit it.

Start by browsing some photos of life under the water.

UNDERWATER PHOTOGRAPHY

http://www.uwsports.ycg.com/magazine/1995/november_december/photo.htm

What you need to get started.

SITES WITH PHOTOS

http://home.navisoft.com/divebo/photos.htm
http://www.cathychurch.com/
http://www.oceanphotos.com/index.html
http://www.campus.ne.jp/~tozawa/
http://www.geocities.com/TheTropics/4785/
http://www.beverlyfactor.com/
http://hawaii.cogsci.uiuc.edu/photos/photos.html
http://www.internetus.net/users/machinm/
http://www.oceanphotos.com/nfthumbnud.htm
http://www.foris.com/uwphoto.html
http://www.naturescreate.com/

MARINE FLOWERS

http://www.e-net.or.jp/user/ncc-1701/owase/osmain.html

Coral Reefs.

HOW YOU CAN HELP

http://www.motherjones.com/coral_reef/

FISHEYE VIEW CAM

http://www.fisheyeview.com/

REEF RESOURCE PAGE

http://www.indiana.edu/~reefpage/

REEF LIFE

http://www.terryparker.duval.k12.fl.us/reef.htm

UNDERSEA EXPLORATION HISTORY

http://www.intrepid-museum.com/

CITIES UNDER THE SEA

http://www.aquanet.com/citysea.htm

UNDERWATER TECHNOLOGY

http://www.benthos.com/index.htm
http://www.cms.udel.edu/mts/

```
http://www.rov.net/
http://www.oii-adtech.com/
http://www.oceanspar.com/
```

PERSONAL SUBMARINES

```
http://www.ivccorp.com/
http://www.deepflight.com/
http://www.subsee.com.au/index.html
http://www.seamagine.com/
http://ussubs.com/
```

BIOSPHERES

```
http://www.paragonsdc.com/
http://www.mabnetamericas.org/home2.html
http://www.biospherics.org/
```

UNDERSEA EXPLORATION CD-ROM

```
http://www.lockegroup.com/maninsea/maninsea.html
```

CARIBBEAN MARINE RESEARCH

```
http://www.cmrc.org/general.htm
```

UNDERSEA

```
http://sln.fi.edu/oceans/oceans.html
```

NATIONAL UNDERSEA RESEARCH PROGRAM

```
http://gopher.uconn.edu/~wwwnurc/nurphome.html#nurp
```

Now that you have seen some of the wonders of the ocean, answer these questions:

> What do humans use to explore the depths of the ocean?
> What technologies were used to explore the *Titanic*?
> How can humans live underwater?

Writing. Write a journal or diary entry about a week in a submarine or submerged biosphere

Visual output. Create a presentation, poster, chart, or other visual and text presentation displaying the technologies and/or the life forms found under the sea.

LESSON

SEARCHING: SCAVENGER HUNTS

The object of this lesson is to practice keyword searches. On the following pages you will find sixteen "scavenger hunts" that cover each major school subject, with one just for the younger kids and one general one. The hunts are designed to show you the depth of information on the Internet. Each hunt requires that you search by keyword.

These lessons are appropriate for any age group learning to search, but some of the hunts might be more appropriate for middle or high school students.

If you have only one computer in your classroom, you can divide up the requirements and give each student or pair of students certain information to look for, keep track of, and share with the group. If you have the capability of displaying your findings on a large screen or TV, you can also do some of the searching as a group activity. This is less effective than having the students search, but is better than not showing them how to search.

To begin with, look for sites in this book that might help in the scavenger hunt. Follow a link if necessary. Search the book again or try one of your favorite search engines.

Good luck, and have fun!

For the first hunt, I have put in bold the most likely keywords to search for.

3.1   *Foreign Languages: A Whirlwind Tour*

HUNT

QS

Grade Level: Any

For Fun

SPANISH MAGAZINE ONLINE

    http://www.elperiodico.es/

THE VIRTUAL BAGUETTE

    http://www.baguette.com/cur/index/maquette/french/

Locate the following:

1. A **country home** outside of **Paris** — list the URL of the site where you found the map.
2. A **map** of **Spain** — list URL.
3. An online **magazine** from a **Spanish**-speaking country (list the links on the home page).
4. List the URL of a **museum** in a **Spanish**- or a **French**-speaking country. *Extra points:* What artists are featured?
5. The **weather** from a **Spanish** or **French** city.
6. Entrance requirements for any **college** in a **Spanish**- or **French**-speaking country. *Extra points:* Find an apartment or home near the college.
7. Locate the **weather** in the city where the college is located.
8. List the name of a sports **team** in a **French**-speaking country.
9. Find **music** from a **Spanish**-speaking country. List the URL.
10. Locate a **restaurant** or a recipe for a main course from a restaurant in **France**.
11. Locate **jobs** for **linguists**. List one opening you find.
12. What is the e-mail address of a **Spanish**- and **French**-language **magazine** online for **teens**?

Keyword Order

To make your search time effective, remember — the order of the keywords is important. For the first search, try the keywords in this order. Use this as a guide for any of the searches you do.

For a country home:	Try **France, countryside, homes**
For a map of Spain:	Try **Spain map**
For an online magazine:	Try **Spanish magazine**
For a museum:	Try **museum Spanish** or **museum French**
For weather:	Try **weather, France** or **Weather, Spain**
For college entrance requirements:	Try **Spanish** or **French college**
For the weather:	Try **weather** and the name of the city or country
For the name of a sports team:	Try **sports France**
For music:	Try **music Spanish**

For a restaurant:	Try **restaurant France**
For jobs for linguists:	Try **linguists jobs**
For the e-mail address:	Return to the site of the magazine you found in item 3 and look for the e-mail address

-+++-

3.2 *English/Literature: Superbard Search*

HUNT

QS

Grade Level: High School

For Fun

ENGLISH LITERATURE: RESOURCES, INTERPRETATIONS, AND DISCUSSION
    http://www.thinkquest.org/

Locate the following:

1. A picture of Marseilles, France — list the URL of the site.
2. A biography of Mark Twain — list the URL of the site.
3. A reference to the Globe Theatre — list name of site.
4. The weather in Stratford-on-Avon — for the day you search.
5. A newspaper from Germany — list the headline.
6. A review of a production of a play
7. A story about love — what is the title?
    Extra points: If it's about lost love.
8. The cost of a ticket to a concert in any country — list the e-mail address.
9. The name of a city where you could see any upcoming theater production — list URL.
10. Sample from the soundtrack of one of the *Romeo and Juliet* movies or *West Side Story* — title?
11. A literature magazine for teens — list the links on the home page.
12. The URL for a site with literary terms.

-+++-

3.3 | *History: Traveling through Time*   `HUNT`

QS   **Grade Level: Any**

For Fun

ANCIENT SITES

`http://www.ancientsites.com/`

Locate the following:

1. A map of Ancient Athens — list URL.
2. The URL for a site about the history of the Olympics.
3. A biography of any king in power prior to 1900 — list name of king.
   Extra points for a picture.
   Extra, extra points: for a map of the country at the time of the king's rule.
4. The name of a navigational calculator Columbus would have loved to have used.
5. Three of the links on a home page about Vikings (not Minnesota!).
6. The title of an article from "Godey's Ladies Magazine"
7. Pictures of ancient ships. List the name of their country of origin.
8. A newspaper or historical document over 100 years old — list a headline.
9. A speech written over 50 years ago — list the title.
10. A Web site about World War II — list three links on the home page.
11. The URL of a site about ancient costumes. Tell what year the costume is from.
12. The URL of a site about people salvaging ancient ships.

3.4 | *Computer Science: New for the Millennium*   `HUNT`

QS   **Grade Level: Middle or High School**

For Fun

NEWS.COM

`http://www.news.com/`

Locate the following:

1. Information about CU SeeMe — what is the cost to get started?
2. Any article about Netscape versus Microsoft Explorer Browsers — list URL.
3. A site online for kids to paint or draw — what is the e-mail address for the Webmaster or for submitting drawings?
4. The URL of a site with free graphics for your Web page.
5. A biography of Bill Gates — list URL.
   Extra points: For a picture of Bill Gates' house.
6. A game download page. List three popular games.
7. The names of three computers in a computer museum.
8. The titles of three high-tech job openings.
9. Go to the city where one of those jobs is. List the URL of a site where you found a picture of the city.
   Extra credit: For an apartment for rent nearby.
10. The URL of a Web page design tutorial.
11. A computer magazine or journal — what is the lead article?
12. A college east of the Mississippi for computer science majors — name?

3.5　*Science: Around the World*　HUNT

QS　**Grade Level: Any**

For Fun

SCIENCE QUEST

http://tqd.advanced.org/3542/

Locate the following:

1. A picture of the heart — list the URL.
2. Weather satellite photos — list the URL.
3. The URL of a tornado or hurricane information site.
4. The URL of a site about cloning.

5. The first three requirements for a science major at a college in another country.
   Extra points: For pictures of the city the college is in.

6. Three job openings in marine biology.
   Extra points: For the salary.
   Extra, *extra points:* For an apartment in a city where there is an opening.

7. Three links on the home page of any aquarium site.

8. One interactive activity at a science site (not the frog) — what is the activity?

9. A science magazine for teens — what is the e-mail address?

10. The URL for any science site for elementary students.

11. List three images will you find in the Image Gallery of the Singapore Science Centre

12. What is one of the teacher tips for physics at the Fisher Scientific site?

3.6   *PE/Health: Fit for Life*   **HUNT**

QS   **Grade Level: Any**

For Fun

PE TEACHER

    `http://pe.central.vt.edu/`

Locate the following:

1. A picture of the Basketball Hall of Fame — list URL.

2. Scores from any sporting game of the last few days — list scores and teams.

3. A biography of Mark McGwire — list URL.

4. The sports section of a newspaper in a foreign country — list e-mail address.

5. The URL of a site with health/nutrition/fitness information for teens.

6. The URL of a site discussing health care.

7. The URL of a site with coaching tips for any sport.

8. Three links on the home page of a fitness magazine for children.

9. Three links on the home page of a college offering a major in sports medicine.
   Extra points: Address of an apartment for rent in the city.

10. The URL of a tour of the human body.

11. The links on a home page of a sports hall of fame.

12. Locate bicycle safety information for younger kids — links on the home page.

3.7   *Banking and Finance: Doing Business on the Web*

HUNT

QS   **Grade Level: Middle or High School**

For Fun

CHICAGO BOARD OF TRADE

   http://www.cbot.com/

Locate the following:

1. The URL for a site listing Fortune 500 companies.
2. The first three requirements for a degree in marketing at any business school.
   Extra points: Picture of the city the college is in.
   Extra, extra points: Information about an apartment for rent nearby.
3. Main article from a CPA or accounting journal.
4. The home page of any software company — list e-mail address.
5. The URL of a site for money management for teens.
6. The areas addressed at the home page of a bank in any state.
7. The URL of any online stock market demo.
8. The URL of any site with business information for teens (young entrepreneurs).
9. Any site with small business information — list three links on home page.
10. The URL of any school of economics.
11. Three main topics of discussion at a site offering international business information and concerns.
12. The URL of the United States Department of Treasury.

3.8 *Government: It's the Law*

HUNT

QS   **Grade Level: Middle or High School**

For Fun
COURT TV

http://www.courttv.com/

Locate the following:

1. The URL of a site with election results or coverage.
2. A headline from a law journal.
3. The URL of the commercial site of a lawyer in New York City.
4. Any politician's home page — list three links on the home page.
5. The first line from an article about a crime from a foreign newspaper.
6. Election information aimed at teens — e-mail address.
7. The name of any historical document — United States, pre-1890.
   Extra points: For any pre-1600.
8. Any law school home page — list three links.
   Extra points: For three items in the curriculum for first-year law.
9. The URL of a site that teaches how a bill becomes a law in the United States.
10. The URL of a site discussing the year 2000 issue.
11. The URL of a site discussing Internet legal issues.
12. The URL of any foreign embassy.

–ııı–

3.9 *Technology Education:*
If You Can't Fix It, Don't Break It

HUNT

QS   **Grade Level: Middle or High School**

For Fun
INTERNET MAGAZINE

http://www.internet-magazine.com/

Locate the following:

1. The headline from any automotive journal.
2. Three enrollment requirements for any technology school.
   Extra points: For a picture of the campus.
3. Two areas of study at any technology school.
4. The URL for a site listing the job outlook for tech careers.
5. Any Web site developer — list three links on the home page.
6. The specifications of the new iMac.
7. The URL of any computer dictionary.
8. The main article from any carpenters' journal.
9. Three links on the home page of a technology magazine.
10. The URL for a site with technology information aimed at teens.
11. List two **technowise** skills you can learn at http://www.learn2.com/
12. List three of the exhibits at any computer museum.

—III—

3.10 *The Arts: A New Canvas*   **H U N T**

QS   **Grade Level: Any**

For Fun

THE GREATEST PAINTERS

   http://www.kultur-online.com/greatest

Locate the following:

1. The URL of any museum tour inside the United States.
2. The name of any online graphics journal.
3. Three entrance requirements for any arts college.
   Extra points: For a picture of the campus.
   Extra, extra points: For information about a restaurant in the college city or nearby.
4. Names of two African sculptures pictured online.
5. The hours of operation of an art museum.

6. The e-mail address of any 3D art site.
7. E-mail address of an online quilting magazine.
8. Arts magazine online for teens — name of magazine.
9. The URL of any site for posting student art.
10. URL of a site with pictures of underwater creatures.
11. The URL of any site with a history of jazz and samples of the music.
12. The URL of any site where you can listen to the radio online.

3.11   *Counselors: Planning Ahead*   HUNT

QS   ## Grade Level: Middle or High School

For Fun

PETERSON'S EDUCATION CENTER
      http://www.petersons.com/

Locate the following:

1. The URL of any site with financial news.
2. Three links on the home page of any college or university east of the Mississippi with an instructional technology major.
    Extra points: For a picture of the city the college is in.
    Extra, extra points: For information about an apartment for rent in the city.
3. The title of any article from any journal for school counselors.
4. The second question asked at any virtual interview site.
5. The URL for any site which helps with SAT preparation.
6. The first three requirements for a graphics design major at a tech school or college.
7. The approximate costs for tuition for one year at the college.
8. The e-mail address of any counselor online from another school.
9. The URL for any site with financial aid information.
10. The URL for any site with dictionaries online.
11. Any site with an interactive résumé. List the URL.
12. Three links on any site with career information for high school students.

3.12 *Writing Skills: Put It Down —*
But Not on Paper

HUNT

QS   **Grade Level: 5th and up**

For Fun

KIDNEWS

http://www.vsa.cape.com/~powens/Kidnews.html

Locate the following:

1. The URL for any online book store.
2. The e-mail address for any site where teens can get homework help.
3. A headline from any English-language newspaper in Asia.
4. Three links on the home page of any magazine for writers.
5. The URL of any site with movie reviews.
6. The URL of any grammar instruction or practice site.
7. The title of any story from South America (in English).
   Extra points: For a story in Spanish.
8. The URL of any newspaper with searchable archives.
9. Three links on the St. Cloud University OWL home page.
10. The main article at an e-zine written by teens.
11. The title of one of the albums reviewed at any music site.
    Extra points: If it's reviewed by teens.
12. The URL of any site with at least one dictionary and a thesaurus.

+++

3.13 *Math: It Still Adds Up*

HUNT

QS   **Grade Level: Any**

For Fun

CORNELL MATH/SCIENCE GATEWAY

http://www.tc.cornell.edu:80/Edu/MathSciGateway/math.html

Locate the following:

1. The URL for any site with information about navigational calculators.
2. The URL of any site with picture of fractals.
3. The first three terms defined in any mathematics dictionary.
4. An e-mail address of any site with collaborative online math projects.
5. Three links on the home page of any general math practice site.
6. The headline of any math journal.
7. The URL of any site with information about jobs for mathematicians.
8. Links on a page aimed at renovators, builders, or architects.
9. One piece of information about any woman in mathematics history.
   Extra points: For a picture.
10. The first three ingredients and their quantity from any European recipe.
11. Locate *Kids'Money*: `http://pages.prodigy.com/kidsmoney/` What are three of the links on the home page?
12. Locate any college in New England with a mathematics major. List the first three requirements for graduation.
    Extra points: For an apartment for rent in the city where the college is located.

———

3.14 *English/Drama: Superbard and Friends*   **H U N T**

QS   **Grade Level: 5th and Up**

For Fun

ENGLISH LITERATURE

`http://englishlit.miningco.com/`

Locate the following:

1. Pictures of Verona in Romeo and Juliet's time — list URL.
   Extra points: For pictures of Verona today.
2. The URL for a biography of Charles Dickens.

3. The URL for a site that describes the Globe Theatre.

   Extra points: For the URL of a site detailing the renovations of the Globe.

4. The URL of any site which gives background information for the novel *Escape from Manzanar.*

   Extra points: For any picture of Manzanar.

5. The URL of any site about Greek mythology.

6. The URL of a site about American authors.

7. A headline for any newspaper from Italy.

8. The URL of a site with a map of Italy.

   Extra points: If Verona is on the map.

9. The URL for any site with information about the making of the movie *Titanic.*

10. The URL of any science fiction site. What are three links on the home page?

11. The title character of any interactive online mystery story.

12. The name of any online literary magazine designed for teens.

3.15   *A Kid's Search of the Net*

HUNT

QS

Grade Level: Any

For Fun

After School Clubhouse

> http://www.eduplace.com/kids/index.html

Locate the following:

1. A map of England — list the URL.

2. A hands-on science museum — list an activity you can do there.

3. The URL of a site about roller coasters.

4. A villa to rent in Spain for a vacation — list the price in their currency.

5. A site where you can buy toys from Europe — list the name.

6. A tour of The Palace of Versailles — list the URL.

7. A tour of Sturbridge Village in Massachusetts — list the URL.

8. A math site where kids (K–8) can practice math — the name of the site.

9. Information about bugs — list three links on the home page.

10. The URL of a site about national parks in Canada.

3.16   *A General Scavenger Hunt*

HUNT

Subjects: General

QS   **Grade Level: Any**

Starting Point

```
http://www.yahoo.com/
```

1. Find a site about butterflies. List the names of three butterflies mentioned there.

2. Locate a picture of Old Faithful geyser in Yellowstone National Park. What state is that in?

3. Find an online newspaper near your town. List the headline

4. Oundle, in England, is holding the World Conker Championships in October. What is a "conker?"

5. List the URL for one site that offers hints for computer game players.

6. List one company that takes people on tours of Buckingham Palace.

7. What country is the city of Flin Flon in?

8. You are eating SMORGASTARTA. What are you eating and what country might you be in?

9. List the name of one horse enthusiasts' magazine online.

10. List the URL of a site for people who like *Star Trek* movies.

11. List the URL of a site for people who like jazz music.

12. Locate a site for a bookstore online. What is one of the featured books?

3.17   *Start the Fire: An Ambitious Search*   **HUNT**

ES

**Subjects: History, Current Events
Level: 4th and Up**

An online and offline exercise to broaden students' knowledge, using the song "We Didn't Start the Fire" by Billy Joel:

http://witten.hartwick.edu/students/ronin/bj-wdstf.html

My students broke up into groups of 3–5. They were encouraged to work with students from another class period and to combine within groups, those with the Internet at home and those with no connectivity outside school. They were to correspond by e-mail and present their findings on paper. The walls of our rooms eventually displayed some wonderful pictures and text explaining the contents of the song.

For those of you not familiar with the song, it is an overview of history from the 1940s to the 1980s, mentioning significant people, places, and events. My students' task was to illustrate and explain each reference. Using Net and other resources, this homework assignment kept the kids busy for over a week. They first divided the song into decades and focused individual attention on just one part. When each student finished their research, they decided on a presentation format. Many students were amazed to find that the references in the song were helpful not only in our literature class, but in history and government classes as well.

One ambitious person has posted the lyrics online with links for most of the references. Unfortunately, not all of the links are to the exact reference. For example, the link for the mention of hypodermics on the shore takes you to a site about hypodermics. My students researched more and found the event Billy Joel referred to.

Billy Joel song lyrics with links:

http://users.aol.com/jdsweeney/fire.html

CHAPTER

4

GETTING DOWN TO BASICS

PREPARING TO USE THE NET

IN THIS CHAPTER

- Preparing to Use the Net
- How We Use the Tools

Now that you have learned to get on the Internet, access sites, browse, and search, it's time to begin the process of preparing to use the Internet "teaching tool" in your classroom with your students.

See What's Online

Teachers, look at your curriculum. What unit or concept is coming up in about a month? Students, look at the classes you are taking. What are you studying now that might be enhanced by more information — information you can find on the Net?

Whether it's counting or calculus, *Charlotte's Web* or Chaucer, start looking for sites that add, in some way, to your areas of study. Check the sites in this book, then use your search tools to help you find more. Bookmark these sites.

Plan the Outcome

What kind of physical representation would be logical, interesting, or necessary from this exploration? We were aiming at writing an essay after one exploration, but the students realized a chart or graph would be just as informative, especially if they could explain it aloud or with added text.

59

My students have created posters, written essays, completed research papers and book reports, and stapled them on our walls. What kind of activity is appropriate for the lesson and for your students?

Plan Your Time

How long do lessons take when using online resources? There are many variables; I can give you some idea of how long certain lessons took us. We spent one class period, 45 minutes, on a common link, and six to seven class periods on the Web search "Find Your True Home" because of the output. We also spent fifteen hours creating a Hypercard stack of sites. We spent two weeks creating a three-column, three-page travelogue of a boat trip with extensive research and writing.

The amount of time needed for any exploration will vary depending on the scope of the project, yours and your kids' Internet access skills, and the amount of connectivity you have.

Speed Up Your Search

Decide on keywords before you begin — brainstorm with the kids and bookmark sites you want to use in your lesson. Thoroughly check out sites you want to use and make note of those sections that are more appropriate. For example, The Exploratorium has a lot to offer, but you may only be going to their site for the "Science behind Sports" section. Provide the URL for kids to go directly to a section of a site. Your prep time before you go online makes the kids' online time more efficient. With extensive projects, I always provide starting points.

Get to Know Sites Outside Your Teaching Area

The more you know about what's on the Internet, the more you can extend your lessons. Knowing that we could find pictures of galleons, Marseilles, and French chateaux expanded the scope of our *Count of Monte Cristo* exploration. If you weren't aware that Matchbox Toys or Legos are online, it might never occur to you to build a lesson around them, much less expand it to the history of toys, to inventions and tools of earlier times, to stories about toys to costs of toys to. . . . Stop any time you want, or carry on if you choose!

Look Up Sites for Your Kids' Interests

If you are a bit interested in affairs in their world, perhaps they'll spend more time in worlds you'll want them to tour. Take them to sites they'll enjoy (of course, preview the sites) and then take them to sites you select for them. Encourage your kids to take you to sites they like. I post on the board "Site of the Week," or sometimes "Site of the Day," if any of us find something particularly interesting. Reluctant learners can sometimes be lured into your world just by taking them somewhere they would want to go first, before you make an assignment of it.

How Accurate Is the Information?

You'll need to evaluate the accuracy of information on a site-to-site basis. From what we have seen, most of the sites are making every attempt to be accurate. Inaccurate or badly presented information means few people will return to a site, and the number of return hits is important to those who create a site. Most Webmasters seem to be making an effort to be accurate as well as visually exciting.

Web sites must be readable, accurate, well written, and well presented. If they are, chances are your students will respond favorably, enjoy the experience of locating information, and become a more active part of the learning process. My students seem to like sites with a mix of graphics and text. They like *interactive* sites or those that make them feel like they are part of an experience, like the tours of ancient countries and cities, or letters home from soldiers of the Civil War. They also like the connectivity of the Net, especially the ability to e-mail the site creator, or Webmaster. If we like a site, we can tell the Webmaster directly. And if we don't, we can also share that input and perhaps even act as agents of change.

One way to check accuracy is to teach your students to cross-reference. If, for example, my students are researching information about Charles Dickens, they cross-reference to several other sites, compare the information, and judge for themselves the accuracy. Because cross-referencing is easy, students do not argue about the need to verify information, nor do they hesitate to check for accuracy when required.

What Suffixes Can Tell You about Accuracy

All sites must be checked for accuracy and appropriateness before you send your kids there, but here are some general guidelines:

.edu   Sites that end in `.edu` are those connected in some way to an educational organization or school. Rarely, especially now with competitive information showing up, will schools allow anything inaccurate or embarrassing to show up on their site.

.com   Commercial sites, those created by companies, follow the same guidelines as educational institutions. They want nothing on their site that will chase away viewers. Sites with a `.com` that are created by individuals, connected to no one, must be looked at thoroughly.

.gov   Government sites follow the same rules for accuracy and appropriateness as do educational institutions.

.mil   Military sites are also strong on accuracy and appropriateness.

.org   Most organizations also do not want inaccurate or inappropriate material on their sites.

.net   Networks are similar to organizations, but also can be individuals posting, so check them out carefully.

Longevity of Sites

Posting Web pages on the Net is fluid, and sites come and go. There is no telling if the one site you have come to depend on for a lesson will always be online.

New software is emerging that will help you archive sites that you really would hate to lose. Also, with the addition of ZipDrives for both Mac and IBM platforms, you can easily store larger files.

Many sites are constantly updated by the Webmaster, but others are not maintained and are taken off their servers.

Archive software, in the form of add-on utilities, runs with your browser and makes archiving possible. Check out Freeloader at `http://www.freeloader.com/` and WebWhacker at `http://www.ffg.com/whacker` to learn more about archiving sites with software.

Or check out Surfsaver at `http://www.surfsaver.com/` if you want to learn about one archival program. A 30-day demo is free, and if you feel you need to hang on to sites, this might be the answer. Also check out other sites and software listed on the CD-ROM with this book.

Archiving sites takes up a great deal of memory. If your computer has little to spare, then find as many sites as you can for your lesson and bookmark them. Print what you need and hope for the best.

You may want to encourage your school to purchase a small server to be placed in the library for archiving sites. Advanced Technologies

Academy is in the process of doing just that. You can always contact their web team for more information at

http://www.atech.tec.clark.nv.us

Kid's Tips: Finding new sites. For the younger kids, check out Yahooligans! at http://www.yahooligan.com/

Teachers: You can check out What's New at Yahoo! at

http://www.yahoo.com/

by clicking on the icon of the baby from their home page. They offer a categorized list of new sites they have found.

Also check Kathy Schrock's site at

http://discoveryschool.com/schrockguide/

She offers a new site list each month.

Inappropriate Material on the Internet

As I was preparing the first edition of this book, I came across an article in *NetGuide* magazine pertaining to the research that prompted *Time* magazine's cover story on the perils of the Net. It seems the researcher, who located more than 900,000 pornographic images on the Internet, found most of them on BBSs (Bulletin Board Services), not on the World Wide Web. My students, and more than likely yours, too, will access few, if any, BBSs. My students will also not enter chat rooms, e-mail outside school for a school assignment without my knowledge, download software, or give out personal information without my permission. There are software packages available that will help limit students' access to the Net and minimize the chances of finding anything objectionable.

We experienced two drawbacks to using safe surf software last year. In one instance, an elementary school, thinking that .com meant commercial, blocked all .com sites with their safe surf software. That meant the kids could not access nationalgeographic.com, discovery.com, mathboxtoys.com, and many other wonderful sites. Be careful not to exclude on the basis of generalities.

The other result of blocking sites was to keep teachers and students out of sites that are quite useful, because they have some aspect that gets them blocked. We tried to access The San Francisco Exploratorium (http://www.exploratorium.edu/) site from a high school connection and were blocked. We could not get at the "Science behind Sports" section, the cow's eye dissection online, or any of the other wonderful parts of this site because of something that got it blocked. What that something is, we never could find out. If a site contains one part that is objectionable, make use of the other parts as best you can, even if that means printing the material.

I really believe that with proper supervision, including room setup, a well-thought-out and challenging lesson, and a word of caution to kids, most Internet use will be safe.

One bright note on the horizon was a suggestion I first saw in Jesse Berst's column that mentioned placing an xxx in any site with inappropriate material. Watch for changes to software and Net domain names and as you set up your school Internet connection, try to find appropriate ways to block sites as well as to use them.

Kid's Tips: To learn more about software you can use to filter sites:

NET NANNY

http://www.net/nanny.com/

CYBER PATROL

http://www.microsys.com/cyber

SURF WATCH

http://www.surfwatch.com/

HOW WE USE THE TOOLS

Before we explore the lessons, it's important to know which tools we will be using and to what degree. Although, most of the time, the Internet and the World Wide Web are sufficient for all our research needs, in class and out, there are other tools on the Internet at our disposal as well. Here is how we have made use of many of the tools.

Browse

Me: I browse Yahoo, Yahooligans, Lycos, and Looksmart as often as possible to check for new sites.

In class: We rarely browse in class — browsing implies "just looking" and usually the kids have a specific purpose for being on the Internet. If they want to spend time seeing what's new, I send them to Yahooligans.

Kids: They browse at home or in the library for sites of interest to them — usually games, sports, fashion, TV, music and movies.

Search

Me: I search for personal and school information. I tend to use Yahoo, Excite, and Northernlight.com for my searches.

In class: We search in response to specific assignments and use Excite, Lycos, Altavista or sometimes a multiple search site like Dogpile at
```
http://www.dogpile.com/
```

Kids: They tend to search for school as well as personal information and use the same tools at home as we do at school.

E-mail (Electronic Mail)

Me: I use e-mail to correspond with colleagues, friends, students, my editor, and a host of others. It is an indispensable part of the Internet for me.

In class: We found a way around the problem of e-mail for all students. After each one of them signed, along with their parents, an e-mail permission slip, we signed them up for an online service.

Free e-mail is available online in several places. For ease of organization, we used Hotmail, which we also chose because of its handy spellchecker, thesaurus, and dictionary. Students e-mailed as part of discussion groups, research teams, or readers sharing their interests. E-mail became another way of communicating, from asking advice on a rough draft to sending in a final draft or sharing some wonderful new site.

Each student had a signed permission slip from parent or guardian allowing them to use e-mail, and later this was made part of our acceptable use policy.

Problems We Faced

1. Inappropriate e-mailing — student to student. The writers were taken off all electronics for an agreed-upon time.

2. Too much mail. Students took up too much library computer time answering their personal e-mail.

Solutions

1. Monitoring e-mail from class — I can request that all students send me a carbon copy of any e-mail going out from class or that is class related. I can monitor that in class, but not outside. I also do not allow personal e-mail during class time. Inappropriate e-mail, like inappropriate Web sites, is hard to monitor outside of class, but once found, it can be dealt with. Most students who are truly incorporating the Internet into their learning style will not want to be removed. For some, time away is punishment enough, and for others, more monitoring is required.
2. Coordinate with other teachers who might be using e-mail for communicating with students to avoid electronic overload and restrict personal e-mail to nonclass times.

Ftp (File Transfer Protocol)

Me: All of the files related to this book were sent from where I live on the West Coast to my publisher on the East Coast. I have also downloaded files and software by ftp.

In class: We have had to access plug-ins and transfer some student files electronically, but usually students have not needed to ftp.

Kids: Many use ftp to download games to their hard drives or to upload their Web sites to their servers.

Usenet (Sources of Newsgroups)

Me: I look for educational newsgroups with information relating to my curriculum or school needs. I don't spend much time at newsgroups, but they can be very worthwhile.

In Class: I still have not had the time or need to send kids to newsgroups. But, if I find appropriate ones, and the need arises for us to find our information there, we will use newsgroups.

Kids: Most students will find newsgroups that fit their personal interests — games, sports, movies, etc. — and will explore the postings.

Telnet (Electronically Connecting to a Remote Computer)

Me: I could access the public library system in Las Vegas from a remote terminal. Other library systems can also be accessed. At this time, I still have made no other uses of telnet.

In Class: We access the public library to find out if books are available. Other uses might come later as our needs grow. But at this time, we have made limited use of telnet.

Kids: Other than accessing the public library and for use in high-end Web page creation, most of our students do not use telnet.

Gopher (Information Databases)

Me: From time to time, the information that I am seeking on the Internet is stored in a Gopher data base. I tend not to search Gopher for sites for students because the sites tend to be text-based and less effective at meeting the needs of our visual learners. For honors-level and gifted students, the information on Gopher servers is very useful.

In Class: The students also find some of the information they need from Gopher servers, but most of the time they find what they need on other parts of the Internet.

Kids: At home, kids will find the same uses and needs for Gopher servers.

PRACTICE LESSONS

IN THIS CHAPTER

- Browsing for Specific Sites or Information
- Searching for Specific Details
- Using Hyperlinks
- Planning an Outcome
- Creating Output
- Adapting Lessons to Your Curriculum

I t's inevitable that when you and your kids go online, you're going to learn a lot. You'll learn about people, places, things, ideas. You'll learn with new tools and other people and you'll see what you came into teaching to see; kids, all ages of kids, loving the process of learning. But as with any instruction, it's wise to have a purpose and direction. Random browsing is fun, but it's more beneficial to direct your students to information you need them or want them to have. If your lessons are purposeful, students will accomplish far more than you ever imagined.

Some of the lessons in this book fit into the category of queries, learning more about something you and your kids are curious about. Others are more extensive and involve more than the gathering of information, but require the thoughtful use of the information to answer a question, solve a problem, predict an outcome, or create something new.

For more information on what to include in an Internet lesson, read Dr. Jamie McKenzie's article "Grazing the Net: Raising a Generation of Free Range Students" at

```
http://fromnowon.org/
```

Read, too, Dr. McKenzie's article "We Weave the Web," and as you prepare your lessons, keep in mind his overview of the Research Cycle:

Questioning

Planning

Gathering

Sorting and sifting

Synthesizing

Evaluating

Reporting

After you use some of these lessons, and I hope you do, substitute freely with the formats or invent your own. I've test-driven as many of the lessons as I can with my kids, and bit by bit, they are getting so fast with the tools that getting information is easy and fun. Learning as fun . . . an amazing concept. But for my kids, no challenge is beyond them, no quest for information too difficult. When we put our heads together — and with the Internet, we have a lot of heads to choose from — we increase our knowledge, our power; our empowerment. So, start your kids browsing, then move into searching and finally, explore.

THE PRACTICE LESSONS

I've attempted to indicate what grade level I think would be most appropriate as a starting point for any lesson. I can't say whether a particular lesson will or will not work for, say, 3rd grade. I judged some of the levels according to subject matter, amount of reading and research needed, and interest level. If I've misjudged the placement of these lessons, please let me know.

The following are some lessons for you and your students to practice with.

Remember that *BR=Browsing, QS=Quick Search, ES=Extended Search, EO=Extended Search with Output,* and *PD=Package Deal* (complete lesson).

LESSON

4

THINGS YOU CAN DO EASILY ON THE NET

Browsing and Searching

Some areas of research have been difficult for students because they lack the necessary resources to gather enough information. The Net puts vast quantities of data at your kids' fingertips. Here are some lessons, designed for practice in using search tools, that also add to students' frame of reference and knowledge base.

4.1 Hurry on Down

BROWSING

BR **Grade Level: 2nd and Up**

Type in these URLs as one of your first practice sessions. Follow some links and enjoy. Try bookmarking.

If you are using Navigator, you can use a shortcut by simply typing in the name in the middle, as in `discoverychannel` or `pathfinder`. Navigator fills in the rest as it takes you there. MSIE needs the entire address. AOL will take just the middle because it now uses Navigator as its Internet browser.

Type these:

`http://www.discoverychannel.com/`

Just look around and enjoy.

`http://www.pathfinder.com/`

If you look around, you'll find games on their menu. Click on the word "games" and once that menu opens, look for a game called SPQR; an ancient tour of Rome.

`http://www.raingod.com/angus/Misc/SiteMap.html`

Go to maps and check out Angus's tours or his art.

`http://www.si.edu/`

Take a tour of the Smithsonian Institute.

`http://www.geocities.com/`

Check out "Neighborhoods" in Geocities.

```
http://www.nationalgeographic.com/
```
Take a look at their projects and photography.

—+++—

4.2   *Newspaper Search*   **B R O W S I N G**

ES

Subject: Any
Grade Level: 3rd and Up

Because more than 1400 worldwide newspapers are available on the Net, this opens up an entire world of information. Newspapers, most of them, are updated daily, bringing students a constant source of worldwide information.

Here are some good places to start for access:

```
http://www.webwombat.com/.au/
http://newo.com/news/
http://www.hotcc.com/newspapr.html
```

Find one event in your local newspaper (or one close to you), then access other newspapers in other parts of your country or in the world and compare the coverage. To whom was the event most important (front page)? To whom was it least important (no news or little coverage)? What do you suppose accounts for this? Is the coverage different throughout one country or state?

—+++—

4.3   *A Hockey Team's Secret Weapon*   **B R O W S I N G**

Another lesson to practice searching.

ES

Subjects: Science, Sports, Ecology
Grade Level: 4th and Up

We live at 5500 feet above sea level, and my son plays ice hockey at a rink at 6000 feet above sea level. Whenever our team plays against a team from the Los Angeles Valley area, our players wonder how long it will take for their secret weapon to kick in — during the first period of play, or not until later in the game?

But, it usually hits at some time during the game and gives the mountain players the advantage.

Have you figured out our secret weapon yet?

The ice rink, by the way, is outdoors with no air conditioning or controlled climate to skate in. Also, some days the valley teams drive through 30–100 miles of smog to get to our rink. The last 10 miles of the trip is through cleaner air and bluer skies, however.

Figured out our secret weapon yet?

For the teacher. Our secret weapon is the visiting team's lack of ability to adjust to the thinner air.

1. Once you figure out our secret weapon, tell what effects we will see in the visiting team as they play? Why will we see them?

2. What online sites did you find to help you answer this question?

3. Conversely, what effects can the mountain teams expect on their level of play when they travel from 6000 feet to 1000 feet and into the smog?

Starting point.

HIGH ALTITUDE MEDICINE

```
http://www.highaltitudemedicine.com/
http://www.princeton.edu/~oa/altitude.html
```

Bonus question. What American city, with several sports teams, feels they have the same advantage for their teams for the same reason as our mountain teams? (Denver)

---┼┼┼---

4.4 *Getting Down to Business* BROWSING

EO ### Subject: Math/Business/Careers
Grade Level: 4th and Up

Practicing search skills with output can be accomplished in many ways. One way, which includes using math skills, is to set up your own office.

You have just been hired as an assistant to Bill Gates' assistant. For more information on Bill Gates, try **PBS Triumph of the Nerds**:

```
http://www.pbs.org/nerds/
```

You are not only moving to Redmond, WA (I wonder what kind of weather they have there? `http://www.weather.com/`), but you are moving into an empty office.

Your job is to furnish your office by locating everything you need, from furniture to computer equipment to plants and paintings, online. Be creative. Your budget is $25,000 (teachers: don't forget, "the sky's the limit" can be fun, too!)

Start with:

```
http://www.zdnet.com/
```

Check for **links**.

Don't forget: cell phone, fax, copier, stationery, tables and chairs, and a desk.

Keywords

computers shopping
furniture
shopping + furniture
art galleries

Extension.   Find a building or office space for rent near Redmond, about 30 miles away in any direction. Can you find places to shop for your home online? Oh, your budget for a company car is $20,000, since you might be commuting.

Keywords

rent
rent office
shopping + name of city
name of city

Extension.   You are doing a terrific job. We want you to head up the office in (pick a city any where in the world). You'd like to get to know the city; where to shop, to browse, to buy lunch. What can you do there? You need a place to live. Until then, what hotel can you stay at? Can you find a map of the area?

Keywords

name of city
name of city + tour
name of city + shopping
name of city + maps

VIRTUAL TOURIST

```
http://www.vtourist.com/
```

TRAVEL EXCHANGE ONLINE

```
http://www.travelx.com/
```

VACATIONS

    http://www.vacations.com/

TRAVEL

    http://www.lonelyplanet.com/

Possible Substitutions

    Outfitting a science lab
    Packing for an excavation in Africa
    Furnishing an art studio

—ııı—

4.5   *Plan Your Next Vacation*   B R O W S I N G

ES   **Subject: Geography, Travel, Math**
       Grade Level: 2nd/3rd and Up

You can use the Internet to improve kids' math skills with real-life simulations. You can shop for a car online, comparison-shop for electronics, or look for a place to live. You can also plan a vacation.

    Many travel agents and services are online and will gladly help your students do this.

    Pick a destination, locate some wonderful pictures and text from several sources, and make a travel brochure of your own. Where will you go? How will you get there? Where will you stay? What sights will you see? Where will you eat, shop, take side trips?

A good place to start:

    http://www.vtourist.com/
    http://www.vacation-inc.com/
    http://travel.org/
    http://www.expedia.msn.com/
    http://www.travelocity.com/
    http://www.lonelyplanet.com/

Or try a Lycos or Altavista search specifically for your destination.

Extensions.   Can you locate information about cruises? Unusual vacations? A safari?

Note.   Give the kids a budget and have them keep track of where the money went.

—ııı—

4.6   *Let's Move*

ES   **Subject: Geography**
Grade Level: 3rd/4th and Up

Another way to practice using math skills is to simulate moving out on your own. Even the younger kids enjoy the grownup idea of finding their own place.

Apartments for rent and homes for sale, around the world, are available on the Net. Pick a destination. Locate an apartment or home. You can even find villas for rent or sale.

Note.   Give the kids a budget for their rental or purchase and see what they can get. Raise or lower the budget and see what effect it has.

4.7   *A Money Tour of the World*

ES   **Subject: Math, Geography**
Grade Level: 3rd and Up

As the economy becomes more global, it's interesting for kids to learn more about the economies of other countries. One starting point is with money.

HISTORY OF MONEY

```
http://www.ex.ac.uk/~RDavies/arian/llyfr.html
http://woodrow.mpls.frb.fed.us/econed/curric/history.htm
http://www.globalfindata.com/eurohist.htm
```

Determine the exchange rate for your money to the money of two or three other countries:

```
http://www.xe.net/currency/
```

How does your money compare? Worth more or less? How is the appearance of the money different from yours?

Extension.   Do some research on the history of money. How has money changed from early times? What is the future of paper money? What is the problem being discussed in Europe now that pertains to money?

Another Extension.   Explore the history of counting machines (abacus and others). Explore the history of computers and calculators.

4.8 Children's Games around the World/History of Games

BROWSING

ES

Subject: Geography, History
Grade Level: 2nd and Up

When he was 8, my son played for hours with a young boy from France. They spoke no common language but they were able to cross language barriers because they shared something else: their knowledge of outdoor games.

One way to increase multicultural awareness is through an examination of such common interests:

```
http://www.gamecabinet.com/GameCabinet.html
http://www.inmet.com/~justin/game-hist.html
http://www.historychannel.com/cgi-bin/framed.cgi
http://www.ftech.net/~regia/games.htm
```

What can you learn, from your research, about the history of games or games other kids play? Do you still play any games that were played in olden days? Have the rules changed? Do you play any of the same games as kids in other countries?

4.9 Your Favorite Sport around the World

BROWSING

ES

Subject: Geography, Sports
Grade Level: 2nd and Up

Where else do they play your favorite sport? Professionally? In school? Public recreation leagues? Compare rules, costs, equipment, training, schedules, competitions, professional opportunities, etc.:

```
http://www.sportsquest.com/
http://www.nerdworld.com/users/dstein/nw26.html
```

4.10 Where in the World Is the Weather Just Like Yours?

ES

Subject: Geography, Weather
Grade Level: 3rd and Up

Here is another way to search for common factors and increase multicultural awareness.

Start here.

    http://www.weather.com/

Plot weather patterns on a map. Color code by weather pattern.

Example. Las Vegas is red hot. What other states, countries, cities have similar weather? Where is the weather the opposite?

Questions. What crops grow there? How does weather affect lifestyle? **Example**: When it's hot, what do you do for fun? Do kids in other states, countries do similar things? How about when it's very cold — what do kids do for fun?

What are the high and low extremes of temperature where people live? How do they build houses, public areas with the weather in mind? (For example, look into the underground shopping in Canada.)

4.11 Other Tours to Take

QS

Subject: Any
Grade Level: All

If you are looking for other search and research ideas, here is a small list that can grow to boundless proportions, fitting into any area of the curriculum:

    Art museums
    Lighthouses
    Zoos

Gardens
Aquariums
Gardens
Science museums
Monuments
Seven Wonders of the World (ancient and modern)
Festivals
Parks
Solar system
Bed andBreakfast Inns

Can You Find Information About This?

Another short list that you can lengthen.

Rapids
Lakes
Rivers
Mountains
Birds
Trees
Farms
Waterfalls
Ships
Pony Express
Bungee jumping

4.12 *College Search*

BROWSING

ES

Subject: College Prep, Geography
Grade Level: 8th and Up

In the old days, pre-Internet, colleges would send catalogs to prospective students, giving them the opportunity to learn more about the school, its requirements, the courses taught, etc. Today, this information is online. Most major universities and colleges worldwide are posting online the information that formerly went into the catalog.

Have your students prepare more effectively for their post-secondary options by exploring online.

Decide on your college major. Where can you study near home? Another country? How are the curricula the same from one college to another? How do they differ? What are the costs? What can you learn about the city you would be living in if you chose one of the schools far from home to attend?

    http://www.petersons.com/

4.13 *Ecology Efforts around the World*

BROWSING

ES

**Subject: Ecology, Geography
Grade Level: 4th and Up**

Something the Internet makes possible are shared projects your kids can get involved in with kids from around the world. One site for a listing of such projects is at:

    http://www.gsn.org/

You can join in with projects or start your own. This lesson is one suggestion for a possible starting point.

Questions.   What are the ecological problems in your town, city, area?

Who in the world shares your problem?

What are the causes?

Solutions?

Problems with cleanup?

Clean up costs?

What part do kids play in helping with ecology measures?

Can you share information electronically?

Plot your findings in charts or on a map. Can you find statistics? Pictures?

4.14 *Borrow from the Best*

BROWSING

ES

Subject: Geography, Critical Thinking
Grade Level: 4th and Up

Use the Net to bring more of the world to your kids. The ability to explore the best of things from around the world is one of the wonders of the Web. This type of lesson is designed for practicing online skills, as well as synthesizing information and planning an outcome.

Using commercial, travel and other sites, plan your own restaurant:

It would have the menu like _____

It would have the decor of _____

It would have entertainment like _____

Name your restaurant and make a brochure about it using text and graphics from the Net.

A place to start: http://www.epicurious.com/

What would it cost to put your restaurant together? Can you figure out costs?

Also. Plan your own hotel, amusement park, roller coaster, TV or radio station, fashion store, car emporium.
For this search, since you are looking for information from all over the world, note where the sites are located.

Note. Try changing the point of view of your students as they create their hard-copy projects. If they explored a city from the POV of a travel agent, they'll offer one perspective. If they work from the POV of the Chamber of Commerce, realtors, historians, scientists, etc., then they'll offer information from a different perspective.

Note. You can also ask your students to use the Net for find other media that add to their exploration. CD-ROMS, films, books, music, etc., are all available on the Net.

4.15   *Waterfalls in Our World*

BROWSING

EO

Subjects: Geography
Grade Level: 3rd and Up

There are some incredible waterfalls around the world. Search the Internet for information and pictures of waterfalls and chart the following:

Continent

Country

Height

Lake nearby

Source of water

Interesting characteristics

Volume of water over the falls each hour or day

Those used as a power source

Output.

Charts and maps

Well-written communication

Web page, PowerPoint, or Hyperstudio

Pick one waterfall from each continent (six in all).

Set up a tour of your waterfalls.

Include the following:

Nearest city with an airport

Hotel you would stay at

Guides to take you on tour

Time of year for best viewing — weather conditions for best visit

Other interesting sights worth seeing nearby.

Answer the following questions from your research:

1. Which waterfalls are major tourist attractions with many visitors each year (aside from Niagara Falls)?

2. If the waterfall is not used as a power source, why not?

3. Other than Niagara, which falls are the most dangerous to climb near?

4. Are any of the waterfalls in danger of being polluted?

5. Which falls had to be navigated around or built around for travel?

6. What formed your waterfalls? (Glaciers, on a faultline, on the edge of a plateau, etc.)

7. Year discovered and by whom?

LIST OF WATERFALLS

    http://www.waterfallsonline.com/docs/unlimited/library1.html

WATERFALL SAFARIS

    http://www.geocities.com/Yosemite/2687/

MICHELLE'S WATERFALL PAGE

    http://www.ilstu.edu/~dmmaki/waterfal/waterfal.htm

WATERFALLS

    http://www.bigbenpublishing.com/.au/victoria/waterfall.html

WATERFALL LINKS

    http://twilight.vtc.vsc.edu/~pchapin/water/other.htm

LESSON

COMMON LINKS

Using Internet Search Tools in Cross Curriculum Lessons

Samples of Possible Keyword Searches

Helping kids learn to search effectively is a valuable skill. It is even more valuable when combined with learning about a subject. These lessons are designed not only to give kids practice searching, but to approach a subject from a different viewpoint. Feel free to substitute your vocabulary, people, places, things, or ideas

Each of these groupings has one common factor. Using search tools, locate as much information as you can to find that common link.

Extensions. As you explore, keep track of the sites, addresses (URL), information that pertains, maps that help locate, and anything else that helped you find the common factor.

Use these search vehicles: Lycos, Altavista, Excite.

Note. When I use these searches, I merely put the references on the board, and if I have a good starting point, I direct students there. I don't tell them the common link until they have spent at least one class period searching. Many students have even gone back, once they have learned the link, and tried to verify it with varying results.

5.1 *MidEast and Minerals*　　COMMON LINKS

ES　　**Subjects: Geography, History, Science, Technology**
Grade Level: 5th and Up

Red Sea
Sudan
Saudi Arabia
Minerals (iron, zinc)
Technology
Middle East Politics
Exploration

The link. Undersea mining of minerals

A good place to start (for those who need help).

    http://www.mapquest.com/

Note. Your students will be able to locate information about the Sudan, Saudi Arabia, the Red Sea, and minerals but they may not be able to find direct links to the undersea mining. With my students, after they had searched and found the locations and some information about the undersea mining, we made the connections to politics, technology, and exploration by inference.

5.2 *Storms and Stories*

COMMON LINKS

ES

Subjects: Literature, Geography, Oceanography
Grade Level: 5th and Up

Strait of Messina

Sicily

Homer's Odyssey (Charybdis)

Naruto Strait

Edgar Allen Poe (Norway)

Corryvreckan (Scotland) (also spelled Corrievreckan)

Jura

Scarba

Maelstrom

The link. Places with whirlpools/maelstroms

A good place to start (for those who need help):

    http://www.drcasey.com/cabinet/maps/MediterraneanSeathe.shtml
    http://www.stores.demon.co.uk/page2.html

Note. My students found the reference to whirlpools and the Odyssey, but overlooked it in favor of the reference to sea monsters found at the same site. Once they had tried to cross-reference sea monsters with the other locations, they got stumped until I sent them back to the original site (Casey's horror site) and made them read what they had found again. From there, they were able to focus in on whirlpools.

—+++—

5.3   *Magic Mineral*

COMMON LINKS

ES   **Subjects: History, Science
Grade Level: 5th and Up**

Chrysotile

Salamander

Wool

Magic flax

Charlemagne (magic tablecloth)

Marco Polo

Mineral

Fireproof

Romans (cremation) and Arabs (armor)

Tartary, The Great Khan (precious jewels)

The link.   Asbestos use throughout history

Note.   I told my students to start with chrysotile and see if they could find any of the references I had found in the article I took this idea from. They had a good time searching, but could not yet narrow (we only searched for 30 minutes) to find the exact references to asbestos, so I filled in the blanks. This made some of them want to go back and search for the historical references. So far, they have not had class time to do this.

—+++—

5.4 Before Star Trek

COMMON LINKS

ES

**Subjects: Media U.S. Cultural History (comics/radio/TV/film)
Grade Level: 4th and Up**

Wilma Deering
Princess Ardala
Killer Kane
Doctor Huer

A good place to start. Search in Lycos or Altavista for Wilma Deering or Princess Ardala.

The link. Characters in the original Buck Rogers comic strip

If all else fails, a site to start with (a give-it-away site).

http://www.otr.com/sf.html

Questions to answer. Who are these people connected to? When were they created? What information can you find about their stories? Who created them? What additional information can you find about these characters?

Extension. Create a search using your favorite comic strip characters. Make sure you do a search first just in case your favorites are not online. Be sure your comic strip has at least four characters with uncommon names.

Another extension. Do some research on old comic strips. Use your word processor to copy and paste pictures and information from the Net and create a picture tour of the old comic.

Note. This is a simple search, with information that is not difficult to locate. Thus, it's is good starting place for younger kids or those new to search tools.

LESSON

6

BRANCHING OUT — OTHER THINGS TO SEARCH FOR

Practicing the Vocabulary and Other Elements of a Subject with Keyword Searches

The following searches, which I hope can serve as templates for your curriculum, have no common link. They are filled with interesting people, words, ideas, or inventions. Your job is to locate the information asked for. Appropriate starting points are listed. Substitute with people, ideas, and words from your curriculum.

6.1 *Follow the Yellow Brick Road*   **BRANCHING**

EO.PD   **Subjects: Literature, History, Politics**
Grade Level: 6th and Up

This lesson requires that students read *The Wizard of Oz* by L. Frank Baum

In the United States, at the turn of the century, an economic battle raged over the use of gold or silver as the national standard for backing up U.S. money. Many favored changing to the silver standard, while others voted for remaining with the gold standard. One of the most famous proponents of the silver standard was William Jennings Bryan, who in the 1890s led a Midwestern political movement called *populism*.

The populists of the Midwest were challenging the banks and railroads of the East, feeling that the farmers and industrial workers of the Midwest were being harmed because U.S. currency was not backed with a silver standard. Bryan delivered a famous speech called "The Cross of Gold" when he was running for President of the United States in 1896.

Another populist named L. Frank Baum, an editor of a South Dakota newspaper, was moved by Bryan's loss in the election and wrote an allegory, the first in a series. The series was about a place called "Oz" and concerns a young girl named Dorothy, a Cowardly Lion, a Tinman, and other characters who became beloved characters in American literature and film.

1. Read The Wizard of Oz.

2. Research:

    The Populist movement
    William Jennings Bryan
    L. Frank Baum
    The Cross of Gold Speech
    The gold and silver standards
    Late 1890s Midwest America

3. Compare your findings to the following: If this is an allegory, the story could mean that:

    Oz is short for ounce, the measure for gold.
    Dorothy, coming from Kansas, represents the common person.
    The Tinman represents the industrial worker who lost his job when factories shut down in the 1893 depression.
    The Scarecrow stands for the farmers who lacked the brains to know their best political moves.
    The Cowardly Lion is Bryan, who spoke loudly but did little else.
    The Wicked Witch of the East is the Eastern bankers.
    The Emerald City is Washington, D.C.
    The Wizard is the President of the United States.
    Dorothy frees the Munchkins by using the silver slippers (the silver standard).

Other items that are part of the allegory are:

    Munchkins
    The Wicked Witch of the West being doused with water
    The Yellow Brick Road

What might they represent in the allegory?

4. Read parts of the book again, keeping in mind the allegorical nature of the story:

   Scene: On the road through the forest where Dorothy and the Scarecrow discuss Kansas and having brains.

   Scene: The Scarecrow discussing his need for a brain and how the birds treated him as he guarded the corn.

   Scene: The Tin Woodman tells the Scarecrow his story of how he became tin and lost his heart.

   Scene: The Cowardly Lion tells Dorothy about his lack of courage and desire for bravery.

5. In what ways is the author trying to explain the plight of the Midwesterner, the farmer, the factory worker? Support the silver standard? Question the judgment of the Eastern bankers and railroaders? Propose solutions to the problems? (Who ends up in charge of Oz? Who rules the East in the end?)

Note.   In the film with Judy Garland, the silver slippers of the novel were turned into ruby, thus straying from the author's original point.

For a copy of the book online:

http://www.literature.org/Works/L-Frank-Baum/wizard/

Starting points.

WONDERFUL WIZARD OF OZ — A PARABLE

http://www.amphigory.com/oz.htm

POPULIST HISTORY

http://incolor.inetnebr.com/dennis/populist.shtml

WIZARD AS POPULIST TALE

http://www.uncg.edu/psc/courses/jktullos/policy/oz.html

OZ POPULISM THEORY

http://www.halcyon.com/piglet/Populism.htm

THE WONDERFUL WIZARD AS A MONETARY ALLEGORY

http://www.switzerland.isyours.com/FXM/MH/Crime/WWIZOZ.htm

THE TRUE STORY

http://www.mangonet.com/~doog/kruft/oz.html

POPULIST READER

    http://www.eden.com/~reporter/Populist.Reader.html

WILLIAM JENNINGS BRYAN *CROSS OF GOLD* SPEECH

    http://www.tntech.edu/:8080/www/acad/hist/crosgold.html

WILLIAM JENNINGS BRYAN

    http://mission.lib.tx.us/exhibits/bryan/bryan.htm
    http://144.92.37.98/hist102/bios/html/bryan.html
    http://www.law.umkc.edu/ftrials/scopes/bryanw.htm

Extension.   What part did William Jennings Bryan play in the famous Scopes Trial?

    http://www.bryan.edu/scopes/inherit.htm

Read *Inherit the Wind* by Jerome Lawrence and Robert E. Lee, available at

    http://www.amazon.com/
    http://www.barnesandnoble.com/

6.2 *Interesting Folks*

BRANCHING

ES

Subject: History, Geography
Grade Level: 4th and Up

People you might meet along the way.   Each of these people is mentioned in a book as being interesting. What did they do in their lives that made them so interesting? When you have gathered your information, compare notes with your teacher.

Henrietta Lacks and Dr. George Gey

Daniel Dancer

Alexander Wortley

Jean Baptiste Jolly

Notes for Teachers

Henrietta Lacks and Dr. George Gey.   Dr. Gey used cancer cells from Henrietta to develop HeLa Cells that helped develop a polio vaccine and are contributing to finding a cure for cancer. Her cells were used because they grew so rapidly. Check also sites with information about African-Americans for information about Henrietta Lacks.

Daniel Dancer.   1760s London — had a reputation of being a miser. Well-documented evidence points to his miserliness especially as it pertained to his sister.

Alexander Wortley.   Died in 1980 — lived in England and slept in a box on wheels. He moved around a great deal with his box on wheels. He also suffered from a rare speech problem called Klang Association.

Jean Baptiste Jolly.   Paris, France — developed a chemical for dry cleaning.

A good place to start.   Besides searching for their names with a search engine, try the biographical dictionary or other biography sites:

```
http://s9.com/biography
http://www.biography.com/
http://www.wp.com/Hirsane/women.html
```

6.3   *Who Said That?*   **BRANCHING**

ES   **Subject: Any**
             Grade Level: 4th and Up

Each of these phrases has become a cliche. Who originally said or wrote it, and in what context?

   a. Absence makes the heart grow fonder
   b. Greek to me
   c. Ax to grind
   d. The best laid schemes of mice and men
   e. Gone with the wind (not the novel)
   f. Hold the fort

g. Keeping up with the Joneses

h. Eaten out of house and home

i. In the dog house

j. Mad as a hatter

A good place to start.   Sites about quotations.

```
http://www.quoteland.com/index.html
http://www.geocities.com/Athens/7186/
http://www.columbia.edu/acis/bartleby/bartlett/
```

‡‡‡

6.4 *Word Origins*

Another approach to vocabulary.

ES

Subject: Any
Grade Level: 3rd and Up

Where did these words come from? Be prepared to tell the story behind each word's origin.

balderdash
ballyhoo
butterfly
gremlin
hobo
hoodlum
yankee

A good place to start.

```
http://thorplus.lib.purdue.edu/reference/index.html
http://www.iTools.com/research-it/research-it.html
http://philby.ucsd.edu/cgi-bin/http_webster
http://www-sci.lib.uci.edu/HSG/Refl.html#OVER2
```

‡‡‡

6.5 : *What Subject Am I Studying?* **BRANCHING**

Vocabulary study again.

ES

Subject: Any
Grade Level: 3rd and Up

Once you know more about these words or names, you will know what subject they refer to.

- Andromeda galaxy
- Asteroid
- Atmosphere
- Edwin Hubble
- Galileo
- Big Bang theory
- Comet
- Nicolas Copernicus

Extension.   Add some words or names that you found that fit with these. Explain how they fit.

A good place to go, if you get stuck.

```
http://www.npac.syr.edu/:80/textbook/kidsweb/astronomy.html
http://buckman.pps.k12.or.us/room100/abcspace/spaceabc.html
http://db.cochran.com/li_showElems:theoPage:theo:3548:0.db
```

Another extension.   As you were exploring, did you find any other Internet site with great information about this subject? What is the URL? What did you like best about that site?

LESSON

7

ADDITIONAL IDEAS FOR SEARCHES

For each of these searches, you will find sites in this book that will help your students locate the information.

7.1 *How Prepared Are You?*

MORE SEARCHES

EO/PD   **Subjects: Literature, Natural Sciences**
Grade Level: 3rd and up

A few years ago, my students and I played a software game called "Swiss Family Robinson." Based on the novel and closely paralleling the Disney movie (http://www.disney.com/), the software required us to really think and use everything in our environment to survive. We even had to learn what ingredients to gather from our surroundings and how to mix those ingredients in the proper order to create a candle. We had to locate a suitable place for shelter and begin to prepare a roof over our heads. And we had very few chances for error.

Other simulation software, such as "Oregon Trail" and "SimCity," accomplishes the same goals, teaching survival and thinking skills. These pieces of software can be linked to books, stories, films, and often history as well.

If you have not played one of these simulations, read one of the novels, or seen one of the films, it would be helpful to choose one as a starting point, or try some of these sites. Listed here are tours of historical locations, mostly in the United States. Some provide insight into what skills and materials the inhabitants needed to survive. Aside from Old Sturbridge Village (http://www.osv.org/) and Greenfield Village (http://www.hfmgv.org/), here are some other tours.

NATIVE ALASKAN HISTORY TOURS
   http://www.alaskaone.com/eklutna/

FURNACE TOWN
   http://www.dol.net/~ebola/ftown01.htm

Golden Pioneer Museum

http://hengel.henge.com/~goldenpm/

Heritage Farmstead

http://www.heritagefarmstead.org/

Edgewood Heritage Park

http://www.vzinet.com/heritage/index.htm

Knife River Indian Villages

http://www.nps.gov/knri/

Oak Hill

http://www.berry.edu/oakhill/

The Fort at #4

http://www.chesulwind.com/fort-at-no4/index.htm

Gibbs Farm Museum

http://www.rchs.com/gbbsfm2.htm

Claude Moore Colonial Farm

http://www.geocities.com/Heartland/Acres/1344/

Outside the United States.

Ameliasburgh Historical Museum (Ontario, Canada)

http://www.pec.on.ca/ameliasburghmuseum/

Heritage Park (Alberta, Canada)

http://www.heritagepark.ab.ca/

Moncur Gallery (Manitoba, Canada)

http://www.town.boissevain.mb.ca/moncur/

Take some time and add to this list historical sites you find in other countries. Also in this book are tours of Mayan ruins (http://www.mecc.com/mayquest.html) and the ancient city of Petra:

http://www.tardis.ed.ac.uk/~angus/Gallery/Photos/MiddleEast/Jordan/Petra/
    MapIndex.html

More explorations might include the Nile, Ancient Greece and Rome, or ancient China.

While students are learning about just what it takes to survive in conditions where nothing is provided for you and you must provide for yourself, ask them to collectively help each other prepare.

Begin with this scenario: You suddenly find yourself living where you are now, but you have just arrived with the first settlers, pilgrims, tribe, etc. Many of you, around the world, live in areas first populated thousands of years ago. Go back to that time.

Where are you?

When was the year of first settlement?

What are the settlers called?

What are some items used for survival that you probably brought with you?

Was the area different, topographically, back then?

Now it is time for you and your family to build all the things you need to survive.

1. *Without electricity, gas, oil, propane or butane in ready supply, what type of power will you use for energy and light?*

   Online resources for candle making:

   http://candleandsoap.miningco.com/
   http://homepage.interaccess.com/~bmolo/

2. *Of what material, and in what style, will you build shelter?*

   Online resources to help you with building instructions:

   http://www.logcabinhomes.com/
   http://www.woodworking.com/loghomes/

3. *Immediate food supply? Long-range food options?*

   http://www.fieldandstream.com/

4. *Other survival needs: clothing?*

   History of Costume from Ancient Moors to the Renaissance

   http://www.siue.edu/COSTUMES/history.html

Additional resources.

SOAP MAKING

http://www.fragrant.demon.co.uk/makesoap.html

After you learn what you can about what it took to survive years ago, assess your skills. Which of the skills that your ancestors used can you use as well?

Your output can take various forms: diaries, letters, newspapers, collages, Web pages, etc.

7.2   *What Job Do I Do?*

MORE SEARCHES

QS

Subject: Any
Grade Level: 4th and Up

What else do historians, mathematicians, and people who read do besides teach? Introduce kids to some of the jobs your curriculum prepares them for.

List words associated with a job, career or profession. See if the students can find out what job they relate to. What additional information can you find about that job? Is there anyone online with a home page who does that job? What training do you need? Where are the job openings? Can you find out the salary? Can you locate an ad in a newspaper for an opening?

Sample.

Best boy

Key grip

Gaffer

Extra

Foley artist

Stand-in

Casting

Set dresser

2nd assistant director

Costume designer

Try this site.

    http://www.imdb.com/Glossary

Or try.

    http://www.telefilm-south.com/index.html
    http://www.mandy.com/

7.3 | *What State Am I In?* MORE SEARCHES

QS

Subject: Geography
Grade Level: 3rd and Up

List city names, famous universities, parks, or places of interest all relating to one state. Then see if the students can find and post a map of the state. Can they locate the cities, parks, or other places in the state? Can they locate pictures? Are there any famous people from that state? How far is it from your state? How can you get there?

Can you locate a newspaper from that state?

7.4 | *Where in the World Do I Live?* MORE SEARCHES

QS

Subject: More Geography — Substitute Terms to Fit Your Curriculum
Grade Level: 3rd and Up

List city names, famous museums, landmarks, historical sights, music, type of dress, foods commonly associated with this country, universities or public schools, famous citizens, etc. See if your students can create a pictorial and text tour of the country once they have narrowed their search.

Sample.

The Sacred Turtles Of Kadavu

The Tagimaucia Flower

Viti Levu

Mount Uluiqalau

English language

Archipelago

Pacific islands

"Ni sa Bula!"

Capt. William Bligh

Lovoni

If you get stuck.

```
http://www.fijiguide.com/
http://www.en.com/users/laura8/index.html
```

7.5 *Find a Book or Story*   **MORE SEARCHES**

ES

Subject: Any
Grade Level: 3rd and Up

How about a story dealing with your subject?

Have your students select an age group other than their own (younger usually works best, or for the youngest kids, try finding something for a friend or older sibling). See if they can find an appropriate story, book, fable, or myth that someone in that age group might like to read.

Browse here through any category:

```
http://www.books.com/scripts/default.exe
```

Look here for text of fairy tales:

```
gopher://ftp.std.com/:70/11/obi/book/Fairy.Tales/Grimm
```

Look here for an online story:

```
http://www.ucalgary.ca/~dkbrown/stories.html
```

Extension. Put together a list of recommended reads for the age groups or subject selected. Print reviews when you find them. Print author information as well. Copy and paste any pictures from the book or book jacket to add to the printed information generated by your students.

Another extension. What information can your students locate about the authors they have chosen? Can they locate a book that was made into a film they can watch?

7.6 *Holidays*

MORE SEARCHES

ES

Subject: Multicultural Studies
Grade Level: 3rd and Up

From these sites, select a holiday you either do not celebrate or have not heard of and put together an informative booklet or paper with pictures and text explaining the history and traditions behind that holiday.

```
http://www.kidlink.org/KIDPROJ/MCC/
http://www.candlegrove.com/
http://www.holidays.net/
http://www.auburn.edu/~vestmon/christmas.html
http://www.katsden.com/webster/holiday.html
http://www.zapcom.net/phoenix.arabeth/1world.html
http://www.classnet.com/holidays/
```

7.6 *When the Gas Runs Out*

MORE SEARCHES

EO/PD

Subjects: Economics, Transportation
Grade Level: 4th and Up

It is predicted that in less than 50 years, the supply of oil in the world will diminish drastically. America is very dependent on cars, and the oil and gas that keep them running, for almost all our transportation needs.

Read more about the energy crisis in "Future world oil supplies: There IS a finite limit" at:

    http://users.knsi.com/~tbender/ivanhoe.html

What will you do when the gas runs out?

1. Write a plan for your family telling how each member will get to work, school, shopping (groceries), and medical treatment without using a traditional car.

   In your plan, use only the following: public transportation, bikes, in-line skates, walking

   You may also choose one alternative fuel automobile: battery or solar powered

   Make a chart for your family for one week of alternative transportation that gets everyone where they need to go — for necessities only

2. *Additional exploration:* U.S. public transportation vs other countries. Many countries rely on public transportation to move the majority of their people. They use buses, trolleys, and trains that run on alternative fuels.

   Compare the United States with other countries:

   Use of alternative fuels in public transportation (chart)

   Number of electric buses

   Number of electric trains

   Number of electric trolleys

   Number of people transported daily by each method of transportation

Try this site called Carfree Cities:

    http://www.carfree.com/

Other sites that might help.
ALTERNATIVE FUELS VEHICLE PAGE

    http://geocities.com/RainForest/Vines/5134/index.html

ALTERNATIVE METHODS OF PROPULSION

    http://www.pipelin.com/~bkyaffe/altfuel/

ELECTRIC VEHICLES HOME PAGE

    http://www.ev.hawaii.edu/

DEPARTMENT OF ENERGY TRANSPORTATION TECHNOLOGIES

    http://www.ott.doe.gov/

EV WORLD

    http://evworld.com/

Information about vehicles of the 21st century.

TOYOTA'S GREENER CARS

    http://www.toyota.co.jp/e/green/

DIDIK

    http://www.ddgn.com/carman/didik_ev.htm

Alternative fuel vehicles profiled here.

JAMES KUNSTLER SPEECH

    http://www.kunstler.com/spch_rails_to_trails.html

ECOPLAN INTERNATIONAL

    http://www.the-commons.org/ecoplan/consult/eb-home.htm

BIKE PEOPLE

    http://home.earthlink.net/~rickrise/bikepeople/

AUTO FREE TIMES

    http://www.tidepool.com/alliance/aft.htm

CYBURBIA

    http://www.arch.buffalo.edu/pairc/index.html

LESSON

8

SEARCHING THE NET

Sometimes searching for fun is a good way to practice the tools and learn a little along the way. Again, give the kids a choice. I don't let them all gang up on one area because the more width and depth to our explorations, the more we all learn.

8.1 *Highways, Byways, and Subways*   `THE NET`

EO/PD **Subjects: Geography, Ecology, City Planning, Tourism**
Grade Level: 4th and Up

Things to discuss before going online. How air quality is measured, how people are transported around modern cities

Skills to have. Reading maps, measuring miles and kilometers, reading statistics, charting/graphing

I lived in Toronto for several years, using a transportation system that lets me nominate that beautiful city as "the easiest city I ever got around in." I rarely had to wait for a bus, streetcar, or subway for longer than 15 minutes, they took me every-where in the city, and they were clean.

I also lived in Las Vegas, Nevada, which has a transportation system built to accomodate a much smaller city. The explosive growth has made it necessary for them to add to an already confusing freeway overpass system called "The Spaghetti Bowl." I also walked three miles on one street before a bus caught up with me, and I wasn't jogging. Las Vegas now has to warn citizens, broadcasting over the local television stations, about air quality.

Now, I live in Southern California and have to learn freeway numbers again to know what people are talking about when they give directions, as most traveling is done by car and on freeways. It also took my father all day to go 5 miles by bus in one Southern California city. Some days, the mountains I live in disappear behind a wall of smog caused by exhaust fumes and other pollutants.

Cities have to transport their citizens or make it possible for them to transport themselves. Cities also should remain clean. Which of these cities does both best:

Toronto, Ontario, Canada

Las Vegas, Nevada, USA

Los Angeles, California, USA

1. *How do these cities transport their people?*

Subway

http://metro.jussieu.fr:10001/bin/cities/english

Highways and/or freeways

http://www.mapblast.com/
http://www.mapquest.com/

Buses (number per population)

Which system offers transportation by fewer cars?

Which is the most reliant on cars?

What other options do citizens have? (Statistics: Ratio of cars to people, buses or public transportation to people)

Side exploration. How are bicycles still used as transportation? What are some other, unique forms of transportation? Cross-reference. with geography, then extend to history.

2. Check out some statistics about the air quality of Toronto, Los Angeles, and Las Vegas. I think Toronto will come out the cleanest.

What do the governments of Toronto, Ontario, and Canada do to keep their air clean?

What do Las Vegas, Clark County, and Nevada do? Los Angeles, Los Angeles County, and California?

What are the causes of the pollution in these cities?

How do they rate foul air days? What constitutes a moderate air quality or heavy smog day? What are recent statistics for days of bad air quality?

Extra credit extension. Some foul air comes from Mexico. Cross-reference this with geography. Extend to ecology studies.

3. Do some measuring.

What is the physical size (miles and kilometers) of the three cities? In the case of Los Angeles, where freeways connect many small cities, measure the city of Los Angeles itself. Just for curiosity's sake, because people around L.A. commute 60–70 miles into the city for work, what is the physical size of L.A. from the Civic Center, north to Ventura, east to Redlands, and south to Laguna Niguel?

4. Compile your statistics

5. What city do you nominate as "Easiest to get around in"? Cleanest? Easiest and cleanest?

6. How do you rate your city using the same criteria used above?

7. How do you get around your city? How many miles do you travel each day? Week?

Extension. Compare your miles with those of people from other cities. Set up by country, state/province. Where do the mobile people live? Least mobile? Does that have anything to do with the transportation?

Output. Charts, data base, spreadsheet, narrative from the perspective of a tour guide to the city or from the point of view of a tourist who is trying to see all the sights. (This requires taking a tour of the cities.)

Start here for tours.
        http://www.lonelyplanet.com/
Add to your output any additional sites you found useful and any tour of your area.

Extension. Montreal had wonderfully clean subways, too, but New York's and Philadelphia's could use some tidying up. Perhaps they have. What can you learn about efforts to keep their public transportation graffiti-free?

Extension. Research and discuss why the transportation systems evolved as they did in the three cities. Example: The effect on the transportation system of a sudden growth in population. (This applies to Los Angeles or Las Vegas. L.A. had a growth spurt starting after World War II and lasting until the 1980s. Las Vegas's growth has been within the past decade and still continues.)

Or, look into:

- The effect of weather on the transportation system that evolved over the past 50 years
- The amount of physical space available for the city and its environs
- Existing boundaries — natural, manmade, or those of another city — that may have contributed to the growth or lack of it. (Can you learn about Toronto's Green Belt or the manmade lake, Lake Mead, outside Las Vegas?) How do things like that affect transportation systems?

Starting points. Living Together in Harmony with Nature

http://www.stratosphere.org/projects/fpage008.html

From future cities and ecology in housing, this site teaches how to live in harmony with nature.

CARFREE CITIES

http://www.carfree.com/

JAMES KUNSTLER SPEECH

http://www.kunstler.com/spch_rails_to_trails.html

ECOPLAN INTERNATIONAL

http://www.the-commons.org/ecoplan/consult/eb-home.htm

BIKE PEOPLE

http://home.earthlink.net/~rickrise/bikepeople/

AUTO FREE TIMES

http://www.tidepool.com/alliance/aft.htm

CYBURBIA

http://www.arch.buffalo.edu/pairc/index.html

8.2 *Share and Share Alike Search* THE NET

ES **Subject: Any**
Grade Level: All

You've learned a lot about the Net by this time. You have bookmarked, and created folders for all your overflow and you breeze through those search descriptions. Now's the time to share.

What sites would you share with:

a. A 10-year-old girl in Sydney, Australia
b. A 12-year-old boy in Amsterdam

c. An 8-year-old boy on a farm in Iowa

d. A 14-year-old girl in Venice, Italy

e. Any mom your mom's age

f. Any dad

g. Grandparents like yours

h. A new college graduate in your state, province or area

Extension.   If that person, or those persons, were to come visit you, how would you have them prepare? What sites could they visit that tell about your city/state/province/area?

Can you make a map to your house?

```
http://www.mapblast.com/
```

Can you recommend a local online newspaper?
Where can you shop nearby?
What attractions are there to see?
What is the closest university like?
If they like to ski, how far do they have to go, and what will it look like?
What movies are playing nearby while they visit?
What TV shows do they watch back home that they can watch with you?
Can you show them houses/apartments/domiciles that look like yours?
Are there any historical sites nearby to show them?
Any museums? Art galleries? Amusement parks?

8.3 *The Front Page*   **THE NET**

ES   **Subject: Any**
               Grade Level: 4th and Up

Not too many of my students read their daily newspaper, but among the wonderful tools of the Net are sites like CRAYON (www.crayon.net/) and Pointcast (http://www.pointcast.com/) where you decide just how you want your daily newspaper to be set up. Do you want the front page of a newspaper from Australia, Canada,

Belgium, or another of more than 900 countries? From where do you do want your weather, your comics, your sports gathered? These personalized newspapers, once organized, are updated automatically whenever the sites you have chosen are updated. Your choices are amazingly broad and well worth the effort.

Aside from reading the newspaper, it's good for the kids to use such sites as the tools for information they are. Here are a group of lessons designed to involve kids in using the news and newspapers.

Because there are so many newspapers online and from all over the world, it's possible to access news with just a touch of a few buttons.

1. **Browse** through some of the newspapers that interest your students at this site:

NEWSPAPERS AROUND THE WORLD

        http://www.geocities.com/~oberoi/newspapr.html

2. Focus on a global area of class interest:
   Environment
   Business/economy
   Peace
   Health
   Media
   Technology
   Arts
   Weather
   (Or one of your own)

3. Decide which headlines from the newspapers have the most interest, globally. (This presumes an understanding by your students of how events in any one of these elements can have a global impact.)

4. Copy and paste the most important headlines into another medium or print selected text and pictures to create a layout of Global Headlines.

Extension. Put together an historical newspaper, dating back over 50 years ago, for any one of the newspaper sections listed above.

Extension. What sports would you emphasize in a global newspaper?
   Put together a sports section for your global newpaper. Explore some of the online sports networks. Is their coverage global? Did they leave any sports out that you found covered in the newspapers?
   Why should Internet coverage be global?

Extension. Take an event you read about or a featured story from the recent news and track it *Forward and Back.* Example: from the news of 11/24/96: Hijacked plane crashes into sea.

Extension. Go back 10 or more years and follow an international or more local story as far as you can.

Extension to another medium. Watch "Time and Again" on MSNBC for similar news coverage.

LESSON

9 — WANT ADS

These lessons are designed for kids to learn how to read help wanted ads, create résumés, and use the newspaper. They are also designed to have kids learn more about different jobs. It's easy to use the Internet to expose kids to a wider variety of jobs, occupations, and careers than ever before. Showing them people at work helps them plan for their future.

All of these jobs can be adjusted to trainee/entry level as well.

9.1 — Internet

WANT ADS

EO

Subject: Any
Grade Level: 4th and Up

Small but growing, online newspaper needs experienced Webmaster to pull all the pieces together. E-mail your résumé and show us online what kind of work you do.

1. What are the job responsibilities of a Webmaster?
2. What training do you need? Where can you get the training?
3. What is the salary for a starting position?
4. Can you locate a résumé for a Webmaster, online?
5. What is the outlook for the job of Webmaster in general?
6. List three URLs for sites where you think the Webmaster is doing a good job. Ways to tell:
   a. Is there anything that is part of the site that is designed to bring you back again?
   b. Is the site speaking to one audience, or is it serving many audiences? Does it serve its audience/audiences well with enough information or things for that group to do?
   c. Can you tell, up front, what you will find at the site?
   d. Did the site get you involved in any way — signing up for updates, a newsletter, an e-mail address for comments, a questionnaire?
   e. Did the site create networks within the Net using hyperlinks?

    f. Is the site overloaded with bells and whistles, or are they used to good effect to add something terrific?

7. Can you find an ad for a job opening online? In your local newspaper?

9.2   *Archaeologist*

WANT ADS

EO   **Subject: Any**
Grade Level: 4th and Up

Small, but financially secure university seeks an Indiana Jones–type professor interested in arts and antiquities to work with a professor of cultural studies, a Margaret Mead–schooled anthropologist, to search the world over for links to man's history. Assignments available immediately in China and Ethiopia.
    E-mail your résumé and URL of samples or your work.

1. Define archaeologist.
2. Locate a biography for one archaeologist currently working and one deceased.
3. Where are current explorations taking place? Are any near you?
4. Where can you study to be an archaeologist? What classes do you take in your major? List four.
5. List URLs for three museums with archaeological finds on display.
6. What is the most recent find?
7. What find is dated as the oldest?

9.3   *Architect*

WANT ADS

EO   **Subject: Any**
Grade Level: 4th and Up

Creative team of four architects needs one more to head our global studies division. We are planning pavilions now for the next World's Fair. Check out Grassroots Catalyst for Change:

```
http://health.acor.org/grassroots/
```

E-mail your résumé and the URL of any site with a display of your work.

1. Locate the biographies of two famous architects with pictures of their work.
2. If you were designing in Europe in the 1800s, what might some of your work look like? Who would have been designing at the same time? Who were your influences?
3. Locate the home pages of two architects. What do they specialize in? Are there samples of their work? Did you find e-mail addresses?
4. Where can you study to be an architect? List three classes in your major.
5. Can you list the URLs for three modern designs you like? Three older ones?
6. Can you find a résumé of an architect? A job opening? Salary?

9.4 Stockbroker

WANT ADS

EO

Subject: Any
Grade Level: 4th and Up

New, progressive brokerage needs your youth, energy and talent. You will be trading globally, so résumé should reflect your experience with other markets ourside your native country.

1. Find home pages or résumés for three stock brokers. What information do they provide?
2. Where do you study to be a stock broker?
3. What do you study? List three classes in your major.
4. What kind of salary can you expect for someone with 3–5 years' experience?
5. If you live in Japan, what market do you trade on? Europe? Australia? South America?
6. What can you learn about the history of the stock market?
7. Where can you trade or see stock quotes online?
8. Where, online, can you get involved in a stock market simulation?

9.5 Editor

EO

Subject: Any
Grade Level: 4th and Up

Online magazine for kids needs editors for various departments. Send résumé by e-mail and URLs of any sites online with samples of your work. Departments needing editors are sports, games, school, music, and TV.

1. What does an editor do?
2. Locate the e-mail addresses of three editors of online kids' magazines.
3. How can you tell when a magazine has a good editor?
4. List three stories you found online that you liked.
5. What skills does an editor need?
6. What do editors study in school?
7. Did you find one article or story you did not like because of its presentation? What would you do to improve it?
8. What kind of salary can an editor expect?
9. Locate an online ad for a job opening for an editor.

9.6 Marine Biologist

EO

Subject: Any
Grade Level: 4th and Up

Distinguished aquarium and research center needs an experienced marine biologist to assist in ecological research. Send résumé via e-mail and URLs of any projects in which you assisted.

1. Locate online aquariums. Which one would you like to work at?
2. Where can you study to be a marine biologist?
3. What do you study? List three classes in your major.

4. What salary can you expect?

5. Locate some marine biologists online with samples of their projects.

6. What equipment do they use?

7. What are marine biologists studying in Australia? Japan? Vancouver? San Diego?

Possible Substitutions. While I tried to present one job for every main curriculum area, extensions from your subject, showing your kids what people who study your subject do with the knowledge, gives them choices and possibilities. Find those people online and show your kids how your subject is used.

Too often, students have no idea what people who love math, history, or literature do besides teach or some of the better-known professions. The world is full of unique, exciting, challenging, and enjoyable ways for people to spend their lives productively and be compensated for it. Expose your kids to as many ways of making a living as you can.

LESSON

10

ADDITIONAL EXPLORATIONS

Background information can be interesting and help fill in some gaps in the gathering of knowledge. This approach focuses on one area and sends the students looking for specifics. These details, added to those gathered by other kids, provides a broad perspective.

I also tried to include all core subjects in the total exploration, giving the kids the choice of area to explore but making sure all areas are covered.

These explorations can become quite visual, using a lot of paper. If you have the option of doing computer presentations or publishing your results on your own Web page, this is very effective and will save trees.

10.1 *Change Your Latitude*   EXPLORATIONS

EO   **Subjects: Geography, Latitude and Longitude**
Grade Level: 4th and Up

Nominate your favorite city in the entire world by listing its latitude and longitude only.

1. Students will locate cities, search quickly for information and pictures, and nominate their favorite
2. Tease the voters with pictures of the city without naming the city or giving away its name and location.
3. Tell why it is your favorite city.
4. Post all nominees online or on a bulletin board.
5. Students locate, research, and vote for their favorites.
6. Post the top 10 choices.
7. Extend to rivers, mountains, lakes, beaches, lighthouses. . . .
8. Plan a trip to your favorite of the winners:

    Write a travel brochure or a narrative account of a visit;

    prepare a visual presentation about the city;

    compute the costs of a visit.

Starting points. For some maps with latitude and longitude:

```
http://www.mapblast.com/
http://www.mapsonus.com/
http://www.mapquest.com/
```

For some tours:

```
http://www.lonelyplanet.com/
http://www.expedia.com/
```

10.2 *Through the Core Subjects and Beyond*

EXPLORATIONS

EO   **Subject: Any**
Grade Level: 4th and Up

Explore what's behind.

1. The science/health of training for the Olympics
2. The business of training for the Games
3. The history of the Games.
   Where did they originate? When? Why there?
4. Stories about Olympus and Olympic heroes
5. Sculptures of athletes, mythological figures from Olympus, or Olympic heroes

Explore what's behind.

1. The science/technology behind making a CD, record, or cassette
2. The business of getting recorded:
   Who are the leaders in the recording industry; the producers? Who's up and coming?
3. The history of the recording industry. What inventions led up to the first recording? What was the first recording? Who are Motown? Why is Nashville important in the recording industry?
4. Locate some biographies of music industry recording stars from the 1930s, '40s, '50s, '60s, '70s, '80s, '90s
5. Locate samples of album or CD covers. How has the art changed over the years?
6. What other countries have strong recording industries?

Output.
- Hypercard stack of info
- Report with charts, timeline, and maps
- Biography of one artist or producer
- History of one company with pictures and information
- PowerPoint presentation of one aspect of search — especially the artwork

10.3 *Faraway Places with Strange-Sounding Names*

EXPLORATIONS

EO   **Subject: Geography**
Grade Level: 3rd and Up

A worldwide search for kids of all ages.

You can learn some interesting things about a country by exploring the history behind its place names.

Here are some unusual names found in Canada:

Bay of Fundy	Flin Flon
Regina	Manitoba
Toronto	Vancouver
Goobies, Newfoundland	

Can you locate these places online and find out how they got their names? Keep track of the timeline for the establishment of the places and plot their locations on a map.

You may not be able to find each of these names, but sometimes your search will lead you to other places with interesting names.

Writing idea.   Write the newspaper story of the birth of one of the places. Don't forget to mention all the interesting details of how the place got its name.

Some unusual names in France:

Nice
Paris
Nancy

Lyon
Marseilles

Some unusual names in Louisiana:

Baton Rouge
New Orleans
Lafayette
Lake Pontchartrain
Point a la Hache
Some unusual names in Texas:
Amarillo
Lubbock
Sweetwater
Odessa
El Paso
Monahans

10.4 *In Their Own Words*

EXPLORATIONS

EO

Subject: Literature, History
Grade Level: 3rd and Up

Journals often give an interesting account of history. Online, you can find many examples of journals, ranging from Alice Williamson's Civil War Diary at:

http://scriptorium.lib.duke.edu/williamson/

to first-person accounts of settlers crossing the country along the Oregon Trail:

http://208.206.78.232/daver/1sthand/atp/atp.html

Read some of the real-life accounts you find online for one era, generation, or event.

Example.
WPA LIFE HISTORIES

http://rs6.loc.gov/wpaintro/ctcat.html

First-person accounts from people who lived during the American Depression.

Writing idea. In your own words, what was a typical day like for someone living during the time you read about?

Just wondering. If you were crossing America in a covered wagon, there are some skills you would need that would get you through tough times. What are some of the skills possessed by the people you read about? Which of those skills do you not have? What skills do you have that they did not have?

EXTENDED STUDENT ACTIVITIES

BASICS AND BOOKMARKS

IN THIS CHAPTER

- Samples of Lessons for One Subject Area
- Sample Lesson for Writing Skills
- Samples of Cross-Curriculum Lessons
- Suggestions for Using E-mail with Students

It still amazes me that after having had one computer or another in my classroom since 1981, there are colleagues who have never had a disk drive or monitor grace their room. How terribly sad it will be if they have to wait another 18 years for this tool.

My plea to administrators at all levels is for two things: first, go online often. Second, put one Internet-capable computer in every classroom, in every workroom, and on every desk, and then invite the parents in to learn along with you and their kids.

At The Advanced Technology Academy, our internal e-mail conneced me to everyone. I could e-mail the facilities supervisor, the nurse, all counselors, teachers, and support staff. Our principal's secretary provided us with the "trivia of the day," and one of our math teachers offered "bumper sticker of the day." We also e-mailed notices, reminders, lessons, stories, and all manner of friendly advice. If we could have e-mailed the parents with the same ease, communications would have been astounding. Everyone needs, not only to be connected to the Internet, but also to be supplied with word processing, data base, spreadsheet, and publications software . . . to begin with.

Our Internet connection supported 650 stations and while there were some startup glitches, it's been remarkably reliable. For many students, it has moved from an oddity to a necessity.

Don't bunch your only computers into one room that must be scheduled for use. These are immediate tools, your word processor and your Internet connection. And they are the basics for every teacher. (A printer is not optional, by the way. I see it as part of a total system. Laser, preferably . . . ink jet for the budget conscious.)

Suppose your class reads "The stalwart soldiers marched ramrod straight. Their tall shakos, red feathers on white, swayed in the summer breeze as they moved toward the fort." (I made this up so there's no credit needed!) It's important that the readers immediately get to their dictionaries online. Of course offline is OK but while you're online, you can cross-reference to a thesaurus with ease, and then move over to a reliable search engine to find pictures of shakos and perhaps pictures of forts and stalwart soldiers. When one hand goes up and asks, "Teacher, what's a shako look like?", it's time to find out.

It does no good to tell the kids at this point, "Well, write down the word 'shako,' kids, and next week or month when we're in the computer lab, we'll look for pictures online, and if we have enough time, we'll look for some pictures of forts."

Remember, the more connections teachers and students get at their immediate fingertips, the more input comes into the room on a constant basis. And that input finds its way around the room for everyone to see.

With all that in mind, it is vital that everyone learn to use their tools with ease. Sites should be bookmarked for easy access. Better yet, when you create your own page, put your most used tools on your page as hyperlinks.

Here are some extended lesson ideas that will work much better if you and your kids search quickly, bookmark often, and practice using the tools.

ABOUT THE NEW LESSONS

In updating the material for this edition of the book, I moved some of the template-type lessons to the CD-ROM and added here more project-based explorations that are, by the nature of their subject matter, cross-curriculum. One of the aspects of our new style of learning that most appealed to my kids was this, the cross-curriculum parts. From one basic starting point, we found so many obvious areas to branch into, and the concept of linked learning became real. One subject, no matter how we have to set up our schedules, is not isolated from others. My kids liked broadening their scope. I hope yours will, too.

LESSON

11

EXTENDED STUDENT ACTIVITIES

My first lesson using the Internet with my students was focused around *Great Expectations* by Charles Dickens. Teaching the novel was part of our ninth grade curriculum, and I wanted to see what was online that would add to our knowledge base. The outcome was a sequential lesson with pieces that can be infused into your study of the novel as you progress through it. This is not like the other lessons, which work through a process to answer a question. The sites in this lesson parallel the reading of the novel.

Our second lesson pertained to *Romeo and Juliet* and served as an introduction to the work by building a frame of reference for my students who knew nothing about Verona or Italy. Other pieces of the lesson were added to broaden the kids' frame of reference and understanding of the concepts of the play, the author, and the times in which Romeo and Juliet lived.

"Where the Wind Blows" was planned to explore one central idea, branch out to logical extensions, and end with constructive planning on the part of the students.

"Of Castle and Kings" grew out of the quantity of information I found all pertaining to one general area of study. As I found more sites all relating to King Arthur, it became easy to develop them into one extensive learning experience.

"High Jumps, Hockey Pucks, and History" approaches a subject from a different starting point and then uses the extensive information available on the Net to expand students' knowledge.

The "Writing Help" lesson is designed to provide a variety of sites aimed at helping your kids with their writing skills as well as informing them in the correct methods of documenting online materials.

The Civil War lesson is constructed with the idea of personalizing the war experience for students and providing more background and insight.

I devised the "Exploring the Web" lesson, the French and Spanish lessons, and "Making a Path to Your Career" as a way of demonstrating the depth of information on the Net. I wanted the kids to see just how much you can learn about one particular area, as well as see the kinds of extensions you can make from one starting point.

The final lessons are cross-curricular. I find using the Net lets us make connections away from our set curriculum that were difficult before. With the Net, we can explore relationships between one concept and another. We can use one idea as a springboard to another, reinforcing the concept that one subject area is not isolated from another, even though we are structured to teach it as such. Science overlaps into history, literature can be taught with the times of the author or work presented as well, math can cross over into other subjects — and suddenly, common threads link our kids' studies together.

Use these lessons as guides for creating your own. Begin to explore the side trips you can make from your original starting point. My favorite lesson, at the moment, is "A Long Non-fatal Net Search," based on the novel *A Long Fatal Love Chase* by Louisa May Alcott. Within the design of this lesson I was able to start with the contents of a novel set in a particular historical time period and create 14 side trips or extensions for further exploration. With the shared input of all my students, we are now able to create a broad picture of that time period; a visual and informational knowledge base that goes beyond just the reading and understanding of the novel.

I realize that for some, lessons using the Internet are focused on projects involving other kids, other schools. I have chosen to focus on the existing curricula, creating lessons to enhance or expand what we already teach — because as a classroom teacher, that is what I am charged with covering. Most teachers have very little power over the curriculum guidelines, and the process of changing them is cumbersome. Therefore, I see our starting point with the Net in our curriculum as building lessons around what is already in place. With time, the existing curriculum will reflect the impact of this new medium. In the meantime, I hope that practicing the skills of using the Internet combined with your present curriculum will provide your students will new skills, new outlooks, and new approaches to learning.

11.1 *Great Expectations*   ACTIVITIES

PD   **Subjects: Literature, History**
Grade Level: 8th and Up

The novel by Charles Dickens has received quite a bit of attention from online participants. Start your exploration with a brief **biography** of Dickens provided by Brown University.

> http://www.stg.brown.edu/projects/hypertext/landow/victorian/dickens/
>   dickensov.html

Next, take a **Tour of Dickens' Kent.** Earmark those locales that directly pertain to the novel. You can also **cross-reference** to architecture sites for those who are interested.

> http://lang.nagoya-u.ac.jp/~matsuoka/CD-Kent.html

At this site, you can also see what a Victorian gentleman or lady might have worn:

```
http://www.autopen.com/romance.well.dressed.shtml
```

Or check The Regency Fashion Page at:

```
http://locutus.ucr.edu/~cathy/reg3.html
```

Or see more Victorian Styles here:

```
http://www.victoriana.com/
```

Follow with **discussions of the Victorian Era** by students and staff at Brown University (same site):

```
http://www.stg.brown.edu/projects/hypertext/landow/victorian/dickens/dick-
    ensov.html
```

and, go to

```
http://www.indiana.edu/~iupress/journals/vic.html
```

for more discussion of the Victorian Era at the Victorian Studies Home Page. Students looking for other authors of the same period will find information here.

Use the **same Brown site** for discussions of the novel itself. One interesting part of the Brown site discussed the ways in which Dickens usually developed characters. That information, at the beginning of our reading, led students to look for those elements as they read.

Finally, end with a **review of the novel** written shortly after it was published:

```
http://www.theatlantic.com/atlantic/atlweb/classrev/greatexp.htm
```

There are many ways in which other material at these sites can be used to extend the study of the novel. Dickens material on the Net is quite extensive; the Nagoya site offers several links.

One extension. **Literary terms** from:

```
http://fur.rscc.cc.tn.us/OWL/ElementsLit.html
```

My students especially enjoyed discussing static and dynamic characters; what is your proof that one character is either static or dynamic?

Putting it all together. We used **Hypercard** and created a Dickens stack. Our main card held general literary elements: plot, characters, setting, conflicts, tone, etc. Each topic led to more information that was added as we read, discussed, or gathered information from the Internet or any source. We especially focused on themes, characters, and setting.

At the very least. For teachers with minimal Internet access (you have it at home and nowhere else), most of what you find online can be printed, including pictures. So, until you have more widespread access, you'll print what you can and share with your students. Post a map and pinpoint the cities. Locate a more detailed map and post pictures. Write a modern review of the novel based on the information from the old one. Locate other Victorian pictures and post them for a visual perspective.

11.2　*Romeo and Juliet:*　ACTIVITIES

PD

Subjects: Literature, History
Grade Level: 8th and Up

Before we started reading the play, I asked my Honors Freshman English class to tell me all they knew about Verona and Italy.

"Italy is shaped like a boot," they informed me, before they impressed me with the bulk of their knowledge. "Italians eat pizza and they have a tower that leans."

A frame of reference, not only for Verona but for Italy, was in order. The Net offered us a nice range of information.

We began with a tour. One site provides a **Romeo and Juliet Itinerary**: a tour from their point of view. The same site also provides a tour of **Ancient Verona**.

Tours of **Italy** can also be found online.
http://www.intesys.it/Tour/

Try The Virtual Tourist:
http://www.vtourist.com/

Another tour of Verona:
http://www.immagica.it/verona/

A **study guide** has been prepared for use with the play *West Side Story* and Franco Zeffirelli's film version of the play at:
http://www.wsu.edu:8000/~brians/love-in-the-arts/romeo.html

Essay: A Plague on all our Houses:
http://www.geocities.com/CapitolHill/Senate/1088/

A complete **text** of the play and discussions can be found at:
http://the-tech.mit.edu/Shakespeare/works.html

A literature Cyberguide for the play can be found here:
http://www.bell.k12.ca.us/BellHS/Departments/English/SCORE/webguide.html

Other **links** to Shakespeare sites can be found at:

`http://www.palomar.edu/Library/shake.htm`

This site also includes a biography, criticism of the works and performance information.

One extension. The following site offers an analysis of the **Shakespeare Mystery**: who really wrote the plays.

`http://www2.pbs.org/wgbh/pages/frontline/shakespeare/tindex.html`

Putting it all together. Research other literary or film star-crossed lovers and have your students compare. Or, taking the main characters and the plot, write a synopsis of a film but change the locale and/or generation, title it, cast it with modern actors, and make a visual representation. We did a movie poster.

At the very least. Print the itinerary information and pictures. Give them the information from the other sources. They can take notes, discuss, react, and respond.

11.3 *Where the Wind Blows*   ACTIVITIES

PD   **Subjects: Geography, Science
Grade Level: 3rd and Up**

Part 1

On the highway from Los Angeles, California to Palm Springs, California, (`http://www.mapblast.com`), as you approach the outskirts of Palm Springs (`http://www.palmsprings.com/`), you will pass by fields of modern windmills, huge, wind-powered fans (`http://www.palmsprings.com/services/wind.html`).

What topography in that area creates so many strong winds? (`http://www.palmsprings.com/points/canyon/`)

What kinds of power does wind power replace?

Where else in the world are windmills, old and new, used as a source of power?

What statistics can you gather about wind power? Costs? Strengths? Weaknesses? The technology behind it?

Where else in the world does the wind blow strongly enough and consistently enough to allow the use of wind power?

How many people will be able to use wind power in the Palm Springs area?

Part 2

In Eastern Canada, in the Province of Ontario, near the city of Toronto, water supplies much needed power to people. (http://www.hydro.on.ca:80/)

What is the source of the water that powers the area?

Where else in the world is water power used?

As You Explore

Did you learn of any unusual sources of power?

What did people use in the days of old, before electricity, to provide power? (Horse power, paddle wheel, gas, steam, coal)

What kinds of machines were powered by these means?

What does the future hold for your city or town in terms of power use? What is used now? What else can be used? What do you think is the best power source for your area?

Did you learn about any areas that use power wisely? Unwisely?

You're in Charge

What kind of power would you use for your area? Would you use one source? A combination of sources? What factors influenced your decision?

11.4 *Of Castles and Kings*   ACTIVITIES

PD   **Subjects: History, Literature, Travel**
Grade Level: 3rd and Up

With the popularity of films such as *First Knight* and *Dragonheart* comes an interest in lives lived long ago. Camelot has long been a source of interest for many. Go back in time and explore an exciting era online. As you explore, try to learn more about what kind of ruler Arthur was. What laws did he devise to govern his people? Was he a fair and just ruler, or harsh?

Background

CAMELOT PROJECT

http://rodent.lib.rochester.edu/camelot/cphome.stm

KING ARTHUR

http://www.britannia.com/history/h12.html
http://www.xs4all.nl/~iman66/
http://www.users.globalnet.co.uk/~tomgreen/arthur.htm
http://www.geocities.com/Area51/Lair/5459/arthur.html

NET SERF

http://www.cua.edu/www/hist/netserf

MEDIEVAL SOURCEBOOK

http://www.fordham.edu/halsall/sbook.html

KING ARTHUR

http://www.geocities.com/~gkingdom/saxonshore/index.html

SAXON SHORE

http://www.geocities.com/~gkingdom/saxonshore/index.html

Frame of Reference

CASTLES ON THE WEB

http://www.castles.org/
http://www.castlesontheweb.com/

Take a Tour: Find a Place to Stay

UNITED KINGDOM GUIDE

http://www15.pair.com/cir/index.html

VIRTUAL TOURIST

http://www.vtourist.com/

Find an Ancient and Modern Map of the Area

MAPQUEST — WHO LIVES THERE NOW?

http://www.mapquest.com/

HISTORICAL MAPS

http://www.carto.com/links.htm

Study a Little History

ANCIENT HISTORY

http://rome.classics.las.umich.edu/
http://eawc.evansville.edu/
http://www.julen.net/aw/

WOMEN IN HISTORY

http://www.uky.edu/ArtsSciences/Classics/gender.html

MEDIEVAL HISTORY

http://history.hanover.edu/medieval/crusades.html

Check Out Who Rules

RULERS

http://www.geocities.com/Athens/1058/rulers.html

Read Some Stories

FOLKLORE, MYTHS, AND LEGENDS

http://www.ucalgary.ca/~dkbrown/storfolk.html

Listen to Some Music

REAL MUSIC FOR THE REAL WORLD

http://www.rootsworld.com/rw/

Role Play

AVALON

http://www.avalon.co.uk/avalon/

Cross-Reference

CZAR ALEXANDER'S PALACE

http://www.alexanderpalace.org/palace/

THE KNIGHT'S COAT OF ARMS

    http://biz/ctol.net/knights/

SWORDS AND STUFF

    http://www.swords-n-stuff.com/index.html

ELECTRONIC TEXT OF *LE MORTE D'ARTHUR*

    http://www.geocities.com/~gkingdom/saxonshore/index.html

Search on your own.   What movies are there about King Arthur? Books? What art, literature, theater came from that era? Watch the old film musical *Camelot*. Watch *First Knight*, if you're allowed. Can you find the fashions of that time described and pictured? What was the political structure of Camelot? Where, if anywhere, is that stucture still in existence? What can you learn about Guinevere and Lancelot?

Putting it all together.   Why not make a castle or a coat of arms? Put together a newsletter for Camelot or a radio or TV broadcast.

Extension question.   What other leaders, kings, rulers at the time were similar in their style of rule and thoughts on laws to King Arthur? Who, ruling today, is similar to King Arthur? Similar in what ways?

11.5 *High Jumps, Hockey Pucks, and History*

ACTIVITIES

PD   **Subject Areas: Sports, History, Politics**
Grade Level: 4th and Up

Every four years, two selected cites host the Winter and Summer Olympics. Much can be learned from a tour of the cities that played host.
    Begin with a search (both/either Winter or Summer Games) of one of the cities.

Questions.   How far back in history can you go with your search? Make a chart: medal winners, sport, country.

What inferences and conclusions can you make? What can you learn about the following:

>   Country name changes — which, when, why?
>   Each competition's hero/heroine
>   The costs of training
>   Success stories
>   Tragedies
>   Defections
>   Training
>   Who went on to play pro?

Arrange a tour of the city with sports and activities for visitors in mind.

Extensions.   Database, spreadsheet, and Hypercard opportunities for tracking information.

SYDNEY 2000 GAMES

    http://www.sydney.olympic.org/

VIRTUAL TOURIST

    http://www.vtourist.com/

LONELY PLANET

    http://www.lonelyplanet.com/

TRY HOSTELING

    http://www.cs.cmu.edu/~mkant/Public/Travel/html/hostelling.html

FLAGS OF EACH COUNTRY

    http://www.imagesoft.net.flags/flags.html

NATIONAL ANTHEMS

    http://www.rootsworld.com/rw/

Can you locate an address for maps?

11.6 *Writing Help*

PD

Subjects: Any
Grade Level: 5th and Up

Many sites exist to provide writing help online. One place to start for students who seek *specific help* is

```
http://leo.stcloud.msus.edu/
```

"My writing is choppy." "I have difficulty organizing my writing." Specific help is offered in response to these types of complaints.

More help is available from the University of Victoria:

```
http://webserver.maclab.comp.uvic.ca/writersguide/welcome.html
```

Types of essays, paragraphs, and sentences are explained in easy-to-understand language with brief samples.

MLA Format — giving credit to sources — help can be found here:

```
http://owl.english.purdue.edu/Files/110.html
```

APA Format information and guidelines are available here:

```
http://www.writeplace/com
```

More writing tips and a place to post writing is found at The Write Place:

```
http://www.writeplace.com/
```

Extension. Purdue's OWL offers a step-by step guide to writing research papers.

```
http://owl.english.purdue.edu/Files/Research-Papers.html
```

Putting it all together. Now that your students have information about writing, let them write. Explore a topic online. Start by determining what kind of paragraph, essay, or paper to write, arm them with the helpful writing hints they might need, and have them write about what they learned.

At the very least. Print the specific information for them as needed. Read some common sections to them, and have them take notes and then write.

11.7 *The Civil War*   ACTIVITIES

PD

Subjects: History
Grade Level: 4th and Up

To bring a more personal experience to the study of the war, begin with a detailed timeline to create a frame of reference:

    http://lcweb2.loc.gov/ammem/tl1861.html

Add the background and experiences of two towns divided by the Mason–Dixon Line. Read their accounts, using actual historical documents, in *The Valley of the Shadow*:

    http://jefferson.village.virginia.edu/vshadow/vshadow.html

Cross-reference with letters from soldiers:

    http://www.ucsc.edu/civil-war-letters/home.html
    http://home.pacbell.net/dunton/SSDletters.html
    http://www.genealogy.org/~ajmorris/cw/cwletter.htm

Cross-reference for more information at the Museum of the Confederacy:

    http://www.moc.org/

Locate maps online, print a copy of a U.S. map of the Civil War era, and begin plotting the location of the soldiers as they mention places where they were stationed or fought:

    http://scarlett.libs.uga.edu/darchive/hargrett/maps/maps.html

Students can then begin to compare the experiences, emotions, and conditions of the soldiers. Compare the soldiers' feelings about the war: in 1861, by 1864. Can students get a sense of their moods? Changes in attitudes, if any? Physical conditions? Continue the study with Lee's retreat to learn more about the total experience of the war:

    http://www.chr.vt.edu/CivilWar/Retreat/Retreat.html

Extension.   Add the experience of the Underground Railroad by reading of the experiences of one man tracing the path of the railroad in *A Walk to Canada*. Plot the route on your map.

    http://www.npca.org/walk.html

Another extension.   Use one of the historical documents sites to locate any pertinent documents.

    http://www.chico.rice.edu/
    http://www.msstate.edu/Archives/History/index.html

Additional extension. Photographs, listed by year and event, can be assessed to cross-reference with the letters from the soldiers or other events covered.

```
http://sunsite.utk.edu/civil-war/
http://rs6.loc.gov/ammem/t11861.html
```

Putting it all together. Perhaps students could create a diary of one of the soldiers, a family album or a journal of one soldier with maps, pictures, letters, newspapers, etc.

At the very least. Print — letters, pictures, maps, newspapers, documents — and still bring them the experience from the soldier's perspective.

‖‖

11.8 *Find Your True Home*

ACTIVITIES

PD

Subjects: Geography, Math
Grade Level: 3rd and Up

One interesting way to explore the possibilities of the Net is to try to find your "true home." Given certain factors, where might you like to live? Once you find that information, what can you learn about that city? See:

```
http://pathfinder.com/@@JU1MFAcALQWWfyPh/money/best-cities-96/index.htm
```

Another way to get to this site

1. Type: *Pathfinder*
2. Click on *Money*
3. Click on *Best Cities*
4. Click on *Find Your Best City*

Using the 63 factors is very slow, and the use of nine general categories is more limited. We used one to three of the nine categories, looked for one or two common cities, and then explored one of them.

Once students have factored in all the necessary information and gotten a list of the cities meant for them, go to the next site and explore one of the cities in depth.

```
http://usacitylink.com//
http://www.travelocity.com/
http://www.citysearch.com/
```

Cross-reference.

```
http://www.city.net/
```

Extension.   Can you find a place to rent in your selected city?

```
http://www.rent.net/
http://www.infoconnect.com/h-search.html
http://www.realtorads.com/ (Homes for sale)
http://www.homescout.com/
```

Go to *Apartment Search* (your students might not find their exact city, but perhaps they'll find something close).

Extension.   Use *MapBlast, The Interactive Atlas*, to find your city and zoom in. You can start with the state, zoom in, pan around until you find the city, then zoom in again. Once you locate an address or street, use the *BigBook* site (go to the bottom of the page to the *Maps* link)

INTERACTIVE MAP BUILDING SITES:

```
http://www.mapblast.com/
http://www.mapquest.com/
http://www.bigbook.com/
http://www.mapsonus.com/
```

MapBlast or BigBook.   Type in an address that appears in the city you are exploring. Most of the apartment sites give at least a street address. MapBlast will show you exactly where the location is. BigBook will zoom into the city and even show businesses in the area you found.

Students also enjoy typing their home address into MapBlast and exploring this site.

Still another extension.   How far is it from Las Vegas (or where you are) to your new city?

```
http://www.indo.com/distance/
```

What's the best route to get there?

```
http://www.delorme.com/CyberMaps/   (Use Cyberrouter)
```

Or get Driving Directions from MapBlast.

How's the weather?

```
http://www.weather.com/
```

More extensions.   Will my salary where I live now be enough for me to live in my new city?

Give your students an average salary (over $20,000, please!) and this program will tell them if it is enough to live on with cost of living factored in. Use the Salary Calculator (the moving calculator tells you how much it will cost to make a move):

```
http://www2.homefair.com/index.html
```

One more extension. Is there a newspaper online for your city, state, or place nearby?

```
http://www2.webwombat.com.au/
http://www.newo.com/
```

I looked for Rochester, MN, but the two Rochester newspapers were from New York, so I used the Minneapolis–St.Paul paper for information.

One more. Did the kids learn any of the following:

Any famous people come from the city?
Any major businesses? Universities?
What is the city known for? Proud of?
Any museums nearby?

Cross-reference. Go back to the maps. Now that you've found an apartment, house, hotel, etc., see if you can locate them on a map.

Putting it all together. Keep a journal of what your kids learned about the city that they most liked or other factors that would influence a move there. Why not pinpoint your kids' cities on a big wall map? Did any of the kids have the same city? What were their common factors? What can they find in print about their city?

Kids could put together a travel brochure for their city, complete with postcards, airline tickets, and maps. (These capabilities can also be found online!)

At the very least. Get the common factors from your kids, then find the city or cities for them. They explore in print; you explore online (some can go online at home or the library). You supply the information from their input. Print what you can for them. Try printing some of their newspapers for them.

11.9 *French and Spanish — Trip of a Lifetime*

ACTIVITIES

PD

Subjects: Languages, Geography
Grade Level: Any

If you can't actually get your kids on a plane to a country that speaks the language you're studying, why not go online and do the same?

Check Some Sites

FRENCH AND SPANISH

```
http://www.iway.fr/champs_elysees/
http://edb518ea.edb.utexas.edu/html/spanishmaps.html#Chile
http://www.mapquest.com/
```

TOUR

```
http://www.lonelyplanet.com/
```

General tours can be found at LonelyPlanet.

```
http://www.paris.org/
http://www.tourspain.es/
```

EUROPEAN VISITS

```
http://www.eurodata.com/ev1.htm
```

READ A MAGAZINE

```
http://www.baguette.com/cur/index/maquette/french
http://www.elperiodico.es/
```

CHECK OUT THE NEWSPAPER

```
http://www.ual.mx/opinion/opinion.html
```

CHECK OUT A UNIVERSITY

```
http://www.aup.fr/
http://www.ucm.es/UCMD.html
http://www.iro.umontreal.ca/
http://www.ucr.ac.cr/
```

FIND A PLACE TO RENT

```
http://www.europa-let.com/
http://www.ivacation.com/c109.htm
```

Extensions.   Can you find a pen pal to communicate with?

```
http://www.shadetree.com/~rplogman/
```

What about stories from the region?

```
http://www.worldwidenews.net/HUMANITI/LITERATU/SUBJECT.HTM
```

What museums can you visit? What other cultural events can you learn about?

```
http://wwar.com/index.html
```

Can you listen to any music from the region?

```
http://www.rootsworld.com/rw/
```

Practice a phrase or two:

http://www.travlang.com/languages/index.html

Putting it all together.   Plan a tour, make a brochure for your travels, plan your first year of college at the university. Can you find your university on a map? Can you locate the rental property on a map? What other places of interest are in the area? How's the weather?

http://www.weather.com/

At the very least.   I know it sounds tired to keep saying, "Print everything," but if that's the only way you can include your kids in the global experience, then by all means, print.

11.10 *Making a Path to Your Career*

ACTIVITIES

PD

Subjects: Careers, Work Experience
Grade Level: 8th and Up

Focus: Preparing for a job

For the dream job you have always wanted, what information can the Internet provide to help you with your preparation?

1. *Try an assessment test to find out what career is right for you.*

   CAREER COMPANION
   http://www.careercompanion.com/
   Go into the Career Briefcase and try the assessment tools. Or try:

   AMERICAN EXPRESS UNIVERSITY
   http://www.americanexpress.com/student/
   Go to "The Money Pit"; from there go to "Getting a job," then check out your strengths.

2. *How do you prepare for the job?*
   What colleges or schools will train you? What classes do you have to take?

Peterson's Guide to Colleges
http://www.petersons.com/

Black Colleges and Universities
http://www.edonline.com/cq/hbcu/

College Exchange
http://www.usmall.com/college/

Peterson's Vocational Schools
http://www.petersons.com/preview/votec.html

3. *Where can I find money to pay for school?*

Scholarship Book
http://www.scholarshipbook.com/

Scholarships and Grants
http://scholarship.vweb.net/

Student Services
http://www.studentservices.com/search/

College Money Matters
http://jerome.signet.com/collegemoney/

4. *What interview skills do I need?*

Career Companion
http://www.careercompanion.com/

American Express University
http://www.americanexpress.com/student/

Student Center
http://www.studentcenter.com/

5. *How do I write a résumé?*

Career Mosaic
http://www.careermosaic.com/

THE MAIN QUAD

`http://www.mainquad.com/`

AMERICAN EXPRESS UNIVERSITY

`http://www.americanexpress.com/student/`

6. *Now, where are the jobs?*

HI-TECH JOBS

`http://www.hitechcareer.com/hitech`

AMERICA'S JOB BANK

`http://www.ajb.dni.us/index.html`

CAREER WEB

`http://www.cweb.com/`

CAREER MOSAIC

`http://www.careermosaic.com/`

MONSTER BOARD

`http://www.monster.com/home.html`

ONLINE CAREER CENTER

`http://occ.com/`

Extensions.   Once you've settled on a career and found just the right one, in the right city, what can you learn about that city?

`http://usacitylink.com/`
`http://www.city.net/`
`http://www.vtourist.com/`

Can you find a place to rent?

`http://www.rent.net/`
`http://www.infoconnect.com/`

Can you locate your apartment on a map?

`http://www.mapblast.com/`
`http://www.mapquest.com/`
`http://www.bigbook.com/`

Can you find a newspaper for your city or one nearby?

`http://www.webwombat.com.au/`

Additional sites that help prepare you for college or work.

THE STUDENT SURVIVAL GUIDE

    `http://www.luminet.net/~jackp/survive.html`

THE CATAPULT

    `http://www.jobweb.org/catapult/catapult.htm`

FUTURESCAN MAG

    `http://www.futurescan.com/`

CAREER PATH

    `http://www.careerpath.com/`

Offline extensions.   Put together a brochure for another student to show the best path for getting to one job. What school should they attend? What skills will they need? Where are the jobs? What advice would you give someone looking for this job? What will it cost to prepare? Where can they get financial help?

11.11 *Fractals and Fabrics*   ACTIVITIES

PD   **Subject Areas: Geometry, Technology, Arts, History**
              Grade Level: 9th and Up

Among technology's many new territories, it is steadily finding its way into the arts. Film and television have long used any new advance in technology to their advantage. New technologies are combining with old arts to find new expressions. One of these marriages is MSNBC. On a smaller scale, another is the use of technology in the textile industry.

Places to start.   According to TheSite (`http://www.zdnet.com/zdtv/thesite/`), Sept. 15, 1996, one textile company is designing fabrics for some very big-name companies. If you can find the reference, you'll learn how one woman is combining technology and weaving. You'll learn about the new designs and also about weaving. You can then see some interesting connections among textile design, weaving, technology, and the arts.

Cross-reference.

1. Jacquard's loom: Do a little research to find out how Jacquard established the connection between weaving and technology.

   http://weber.u.washington.edu/~jhaag/osjl.htm
   http://www.ce.vt.edu/evd/Htmls/P415420.html

2. Boston Computer Museum (http://www.tcm.org/) for pictures of Herman Hollerith's Census Machine and early punch cards. Hollerith carried Jacquard's idea into business. See also

   http://www.comlab.ox.ac.uk/archive/other/museums/computing.html#local

   MORE HISTORY OF WEAVING

   http://www.about-turkey.com/halihist.htm

   WEAVERS AND LOOMS

   http://www.miningco.com/

   TECHNOLOGY AND FASHION

   http://www.fashion.net/industry/technology.html

   WEAVING RESOURCES

   http://home.netinc.ca/~rstowe/index.html

3. World Wide Computer Art

   http://WWW.UC.EDU/~KIDART/KIDART.HTML

   COMPUTER ART LINKS

   http://www.nerdworld.com/nw1177.html

   Check here to learn a bit more about what computer art is all about and perhaps find some information about weaving, fabrics, and fashion.

4. Fractals and fabrics: One seems to make use of the other. Access some pictures and information about fractals.

   http://www.kcsd.k12.pa.us~projects/fractal/
   http://www.vis.colostate.edu/~user1209/fractals/index.html
   http://www.itsnet.com/~bug/fractals.html
   http://www.calweb.com/~bjohnson/fract.html

Now you can see how one art, fabric design has its roots in geometry, technology, and history. What other arts share the same connections?

Extensions.   Explore one of the following:

a. Fabric making — U.S./worldwide
b. Fabric making — then and now
c. Computer design hardware — then and now
d. Computer design software
e. Other areas that use computer design: automobiles, film, TV, music, architecture
f. What other areas of the arts that have not yet made a connection to technology can you see connecting? Fashion, costume design, dance, other areas of design? What can you learn about emerging use of technology in one of these areas on the Net?
g. What part does geometry play in the design portion of one of the above arts? In what ways does an art's history influence its present-day manifestations?
h. History of costume and use of fabrics in each period.

    http://www.siue.edu/COSTUMES/history.html

Create.   Use the medium of your choice (PowerPoint, collage, computer design, other) to do one of the following:

1. Create a visual display of the history of one art form.
2. Create a visual display of the evolution of one form of technology that has had an impact on an art form (cameras, moving and still; paints, fabrics, brushes, software, hardware, other).
3. Using fractal technology, design your own fabric pattern for a company of your choice. Take into consideration their colors (if any) and logo. What are some of the other things you would need to know about a company in order to design well for them? (location, age of employees, functions of the fabric, other?)

More extensions.   Access this Web site for more information:

THE FRACTORY

    http://library.advanced.org/3288/

11.12 *Trade Winds and Wagons*   `A C T I V I T I E S`

PD

Subjects: Geography, Science, History, Literature
Grade Level: 4th and Up

Focus: How did weather affect explorations?

Every year, around September, we are reminded of the power of nature when hurricanes strike. Weather is such a powerful force that it must have been a major consideration for explorers. Use online and other resources to find the links between weather and explorations.

1. *Pick an explorer and find out in what month that explorer left on his/her journey.*

   EXPLORERS AND HISTORY

   ```
   http://weber.u.washington.edu/~eckman/timeline.html
   http://www.cr.nps.gov/aad/feature/feature.htm
   http://sunsite.unc.edu/expo/1492.exhibit/Intro.html
   http://history.hanover.edu/europe.htm
   ```

   DISCOVERERS WEB

   ```
   http://www.win.tue.nl/cs/fm/engels/discovery/index.html
   ```

   PIONEER WEBSITE

   ```
   http://members.aol.com/goal1/pioneers.html
   ```

   OREGON TRAIL

   ```
   http://www.webtrail.com/rvs/oregon.html
   http://www.geocities.com/Athens/Ithaca/5531/index.html
   ```

   MARITIME HISTORY

   ```
   http://emporium.turnpike.net/Z/zen/PIRATES/Morgan.html
   http://www.cronab.demon.co.uk/marit.htm
   ```

   MARITIME BIOGRAPHIES

   ```
   http://pc-78-120.udac.se:8001/WWW/Nautica/Biography/Biography.html
   ```

   PIRATES

   ```
   http://hyperion.advanced.org/16438/
   http://www.legends.dm.net/pirates/index.html
   http://emporium.turnpike.net/Z/zen/PIRATES/Morgan.html
   ```

VIKINGS

http://www.anthro.mankato.msus.edu/Vi/vikhome.htm

2. Where did they start? Where were they headed? Can you find a map?

HISTORICAL MAPS

http://www.carto.com/links.htm
http://scarlett.libs.uga.edu/darchive/hargrett/maps/maps.html
http://www.ma.org/maps/map.html
http://www.lib.umn.edu/jfb.html

3. What weather conditions did they face that affected the outcome of the exploration?

CALCULATORS ONLINE (NAVIGATION)

http://www-sci.lib.uci.edu/HSG/RefCalculators.html

WEATHER CHANNEL

http://www.weather.com/
http://www.weather.com/weather/int/regions.htm#europe

Other weather sites.

CLOUDS

http://covis.atmos.uiuc.edu/guide/clouds/html/oldhome.html

STORMS

http://www.geocities.com/SunsetStrip/Underground/3494/wx.html

GOLD RUSH ACCOUNT

http://uts.cc.utexas.edu/~scring/index.html

GEOGRAPHY AND ENVIRONMENT

http://www.netcore.ca/~gibsonjs/geonews.htm

Visual representation.   Chart your work or put it in a data base. Pinpoint the explorations you research on a map of the world.

Extensions.   Focus in on one weather condition and research more about its power: earthquakes, hurricanes, blizzards, ocean conditions, winds, typhoons, tornadoes, floods.

Extended questions or areas of further research.
a. What changes have occurred in weather patterns over the last 200 years?

b. What is the outlook for more weather changes?

c. What kind of shipping is done today? Where? Is weather still a consideration in schedules?

d. How are ballooning explorations affected by weather?

e. Did pirates take weather into consideration in their journeys?

f. What new technologies were invented to combat weather during the time of the exploration you researched?

g. What common factors did you find in weather conditions? Time of exploration? Outcome of exploration? (A chart would be good here.)

h. What weather conditions do science fiction writers show for characters exploring outer space? Are these accurate?

i. Did anybody beat the odds against the weather?

j. What are your conclusions about weather and explorers?

k. What math do explorers rely on? Explain and relate to one exploration.

Branching out. What books can you find about weather? Pirates? Explorers? Can you find any folklore online about weather, the Gods, Norse explorers?

MYTHS, LEGENDS AND FOLKLORE

    http://www.ucalgary.ca/~dkbrown/storfolk.html

Films about weather, explorers? *White Squall*

FILM SITE

    http://members.aol.com/cgcritic/index.htm

Relate an exploration that was scary because of the weather.

Write a new account about an exploration that battled the weather.

Write an imaginary diary account of an exploration or pirate adventure with the actual weather they would have encountered as a factor.

Can you locate any paintings or sculptures of explorers?

MUSEUMS ONLINE

    http://wwar.com/index.html
    http://www.lam.mus.ca.us/webmuseums/

Read *Robinson Crusoe* by Daniel Defoe, *The Hatchet* by Gary Paulsen, or any other book about an adventure or exploration.

11.13   *Motown and Morphing*   ACTIVITIES

PD

Subjects: Automobiles, Design, Geometry, Computer Technology
Grade Level: 7th and Up

You are shopping for new rims/wheels for your dream car. Take a look at samples of **hi-tech rims/wheels** begin designed for automobiles today. Check out samples at one of these sites:

http://www.superbuytires.com/ (Click on NICHE)

or

http://www.albawheels.com/

Notice how many different styles there are. If you take a close look, you'll notice how many of these designs display geometric shapes changed just a little, altered in some ways from the original straight geometric shape.

Can you find the following information?

What shapes can you find in the rim designs?

In what way were the shapes changed, tweaked, morphed?

Do the new shapes have names?

What materials are used in the rims? What are the properties of the material used? Strong, pliable, durable, resist rust?

If you were to design a rim, could you make the interior in the shape of a web with only one thread attached to the outer rim? Would it be sturdy enough? What aerodynamic factors does the rim come in contact with as you drive?

Does the interior of the rim have to be structurally strong or can it be totally decorative?

Extension.   Take a look at other cars and parts of cars. Where else do you see geometric shapes altered by design? For example, look at the difference in headlight and taillight designs, spoilers, and body styles. Do these shapes have names? What aerodynamic principles affect each part and therefore affect design?

For more about aerodynamics:

http://www.nas.nasa.gov/NAS/Education/TeacherWork/RaceCar/
    Aerodynamics_In_Car_Racing.html
http://www.popsci.com/context/events/automotive/indycar/aero.html

For a look at other cars

CAR AND DRIVER

> http://www.caranddriver.com/

Car fans' favorite magazine is now online.

AUTO WEEK

> http://www.autoweek.com/

Another place for car information for you and your driving kids.

FERRARI'S HOME PAGE

> http://www.ferrari.it

Offers a breathtaking musuem of classics some only dream about.

THE AUTO CHANNEL

> http://www.theautochannel.com/

News about cars and the industry; very up-to-the-minute.

HARRIS MOUNTAINTOP

> http://www.mtp.semi.harris.com/autos.html

A page with dozens of links to automotive sites.

MOTOR TREND

> http://www.motortrend.com/

Extension.   Draw your own rim.

1. Begin with a completely filled-in circle and chip away or cut away at it like a sculpture until you have the design you want.
2. Or, begin at one point on the outer rim of a circle with just a dot or line that expands into your design.

Extension.   Into the technology: What kind of computer program is needed to morph a drawing? What sites can you find online that display samples of morphing? When you are changing one of the lines of a rim design, bending it or smoothing it, is that the same as morphing? If not, what would the design technique be called?

11.14 *A Long Non-Fatal Net Search*

PD

Subjects: Geography, History, Literature
Grade Level: 2nd and Up

Creating a Visual Frame of Reference

In a scene from the novel *A Long Fatal Love Chase*, by Louisa May Alcott, after Rosamond is spirited away on Tempest's yacht, the author describes the place to which she has been taken with key phrases such as: "They were together on the terrace of Valrosa." The Mediterranean is "a mile away" and a "curving shore" is visible from the terrace. The city is described as "white walled" with gilded domes, feathery palms, lovely villas, and a "climate of perpetual summer." Roses bloomed in this city, even in January. Valrosa, says the author, means "nest of roses."

The terrace, according to the author, had wide steps, cornices, pillars, and "a curved balustrade." Nearby is a grotto and golden-green lizards, and the heroine has "one hand lying on a cushion of thornless verdure."

From reading the novel, we know that the heroine was kidnapped and taken to this city around the year 1865.

Using the clues above, locate the city and find pictures that illustrate the words above.

(For the teacher — the city is Nice, France.)

A good starting place.   These key concepts that might lead you in the right direction:

> White-walled city
>
> Mediterranean Sea — she is one mile from it, overlooking a curved shore.
>
> Gilded domes
>
> Yacht — harbor, dock or port — 1865
>
> Golden-green lizards
>
> Valrosa — what language might that be?
>
> Cornices — balustrades
>
> Thornless verdure
>
> Grotto

When you have finished your searching, with luck not only will you know what city the characters visited; you will have a visual frame of reference for that city.
If you get stuck:

```
http://www.nice-coteazur.org/francais/index.html
http://www2.ba.best.com/~edelman/europe/Nice.html
```

Extensions.   Pick a side trip.

Given the information above, it is possible to extend your search in a variety of directions. Choose one of the following "side trips" and keep a record of what you locate and learn.

1. **Transportation in 1865** — yachts, trains, ships, boats, carriages. Plan a grand tour from London, England, to Berlin, Germany, in 1865. Travel by as many means as possible and make stops in Spain, France, Italy, Switzerland, and then Germany. Can you find maps? 1865 maps? Modern maps? Can you find pictures of your means of transportation?

2. **Costumes** — What might a wealthy yacht-traveling young woman of 18 wear in 1885? A wealthy man of 35? What jewels, hats, shoes, evening clothes, travel clothes?

3. **Architecture** — villas, walled cities, balustrades, cornices, gilded domes.
   What might Valrosa look like? What other buildings of that time had these architectural ornaments?

4. **Politics** — What was happening in the Mediterranean politically in 1865? In Europe? In America? In other parts of the world?

5. **Landscape Architecture** — Locate verdure, grottos, flora, and fauna of the Mediterranean, gardens of France, Italy, Spain. Gardens of a typical villa.

6. **Art** — What paintings, statues, and other artwork might have been displayed at a villa like Valrosa? Who were the renowned artists of this period?

7. **Literature** — What other works did Louisa May Alcott write? Why was *A Long Fatal Love Chase* not published in 1866? What can you learn about the life of Alcott? What influenced her writing?

8. **Literature of America circa 1866** — Who else was publishing at the time? Are these novels, poems, essays? Are these works similar in theme to those of Louisa May Alcott? What were the influences on the writers at the time?

9. **World Literature** — Who else was publishing in the world at that time? Are these works similar in theme to those of Alcott? Was there a unifying theme in literature in the world of 1865? Themes?

10. **Yacht Travel** — If you were traveling the world by yacht in 1865, what ports would you visit? Can you chart a route from England to three of these ports of call? Can you map them? Can you locate information about the cities in 1865? Today?

11. **Investing** — As a young person of wealth in 1865, what are some of the ways in which you would invest your fortune? What industries, companies, ventures were safe to invest in? Risky?

12. **Colleges of 1865** — Where might the wealthy young man go to college in America? England? France? Italy? Germany? Colleges today in the same countries for any young man or woman? Where would the young lady of 1865 go to college? What did an education in 1865 consist of?

13. **Music/Theater** — What composers would the characters in the book have listened to who were considered modern? Who might they have seen perform on the stage? Who were the modern playwrights of the time? What theaters were popular at the time?

14. **Inventions** — Rosamond and Tempest had access to the modern world's wonders. Aside from their yacht, what were some of the newest, most amazing, time-saving, labor-saving devices they might have used in 1985? Who invented them? Where?

Further extensions.   Some of the short stories in a standard English curriculum lend themselves to this kind of frame of reference search. Try a similar lesson with "Gift of the Magi" or "The Most Dangerous Game" A real challenge would be to develop frame of reference links and pictures for an entire novel.

Extended research.   Authors of certain genres of literature, if they are to be taken seriously, incorporate specific conventions into their work. In the area of mystery, for example, an author is supposed to leave the reader enough clues that when the mystery is solved, the reader can say, "I knew that." Other conventions dictate that no secrets can be withheld from the reader for the sake of a surprise ending.

Romances also have certain properties in common. What are the properties of a "good romance"? Who were the original romance writers? Who are the best in the field today? What novels are considered to be "good romances"?

What are the properties of a "good mystery"? Who are some of the best mystery writers today? 100 years ago?

A place to start.

    http://world.std.com/~swrs/writips.html
    http://www.azstarnet.com/~poewar/writer/pg/fiction.html

Writing ideas.

    Keep a journal of information and pictures

    Create a Hypercard or Hyperstudio stack of information — create a visual tour with captions and text

Write a narrative description of your findings, in the style of Alcott (go online for samples from her other works and check your library)

Write a narrative description, based on your findings, in a more contemporary style (go online for samples of contemporary authors or use other materials for their styles)

Prepare a PowerPoint presentation of your findings — a visual tour with captions and text

11.15 *Using E-mail to Your Advantage*

ACTIVITIES

PD **Subjects: Communications, Writing**
Grade Level: 3rd and Up

The Internet is THE communications tool of the generation you are teaching. All reports indicate that Net use will explode in and outside classrooms over the next few years. Not only can your kids get more information from the Internet, they can communicate with all those people they meet out there. Communication can occur in chat rooms (which we avoid at this time), by posting of writings and art on the Net, and by writing to people. Here are some suggestions for using e-mail to help students practice their writing skills.

Writing Skills and the Net

I noticed a commercial on TV last night that I am tired of seeing over and over and over. If I can find the company online, I can e-mail them and express my thoughts. Use e-mail to help your students find their voice.

1. Have your students watch TV and notice commercials they don't like. Discuss the reasons for their dislike. If they have legitimate concerns, teach them how to write a proper letter, and e-mail it for them.

2. Find one of the sites for Netiquette (etiquette online) and discuss the proper ways to communicate online.

3. E-mail TV shows your students like; tell what it is they like about the show.

4. Tell TV shows you don't like what you might do to make them better.

5. Submit their writings to one of the many sites that post student work.

6. Respond to sites they like; critique sites they would improve or find hard to get around.

7. Give them a voice — find places online that discuss issues they are interested in and make them part of the discussion.

8. Make your own Web page. This is a great exercise for groups. Each student can take on the task they most like: Webmaster (perhaps you), graphic designers, writers, creators of links, special effects designers, code writers (HTML).

Search, then have them bookmark their sites to verify their finds or copy and paste the information into another piece of software, if that's available (a word processor works well). If you have a printer, they can also print their pages of information.

If you start with any of these samples, feel free to add or delete components.

To practice using some of the more commonly used tools — bookmarks and search engines — here are a few quick practice sessons.

11.16 *A Vocabulary Study for the Older Kids: Lunatics and the Moon*

ACTIVITIES

PD

Subjects: Language
Grade Level: 7th and Up

Bookmark the following.

DICTIONARY WITH THESAURUS

    http://humanities.uchicago.edu/forms_unrest/ROGET.html

AN ALTERNATIVE DICTIONARY

    http://www.oed.com/

An Alternative Thesaurus

http://www.xplore.com/xplore500/medium/reference.html

A Site for Word Etymology

http://bay1.bjt.net/~melanie/take.html

Click on "A Letter at a Time."

One Search Engine

http://www.excite.com/

One Bookstore Online

http://www.amazon.com/

Problem.

Define "lunatic."

Give three words the thesaurus listed as related to *lunatic*

Locate the history of the word

Find books with *lunatic* in the title.

How many of them are mysteries? What other subjects do they seem to be about? How many of them have something to do with the moon?

What do you suppose is the connection between the moon and *lunatic*? In what way did the moon provide the basis for the word lunatic?

If you have Hypercard, this is a short (1–2 periods) exercise for vocabulary building. Have your kids keep track of the book titles they find, the words they learned, definitions, etymology, and the suppositions they arrived at to answer the last question.

You can also cross-reference with the Internet Movie Data Base (http://www.imdb.com) to find movies with *lunatic* in the title. Put those in your Hypercard stack, too. Add that information to your students' formation of the reason the moon provided the basis for the word lunatic.

Extension.   What other words can you trace this way?

Further extensions.   What can you learn about themes in literature surrounding the moon: harvest moon, sailor's moon, new moon, eclipse, full moon?

Are any of the books you read about connected to the idea of lunacy?

11.17 *Amazing Jobs*

EO

Subjects: Career Exploration
Grade Level: 4th and Up

Bookmark the following.
INTERNET MOVIE DATA BASE
      http://www.imdb.com/

A SEARCH ENGINE
      http://www.altavista.com/

THE U.S. NAVY ONLINE
      http://www.navy.mil/

NASA
      http://www.gsfc.nasa.gov/NASA_homepage.html

A BOOKSTORE ONLINE
      http://www.amazon.com/

Explore one of these amazing jobs. Try to learn about their job; their daily tasks, and the environment in which they work:

        Nuclear submarine crew member
        Astronaut
        Aquanaut

Read about some movies pertaining to these jobs(or view them if you can — please check the ratings first)

        Hunt for Red October
        Down Periscope
        Apollo 13
        20,000 Leagues under the Sea
        Crimson Tide

What is the most exciting part about the job you explored?

What is the most frightening?

Can you locate books about these jobs?

Write a diary of your time on the job.

11.18 *A Place Like Arcata*

EO **Subjects: Ecology, Geography**
Grade Level: A Spreadsheet Lesson for All Ages

In a *People* magazine story, my kids and I read about the small Northern California town named Arcata. In this town, most of the people recycle. Many use alternative fuels and many are vegetarians.

Read the story at

```
http://pathfinder.com/people/970317/features/arcata.html
```

Search for more information about Arcata. What statistics can you find about the population of Arcata?

Bookmark the following.

THE *PEOPLE* MAGAZINE ARTICLE

```
http://pathfinder.com/people/970317/features/arcata.html
```

SITES WITH DEMOGRAPHICS AND STATISTICS

```
http://dbisna.com/mdd/mddintro.htm
http://www.usadata.com./
```

SEARCH ENGINE

```
http://www.lycos.com/
```

What statistics can you locate online for Arcata?

Population

Ages of inhabitants

TV preferences

Recycling statistics

Alternative fuel use

Transportation use

Number of vegetarian restaurants

Once you get some idea of what the people of Arcata are like, statistically, can you locate any other city with similar statistics for their ecological sense? Did any names of places crop up as you explored Arcata?

Cross-reference with environmental news, universities with strong environmental programs (that's what brought many of the people to Arcata: the nearby university.)

11.19　*The Recent News*　ACTIVITIES

EO　**Subjects: Economics, Geography, History**
Grade Level: An Economic Lesson for the Older Kids (Grades 7–12)

Trace the history of this news story: Hong Kong returns to Chinese rule.

What is the history of the rule of Hong Kong?

http://www.hongkong.org/

Read about the history of China

http://www.china5000pro.com/welcome.html

Read a Hong Kong newspaper

http://www.newo.com/

(Go to news, Asia and Oceania, Hong Kong.)

What treaties, if any, were involved?

What trade goods go in and out of Hong Kong's port?

What can you learn about manufacturing in the city?

What technology is produced there?

What is the average income of a Hong Kong worker?

What projections are there for changes in Hong Kong now that the Chinese have taken over?

What are your projections as to how the change will affect the economy of Hong Kong? Of China?

11.20 *It's Ironic*

EO **Subjects: Geography, History**
Grade Level: A Quick History Search for All Grades

Go online and see if you can find the facts that help you answer this question: Why is it ironic that the Verrazano Bridge in New York City crosses over the Hudson River?

Read some history of the area:

```
http://www.envirolink.org/orgs/hrwa/river.htm
http://grid.let.rug.nl/~welling/usa/nl1.html
http://wwww.hotwired.com/rough/usa/mid.atlantic/ny/nyc/framework.html
http://www.pojonews.com/enjoy/stories/10249610.htm
http://www.hudsonriver.com/
```

Read about Hudson and Verrazano:

```
http://www.hudsonriver.com/halfmoonpress/stories/hudson.htm
```

Read a first-person account of someone caught up in the events of the time:

```
http://www.lib.virginia.edu/etext/readex/8611.html
```

For the teacher. Historical research seems to point to Verrazano as having discovered the river that bears Hudson's name, yet he was never given credit for the discovery. All the recognition Verrazano got for his discoveries was to have the bridge named for him.

Side excersion. Hudson's men rebelled against him. Why?

Writing exercise. Write a newspaper account of the rebellion against Hudson. First, research some historical newspapers for the correct style of the times.
Historical texts available at:

```
http://nwoca7.nwoca.ohio.edu/
http://www.msstate.edu/Archives/History/index.html
http://chico.rice.edu/
```

Another side trip.   What is Hudson's connection with the Netherlands? What can you learn about the history of Dutch settlements in the Hudson River Valley?

11.21   *Who Gets the Credit?*   ACTIVITIES

EO

Subjects: History
Grade Level: A Quick History Search for All Ages

Use your bookmark for a search engine to get you started. If you have not yet book-marked a search engine, try

```
http://www.excite.com/
```

What information can you locate online about Brendan the Navigator? What large land was it possible he discovered?

As good a place to start as any:

```
http://www.geocities.com/Athens/4006/
http://www.mindspring.com/~nesbit/brendanmain.html
```

For the teacher.   Brendan the Navigator was a monk from Ireland around the 1300s. Historical theory says Brendan spent years at sea, and when he finally returned to Ireland, he related tales of icebergs, islands of blacksmiths with fire falling around them, and a beautiful land with no end. There is a theory that he might have discovered America long before Columbus.

11.22   *See the USA*   ACTIVITIES

EO

Subjects: Geography, History
Grade Level: An American Tour for All Ages

Music has always played an important part in the lives of Americans. The styles of music called jazz and the blues were born in America. Also born in America was rock 'n' roll.

Learn more about America through the eyes of its musicians. Take a rock 'n' roll tour of America. From the rise of rock in the south, to the birth of American Bandstand in Philadelphia, and across the nation to San Francisco in the 60s, Americans have been singing a new tune.

Start your search at the Rock 'n' Roll Hall of Fame:

`http://www.rockhall.com/`

Begin with the birth of rock in the 1950s with Bill Haley and the Comets, Chuck Berry, Elvis Presley, etc., and move on through the Motown groups of the early 1960s to the protest rock of the late 1960s with Jackson Browne, The Grateful Dead, Lynyrd Skynyrd, etc.

For each group or singer you find, plot on a map where they came from. Locate their home town or another town nearby. Take a tour of the area they grew up in.

Create a family tree of rock musicians showing their influences and roots.

What other musicians influenced them? Does your research show any areas where rock 'n' roll musicians were concentrated? Are there any states that didn't seem to contribute to the rock 'n' roll bandwagon? What might account for a lack of rock 'n' roll musicians not coming from one area and a large number coming from another area?

Extension.   Go back 100 years and explore the music and musicians who were contributing to the style of the time in any location you choose. Locate the artists' homes on maps and see if you can trace their influences. Try going even farther back to the roots of classical music and trace its geographical locations.

What conclusions can you draw about the growth of music by tracing the paths of its artists? What can you learn about a country by learning more about its musicians?

Extension.   Take a literary tour of an area or country.

Extension for older students.   Cross-reference with the political happenings of the era you are researching. What was going on in the world at the time the music was created? Does the music reflect the political times? In what ways?

11.23 *Swashbucklers and Seafarers*   ACTIVITIES

PD   **Subjects: History, Geography, Literature**
Grade Level: 3rd and Up

Internet resources provide a wonderful opportunity to explore the lives and times of pirates and other seafaring adventurers. One way to start your exploration is to view the film *Treasure Island* (Disney, 1950), or perhaps your students have read the book by Robert Louis Stevenson. The younger kids (ages 4–8) may have read

Edward and the Pirates by David McPhail (published by Little, Brown & Co., 1997) or perhaps you've found *Pirates Past Noon* (*The Magic Tree House,* No. 4) by Mary Pope Osborne, Random Library, February 1994.

Other books about pirates can be found at Amazon Books:

    http://www.amazon.com/

To begin your journey to become steeped in the lore, lands and legends of pirates:

Begin with the history of piracy at:

    http://www.ecani.com/vi/pirates.htm

Follow that with more history at:

    http://www.buccaneer.net/

For a good overview of pirate life, go to:

    http://www.geocities.com/Athens/1108/scurvydogs.html

National Geographic has provided a wealth of information at:

    http://www.nationalgeographic.com/modules/pirates/index.html

The History of Piracy site offers even more pictures and information:

    http://www.ametro.net/~lbyars/

Follow up with some pictures, legends, myths, and more at:

    http://geocities.com/Athens/Parthenon/1500/piracy.html

Add pictures, maps, and more information by going to:

    http://www.ecst.csuchico.edu/~beej/pirates/

More information about pirate maps can be found at:

    http://www.cac.org.uk/pirates/maps.htm

You can learn more about the pirates of the Bahamas at:

    http://www.interknowledge.com/bahamas/bspira01.htm

Try this great cross-reference to treasure stories:

    http://www.ukoln.ac.uk/treasure/links/treasure.htm

Read a brief account of the life of Blackbeard at:

    http://members.aol.com/durhamite/jtht/tale.htm

You'll find a short list of pirate books at:

http://www.indirect.com/www/chivalry/Pirates.htm

How about watching a couple of films about pirates?

> *Mutiny on the Bounty* (1935)
> *The Sea Hawk* (1940)
> *Captain Blood* (1935)

Or go the The Internet Movie Data Base (http://www.imdb.com), search by keyword for "pirates," and get a long list of movies.

Cross-reference your search by typing in other keywords such as buccaneer and swashbuckler.

Don't forget to tour the islands where the pirates lived:

http://www.travelocity.com/

Can you find information about any CD-ROMs that deal with pirates?

Output and writing ideas. Journals, timelines, maps, diaries, stories, Hypercard stacks, PowerPoint presentations — any of these can be used to display what you learned about pirates.

11.24 *Let the Light Shine: An Exploration of Lighthouses* ACTIVITIES

PD

Subjects: Geography, History, Maritime History
Grade Level: 3rd and Up

An interesting way to explore not only the world, but also changes in specific technology, is to explore the world of lighthouses.

"What kind of a guy takes a job keeping a lighthouse?" asked Linus Larrabee in the film *Sabrina*. As you explore the world of lighthouses, perhaps you'll learn more about the people who manned them, the stories around them, the technology that powered them, and some of the places where they are located.

A good place to start.

LIGHTHOUSES AROUND THE WORLD

    http://worldlights.com/world

From their home page, you can find tall tales about lighthouses. Another good starting point is

LEGENDARY LIGHTHOUSES

    http://www.pbs.org/legendarylighthouses/

Once you've read those, check out some of the locations of lighthouses around the world.

Plot their locations on maps and indicate the years they were built. A data base is a good place to store information about the year built, size, capabilities, location, and any interesting facts you learn along the way.

More lighthouse links can be found at:

    http://spider.biddeford.com/~lhdigest/feb97/lthselinks.html

Add to your frame of reference by going to:

    http://zuma.lib.utk.edu/lights/

Along the way, what did you learn about the Fresnel lens? Ships that were saved by lighthouses? The most dangerous coasts? The safest shores where there are lighthouses?

Suggestions for writing. A diary of a lighthouse keeper, a PowerPoint presentation on lighthouses, a ship's log of the dangerous journey saved by the lighthouse, or the account of a ship saved from the perilous shore as written by the lighthouse keeper.

11.25 *Not Another Fish Story: Aquariums Online*

ACTIVITIES

PD

Subjects: Geography, Oceanography
Grade Level: Any

It seems to me that if I were to research different aquariums and kept track of the kinds of sea creatures and plants found in the different locations, I might just learn something new about fascinating lands.

There are many aquarium sites online, from the coast of California, to the shores of Vancouver, to the inland waterways of Iowa. From Japan to Australia and many places in between, aquariums provide an online experience full of surprises. Each of these sites offers a tour of the aquarium plus more information about the facility and its programs.

For a preview of what you might see, check out some undersea photography sites.

Start at The Underwater Photography Web Site:

`http://www.repost.com/uw-photo/`

A couple of other places for great photos:

`http://www.divediscovery.com/Fiji/fiji.html` (click on U/W Gallery)
`http://www.marinediving.com/www/mpl/mplsele.html`

Now, begin your tours of aquariums in the United States on California's Coast at Monterey Bay Aquarium:

`http://www.mbayaq.org/`

Take a drive down the coast to Cabrillo High School's aquarium:

`http://www.rain.org/~conqfish/`

Continue on down the California coast to the Birch Aquarium at La Jolla:

`http://aqua.ucsd.edu/`

Oregon's wonderful aquarium can be found at:

`http://www.aquarium.org/`

Move on to Iowa:

`http://www.iowaaquarium.org/`

Take a trip to Chicago to the Shedd Aquarium:

`http://www.sheddnet.org/Cee.htm`

Now, move to the South and take a look at Tennessee's aquarium:

`http://www.tennis.org/`

Take a drive to Boston to their New England Aquarium:

`http://www.neaq.org/`

Don't leave the United States yet — check out Florida's aquarium:

`http://www.sptimes.com/aquarium/default.html`

No tour of aquariums would be complete without a visit to Sea World:

http://www.4adventure.com/parkcentral/swf/

Before you leave the United States, check out the Smithsonian's Ocean Planet Site:

http://seawifs.gsfc.nasa.gov/ocean_planet.html

Now, on to Canada and the aquarium in Vancouver:

http://www.vanaqua.org/

Work your way East to the St. Lawrence Aquarium:

http://www.northnet.org/slaec/

Don't miss the Fisheries Museum of Nova Scotia:

http://www.ednet.ns.ca/educ/museum/fma/index.htm

It's time to cross the Atlantic Ocean to the Dingle OceanWorld Aquarium in Ireland:

http://www.ksat.ie/ksat/featur.htm

Check out the British aquatic site at:

http://www.cfkc.demon.co.uk/

Travel farther East to Sweden's aquarium site. It's in Swedish, but if you ask, they'll present the slides in English:

http://www.rby.hk-r.se/~pt94fla/aqua/

Now, check out Yoshi's Reef in Japan for more colorful pictures:

http://207.18.184.26/reef.html

Visit the Underwater Observatory and Marine Park in Israel:

http://www.coralworld.com/eilat/

Explore that Great Barrier Reef

http://www.gbrmpa.gov.au/

See some beautiful pictures and get more information:

http://oberon.educ.sfu.ca/splash/tank.htm

For lots of related tours and information, check here:

http://www.wln.com/~deltapac/ocean_od.html

Lots of aquarium links:

http://nic2.hawaii.edu/~delbeek/aquarium.html
http://www.iseshima.com/aquarium/aqua.html
http://netvet.wustl.edu/fish.htm

Read more about personal aquariums at AquaScape:

http://www.netservetech.com/AquaScapeMag.html

Look here for information about careers in marine science:

http://oceanlink.island.net/index.html

As you explore, keep a data base of information about the types of sea creatures and ocean life you discover in each location. It's difficult to predict exactly what information you will find as you explore.

At each site, make note of the following:

Prettiest fish

Largest fish

Most dangerous fish

Most unusual fish

Types of plant life

Types of coral

When you are done, have kids post their entry into the "Most Beautiful Fish Contest," "The Most Unusual Fish Contest," etc.

Some questions to keep in mind.   Do you find any similarities? What are some of the most unusual ocean life forms you learned about? What is being done in the area of ocean conservation on a global basis? Did you learn about any differences between freshwater marine life and seawater marine life?

Extensions.   Learn more about jobs in marine biology, marine conservation, and underwater exploration.

11.26 *Top of the News*

EO

Subjects: Any
Grade Level: 5th and Up

Often, when you pick up your daily newspaper (in print or online) you'll find something interesting. You can usually find more information about the topic by going online.

Example. In the *Las Vegas Review Journal*, 5/21/97, find an article on the "Missing Link": *Unenlagia comahuensis*. For an abstract of the news article describing the find, printed in *Nature*, May 22, 1997, check this site:

    http://www.nature.com/

Sign on and go to the May 22, 1997, issue. Then check the table of contents and look for "New evidence concerning avian origins from the Late Cretaceous of Patagonia" (Letter to *Nature*), by F. E. Novas and P. F. Puerta.
Read the summary of their findings.
Fossils were discovered in Argentina, in the Patagonia region, belonging to a bird that may be a descendant of a dinosaur.

> Can you find the original article?
>
> Can you find a newpaper in Argentina discussing the find?
>
> What other sites can you locate that discuss this find?
>
> As you explore this topic, are there any other links that you find to extend your studies?
>
> Did you learn about the career of being a paleontologist?

A good starting place to learn about the area is this tour of Patagonia (mostly text):

    http://www.cco.caltech.edu/~salmon/argentina1.html

For a long list of dinosaurs, check:

    http://www.yakscorner.com/new/big/dinolist.html

Can you locate a picture of the bird? The area where it was discovered? What dinosaurs and birds is it linked to?

11.27 *A Lesson in Nationality*   `ACTIVITIES`

EO   **Subjects: Geography, History, Culture**
Grade Level: 5th and Up

In an interview (*Las Vegas Review Journal*, May 25, 1997), Puerto Rican actor Hector Elizondo made a point about race when he said, "Puerto Rican is a nationality, not a race." With all of the conquests by explorers and through wars, lineage of any particular country can become very mixed and varied.

Inhabitants of Puerto Rico are descendants of the Spanish. Inhabitants of Spain came from many places. How far back can you trace the lineage of the people of Puerto Rico? Start your timeline with the first exploration and conquest of the island and trace back to their Spanish roots. Then trace the roots of the people who settled in Spain and trace them back to their homelands, too. Then continue your exploration as it branches out in several directions.

Use maps, timelines, and pictures to display the lineage.

Start with a study of the history of Puerto Rico at:

```
http://welcome.topuertorico.org/history.html
http://www.hartford-hwp.com/cp-usa/archives/95-09-23-2.html
```

Continue with a study of the history of Spain and learn about the many influences that settled the country at:

```
http://www.DocuWeb.ca/SiSpain/english/history/hisintro.html
```

From here, you can see that many nationalities settled in Spain. Now your job of tracing backward will take many directions: south to Libya and north to the Celts, as well as into Rome and Greece.

With so many directions and so many influences, it is important to note that while nationality can be established, the issue of race is much more difficult to define when so many diverse influences joined together to form even one country.

Extensions.   Can you begin at another country and trace back the settlement and ancestry?

Further reading.   What novels can you find about the exploration of Puerto Rico and Spain? What can you learn by reading *Don Quixote* by Cervantes?

More.   Spend some time exploring Spanish museums and artists

LINKS FOR SPAIN
        http://www.docuweb.ca/SiSpain/english/index.html

11.28   *Americana: Portrayers of America*

ACTIVITIES

EO

Subjects: Art, History, Geography
Grade Level: 7th and Up

In any culture, there are artists, writers, poets, and musicians who, through their work, personify their people, their land, their culture. In America, this personification can be seen in the art of Currier & Ives and Norman Rockwell, the poetry of Robert Frost, and the writings of Mark Twain, among others.

The problem.   Pick an era in American history and prepare an overview of the artists, writers, poets, and musicians who, through their work, presented a view of America and Americans. Who are the artists, writers, etc.? List samples of their works that represent America. What were the dominant American personality characteristics they portrayed? What were the positive characteristics? Negative?

Extensions.

1. Which science fiction writers, filmmakers, artists seem to be portraying an accurate view of America's future? Why do you think it's accurate?

2. Which TV shows from the 50s to the 90s seem to depict a view of America and Americans? What characteristics are portrayed?

3. Which films from the 30s to the 90s depict a view of America and Americans? Which characteristics are portrayed?

To begin your research, start with an interesting history of Currier & Ives prints and views of many of them at:

    http://www.pev.com/whispers.htm

Get a view of more Currier & Ives prints at:

    http://www.oldprints.com/

Cross-reference with:

> http://www.mcny.org/mcny/set3.htm

To view some of Norman Rockwell's work depicting 1920–1960s America, go to:

> http://www.paonline.com/zaikoski/rockwell.htm

You'll find more of Rockwell's work at:

> http://www.sundial.net/~djarrett/dj-nr1.htm

Another collection of Rockwell's work can be seen at:

> http://www.paonline.com/zaikoski/index.htm

To visit Rockwell's Museum collection, go to:

> http://www.nrm.org/

After looking at the art work for either Currier & Ives or Rockwell, what assumptions can you make about their view of Americans? What activities are depicted? People? Generations? Attitudes? Feelings?

Can you sum up your impression of Americans based on your impressions of the art? For example:

> Americans take part in…
>
> Americans are _____ (descriptive adjective) people who like_____ (activities)
>
> Things that are important to Americans are…
>
> People who are important are …
>
> Activities that are important are …
>
> Places that are important are …
>
> Emotions often displayed are …

Extension.   Locate the poets, authors, and musicians of the same era. If you fill in the above blanks referring to their work, what answers do you provide?

Extension.   Do similar research for another era and fill in the blanks. Can you see any overall pattern of what is considered "American" or the characteristics that depict Americans?

Extension.   Pick another country and an era in that country's history and do a similar search using their artists, musicians, writers, etc.

11.29 *Solving a Problem*   ACTIVITIES

PD

**Subjects: History, Geography, Cartography
Grade Level: 4th and Up**

Problem. The year is 1800; the place is St. Louis, in the Louisiana Territories. You are the owner of the American Fur Trading Co. of St. Louis. You have established a village west of the Mississippi River that is exclusively French. For more than 20 years, from Indian tribes in the vicinity, you have successfully traded for valuable furs. These furs are floated down the Mississippi River to the port at New Orleans (at great peril to your shipment and crews) and then shipped to Europe's nobility.

Your city has begun to prosper, but now Louisiana, which keeps changing possession between cousins in Spain and France, is in the hands of the Spanish. With a valuable load of furs ready to ship or rot, the port of New Orleans, by Royal Spanish edict, has been closed to all but Spanish-owned ships. A gantlet of Spanish warships blocks the harbor entrance. You must move your furs to a port for shipping, but your way is blocked.

1. *What do you do? What is the shortest, fastest and safest route for shipping your furs?*

   Background information you might need:

   > Open ports
   >
   > Ports near St. Louis
   >
   > Dangers and perils on the Mississippi
   >
   > Methods of travel
   >
   > Indians who trade furs
   >
   > Indians who are unfriendly
   >
   > Settlements in the area

   You'll need additional information on the background of the Louisiana Purchase and the fluctuating ownership of the territory

2. *OOPS!* Your settlers cannot build wagons rugged enough to travel the rough trails to another port in time. Your furs will rot and have to be destroyed. They must be shipped out of New Orleans. A French ship (the *Estragon*) is tied up in

East Bay Harbor, outside New Orleans, and is waiting for your furs. You must get past the Spanish blockade.

How?

To find out what really happened, read *Louisiana Purchase* by A.E. Hotchner, or, for further outside reading of this time period, try *A Place Called Freedom* by Ken Follett, or *Burr* by Gore Vidal.

Additional areas to research.

Costumes of this era

Music

Languages

Writers

Artists

Architects

Political figures

Names you might run across.

Thomas Jefferson

James Madison

Meriwether Lewis

Additional question. At 4 cents an acre, how much did America pay for the Louisiana Purchase? How many acres?

Some sites to start with.

LOUISIANA PURCHASE

```
http://www.crt.state.la.us/crt/purch.htm
http://www.crt.state.la.us/crt/museum/cabildo/cab4.htm
http://www.nara.gov/exhall/originals/loupurch.html
http://www.gateway.com/History/LaPurchase.html
```

MISSISSIPPI RIVER — HISTORY AND TRADE

```
http://www.adventures.com/encyclopedia/america/msdelta.html
http://www.greatriver.com/index.shtml
http://www.tulane.edu/~lmiller/Transportation.html
```

MIKE FINK — THE KEELBOAT CAPTAIN

```
http://www.tiac.net/users/stein1/Fink.html
http://www.primenet.com/~psenffne/22da.htm
```

THOMAS JEFFERSON BACKGROUND AND TOUR OF MONTICELLO

http://www.monticello.org/index.html
http://grid.let.rug.nl/~welling/usa/revolution.html

A NEWSPAPER FROM THE ERA

http://earlyamerica.com/earlyamerica/past2.jpg

AN ESSAY ON SLAVERY IN THE EARLY COLONIES

http://earlyamerica.com/review/winter96/slavery.html

A LETTER FROM THOMAS JEFFERSON TO JAMES MADISON

http://earlyamerica.com/review/summer/letter.html

MAPS OF THE AREA

http://www.lib.virginia.edu/exhibits/lewis_clark/home.html
http://scarlett.libs.uga.edu/darchive/hargrett/maps/revamer.html

HISTORY OF EXPLORATION OF THE AREA

http://www.lib.virginia.edu/exhibits/lewis_clark/ch4.html

THE FIRST EUROPEANS IN AMERICA

http://grid.let.rug.nl/~welling/usa/revolution.html

NATIVE AMERICANS

http://grid.let.rug.nl/~welling/usa/revolution.html

MOUNTAIN MEN AND FUR TRADE

http://www.xmission.com/~drudy/amm.html
http://lily.mip.berkeley.edu/classes/history16/pages/img0001.html

POETRY, PICTURES, AND ARTICLES

http://www.history.rochester.edu/godeys/

WHAT PEOPLE USED AND WORE

http://www.foxrivertraders.com/toc.htm

HOW PEOPLE LIVED (CIRCA 1900)

http://www.vzinet.com/heritage/index.htm

ADDITIONAL SITES

```
http://indy4.fdl.cc.mn.us/~isk/maps/houses/housingmap.html
http://www.mvnf.muse.digital.ca/popul/coureurs/index2en.htm
http://www.1856.com/history.htm
http://www.mwd.com/tourism/forts.html
```

REAL-LIFE ACCOUNTS

```
http://www.xmission.com/~drudy/mtman/html/jed.html
http://www.xmission.com/~drudy/mtman/html/sagewntr.html
http://www.xmission.com/~drudy/mtman/html/colter.html
```

Movies you might want to watch.

Davy Crockett and the River Pirates — Disney 1956

Davy Crockett, King of the Wild Frontier — Disney 1955

LESSON

NEW LESSONS

A Note about Output with These Lessons

When your students are ready to participate in these explorations, you may be, as we were, ready to create Web pages, or you may have discovered other ways for your kids to communicate their findings.

I hope you're seeing many different ways to use all the tools at your disposal, not only the computer and Internet ones — that output is varied, adaptable, creative, and fun. And even if you are creating Web pages, I hope your walls are getting too small to display all you and your kids are finding.

Therefore, here are some new explorations.

12.1   *Amelia — Lost and Found*   NEW LESSONS

Suggested by Nick Costa, ROTC instructor, San Bernardino High School, from an article that interested him.

EO/PD   **Subjects: History, Geography, Politics, Technology**
Grade Level: 6th and Up

On June 1, 1937, the American aviator Amelia Earhart attempted to fly around the world. On July 2 of the same year, she made her last radio transmission from her plane. No recovery was ever made of the plane or its pilot.

Recent research has uncovered new evidence in the disappearance of this aviator. There was some speculation that she was flying a spy mission for the Americans because of increased Japanese military activity in the South Pacific. Others say she was just trying to set a record.

What can you learn about:

Amelia Earhart.

Her history — what a story that must be! A woman aviator, the 1940s, the war

The technology in finding pieces of the puzzle of her path

Geography — where was she flying? What does this have to do with World War II and the Japanese?

Politics — spy theory: The South Pacific and the islands there were important in the war . . . was she flying over those to check things out? Was it her cover story? If so, or even if not, creative writing would be a fun way of telling that story.

Was the route she was taking in the right place to spy for the government?

Was she capable, as a person, of carrying out such a dangerous mission?

Why was the area she was flying over important to the American military at that time?

Starting points. Background about Amelia:

```
http://www.ionet.net/~jellenc/eae_intr.html
http://www.worldbook.com/fun/aviator/html/twolegnd.htm
http://www.atchison.org/Amelia/FurtRead.htm
http://www.rochester.k12.mn.us/century/explorers/earhart.html
http://home.sprynet.com/sprynet/robincam/aeimage.htm
http://tesla.csuhayward.edu/cappstreet/urban/hatch/earhart.html
http://www.access.digex.net/~janette/amelia.html
http://www.thehistorynet.com/AviationHistory/images/0797_11.htm
```

Her plane:

```
http://ceps.nasm.edu/GALLERIES/PHOTO1/VEGA.GIF
```

The new evidence:

```
http://www.tighar.org/Projects/AEdescr.html
http://www.cnmi-guide.com/history/ww2/amelia/map.htm
http://www.saipan.com/cnmiinfo/history/earhart.htm
http://www.anya.com/mysteries/hypamelia.html
http://fox.nstn.ca/~dblaikie/n17ma97a.html
http://www.sfmuseum.org/hist6/amelia.html
```

The flight to recreate her flight:

```
http://worldflight.org/
```

The war in the Pacific:

```
http://www.glue.umd.edu/~enola/hist/history.html
http://www.geocities.com/Pentagon/Quarters/6991/usmc.htm
http://www.spectra.net/~burgman/ww2/ww2.html
http://www.geocities.com/Heartland/Plains/6672/canal_index.html
http://www.saipan.com/cnmiinfo/history/spnwar.htm
http://www.gwjapan.com/ftp/pub/newsltr/wjj/1992/win92a.txt
```

The U.S. Air Force:

```
http://personal.trxinc.com./dpixler/
```

South Pacific Islands — what are they? Where are they?

```
http://www.magna.com.au/~hideaway/
http://www.sunspotsintl.com/
http://www.pacificislands.com/
```

12.2 *The Lost Continent*   NEW LESSONS

As suggested by the PBS documentary on the same subject.

EP/PD **Subjects: History, Literature, Geography, Art, Technology**
Grade Level: 4th and Up

Modern technology has been instrumental in solving an age-old problem: if the Lost Continent of Atlantis really existed, where was it? Most scholars have used the text of Plato's writings to determine the existence and scope of the Lost Continent.

PLATO'S WRITING

```
http://classics.mit.edu/Plato/critias.sum.html
```

But, recent advances in sonar and satellite technology, along with some different interpretations of Plato, have led scientists to believe that Atlantis did exist, but not where it was originally thought to be. Scientists have also discovered indigenous peoples who, while they live far from one another, share common traits with people of the Lost Continent.

Using the following sites as starting points, determine:

1. What is the relationship between each part of this exploration and Atlantis — i.e., what relationship to Atlantis do Guanches, Bimini, the Azores, etc., have?
2. What part is technology playing in learning more about the continent?
3. Where do you think Atlantis is? Plot that location on a map. Using your research, defend your results.
4. What were the people of Atlantis like?

ATLANTIS LOST CONTINENT

http://www.atlan.org/

THE LOST CONTINENT

http://www.laketech.com/AD_LC.HTML

ATLANTIS–MU–LEMURIA

http://www.spiritweb.org/Spirit/atlantis-mu-lemuria.html

ATLANTIS

http://thor.prohosting.com/~starbuck/atlantis.htm
http://www.angelfire.com/ri/allfantasy/atlantis.html

THE LOST CITY OF ATLANTIS

http://www.sun2001.com/atlantis.html
http://www.laketech.com/AD_LC.HTML

SANTORINI ISLAND

http://agn.hol.gr/hellas/cyclades/santorin.htm

BIMINI ARCHAEOLOGY

http://www.knowledge.co.uk/frontiers/sf064/sf064a01.htm

BIMINI

http://caribbeansupersite.com/bahamas/bimini.htm

AZORES

http://www.dca.uac.pt/acores/eazores.htm

AT THE TRACKS OF THE GUANCHES

http://www.red2000.com/spain/canarias/g-canari/guanch.html

THE GUANCHES

http://www.cistia.es/cabildotf/ingles/pueblo_tf/historia01.html

AKROTIRI

http://dilos.com/region/cyclad/akrotiri.html
http://www.culture.gr/2/21/211/21121a/e211ua08.html
http://santorinitoday.com/akrotiri.htm

THERA

http://www.vacation.net.gr/p/santor.html

MYSTIC SITES

http://www.dimensional-doorways.com/hmsframe.htm

MEDITERRANEAN HISTORY

http://www.iit.edu/~phillips/personal/contents/medhis.html

THE ERUPTION OF THERA

http://home.fireplug.net/~rshand/streams/thera/thera.html

ORIGINS OF ATLANTIS

http://home.fireplug.net/~rshand/streams/thera/atlantis.html

PELOPONNESE

http://vislab-www.nps.navy.mil/~fapapoul/
http://www.vacation.net.gr/p/pelopon.html

PILLARS OF HERCULES

http://www.jps.net/triumph/p287.htm

ISLAND OF LACONIA — PILLARS OF HERCULES

http://www.ellada.com/pelopo04.html
http://www.geocities.com/Athens/Delphi/3728/cerigo.htm
http://w4u.eexi.gr/~langsett/theo.htm

SONAR MAPPING

http://www.cs.mu.oz.au/~andrbh/SonarMap/SonarMap.html
http://aaron.cee.usu.edu/inse/mapping.html
http://humm.whoi.edu/Smith/TOBI3D.htm

Bonus question.   What part do the Nasca Indians play in putting this puzzle together?

12.3 Dolphins and Bears and Dogs, Oh My!

NEW LESSONS

EO/PD   Subjects: **Animal Behavior, Geography, Dogs, Dolphins, Decision Making, Environmental Issues**
Grade Level: **1st and Up**

Find this article in *People* magazine, 6/15/98, pg. 146: "Bear Scarer."

`http://www.pathfinder.com/`

Look for *People* magazine.

Search the magazine for the article (what key words will you use?).

Here are some key pieces of information you will learn:

Who: Carrie Hunt
What: Teaches bears to stay away from the "pizza, chips, and Twinkies that civilized man persists in leaving about."
When: Now
Where: Yosemite and Glacier National Parks (Now here, you've got to take a side trip — two, actually. Don't forget to see Going to the Sun Highway, and try to find pictures of some bears, too!)
Why: To save their lives
How: By using Karelian bear dogs

1. Where do these dogs come from? (Map it.)

2. Where can you learn more about the following: (List more URLs, and decide how will you keep track of all your information.)

   a. Karelian dogs
   b. Yosemite
   c. Glacier National Park
   d. Other work dogs, like cow dogs
   e. Carrie Hunt
   f. The bears she saved

g. Other animal saving techniques (How was Willy the Whale, from the movie *Free Willy*, moved from Mexico to Oregon?)

h. Other animal saving people or organizations (Who is looking after the Baby Seals in Canada? The endangered species in Kenya?, etc.).

Now that you know more about saving endangered species, read about the endangered River Dolphins in China. They are being displaced by the building of a giant dam. (See also the China Dam lesson.)

Adding in that knowledge, knowing what you know about saving animals and the technology involved, what will you do if the task of relocating those dolphins falls to you? (well phrased communication)

1. Who would you call for advice?

2. Where can you take the dolphins so they can live happily and thrive?

3. What will be the best way to get the dolphins to their new home?

Other things to think about. The bears you learned about are being harmed by the leavings of man. Did your research reveal any other animals that suffer from what "civilized man persists in leaving about"?

Is anyone doing something to help other animals as Carrie Hunt helps bears?

How could you help someone like Carrie?

How do you become someone like Carrie? (What would you study?)

What kind of personality is helpful to this work?

Which animal would you like to help save? Is there a way you can help?

Who can you connect with online (via e-mail) in this quest?

Output. Aside from interesting discussions, some wonderful visual and text projects can display kids' learning and understanding.

List all the URLs you found to add to this exploration.

Show us pictures of the animals being saved.

Tell us how to get involved and what we need to study to help.

Tell us and show us more about the technology that helps.

12.4 *The Million Dollar Sturgeon*

NEW LESSONS

Suggested by a news article about the quarter-million-dollar sturgeon.

EO/PD

Subjects: Oceanography, Technology, Ecology, Geography, Economics
Grade Level: 6th and Up

All over our world, fish are disappearing in record numbers. At the same time, the number of fishing boats, many of them factory ships, not independent smaller boats, has grown dramatically. This combination has caused many of the fish we eat to be less plentiful. The blue-fin tuna is one. Another endangered species is the sturgeon, which is valued for its caviar. One sturgeon recently sold for $250,000. To combate this depletion of the wealth of the ocean, aquariums are developing programs for their nearby seas. Here is one searchable newspaper. Check for articles on sturgeon and caviar:

SAN FRANCISCO GATE

        http://www.sfgate.com/

Using the URLs from the aquarium quest, check out the programs being developed to save ocean life.

Once you have explored aquarium projects, read about the legislation signed in June 1998 by President Bill Clinton in Monterey, California, to establish an organization to protect the oceans.

What does the legislation hope to do? Are there similar laws in other countries? How important is it that such projects and laws are developed?

Extensions.

How is the Internet helping in the quest to save the seas?

Do inland lakes and waterways in your area need protecting in any way? What is being done to save your water?

Is there anything your class can do to help (locally or outside your area)?

What other projects are helping to save the coral around the world?

What are some of the new technologies helping save the seas?

How is overfishing changing the prices of fish? Can you find out how much blue-fin tuna sushi costs in Toyko? How about caviar from Russia? Shrimp from Louisiana?

Starting points.

CAVIAR

    http://www.netroam.com/caviar/
    http://alldata.superlink.net/cavruss/

STURGEON

    http://www.sturgeons.com/

STURGEON GENERAL

    http://www.sturgeongeneral.org/

STURGEON AND CAVIAR NEWS

    http://www.sturgeons.com/news.html

OCEAN AND COASTAL PROTECTION

    http://www.epa.gov/OWOW/ocpd/

OCEAN PROTECTION TRUST

    http://www.mullum.com.au/opt/

CENTER FOR MARINE CONSERVATION

    http://www.cmc-ocean.org/

MARINE CONSERVATION SOCIETY

    http://www.mcsuk.mcmail.com/

MARINE FISH CONSERVATION NETWORK

    http://www.netspace.org/MFCN/

OCEAN AND COASTAL LAW

    http://netserver.uoregon.edu/organizations/oceanlaw/memos/issue44.html

MANAGING GLOBAL ENVIRONMENTAL COMMONS

    http://ps.ucdavis.edu/classes/pol129/TZA/ourpage.html

NEWS ARTICLES

    http://www.washingtonpost.com/wp-srv/inatl/exussr/june/10/caviar.htm
    http://www.washingtonpost.com/wp-srv/frompost/features/june97/caviar.htm

WORLD WILDLIFE FEDERATION ARTICLES

http://www.wwf.org/new/news/prcav.html
http://www.wwf.org/new/news/pr142.htm
http://www.wwf.org/new/news/pr137.htm
http://www.wwf.org/new/news/prmarine.html

THE CLINTON OCEAN POLICY

http://www.wwf.org/new/news/pr147.htm
http://www.wwf.org/new/news/pr123.htm

RELATED ARTICLES

http://www.wwf.org/new/news/prsharks.html
http://www.wwf.org/new/news/prun.html
http://www.wwf.org/new/news/prlac.html
http://www.standard.net/snweb/greatsaltlake/junction/brine/1.html

YEAR OF THE OCEAN

http://www.wwf.org/yoto/yoto.htm

SEA WEB

http://www.seaweb.org/

OCEAN 98

http://www.ocean98.org/

OCEAN PLANET

http://seawifs.gsfc.nasa.gov/ocean_planet.html

PLANKTON NET

http://www.uoguelph.ca/zoology/ocean/index.htm

CORAL ECOLOGY

http://nhmi.org/corals.htm

NORTHERN PACIFIC MAGAZINE

http://np.rybvod.kamchatka.su/

MARINE RESOURCES DEVELOPMENT

http://www.mrdf.org/

EXPLORE UNDERWATER MAGAZINE
http://www.exploreuw.com/aindex.htm

DISCOVERY BAY MARINE LAB
http://ourworld.compuserve.com/homepages/Discovery_Bay_Marine_Laboratory/

12.5 *The China Dam Lesson*   NEW LESSONS

**EO/PD Subjects: Literature, History, Ecology, Economics
Grade Level: 4th and Up**

After we had read *Antigone*, *Julius Caesar*, and *Herland*, I wanted my students to use their knowledge of character to solve a problem. I had heard about the China dam from a news story and, after a bit of research, decided it would make a good problem-solving exercise.

I asked my kids to research the arguments surrounding the building of the world's largest dam in China. This dam, prior to its construction, was highly controversial.

After reading the pros and cons, my students were to respond to the following:

> Creon, the king in Antigone, would/would not build the dam because _____
>
> Julius Caesar would/would not build the dam because _____.
>
> The women of *Herland* would/would not build the dam because _____.

Each response had to reflect the students' understanding of the characters and their values.

Along the way, we found a site where people from around the world had been posting their views on the controversy. Several of my students wrote responses to some of the views they felt were not well thought out. With my permission, they e-mailed their responses. The next day, one response, from a freshman, was posted along with all others from around the world!

To read about the China Dam problem:

```
http://www.chinavista.com/travel/tangtze/main.html
http://www.exim.gov/3gorges.html
http://home.hkstar.com/~daiwo
http://gladstone.uoregon.edu/~chrismc/three_gorges.html
http://www.hrw.org/summaries/s.china952.html
```

To read *Herland* online:

```
http://www.shss.montclair.edu/perkins/herland1.html
```

What would your country, city, state do about the dam? Why do you think that?

In August of 1998, China suffered from severe storms and flooding. Read what the experts think about these events and their impact on the new dam and the people living around it.

Searchable newspaper.

SAN FRANCISCO GATE

```
http://www.sfgate.com/
```

12.6 *The Movement West*

NEW LESSONS

EO/PD   **Subjects: History, Geography, Map Skills**
Grade Level: 4th and Up

After the U.S. Civil War, many Americans headed West. Former slaves, Southerners, and those from the victorious North packed up their belongings and started West. Explore this westward migration.

Research.

1. What year did the Civil war end?
2. At that time, what were some settled territories in the West? (Calif., Oregon, Wash., Oklahoma, Texas, etc)
3. What were considered unsettled territories?
4. What routes did people take to get to the settled or unsettled territories?

The Activity.
1. Pick a person: (a) Former slave, (b) Southerner, (c) Northerner.
2. Pick a starting point: Where might your person have lived during the Civil War?
3. Pick settled or unsettled territory to head toward.
4. Plot your route (find historical maps to guide you).
5. What do you plan to do out West (farm, goldmine, merchant, scout, guide, other)?

Output.
1. Write a letter home telling the folks about the trip you just took out West. What route did you follow? What should they watch out for (good and bad) when they come to join you? Give them directions and advice.

Additional things to research. Reporters who wrote of these journeys (Horace Greeley, Remington). Read their accounts, then write one of your own.

Additional feedback. Well phrased communication.

1. If you are a Southerner, why would you go West after the Civil War?
2. If you are a Northerner, victorious in the War, why would you go West?
3. Where were some of the settlements that were formed by former slaves? (Oklahoma)

Extra Credit. Research and write about your life in the West as (a) a scout for the military, (b) a wild-horse trader, (c) a gold miner, (d) an outlaw.

Starting points.
HISTORICAL MAPS

    http://www.lib.virginia.edu/exhibits/lewis_clark/home.html
    http://www.libs.uga.edu/darchive/hargrett/maps/maps.html

RESEARCHING PEOPLE OF THE CIVIL WAR ERA

    http://www.cwc.lsu.edu/other/genealogy/

CIVIL WAR NEWSPAPER

    http://members.aol.com/Zollicofer/civilweek.htm
Weekly account of the war.

AMERICAN CIVIL WAR ARTICLES

    http://www.historybuff.com/library/refcivil.html

HISTORY BUFF'S HOME PAGE

http://www.historybuff.com/

Links to some wonderful historical information.

EARLY AMERICA

http://earlyamerica.com/

Archiving Early American newspapers and other information.

CIVIL WAR NEWSPAPERS

http://www.cwc.lsu.edu/links/links4.htm#Newspapers

Links to several newspapers.

DOCUMENTING THE AMERICAN SOUTH

http://sunsite.unc.edu/docsouth/

The Southern experience in America.

MANIFEST DESTINY

http://members.aol.com/htmpro/index.htm

"How the Rest was Won" — documenting the settlement of the West.

THE WILD WILD WEST

http://www.gunslinger.com/west.html

Links and information about the gunslingers, the sheriffs and others who settled the West.

ALONG THE CHISHOLM TRAIL

http://www.texhoma.net/~glencbr/index.html

Learn where, when, and who traveled this American trail.

AMERICANWEST

http://www.americanwest.com/

A celebration of those who explored and settled.

JEFFERSON NATIONAL EXPANSION MEMORIAL

http://www.nps.gov/jeff/arch-home/

Dedicated to those who settled the American West.

12.7 *A Man, A Mountain, and the Weather*

NEW LESSONS

EO/PD   **Subjects: Geography, Geology, Biology**
Grade Level: 3rd and Up

What is the effect on the human body when climbing Mt. Everest?

1. Go online and read about Tom Whittaker, who is climbing Mt. Everest. (a) Why is he a special climber? (b) Has he successfully climbed the mountain yet? Why/why not?

2. If you are going to climb Mt. Everest, (a) what is the best time of year to go? (b) What weather conditions are most favorable to climbing? (c) What weather conditions are least favorable?

3. Where is Mt. Everest? What mountain range is it part of?

4. How high is it?

   Extra: How high is Base Camp?

5. According to one source, when climbing Everest, the brain swells and the lungs heave. (a) At what altitude will this happen? (b) Why does this happen? (c) What other effects are there on your body?

6. Why is the air thin at Mt. Everest?

7. If you live in an area closer to sea level (1000 ft) and you fly to Nepal to begin your climb, will you be able to start the day you arrive, or will you need to ease into it gradually? Why/why not?

Output.

   One-sentence answers to questions

   One-paragraph responses

   Responses with graphics

   Narrative account of your journey incorporating all the answers

   PowerPoint presentation of your journey with the answers

   E-mail your response to questions as if you were having a conversation with someone who wants to learn about climbing Mt. Everest.

Extension.

1. If you live at an altitude of 1000 feet or less and are driving within 1–2 hours to an altitude of 8000 feet to hike, ski, or climb, what can you expect to happen to your body? Why? (a) What about the reverse — you leave an altitude of 8000 feet to go hiking at 500 feet. What can you expect to happen to your body (if anything)? (b) At what altitude can you expect to see changes in the human body?

2. List several other mountains popular with climbers, along with each one's altitude, continent, country, airport you fly into, time of year to climb, dangers you might face climbing that particular mountain.

3. What kind of special equipment is available for climbing a mountain like Everest?

4. What kind of special equipment does a disabled climber like Tom Whittaker need to climb Mt. Everest?

5. Who are some other disabled mountain or rock climbers? What is their disability? Where have they climbed?

6. Which mountain, if you could climb the one of your choice, would you climb? Why?

Starting Points.

SEARCHABLE NEWSPAPER — SF GATE

    http://www.sfgate.com/

MOUNTAIN ZONE

    http://everest.mountainzone.com/98/

EVEREST NEWS

    http://www.everestnews.com/

MT. EVEREST CAM

    http://www.m.chiba-u.ac.jp/class/respir/eve_e.htm

NOVA ONLINE — ALIVE ON EVEREST

    http://www.pbs.org/wgbh/nova/everest/

EVEREST ONLINE

    http://www.everestonline.com/

12.8 : *The Count of Monte Cristo*   NEW LESSONS

EO/PD   **Subjects: Literature, History, Geography, Architecture**
Grade Level: 6th and Up

This type of lesson works well with any work of literature. For the kids to really come closer to understanding the story, they needed to have more pictures in their heads, and more background information on which to build their point of view. We wanted to walk as many miles in the characters' shoes as we could. We kept the movie *Titanic* in mind as we read everything. It was the same need to bring authenticity to our conversations about the novel that led us to explore. I told the kids early on that I didn't' want their answer to any question raised in class to be "Duh, I don't know." They found out they liked knowing and they liked the process of finding out.

We didn't mind exploring! We rather enjoyed it!

Bringing Your Literature to Life

Begin by setting the scene.   The novel opens with a ship arriving in the harbor of Marseilles, France. Several sites will show students what Marseilles looks like, as well as what kind of ship the Count sailed on. Remember to check the time period.

This is when kids start to branch out. Some focus on ships while others focus on Marseilles or even the wardrobes. Others focus on events that shaped the times. All this builds a broad context within which we read and talked about the Count.

Marseilles, a Tour.

INTERACTIVE MAP OF MARSEILLES

        http://www.isweb.com/geo/amrs.htm

MARSEILLES HISTORICAL INFORMATION

        http://www.enprovence.com/marseille/anglais/

TOUR MARSEILLES

        http://www.pageszoom.com/pt/villes/marseill/ang/acc.htm

MORE MARSEILLES

        http://www.provenceweb.fr/e/bouches/marseill/marseill.htm

SOUTH STREET SEAPORT MUSEUM

    http://www.southstseaport.org/index.htm

The Count sailed into Marseilles on a merchant ship. Find pictures here.

THE TREASURE FLEET

    http://www.northlink.com/~hauxe/

SCHOONERMAN

    http://www.novagate.com/~schoonerman/

REGENCY FASHION PAGE

    http://locutus.ucr.edu/~cathy/reg3.html

How would the Count attire himself?

LA COUTURIERE PARISIENNE

    http://www.geocities.com/Paris/4432/

HISTORY OF COSTUME

    http://www.siue.edu/COSTUMES/COSTUME15_INDEX.HTML

CAT'S PAJAMAS

    http://catspajamas.com/

VINTAGE CLOTHING.

VICTORIANA

    http://www.victoriana.com/

As the plot progresses. The Count is imprisoned in the Chateau D'If. For more about the prison.

CHATEAU D'IF

    http://www.cogito.fr/marseill/chatif.htm

Soon, The Count moves to Paris — take a tour.

PARIS MAP

    http://www.isweb.com/

PARIS PAGES

    http://www.paris.org/

PARIS TOUR

    http://www.paris-france.org/

Later, he buys a country villa — have your students decide which one might have been his.

FRENCH CHATEAUS

    http://www.chateaux-france.com/

FRENCH VILLAS

    http://www.justfrance.com/
    http://www.francevillas.com/

Miscellaneous Count links.

COUNT OF MONTE CRISTO

    http://i-site.on.ca/booknook/79/adventure/countofmontecristo/
        vivianchow.html

A review.

ELECTRONIC TEXT OF *COUNT*

    ftp://sailor.gutenberg.org/pub/gutenberg/etext96/01jwr10.txt

COUNT CARTOONS

    http://www.bonus.com/bonus/card/scs_montecristo.bottom.html

THE FILM VERSION

    http://www.videoflicks.com/VF/04/004896.Htm

ALEXANDRE DUMAS

    http://brooklynny.com/neighborhoods/stories/dumas.html

DUMAS

    http://www.cadytech.com/dumas/

STUDENT REPORT ON DUMAS

    http://nkasd.wiu.k12.pa.us/vhs/dumasbell.htm

SWASHBUCKLERS AND FOPS

http://legends.dm.net/swash/dumas.html

More about Dumas.

LIFE OF DUMAS

http://www.smithsonianmag.com/smithsonian/issues96/jul96/dumas.html

ALEXANDRE DUMAS

http://www.acamedia.fr/dumas/

In French, with English summaries.

Historical Background.

A major part of the story is a quest for revenge. To understand motivation, the kids had to understand the betrayal and the betrayers first, and then understand their actions in the context of their lives. Who were these men, and why did each betray him?

What part did politics play? The political times began here: On March 31, 1814, Napoleon surrendered and was sent to the island of Elba in the Mediterranean to live out his days. King Louis XVIII took power. What can you learn about both?

NAPOLEON

http://www.ping.be/~ping5895/
http://come.to/napoleon/
http://www.napoleonfirst.com/
http://www.napoleon.org/

FRENCH HISTORY

http://www.france.com/culture/history/napoleons.html

For King Louis XVIII.

EUROPEAN ROYALTY

http://www.eurohistory.com/

FRENCH ROYALTY

http://www.ping.be/~pin12133/conde/english.htm

Trace the history of the monarchy.

FRENCH PERSONALITIES

http://www.pvhs.chico.k12.ca.us/~bsilva/projects/france/franpers.html

Read about Louis XVIII here.

KINGS OF FRANCE

`http://www.beyond.fr/history/kings.html`

A chronology.

MAD MONARCHS

`http://www.xs4all.nl/~kvenjb/madmon.htm`

King Louis is not here, but some of his relatives are!

ROYAL SCANDALS

`http://www.discovery.com/area/history/royal/royal1.html`

More of Louis' relatives are profiled.

ROYALTY IN HISTORY

`http://www.xs4all.nl/~kvenjb/kings.htm`

It seems that many of the royals in Europe intermarried. Read about Louis' ancestors.

THE FRENCH REVOLUTION

`http://www.wtj.com/artdocs/napsum1/`

This is an excellent site for building a frame of reference. But notice the number of references to people, places, and events that your kids should be familiar with. Many of these gaps in familiarity can be filled in with additional research. (You begin to see why there is never enough time!) How can you get reluctant learners to absorb all this? Give them time to look for information they are interested in that adds to the collective understanding, and then have other kids add in what they have learned. This is an extremely collective and collaborative process.

THE FRENCH REVOLUTION

`http://members.aol.com/agentmess/frenchrev/index.html`

A QUIZ ABOUT FRANCE

`http://www.pvhs.chico.k12.ca.us/~bsilva/projects/france/franques.html`

With the answers supplied, you can't miss filling in some gaps in information.

FRENCH HISTORICAL INFLUENCES

`http://www.prs.k12.nj.us/schools/PHS/Social_Studies/CompGovt/France/`
`    FRENCHHISTORY/Napoleon.html`

An essay to fill in more background.

THE ISLAND OF ELBA

    `http://www.elbacom.it/`

In English and Italian.

VIRTUAL ELBA

    `http://www.elbacom.it/v_elba/tour97/`

Part of the last site.

TUTT'ELBA

    `http://web.elbalink.it/tutt'elba/tutt'elba.home.ing.html`

Also in English or Italian, another tour.

NAPOLEONIC WAR SERIES

    `http://www.wtj.com/pl/pages/napoln.htm`

Where Did All This Lead Us?

To conversations, communications, and discussions. Ultimately, our questions about the Count were:

> Was his seeking revenge justified?
>
> If a man does something for his country, does it make it more justified — such as the actions of Cassius and Brutus (for those of you who have read *Julius Caesar*) and the actions of the Prosecutor against the Count?
>
> If a man seeks revenge for personal motives, is it ever justifiable — such as the mother who killed the man who molested one of her children?
>
> Did the Count ever feel remorse? Why?
>
> In what way was this a pro-Napoleonic story? What ties, if any, did Dumas have with the Napoleonic era?
>
> What was the fight all about with Napoleon at the center, and how does that tie into the wars we have read about so far? In the Napoleonic Wars, in France, which side would you have been on? We learned that Caesar was a ruler who courted the people. What was Napoleon like?

So many questions, so little time.

Extensions.   Follow up, in this story; the execution of King Louis and his queen. Write a first-person narrative of someone who had an interesting view of the situation.

We could have spent a great deal of time finding and presenting visually all the references in this novel or in any novel. Worthwhile projects for any English literature class would be to prepare visual guides to the novels you are reading. If you break up the tasks into manageable groups, these can be accomplished in a reasonable length of time and can be extremely helpful for emerging readers. Guides should also include as many references from the time period and place as possible to fill in gaps in kids' understanding.

12.9 *An Artful World*

NEW LESSONS

EO/PD Subjects: Art, Geography, History
Grade Level: With Help, as Young and Emerging Readers;
On Their Own, 4th and Up

Explore our world by looking at the crafts of the people. When a line in the novel *The Count of Monte Cristo* referred to his "stick," my students and I headed online to find pictures of "sticks" circa 1860s. We found beautiful pictures of elaborately carved sticks, of the walking kind. We also found, on our classroom map, where these were crafted. It's interesting when you learn where some of the finest craftspeople create and live. We learned more about what kind of walking stick the Count might have carried . . . and we voted on which we felt seemed to fit his character, just as we voted on which French country manor might have been his. Along the way, we learned about craftmanship. (By the way, listening to the kids discuss the nuances of which stick and which house showed me how well they were learning the character of the Count.)

Let your kids find the crafts of their country, and if you all care to branch out, broaden your boundaries to take in the fine work of crofters and glass blowers, jewelers and weavers, and other craftspeople around your country or the world. Don't forget to plot them on your map. If you don't have a map, go online and print what you need.

Well-phrased communication.

How do the crafts reflect the natural materials available in the area?

How do they incorporate the history of the area?

Are there any themes in the crafts?

Extra credit.   Are the themes of the art in an area the same as those in their literature? Chart the places your kids find crafts and then trace its history. Which craft dates back the farthest

Extension.   Native American crafts and art sell each year in the amount of around $1 billion. What are some other crafts that sell to that degree? Why do you think some crafts sell more than others? What are the names of some books about a particular craft you liked? Are there any magazines about crafts in general or one craft in particular?

Links to crafts.

ARTS AND CRAFTS MOVEMENT

    `http://www.dscweb.com/AandCintro.html`

MASTERS OF THE CRAFTS

    `http://www.cmcc.muse.digital.ca/membrs/arts/bronfman/mcintroe.html`

CRAFTSMAN PERSPECTIVE

    `http://members.aol.com/ac1900/index.html`

ARTS AND CRAFTS RESOURCES

    `http://www.csn.net/ragtime/Ragtime_Resources.html`

WALKING STICKS

    `http://www.walkingstick.com/`

WALKING STICKS AND CANES

    `http://www.folkart.com/~latitude/home/walkcane.htm`

WALKING CANES AND STICKS

    `http://www.folkart.com/~latitude/home/walkcane.htm`

CHATEAUS FOR SALE

    `http://www.le-guide.com/sifex/chateaux/`

INTARTDATA

    `http://www.kulturbox.de/univers/e_intart.htm`

Art directories worldwide.

12.10 *Mudslides and Monsoons*   N E W   L E S S O N S

EO/PD   **Subjects: Geography, Ecology**
Grade Level: 4th and Up

Vocabulary.   Students will need to have discussed these words prior to doing this lab:

Evaporation

Humidity

Condensation

Precipitation

Hurricanes

Typhoons

Tornadoes

Elevation

Low-latitude climates

Dry climates

Middle-latitude climates

High-latitude climates

Highland climates

A city near Naples, in Italy, lost some of its citizens to a terrible mudslide. Several people in Northern California, with houses built on cliffs overlooking the ocean, had to stand by and watch their houses pushed off the side of the cliff and into the ocean below. Nashville, Tennessee, had to clean up after a violent tornado struck downtown. Some towns in China disappear each year because of flooding. Almost no area on the planet seems safe from some form of natural disaster or other.

Locate a news article about a recent natural disaster:

```
http://www.newo.com/
```

Somewhere else.

1. Where was the disaster?

2. What kind of disaster was it?

3. How many lives were lost?

4. Were other things lost as well? Farms, houses, businesses, crops?

5. Was the city or area caught unprepared?

6. What had they done to prepare?

7. What more could they have done to prepare?

8. What new technologies are there that help combat this type of disaster?

DISASTER RECOVERY

http://www.etcentre.org/spills/

AMERICAN CIVIL DEFENSE ASSOCIATION

http://www.tacda.org/

DISASTER PREPAREDNESS ASSOCIATION

http://www.disasters.org/deralink.html

DISASTER PREPAREDNESS, CANADA

http://hoshi.cic.sfu.ca/epc/

FEMA FOR KIDS

http://www.fema.gov/kids/

NORTHEAST COAST WATCH

http://narwhal.gso.uri.edu/cwatch1.html

Your area.

1. What natural disasters are likely in your area? (If none directly affect your area, use the closest geographic area to you that experiences natural disasters.)

2. What time of year does this disaster usually happen? Why that particular time of year?

3. What are the usual damages from the disaster?

4. Has El Niño affected your area by increasing or decreasing the natural disasters?

5. How has your area prepared to combat a natural disaster?

6. In what ways does your area seem unprepared for the natural disaster? (Many lives lost, homes lost, businesses destroyed, etc.) Can you learn of any methods of protecting an area that are not being used?

Output.   Maps, pictures, charts, a newspaper article, a narrative account.

Extensions.

1. Manmade disasters — what are some of the things humans have created that harm an area or environment (Smog, water pollution, over-crowding, war)? Which one has affected your area? Which one has affected the area other than yours that you researched?

2. You have been offered a job in an area that experiences yearly disasters. Of all the disasters, natural and manmade, which one are you most prepared to live with? How are you prepared? Which disaster are you least prepared to live through? Why?

3. Compare the preparedness technology and techniques used in your area or an area you researched with another country.

Starting Points.

DISASTERS

```
http://www.promit.com/d-central/discent.htm
gopher://vita.org/11/disaster
http://www.eqe.com/publications/disaster.html
http://www.disasterresponse.net/
http://www.ag.uiuc.edu/~disaster/disaster.html
http://www.disasterrelief.org (look for mudslide information)
http://gldage.cr.usgs.gov/
http://www.gov.pe.ca (check for information about natural disasters)
http://www.weatherstore.com/
http://www.Colorado.EDU/hazards
```

WEATHER

```
http://weather.yahoo.com/
http://www.weather.com/
http://www.nws.noaa.gov/
```

NEWSPAPERS

```
http://www.newo.com/
http://www.sfgate.com/
http://www.ipl.org/reading/news/
```

EMERGENCY LINKS

```
http://theepicenter.com/emerg.html
```

RESCUE INTERNATIONAL

```
http://www.keyinternet.com/rescueintl/
```

12.11 *A Dog's Life*

N E W   L E S S O N S

EO/PD   **Subjects: Creative Writing, Geography, History, Animal Behavior**
Grade Level: 3rd and Up

People have long waited for some alien species (friendly, we hope!) to arrive from outer space and tell us of faraway galaxies where we might settle and make a new world.

Perhaps the aliens arrived 15,000 years ago . . . and have been patiently waiting for us to evolve to a point where *we* can communicate with *them*!

Dogs Don't Lie About Love is a book that explores, among other topics, how dogs communicate with humans. Wagging tails, barking, and chewing your favorites shoes all mean something. They are trying to tell you something.

Read what you can about domestic dog behavior as well as the history of dogs on Earth. Remember, not all dogs are pets. Some are workers. In some countries they are revered, while in others they are food. But they all display certain behaviors and instincts.

Write a science fiction story, placed in the future, exploring what kind of world humans might develop if we only listened to our dogs. For example, if your dog, the alien, is in charge, how much exercise would humans get? What would you eat? What kind of attitude would a dog have about the environment — the forests, rivers, oceans, lakes, etc.? What are dogs' attitudes about loyalty and friendship? How do many feel about work?

Once you know more about dog behavior, you can write your story about our world . . . according to dogs!"

Starting points.

CANINE BEHAVIOR

```
http://www.doggiedoor.com/
http://www.dogperfect.com/]
http://www.canismajor.com/dog/guide.html
http://www.erols.com/mandtj/
```

CANINE LINKS

```
http://www.ismi.net/iaadp/caninecorner.html
http://www.inch.com/~dogs/
```

TRAINING

```
http://www.totalcaninetraining.com/
```

Extension.   If you do enough research, can you add other animals and their method of communications to your story?

You might want to see two films about communicating animals:

Dr. Dolittle — the Eddie Murphy film of 1998 (PG-13) and the Rex Harrison film of 1967 (not rated). Search for the films at:

```
http://www.film.com/
http://www.imdb.com/
```

Other films about animals communicating:

Homeward Bound: The Incredible Journey

Homeward Bound: Lost in San Francisco

Search online bookstores for books on animal behavior, or perhaps animal adventures:

```
http://www.amazon.com/
http://www.barnesandnoble.com/
http://www.borders.com/
```

Books you might like to read (By Hugh Lofting):

The Story of Dr. Dolittle

Voyages of Dr. Dolittle

Dr. Dolittle's Animals

Try a search of your own for other titles about animals and their adventures.

12.12   *El Niño vs. Banana Splits*   NEW LESSONS

EO/PD   **Subjects: Math, Economics, Ecology**
Grade Level: 4th and Up

El Niño has given Northern and Southern California, as well as other areas in the world, more rain than usual. Almonds in Northern California have been affected. How? What effect will this have on the supply and ultimate cost of almonds? Where are strawberries grown? (Map) How is the current crop? If the crop is good but the roads are wet with rain and slick with snow and the trucking is slow, will the cost of your strawberries go up? If the crop yield is less than normal, what will happen to the cost even if the trucks are rolling?

What will happen to the cost of your banana split because of El Niño? What are some related products (related to almonds and strawberries) that might be affected? (Almond Joy candy bars, strawberry jam, etc.) How can you determine the level of financial impact (loss or gain)?

Some starting points.

EL NIÑO THEME PAGE

```
(http://www.pmel.noaa.gov/toga/tao/el/nino/home.html)

http://www.pbs.org/wgbh/nova/elnino
http://www.pbs.org/newshour/forum/fall_97.html
http://www.coaps.fsu.edu/Lib/elninolinks
http://www.enn.com/specialreports/elnino/index.asp
http://www.disasterrelief.org/Disasters/980227crops
http://www.globegazzette.com/
http://www.usda.gov/
```

By the way. Will your Hamburger Happy Meal be nothing but a sad sack from the kick of El Niño? Try researching collectively and then talking about it in class (sometimes, however, discussion groups happening via e-mail can start the conversational ball rolling before you talk as a group, face to face.)

12.13 *Having a Wonderful Time, Wish You Were Here*   NEW LESSONS

EO/PD   **Subjects: History, Geography, Ecology**
Grade Level: 3rd and Up

Normally, when we read about the great explorers of history, we learn about where they went, how they got there, and what they did when they got there. What we don't read about too often is what they saw along the way.

Can you imagine the reaction of the first explorer who came across the Alps? Or, how would you feel if you were the first wagon headed West and your horse pulled up suddenly and refused to go any farther? As you explore the reason for your horse's stubborn streak, you see in front of you . . . the Grand Canyon!

```
http://www.thecanyon.com/
```

OTHER CANYON PICTURES

```
http://grandcanyontouristctr.com/other.htm
http://forums.msn.com/friendsofeurope/memories/grand.htm
```

Can you imagine the reaction of the first person to see that magnificent wonder?

The Activity.

1. Pick an explorer.
2. Plot on a map, where the explorer went.
3. List the natural wonders the explorer encountered: lakes, waterfalls, volcanoes, craters, mountains, rivers, canyons, islands, deserts.
4. Given where your explorer went, what are some of the natural disasters that he might have encountered: hurricanes, volcanoes, tornadoes, typhoons, whirlpools, etc. Locate and pinpoint on a map both natural wonders found and natural disasters faced.

Starting points.

NATURAL WONDERS

```
http://www.gorp.com/default.htm
http://www.worldwander.com/
```

SEVEN WONDERS

```
http://pharos.bu.edu/Egypt/Wonders/Natural/Home.html
```

PAINTINGS OF THOMAS MORAN

```
http://www.ionet.net/~jellenc/moran.html
```

OTHER PHOTOGRAPHS

```
http://www.felglow.com.au/webpgs/Photographic_Realms/Index.htm
```

EUROPEAN VOYAGES OF EXPLORATION

```
http://www.acs.ucalgary.ca/HIST/tutor/eurvoya/intro.html
```

Learn about the explorers, the routes they took, shipbuilding, and the impact of the voyages.

DISCOVERERS WEB

```
http://www.win.tue.nl/cs/fm/engels/discovery/index.html
```

Find out more about who discovered what.

TRADELINKS

   `http://library.advanced.org/13406/contents.html`

Learn about different trade routes.

ALMANAC OF DISASTERS

   `http://disasterium.com/`

Click on a date and find out where and when disasters happened.

12.14 *Herland*

NEW LESSONS

EO/PD **Subjects: Literature, History, Geography, Social Behavior**
Grade Level: 6th and Up

Organizing our literature chronologically gave us the chance to do some research about the people and cultures that appeared in the stories. During our research, we learned about the status of women in early Greece and Rome. We read about "a woman's place," and the girls in my classes were surprised to learn they would not have attended school with the boys in ancient times.

As our studies progressed, we read *Romeo and Juliet* as well as *Julius Caesar*, and it was after we read about Caesar and while we watched the film version with Marlon Brando that the attitudes toward women really opened the eyes of my students.

In one of the early scenes of the play, Julius Caesar asks Marc Antony to touch his wife, Calpurnia, as Antony runs a race. The superstition was that a woman touched during this race would no longer be barren. What shocked my students was the look of scorn on Caesar's face as he looked at his barren wife.

My students began asking how long it would be before we read literature with more modern attitudes toward women. I knew that would take some time, so we discussed the attitudes and the reasons behind them. I mentioned a little (120 pages) book I had read called *Herland*; a story of a society made up entirely of women. This book, considered a Utopian novel, would give the kids another perspective on women and their role in society.

I went online to find more information about this book and was truly surprised to find the entire book available online. Once I mentioned its availability, the majority of my kids wanted to read it, and that's what we did.

Find *Herland* at:

```
http://www.shss.montclair.edu/perkins/herland1.html
```

Online, there are all manner of texts available for anyone to read. I cannot imagine reading the entire text of *The Count of Monte Cristo* or *Tale of Two Cities* online, but they are available. *Herland*, however, was short enough that we found several ways of accommodating all students.

First, we had to make sure that everyone had access in some form so they could read in the evenings. Those with the Internet at home accessed the site and either copied it to a word processor and read, or printed it and read. Those with e-mail at home, and no Internet, e-mailed it home, chapter by chapter, for reading or printing. Those with word processors at home, but no Internet, copied the book to disk and took it home for reading or printing.

For those with no access at home of any kind, we printed chapters at school for reading at home. I had about 15 students who needed this version. It took a little over three reams of paper to accommodate all my students who needed a print version.

Reacting and Discussing the Novel

I began by developing focus questions for each chapter and e-mailed those to the group leaders for electronic discussion. The questions were designed to focus their attention on several things: setting, characters, attitudes about the women voiced by the male characters. I also asked them to look up words they might not know, as well as develop thesaurus trees for different characters.

After the first six chapters, with the students all discussing electronically, I asked them in class if they felt the need for more focus questions from me. They did not. They knew what we were looking for: Increase your vocabulary, build your frame of reference, understand the plot and characters' motivations and actions, etc.

As time progressed, we began to add to our knowledge of the author and her times. Knowing that the book was written in 1915, I asked the kids to begin researching what was going on in America at that time.

During their research, they discovered the women's suffrage movement, and we added more understanding to the author's motivation for writing. We also came across a list of quotes that told why women should not vote and added these to our base of knowledge.

As we got farther into the novel, all my kids, boys and girls alike, decided they liked the attitudes of the women in the novel and began to understand how different societies develop different ways of being. Many of them, boys and girls, wanted to live in a place like Herland. As additional research, I asked them to compare attitudes and beliefs in an excerpt from Hillary Rodham Clinton's book *It Takes A Village* with those in *Herland*.

Finally, I asked them to research the China dam situation and write a brief statement telling why they felt the women of Herland would or would not build a similar dam. Their answer had to reflect an understanding of the values of the women. Additionally, I asked them to reflect on other characters from our literature and determine what King Creon of *Antigone* and Julius Caesar might have done. Their responses reflected the additional information we had learned using the Internet about those men and their times.

All in all, reading *Herland* proved to be one of the most enjoyable experiences of our year together because it broadened our scope, used our tools, and allowed us to create our own curriculum to answer our questions.

For more about *Herland*:

    http://www.library.csi.cuny.edu/dept/history/lavender/herland.html
    http://hubcap.clemson.edu/~sparks/herland.html

An additional copy of the book is available electronically at:

    http://www.utoronto.ca/util/fiction/gilmanc_her/her_titlepage.html

For the attitudes about women voting:

    http://douglass.speech.nwu.edu/blac_ao5.htm

For suffrage songs and verses from Charlotte Perkins Gilman:

    http://www.cs.smu.edu/People/mmbt/women/gilman/suffrage/suffrage.html

12.15 *Hawking Your Wares*   NEW LESSONS

A lesson for you with no starting links . . .on your own.

EO   ## Subjects: History, Literature, Geography, Trade, Economics
Grade Level: 4th and Up

The opening paragraph of the novel *Mary's Land*, by Lucia St. Clair Robson, offers a wonderful opportunity to link historical research, geography, and other subjects with creative writing.

The year is 1638 and the place is Bristol, England — the same Bristol from which Jim Hawkins embarked for Treasure Island. Flowing into the city are "green ginger and raw brown sugar from Jamaica, wine from Crete, cloth and glass from Venice, hawks from Algiers, and bracelets of Barbary gold. . . ."

What an exciting time to be a trader on the high seas! Bring this historical period alive by "becoming" one of those traders.

First, find those places, including Bristol, on your map.

Now, pick one of the traders and research efficiently enough to tell his tale. What was it like to be a trader in sugar from Jamaica? Or, imagine yourself being a seller of glass from Venice — what was such a trading journey like?

Research. A book like this allows students and teachers to paint a broader picture with their own research. Bring the characters to life and help your students write the story. Explore 1600s Jamaica, Venice, Crete, Algiers, and the Barbary Coast. Describe your traders down to the clothes they would have worn and the attitudes they would bring with them. Much as an actor prepares for a role, to understand and write, your kids need to get into character.

Try to get the broadest picture possible of the kind of person who ventured out on the high seas in 1638.

Ask questions like these:

> What is most likely your home port?
>
> How do traders from your country dress in 1638?
>
> What does your home country look like? (Flora and fauna as well as architecture and topography.)
>
> What kind of ship did you sail?
>
> What was your most likely trade route?
>
> Most common problems during the sailing?
>
> Any problem with pirates?
>
> Any countries you avoid? Why?
>
> What would you bring home from Bristol?
>
> Is Bristol your only stop on your trade route?
>
> Where else would you most likely stop?
>
> What else would you trade for along the route?

Creative writing. Captain's log, letters home, journal, newspaper account, diary from the perspective of a crewman, etc.

Cross-referencing as you research. A quest of this nature can be broadened as time and interest permit. If you and your students can build a broad picture using one work as a stimulus, successive reading will be easier and more enjoyable. So, expand and add as much as you can. And don't be surprised when one student asks to add to the original quest with a related set of research (that's how we got the information on medieval science and medicine). Soon, others will be doing the same. (We got an introduction to Renaissance art from another student.)

Ask questions as kids pursue the original research:

> If I want good entertainment in Bristol in 1638, what's available? When did William Shakespeare start writing? Would his plays have been on the bill in Bristol?
>
> What kind of music would you hear in home ports of the traders mentioned?
>
> What examples of art can you find that represent each country mentioned?
>
> What mathematical devices would traders use when doing business?
>
> What technology helped sail the ship?
>
> What was the state of the world's exploration and settlement in 1638?
>
> Was anyone at war? If so, with whom and why?
>
> What were the home ports like? Venice, Kingston in Jamaica, Algiers, Crete, and the Barbary Coast?
>
> If your trader happens to be a literary type, what books might be on his bookshelf?
>
> Who were some of the ladies of the high seas?

The possibilities are endless . . . and the ways of displaying knowledge and understanding are just as endless. Let your kids help decide the best way to tell you or show you what they have learned.

12.16 *Your Local News*

NEW LESSONS

EO/PD Subjects: News, Web Site Evaluation, Web Site Design, Geography
Grade Level: 4th and Up

Many TV stations are online, not only presenting information about their prime time shows, but also offering sites about their news coverage. As with most Internet sites, the Webmasters, and the TV station, want you to come back often to check out the news, the weather, and special features. It is handy, in the time of El Niño weather and changing world conditions, to have a ready source of updated information. These Web sites also try very hard to offer special reports, just as they do on the air. Can you find a TV station that is close to where you live? Did you locate several?

Those of us near Los Angeles have several to choose from.

KCBS

    http://www.channel2000.com/

KABC

    http://www.abcnews.com/local/kabc/

KNBC

    http://www.nbc4la.com/

KMEX

    http://www.kmex.com/

KTLA

    http://www.ktla.com/

Take a look at the ones from L.A., then compare those to the one(s) near you.

> What do they cover?
> What do they offer for in-depth coverage?
> What are some of the links you would expect to see from a TV news station Web site (links to other shows, print news, other coverage by sister stations, etc.)?
> What links did they provide?
> Did you learn about any sister stations? Plot them on a map.
> How do you evaluate a "good Web page"?

See the links.

Create a rubric or use one found online and rate some of the TV news Web sites. Where are some of the best sites coming from? What made them the best?

Create a news site for your school, perhaps in conjunction with the existing newspaper or yearbook staff. What will you include as news? In-depth stories? What else will you put on your page? What links will you include? How will you make your news site easy to use?

Links to school news sites.

SCHREIBER TIMES

    http://times.portnet.k12.ny.us/

HiLite

http://www.hilite.org/

Ish-Tak-Ha-Ba Times

http://209.18.240.208/times.html

Eastside Online

http://eastside.cherryhill.k12.nj.us/

The Surfrider Online

http://kailuahs.k12.hi.us/surfrider/

Newspapers worldwide.

News Resource

http://newo.com/news/

Daily Print Newspapers

http://www.zafo.com/news/

MediaInfo Links

http://www.mediainfo.com/emedia/

News Central

http://www.all-links.com/newscentral/

F and H Link Page

http://www.box.nl/~frankhbk/nieuws.htm

The Global Newsstand

http://www.mcs.net/~rchojnac/www/tgn.html

News from around the World

http://www.escapeartist.com/media/media.htm

Newspapers of the World

http://www.geocities.com/~oberoi/newspapr.html

Links to Web design tutorials.

The Web Design Resource

http://www.pageresource.com/

Web Developer's Virtual Library

http://Stars.com/

Web Style Guide

http://info.med.yale.edu/caim/manual/

Wade's HTML Tutorial

http://web.mit.edu/afs/athena/user/w/s/wsmart/WEB/HTMLtutor.html

Student's Guide to the WWW

http://www.slu.edu/departments/english/research/

Evaluating Web resources.

WebResults Web Site Planning

http://www.webresult.com/index.html

Effective Web Pages

http://www.algonquinc.on.ca/pilot/test/eval.html

Links to Web design elements.

Evaluation Rubrics for Web Sites

http://www.siec.k12.in.us/~west/online/eval.htm

Blue Web'n Web Site Evaluation

http://www.kn.pacbell.com/wired/bluewebn/rubric.html

Electronic Portfolios

http://www.essdack.org/port/index.html

Web Page Evaluation Rubric

http://fs04.ael5.ocps.k12.fl.us/tips/hs/Rubrics/HS_General_Rubrics.htm

Links to creating rubrics.

Creating Rubrics

http://mailer.fsu.edu/~jflake/rubrics.html

RUBRICS AND CHECKLISTS

http://www.cyber.crwash.k12.ia.us/compcomp/templates/Assessments.html

MANKATO INTERNET SKILLS RUBRIC

http://www.isd77.k12.mn.us/resources/dougwri/internet.rub.html

BUILDING RUBRICS

http://www.sover.net/~mttop/arts/rubrics.html

WRITING RUBRICS FOR ONLINE PORTFOLIOS

http://204.98.1.1/dist_ed/eng/rubrics.html

RUBRICS

http://www.ebe.on.ca/DEPART/RESEAR/RUBRIC.HTM

ASSESSMENT RUBRICS

http://129.7.160.115/COURSE/INST_5931A/Rubric.html#Class

12.17 *Farewell to Manzanar Project*

NEW LESSONS

A suggested project or two to accompany the reading of the novel. From Jonathan Lyons, English teacher, Pasadena High School, Pasadena, CA.

EO/PD **Subjects: History, Literature, Politics, Culture**
Grade Level: 6th and Up

A Comparison of Two Cultures

During World War II, both the United States and the Japanese suffered devastating attacks on home soil at each other's hands. These attacks have been memorialized.

Spend some time looking at the memorials, the statues, the tributes, and the ceremonies. In what ways are they similar? In what ways do they reflect their respective cultures?

Building your Background Frame of Reference

1. *Some starting points:* When I did a search for American culture, I got Polish-American, Italian-American, African-American. . . .

   Have your students define what they see as the dominant American culture, or break them into groups and research the various cultural contributions to "American culture." You can search by ethnic group (Italian, German, etc.) and/or by geographic area (Southern, Western, etc.).

2. Research Japanese Culture, then summarize your findings:

   The Japanese Culture American Misconceptions about Japan

   http://www.cis.ohio-state.edu/hypertext/faq/usenet/japan/
       american-misconceptions/faq.html

   About Japan

   http://www.csuohio.edu/history/japan.html

   Guide to Japanese Culture

   http://www.io.com/~nishio/japan/index.html

   Hagakure

   http://www.geocities.com/Tokyo/Towers/9151/

   Japan Is Strange

   http://www.hotsushi.com/index.htm

   Anecdotes about the culture written by foreign visitors.

3. *Research the memorials. What are the tributes like? How are they similar? How do they reflect the respective cultures?*

   Japanese Memorials.
   Peace 96 Project

   http://park.org/Japan/Peace96/

   A Bomb WWW Museum

   http://www.csi.ad.jp/ABOMB/index.html

   Monuments and Memorials

   http://www.noguchi.org/monument.html

HIROSHIMA LIVE PROJECT

http://www.csi.ad.jp/hiroshima-live/index.html

TERROR OF THE ATOMIC BOMB

http://www.ask.or.jp/~bigapple/

Very graphic.

PEACE MEMORIAL CEREMONY

http://www.city.hiroshima.jp/C/City/ceremony97.html

PEACE MEMORIAL PARK PHOTO GALLERY

http://www.japan-guide.com/a/html/hiroshima_e.html

NAGASAKI NIGHTMARE

http://burn.ucsd.edu/atomintr.htm

Some graphic photos of the effects of the bomb on this city.

RARE FILM DOCUMENTS — HIROSHIMA

http://www.cnn.com/WORLD/9608/10/japan.hiroshima.film/index.html

From CNN archives — A QuickTime movie.

HIROSHIMA

http://cicada.honors.uiuc.edu/japan/hiroshima.html

More photos of the bombing and the memorials.

CITY OF HIROSHIMA

http://www.city.hiroshima.jp/C/City/3-3-2.html

PEACE MEMORIAL PARK

http://mothra.rerf.or.jp/ENG/Hiroshima-old/Sightseeing/Peace-Memorial-Park/
    Peace-Memorial-Park.html

JOINT MEMORIAL SERVICES

http://www.smn.co.jp/library/0313_0319.95/0023t04e.html

PEACE MEMORIAL PARK

http://hp.vector.co.jp/authors/VA001962/peace/index.html

Pearl Harbor.

PEARL HARBOR REMEMBERED

http://www.execpc.com/~dschaaf/mainmenu.html

USS *ARIZONA* MEMORIAL

http://www.nps.gov/usar/index.htm

ARIZONA MEMORIAL MUSEUM ASSOC.

http://members.aol.com/azmemph/

PEARL HARBOR MEMORIAL

http://www.navyleaguehawaii.org/pearl.htm

USS *MISSOURI* MEMORIAL

http://www.navyleaguehawaii.org/mightymo.htm

A DATE IN INFAMY

http://www.newbie.net/PearlHarbor/index2.html

PEARL HARBOR

http://hawaiianculture.miningco.com/msub19.htm

PEARL HARBOR LINKS AND INFORMATION.

http://www.redstone.army.mil/history/chron1/pearl.html

REMEMBERING USS ARIZONA AND PEARL HARBOR

http://members.aol.com/Buckeye34/pearl.htm

4. *Output:* How can you demonstrate your understanding of how the memorials reflect the special aspects of each culture? (Newspaper article, tour from a new perspective, new type of Web site, etc.)

Extensions. Holocaust memorials and sites about Japanese-American internment camps will reflect not so much a culture, but survival in extreme conditions, and efforts by humans to, on the one hand, eliminate other humans, or in the case of the Japanese-American internment camps, to contain a perceived threat. What can be learned about both the environment of the camps and conditions that gave rise to the Nazis in Germany and the guards in the form of the American Government?

Holocaust Memorials.

HOLOCAUST CENTER

http://holocaustcenter.com/

U.S. HOLOCAUST MEMORIAL

http://www.ushmm.org/index.html

HOLOCAUST MEMORIAL MUSUEM AND EDUCATION CENTER

http://www.tampabayholocaust.org/

HOLOCAUST MEMORIAL RESOURCE CENTER

http://www.holocaustedu.org/

HOLOCAUST HISTORY PROJECT

http://www.holocaust-history.org/

LOS ANGELES HOLOCAUST MONUMENT

http://www.laholocaustmonument.com/

YAD VASHEM

http://www.yad-vashem.org.il/

Holocaust memorial and ceremony.

SHOAH VISUAL HISTORY

http://www.vhf.org/home.html

Archiving the stories of holocaust victimsm

Japanese Internment.

CAMP HARMONY

http://weber.u.washington.edu/~mudrock/ALLEN/Exhibit/index.html

HISTORY OF THE INTERNMENT

http://www.fatherryan.org/hcompsci/

HISTORY OF THE JAPANESE INTERNMENT

http://www.webcom.com/unk/pc/race/intern.shtml

Internment Camps

http://www.lib.utah.edu/spc/photo/9066/9066.htm

Arizona Camps

http://www.library.arizona.edu/images/jpamer/wraintro.html

Manzanar.
Manzanar National Historic Site

http://www.sierra.cc.ca.us/us395/manzanar.htm

Manzanar Project

http://monte.mvhs.srvusd.k12.ca.us/~mleck/man/

Manzanar, America's Concentration Camp

http://members.aol.com/EARTHSUN/Manzanar.html

Remembering Manzanar

http://www.qnet.com/~earthsun/remember.htm
Check teachers' resources.

Japanese Internment

http://www.geocities.com/Athens/8420/main.html

Nazi Concentration Camps.
Survivors' Stories

http://shrike.depaul.edu/~lhandzli/auschwitz/

Virtual Auschwitz

http://www.webgate.net/~rh/

Portal of Auschwitz

http://www.geocities.com/Heartland/7071/Westerbork.html

Auschwitz Alphabet

http://www.spectacle.org/695/ausch.html

Pictures.
Concentration Camps

http://www.us-israel.org/jsource/Holocaust/cc.html

MAP OF CONCENTRATION CAMPS

http://holocaust.tqn.com/library/pictures/nmap.htm

INSIDE THE CONCENTRATION CAMPS

http://www.dnaco.net/~twhissen/

Eyewitness accounts.
FROM ASHES TO LIFE

http://www.webtran.com/lucille/

Memories of the holocaust.
L'CHAIM: A HOLOCAUST WEB PROJECT

http://www.charm.net/~rbennett/l'chaim.html

PHOTOS OF THE CAMPS

http://www.remember.org/jacobs/index.html

5. Why is it important to know about the atomic bomb, Pearl Harbor, Japanese internment camps, Nazi concentration camps, etc.?

   In what way does the novel reflect Japanese culture? American political personality? Misconceptions about Japanese-Americans?

12.18 *E.T.'s Landing Strip*   NEW LESSONS

EO/PD   **Subjects: History, Science, Geography**
Grade Level: 4th and Up

Imagine, if you will, a stone. A stone of immense proportions. A stone weighing 200 tons. A stone you have to have — and you have to have it, oh, about 2 miles from where you found it . . . about 2 miles up a hill, down the other side and pulled into place nearby.

This stone, this megalith, is one of *three thousand* you need. Some are smaller, 100 tons, but some are more than 200 tons.

What on Earth do you need all the stones for?

Megaliths are large stones found in places like Stonehenge, Easter Island, Scotland, Wales, and Carnac, France.

Background information about megaliths in Carnac, France:

Erected 4650 BC
Had magnetic properties
Used by Druids, but not put in place by them
No signs of weapons or war at sites
Dragged for miles and put in place
Perhaps used in sacrificial ceremonies
Some weigh more than the Statue of Liberty
Astronomers think they were a gigantic observatory
Some people feel they were set out as a landing strip for aliens
Other legends include: dwarfs, pygmies, leprechauns, and elves
French girls were brought to touch the stones to increase fertility

Writing assignment. You are the leader of the people who live in the area in 4650 BC. You feel the need to move 3000 large stones and place them in a pattern. What makes you want to move the stones? Write a narrative account of this experience.

For more about these stones and other megaliths:

```
http://easyweb.easynet.co.uk/~aburnham/stone.htm
http://members.alo.com/Bilyjan/page1.htm
http://idcnet.com/~ckarrel/index.html
http://www.pitt.edu/~dash/monuments.html
http://www.weldwood.demon.co.uk/ancient.html
http://www.mystical-www.co.uk/scsite.html
http://www.kirtland.cc.mi.us/honors/ancient.html
```

—|||—

12.19 *Buyer Beware*　　　　　　　NEW LESSONS

Objective: Examining the impact of a merger on consumers; using information to your advantage.

EO/PD　**Subjects: Economics, Math, Automotive Engineering
Grade Level: 6th and Up
Time to Complete: 2 Weeks**

Now that Chrysler and Mercedes have merged, what might be the effect on:

Car prices?
Quality?

Affordability?

Safety?

Marketing — less upscale, or more?

Start with.   Home pages of auto dealers

```
http://www.mercedes.com/
http://www.chryslercars.com/
```

CAR AND DRIVER

```
http://www.caranddriver.com/
```

HARRIS MOUNTAINTOP

```
http://www.mtp.semi.harris.com/autos.html
```

AUTO BODY REPAIR NEWS

```
http://www.abrn.com/
```

OTHER SITES TO TRY.

```
http://www.aftermarketworld.com/
http://www.auto.co.nz
```

STOCK QUOTES.

```
http://quote.yahoo.com/?u
http://fnews.yahoo.com/street
```

Automobile safety.

AUTOMOBILE SAFETY FOUNDATION

```
http://www.cyber.net/asf
```

INSURANCE INSTITUTE FOR HIGHWAY SAFETY

```
http://www.hwysafety.org/
```

ADVOCATES FOR AUTO SAFETY

```
http://www.saferoads.org/
```

Read what the pundits say (look up *pundits*). "Look up" means use a thesaurus and/or a dictionary (preferably, a thesaurus). What's happening to their stock (track it)?

Output: Spreadsheet, data base, chart

What about other car companies' stock (VW, Fiat, Toyota, etc.)? Are any other mergers in the works?

Output: Well-phrased communication

Why should you care about a car merger?

Output: Well-phrased communication

Geography.   Where are the home offices of the companies? Where are parts manufactured? (Map this.) Where is labor inexpensive? (Research and map.) Are any of those places involved with the manufacturing of auto parts? (Map after research.)

Math.   Chart safety statistics for the autos involved (chart, data base, spreadsheet, etc.).

Chart performance statistics (similar output).

Who has what to offer whom? Does Chrysler offer Mercedes expertise in auto safety or vice versa? What are the cars most lauded for? (Look up *lauded.*)

Output: Well-phrased communication

Note.   A "well-phrased communication" can take many forms: paragraph, essay, e-mail, conversation, letter, journal entry, etc. Let your project and technology dictate your forms of communication.

Time on task.   Begin with information gathering — 3 to 5 hours (encourage collaboration).

Spend time on communication of findings; preparation/prewriting, rethinking/editing, final communicating/writing — 2 to 4 hours

---

12.20 *Shopping Tips for Mountain Climbers*

NEW LESSONS

EO

Subjects: Geography, Science
Grade Level: 4th and Up

A quick search with discussion as output.

I work and often shop at 1035 feet above sea level, but I live at 5500 ft. above sea level. I drive 15 winding miles from the valley up to my mountain home in about 20 minutes. Why did the 2-liter Dr. Pepper I bought down in the valley explode all over my kitchen when I opened it in the mountains?

Go online and see what you can learn about this phenomenon. What scientific principles are at work here? What fields of science do I study to understand why my Dr. Pepper explodes? Can anything be done to stop it from exploding?

Starting points.
HIGH ALTITUDE STUDIES

    http://www.princeton.edu/~oa/altitude.html

SUBMARINES AND AIR PRESSURE

    http://www.eecs.umich.edu/mathscience/funexperiments/agesubject/lessons/subs.html

EFFECTS OF FLYING

    http://www.softrain.co.uk/pet_v3/hp_av_illness.htm

EARS, ALTITUDE

    http://pakistanlink.com/health/health-09-19-97.html

Extensions. What other foods might explode when they are carried from one altitude to another? Can I expect to see any other effects on my food because of this phenomenon?

Extension. Why do my ears plug up on the drive down the mountains and I have to keep yawning to clear them?

12.21 *Pork Barrel Politics*

NEW LESSONS

A search lesson for the upper grades.

EO

Subjects: Economics, Political Science, Critical Thinking, Government, Decision Making

Grade Level: 8th and Up

The United States government recently passed a new transportation bill worth billions of dollars in funding. As the original bill was being passed through the system, several items were added on: road repair for horsedrawn carriages, $4 million to study replacing a bridge, bike paths, etc.

What was the original bill intended to pay for? How much was asked for? Where would the money go? (which states and for what?)

THE LEGISLATION

    http://www.fhwa.dot.gov/tea21/index.htm

READ ABOUT THE ADD-ONS:

    http://www.manufacturing.net/magazine/logistic/archives/1997/log0301.97/
        03news.htm
    http://www.du.edu/~transplj/

> Who added on funding? (Who asked for bike paths, etc.?) Name? State represented? Political affiliation?

> What did they add money for?

> How much money was funded?

> If you were in charge, which pieces of this bill would you fund?

> Were some things left out of the bill that you feel should be funded? (Is there a road or bridge where you live that needs repair? Something else?)

Extensions.

1. If you have a transportation project you would like funded, what do you need to research to know how much money to ask for?

2. How do you, as a citizen, get the government to spend money where you feel it is needed?

3. Why is this practice called "pork barrel politics?"

12.22 *Protocol*

NEW LESSONS

EO/PD **Subjects: Careers, Government, History, Math**
Grade Level: 6th and Up

The President of the United States, just like any head of state, is usually surrounded by people who do different jobs for him. He has people whose job it is to run his political campaigns. There are also a host of other people who, in one way or another, take care of the needs of the President, the First Family, and the White House.

TOUR THE WHITE HOUSE:

    http://www.whitehouse.gov/WH/Tours/White_House/Welcome.html

After your tour and after following any links you find, see if you can list the names of any of the people who are in charge of the following:

Transportation
State dinners
Housekeeping
Security
Protocol
Gardening
Chef

From that list of jobs, two people, the person who plans State Dinners and the person in charge of Protocol, probably work together quite closely for some very important aspects of the President's job: dinners for visiting dignitaries. These people probably have to know a lot about etiquette, foreign countries, kings, queens, and many other things.

Building background. What can you learn online about *etiquette* and *protocol*? How are they different? How is etiquette similar to *Netiquette*?

SCHOOL OF PROTOCOL AND ETIQUETTE

    http://www.denversearch.com/prod03.htm

PROTOCOL

    http://www.drcomputer.com/protocol/menutips.htm
    http://www.image360.com/etiquette.html
    http://www.gsia.cmu.edu/afs/andrew/gsia/coc/student/etiquette.html

ETIQUETTE AND MANNERS RESOURCE PAGE

    http://www.mindspring.com/~thinds/jmh/etiquetteurls.htm

If you are planning a state dinner at the time you read this, who might be an appropriate guest of honor? (What head of state is in the news today?)
    Research newspapers online to learn more about your guest of honor and any guests you might invite. Keep notes on your findings.

NEWSPAPERS ONLINE

    http://www.newo.com/

RESEARCH ARTICLES ON STATE DINNERS:

    http://www.northernlights.com/

When was the last state dinner in the United States? When was the last time an American President or a member of his family was honored as the guest at a state dinner in another country? What can you learn about that state dinner from the news? More notes to be kept.

The task at hand.   Plan a state dinner — from the salad and the singing to the seating.

Your research.   As you research, note whether the decision is one of (P)rotocol or (E)tiquette. Also decide what is the best tool for keeping track of the information you find — note cards, Hypercard, word processor, etc.

> Who will you invite as your guest of honor? A king, a prime minister, a president?
>
> Your guest list: Who will you invite? How are guests selected? Are particular guests invited because of particular guests of honor? List 10 people you would invite for this dinner.
>
> What foods will you most likely serve this particular guest? Will you serve them food from their land, yours, or another? Plan your menu.
>
> What china, crystal, and silverware will you use?
>
> Shop online at different florists for centerpieces. What might detemine the colors you choose? Will the colors of the guest of honor's flag have any influence on your choice of colors?
>
> What music will you have playing? Who will play it? What determines this aspect of the dinner?
>
> Oh yes, you're invited — shop online for your attire. Print pictures of what you would wear.
>
> By the way, if you were invited to a state dinner, what might your work be that got you invited? Write a brief description of who you are and why you got invited to a White House state dinner.
>
> Who do you want to sit next to? Why? What might you talk about? How do you find out beforehand (online) what your table companion might be interested in?
>
> Since not everyone can sit at the President's table, how is seating organized? If this is not available online, did you find the e-mail address of someone at the White House who might be able to answer you?
>
> What does all this cost? Did you locate any information about the costs of such a dinner? If you had to price it out, what are some of the things that would have to be purchased?
>
> Decide on the number of guests. (Don't forget the President and the guest of honor!) Take a look at your menu. Can you figure out some of your costs for food?
>
> Can you figure the cost of your centerpieces? How many do you need? How do you figure the number of tables you'll need for seating all your guests?

Writing about it.

Respond to the following newspaper help wanted ad:

Wanted: Chief of Protocol for the White House. Must present a résumé clearly indicating your understanding and previous performance of the job duties accompanying this position. Detail your actual on-the-job experiences with foreign dignitaries as they relate to protocol."

Write your invitation: How would you write, in proper language, "come have dinner at the White House"?

Put together a photo collage of your table settings.

Put together a photo collage of your guests, including the guest of honor.

Chart your costs or put them in a data base.

In a formal style, write out your menu.

Research extensions. Some of the job titles of people who work around the President are:

Chief of Staff

Press Secretary

Personal Assistant

Domestic Policy Advisor

Foreign Policy Advisor

Are these White House jobs, or does the job have anything to do with politics as well? Who presently does each job? What are some of their job responsibilities? What is their salary? Who pays their salary?

For the Chief of Protocol job. What does a person study in college for this job? Where can you go for those classes? What might be a starting job after college graduation on your career path to being Chief of Protocol? What are some of the online magazines you, in your job as Chief of Protocol, need to read regularly? What newspapers should you glance at every day?

Other questions you might be able to answer after you research:

Does the President use a new set of china or an old set from previous Presidents?

Can you visit, online, the China Room of the White House?

Starting points.

CUTLERY

```
http://www.occc.com/treasure_house
http://www.bgface.com/slavov/cutlery.htm
http://www.atlanticsilver.com/
```

CRYSTAL

```
http://www.bohemiae.com/
http://www.krystalkonnecton.com/
http://www.cavancrystal.com/showroom.asp
```

MENUS AND FOOD

```
http://www.epicurious.com
```

FLORISTS

```
http://www.net-conx.com/fabulous/fabulous.htm
http://www.widdl.com/florists/american.html
http://www.fnd.com/online
```

FORMAL ATTIRE (MALE AND FEMALE)

```
http://www.maui.net/~formals
http://www.pzaz.com/
http://www.loriann.com/latnl.htm
http://www.alfredsungbridesmaids.com/
```

12.23 *You Be the Scout*

NEW LESSONS

EO/PD

Subjects: Sports/Math
Grade Level: 5th and Up

Objective. To develop criteria, research, analyze statistics and report findings

Starting points.

```
http://www.hitdoctor.com/all_american/players
http://www.pcscouting.com/index/sample
http://buffaloes.colorado.edu/sports/football (check for football records)
http://heron.tc.clarkson.edu/~odonnell/data/9697/roster (check team stats)
http://www.pruitt-vaughn.com/
http://www.sportsview.com/public/tryout.htm
http://www.sportsbase.com/sb_collg.htm
```

Start. Begin with a sport you know something about.

1. Brainstorm the qualities you are looking for in a player (pick a specific position if necessary).

2. Make a chart with the qualities you need. (a) Rank the qualities in order of importance to a team. (b) Give each quality a value (1–10, 0–99%, etc.).

3. Scout the Internet for players. (a) Check school home pages. (b) Check the draft choices for your sport. (c) Check team home pages.

4. Keep track of the statistics for each player.

5. Chart the qualities, assign values, and rank the players.

6. Choose your player.

Questions.

What qualities are you looking for?

How did you assign values to each quality? (Did your online research help you decide on qualities and how to evaluate them?)

Describe how you determined which player you would choose.

Output.

Chart

Poster with qualities and values assigned

Newspaper article about your pick

Scouting report for the coach

Make sure you clarify the qualities you are looking for, which are the most important, how you determined their value, how you assigned values, and how you picked your winner.

Extensions.   Scout for one of the following:

Model (male or female) (make it clear what they will advertise)

Actor/actress (for what role)

Drummer (for what kind of band)

Lawyer (for what kind of law)

Accountant

School (university or post-secondary)

Lead singer (for what kind of band?)

Offline.   Prepare the qualities and make a chart (1–3 hours).

Online.   Research — 3–5 hours

Output.   1–3 hours

12.24 *SUVs*

EO/PD   **Subjects: Geometry, Auto Technology, Aerodynamics**
Grade Level: 4th and Up

Recently, newspapers covered the story of the problem of sport utility vehicles (SUVs) and how dangerous they can be when they are in an accident with a smaller vehicle. According to the news, the manufacturers of the SUVs are considering redesigning them to make them less harmful on impact.

What sciences should you study if you are trying to solve the problem of SUV impact and damage to smaller cars?

Read up on the following:

What is being done to make SUVs less destructive to smaller vehicles?

What is being done to make smaller cars safer — better able to absorb an impact?

What is the safest small vehicle?

What is the least destructive SUV? Why is it the least destructive?

What part does geometry play in solving this problem?

Research the following:

Volkswagen and Porsche SUVs

Mercedes SUVs

Cadillac Escalade

Ford Expedition and other SUVs

More research:

Insurance Institute findings

Automobile safety research

What should the geometry of the SUV be?

Which SUVs are already taking geometry into consideration when they build?

Some starting points.

SUV ONLINE

    http://www.suv.com/

Information about SUVs.

SPORT UTILITY VEHICLE

> http://www.todayssuv.com/

A magazine for the users.

SUV — POPULAR SCIENCE GUIDE

> http://www.popsci.com/suv_site/

SUV REVIEWS

> http://www.auto.com/reviews/sportutility_index.htm

SUV ANTI-FAN CLUB

> http://www.howard.net/ban-suvs.htm

Learn about safety factors and environmental impacts.

ROADHOG

> http://www.suv.org/

More information about SUV safety.

CONSUMER REPORTS

> http://www.consumer.org/

12.25 *The Politics of Trade*   NEW LESSONS

EO/PD **Subjects: Political Science, Economics, Geography
Grade Level: 9th and Up**

The United States relies on many other countries for goods we do not grow or produce in quantity ourselves: tin, cadmium, bananas, chicle (for gum), rubber, silk, diamonds (for industry and jewelry), coffee, cocoa, sugar, wool, lead, copper, and oil.

1. What countries do we get each product from?
2. Where are they (plot on map)?
3. How much do we import in one year? (chart)

4. Who is the leader of the country? (a) How long has he/she been in power? (b) What is the name of their political party or affiliation?

5. Do we have diplomatic ties with each country? An embassy in their country, or a liaison?

6. Is the country at war with anyone today? If so, who and where?

7. What does each country buy from us? How much in one year?

8. Do we have industry or manufacturing in any of the countries we buy from?

9. What does most of each imported good get used for? Example: diamonds — mostly for industry (what uses) or jewelry?

Conclusion. Are we friends with the countries that we buy from? Do we protect those countries? If so, from whom? How do we protect them? What would happen if we did not protect them . . . other than losing the product we import?

How important are diplomatic ties in our modern world? Who is the person in charge of maintaining those ties?

Starting points.

ECONOMIC POLICY AND TRADE

```
http://epn.org/econlink.html#international
http://www.ups.edu/faculty/sousa/converge.htm
http://www.iie.com/atp.htm
```

INTERNATIONAL TRADE ADMINISTRATION

```
http://www.ita.doc.gov/media/
```

INTERNATIONAL BUSINESS KIOSK

```
http://www.webcom.com/one/world/
```

INTERNATIONAL TRADE LAW PAGE

```
http://ananse.irv.uit.no/trade_law/nav/trade.html
```

INTERNATIONAL TRADE COMMISSION

```
http://www.usitc.gov/
```

FEDERATION OF INTERNATIONAL TRADE ORGANIZATIONS

```
http://www.fita.org/fita.html
```

U.S. DIPLOMATIC HISTORY

```
http://www.tamu-commerce.edu/coas/history/sarantakes/stuff.html
```

12.26 *Hot Wheels Online* **NEW LESSONS**

EO/PD **Subjects: Math, Automotive, Financial Planning, Economics, Auto Safety**
Grade Level: 6th and Up
Interest Level: Teenagers 14/15 and Up

Output. Charts, graphs, spreadsheets, data base, discussion or other form of communication of findings.
Terms to discuss before you go online:

Invoice pricing

Used car values

Residual values

Dealer holdbacks

Factory-to-dealer sales incentives

Introduction

If you have ever gone car shopping or have gone with your parents, you know it can be an aggravating experience. Shopping online, evidently, is a way to diminish much of the frustration of shopping in person.

Acccording to Peter Bohr's article in the May, 1998, *Road and Track*, "Kicking Tires Virtually," the Internet is already having a profound impact on the way cars are sold. He goes on to quote Matt Ericksen of the Boston Consulting Group, who states, "Research shows that 20 to 25 percent of buyers use the Internet for research. Given that just three years ago the percentage was zip, that's incredibly impressive."

Your Job

Go online and search for your dream car to drive

1. Make sure it has an acceptable level of safety before you start searching:

   NATIONAL HIGHWAY SAFETY TRANSPORTATION ASSOCIATION

   http://www.nhsta.dot.gov/

2. Now that you've picked a safe car, continue online, to find the following:

   Invoice price

   Used-car value

   Residual value

   Dealer holdbacks

   Factory-to-dealer incentives

   Check the list of sites at the end of the lesson. Create a chart, graph, spreadsheet to display your findings.

   Find online.   Calculators to help you with your data:
   THE BIG CALCULATOR SITE

   http://www-sci.lib.uci.edu/HSG/RefCalculators.html

   ROAD AND TRACK MAGAZINE

   http://www.roadandtrack.com/

   AUTO-BY-TEL

   http://www.autobytel.com/

   AUTOWEB

   http://www.Autoweb.com/

   CADILLAC'S INTERACTIVE DESIGN STUDIO

   http://www.cadallic.com/

   FOR A LITTLE FUN, GO TO:

   http://www.matchboxtoys.com/

   In the Custom Auto Body shop, create a truck.

3. Now that you are ready to go shopping in real life, what price would you reasonably expect to pay for your car according to your research?

4. Check want ads online and off for cars advertised just like the one, or close to the one, you want. Compare prices with an online service. Compare your findings with other people (online or off). Chart your findings.

5. How close were the prices, online and off?

6. Where did you find the best deals, online and off?

7. Were there any particular places offline where the car prices were closer to the online prices? (Did geography play any part in the selling price?)

Starting points.

```
http://www.autosite.com/
http://www.carpoint.msn.com/
http://www.edmonds.com/
http://www.intellichoice.com/
http://www.kbb.com/
http://www.nhsta.dot.gov/
http://www.bmwusa.com/
http://www.ford.com/
http://www.gm.com/
http://www.mercedes.com/
http://www.toyota.com/
http://www.chryslercars.com/
```

At *Intellichoice* you'll find information relating to the economics of car ownership, evaluation of leases, and the BOVY awards for the cars and trucks that are least expensive to own and operate.

At *Edmonds* you'll find critical reviews of automobiles, descriptions of warranties and standard equipment, performance data, insurance ratings, fuel consumption, invoice and suggested retail price, rebates and incentives.

Autosite offers the "Build the Window Sticker" section with invoice and retail prices for vehicles and options.

Microsoft has *Surround Videos* for investigating car interiors and an area called CarPoint which has an affordability calculator to see if you can truly buy that car.

Mercedes has an affordability calculator as well.

GM has BuyPower, where you can search dealer inventories for your dream car. (But only in California, Washington, Oregon, and Idaho.)

Toyota has QuickTime movies which provide a 360-degree tour of your favorite Toyota.

Ford lets you build a Mustang.

Extra credit.

    Locate information about the founder of Auto-by-Tel, Pete Ellis

    Locate stock prices of Auto-by-tel (if it has gone public)

    Did you know you can investigate loans and leases online? Can you find some sites? Use one and communicate your information about loans and leases?

    Where can you find recalls and owner complaint records for cars? For your car? Knowing what you know now, would you still buy the car you originally planned to buy? Why/why not?

12.27 Watership Down *Book Club*

NEW LESSONS

Electronic Discussion Groups organized around literature — any book title can be substituted for Watership Down.

PD

Subjects: Literature, Reading
Grade Level: 3rd and Up

One of the first things I learned about my kids was how grade conscious they are. "What can I do to bring my grade up?" That was a constant question from many. To respond, I finally told them I was going to be rereading one of my favorite books, and if they would care to read it along with me and discuss it, we could do that for extra credit.

    The book I chose was one that was not only a fun read but also would add to the kids' frame of reference and give us plenty to talk about. With my copy ready to go, I told the kids to do two things:

1. Get a copy of the book
2. Get an e-mail address so we could talk electronically

The word went out. Copies of *Watership Down* began to disappear off bookstore and library shelves, and soon I had 30 kids ready to go. As we began to read and the word in my classes spread about this particular book, more joined. Eventually, there were 52 of us reading and discussing this wonderful book.

E-mail addresses were given to those who did not have them. Permission slips were printed and returned to make sure the parents were aware their student would be discussing electronically. Those with personal e-mail addresses that we could not access at school switched to Hotmail. Eventually, all of my students had a Hotmail address, but most of them started using e-mail for this project.

Procedure

As I read, I e-mailed the entire group with questions, comments, observations, words I had to look up, etc. (I also had to break the readers into three groups for the sake of bulk e-mailing.)

In the beginning, we were building our frame of reference for the setting by looking for pictures of the English countryside. At one point, we read about an ilex tree, which none of us had a visual frame of reference for. The word went out, and soon enough, we all got e-mail from Carlos telling us where to see a picture of such a tree. This process continued as we read. Anytime we did not have a frame of reference for something, we collectively researched it and helped each other out.

As the plot of the novel thickened and the kids began to get caught up in the story, issues arose about the plot that were discussed by e-mail.

Handling the Volume of Mail

Shortly after we started reading, I opened up my e-mail one day and found 52 messages. There was no way I could teach and read that large a volume of e-mail, but since the kids were eager to put their two cents into each discussion as well as to share findings that enhanced our reading, I could not ask them to stop. I did ask them to be brief and only e-mail if they had something useful to offer. I also had them discuss things among themselves before they e-mailed me, and I used the concept of discussion leaders and discussion groups to coordinate the discussions.

Lessons Learned

Handling the volume of e-mail was my first task, and the discussion groups solved that.

Having enough copies of a book handy for all interested readers would have been helpful. Some of the kids got a late start because they could not find a copy, and others could not participate with this book due to a limited supply locally.

Keeping the momentum going was easy. All I had to do was post ideas for another book to read, ask for votes from interested readers, and then round up copies. Either I bought them, or the kids gave me money to buy theirs. I also took suggestions from the kids and added those to our list of possible books. The kids voted by e-mail and the majority ruled.

The book club was optional: join in if you want, or if the book we are reading is not to your liking, join us again later.

Success

I submitted our book club idea to Compaq Computers for their mini-grant contest, and we were one of the three winners in the State of Nevada. For our idea, we got to use $1000 to buy more books. There are now more than 100 new novels and other types of books in ATECH's library that have bookplates in them stating they came from the *Watership Down* Book Club.

Continuing

Even though the original members of the book club and I are separated by 200 miles, we still share our thoughts on what we are reading. We share electronically, and one of our Webmasters posts our comments. We recommend books, review books and generally share our love of literature. Once my new school gets connected, I hope to combine the two schools and have one very large book club online.

WATERSHIP DOWN PAGES

```
http://www.geocities.com/Athens/Delphi/3632/literary.htm
http://www.inil.com/users/edamoth/water.html
http://pages.prodigy.net/mgpjlp/watershipdown.htm
http://web.nwe.ufl.edu/~dms/water.html
http://members.aol.com/Bla3288/TheBurrow.html
```

12.28 *The Wave*   NEW LESSONS

EO   **Subjects: Literature, History, Sociology**
Grade Level: 4th and Up

To improve literacy within our school, we adopted the suggestion of a staff committee that the entire school; teachers, students, administrators, and support staff, read the same book, at the same time. In addition to reading it, teachers would incorporate the novel in their curriculum.

As an English teacher, I chose to "teach the novel" as I have taught many novels before. This time, however, we would have total access to the Internet.

I read the book beforehand and got a feel for the main idea, the point of it. It was based on a true incident: A social studies teacher, in 1969 Palo Alto, California, wanted his seniors to understand why German citizens did nothing to stand up, as a concerted body, against the atrocities of the Nazi regime. His kids did not understand how anyone of good conscience would say or do nothing. The teacher's efforts to help them understand led to a movement on campus, a movement that got progressively more violent. The kids who got caught up in The Wave got carried away in their zealousness, but what was also sad was that other students stood by and did nothing.

When I started reading the book again, with the kids, I provided them with online time to learn more about Germany and Germans of 1930–40 and teenagers of Palo Alto, 1969. I brought in samples of the music teens of both times would have listened to, swing and rock 'n' roll. We took a look at what movies they might have watched, and we found a site that gave us great information about German propaganda. We looked for economic information, historical information (later we learned more about the character and history of the Germans during our Medieval Project, and that added more pieces to the puzzle for the kids). We wanted as clear a picture as we could get about the lives of the people in the novels. Why, we wanted to know, were they, and not others, so susceptible?

As we read, researched, and discussed, a logical thought took root. In what ways were we — Las Vegas, 1997, and even America — similar to both the Germans and the Palo Alto kids? As we did our research, we began to see hints.

We began researching our economic statistics and media influences to see in which ways we are "turning a blind eye or a deaf ear" to events in our country. We acknowledged that our country has problems, but what we wanted to know was, to what degree do we personally and collectively ignore things that should not be ignored?

First we wanted to see what kind of images and themes America presents to the world. Are the messages ones we endorse or merely accept as "what the public wants"? Homework became watching TV. We charted what types of shows and main characters are on our most-watched TV programs. We added in information about our movie themes and bestselling book themes, and we collectively tried to get a view of the face America shows the world through our media as well as whether that face reflects who we really are or not. Along with understanding who we are came discussions of how much we put up with. We discussed trash on our streets, homelessness downtown, R-rated TV compared to the days of yore when no rating was needed at all.

We researched and discussed and finally got to the question of, "So, if we see all this that we want to change, what can we do about it?" More discussion ensued and the kids realized they could not change all that needs to be changed in one movie or in one 60-minute TV drama, but they could at least speak up, if they wanted to.

Our last piece of research was to learn which of our TV stations presented the most unrealistic portrayal of America and Americans. Which shows give us the most stereotyped or negative images? Charting followed research, and finally we located, online, the e-mail address for the TV station we deemed the worst portrayer of Americans. One fine day in December 1997, a television station got more than 70 e-mails expressing displeasure at their programming policies.

Did we make an impact? On the TV station — probably not . . . maybe. On the kids? They certainly see themselves and their role in society differently, and they found their voice.

One Additional Note

As a cumulative part of the total literacy project, our school beamed, to most classes, the film version of *The Wave*. Classrooms with viewing capabilites shared their room with those who had no overhead monitors. After viewing the film, a discussion was to be held. Thus, my sophomores hosted a group of seniors coming from a Law class.

I got the discussion going by asking the question, "In what ways are you guys just as susceptible to becoming like the kids in the novel?" My sophomores waited to see what the seniors would say. It's hard for a sophomore to speak up first. Not much happened, so one of my kids got brave and spoke up with just a bit of what we had learned and then they were off. With confidence, referring not only to the novel but to their additional research and discussions, my kids brought out every-thing they had learned and soon pulled the seniors in with some of the questions they had asked and answered for themselves. It got lively and animated, and I have to say I was proud of my kids.

Finally, when one senior asked, "Well, what can you do about it?" my kids proudly said, "We e-mail when we have something to say."

As the seniors left our room, we heard one say, "They read the same book we did?"

Well, that's how we read in our Internet classroom.

12.29   *Show Me the Money*   NEW LESSONS

ES/EO   **Subjects: Geography, Math, Reading**
Grade Level: 4th and Up

A lesson suggested by a link from another teacher's terrific site:
GEOGRAPHY WORLD

    http://members.aol.com/bowermanb/101.html

Brad Bowerman, Lakeland High School, Jermyn, PA.

As students progress through their school years, you often hear them ask, "What good is this subject?" This lesson is designed as a template for you to insert appropriate URLs for sites that help your students understand who uses the skills and knowledge of your subject in the "real world."

Geography at work: What are some of the occupations that use the skills and knowledge you learn in your geography class?

A starting point.

THE VARIETY OF GEOGRAPHY FIELDS

http://www.muohio.edu/~geocwis/careers/frames/geo_fields_fram.html

Want Ad: Location Scout

Do you like to travel? Do you like movies? We are looking for a location scout for our latest film. Must be free to travel anywhere in the world. Salary negotiable.

How would you go about getting a job like this?

What and where would you study?

Which geography skills will you need?

What important pieces of geography knowledge might you need to know?

Would you need to know some of the history of countries you are scouting? Why or why not?

Scout locations for a film that requires the following:

An ancient sea port, preferably Marseilles, France

A mansion in Paris

The Paris Opera House

A country chateau outside Paris

Ancient Mediterranean caverns

An ancient prison on an island

A small island in the Mediterranean

You have just scouted locations for the novel *The Count of Monte Cristo.*

Locate a screenplay or script online and find pictures for the various locations, exterior and/or interior.

ONLINE SCRIPTS

http://www.yahoo.com/text/Arts/Drama/Plays/Web_Published/Works/

Links to scripts published online.

DRAMATIC EXCHANGE

    http://www.dramex.org/

A site devoted to archiving and sharing scripts of plays.

RESOURCES FOR SCREENWRITERS AND PLAYWRIGHTS

    http://www.teleport.com/~cdeemer/scrwriter.html

Online scripts, advice for those interested in theater, and more links.

SCRIPTS-O-RAMA

    http://home.cdsnet.net/~nikkoll/scripts.htm

The Webmaster at this site promises more than 500 TV and movie scripts available online.

Want Ad: Tour Organizer

Enjoy travel? Enjoy kids? Take a terrific bunch of kids on vacation this summer. All expenses paid plus small salary.

> How would you get a job like this?
>
> What geography knowledge would be helpful?
>
> If you take a group on a tour, what kinds of information should you have for them? Historic, topography, cultural, fun, etc.?

Check.

    http://www.expedia.com/
    http://www.lonelyplanet.com/

Plan a tour for 2 weeks in one geographic area of interest to you.

Starting points.

> Ancient Mayan Civilizations
>
> Shakespeare's England
>
> Rome of Julius Caesar
>
> In the footsteps of Odysseus
>
> Along the trail with Marco Polo
>
> The early American authors of New England
>
> A literary tour of England
>
> An African adventure
>
> Into China — ancient or new
>
> The New Siberia

Locate URLs for sites that will give your travelers some idea of where they are going and what they might see.

Plan your itinerary — Where will you go? What will you see? Where will you stay? Where will you eat? What will you buy to remind you of the area? What adventures will you have? What topography will amaze you? What flora and fauna will astound you? Who are some of the famous people associated with the area?

Wanted: Spy

The Central Intelligence Agency needs your geography and language skills. Salary negotiable. Must be able to travel anywhere, anytime, and on a moment's notice. Must also communicate quickly and effectively and be discreet.

Starting points.

CIA

    http://www.cia.gov/cia/index.html

INTERPOL

    http://193.123.144.14/interpol-pr/

INTERNATIONAL INTELLIGENCE STUDY GROUP

    http://intelligence-history.wiso.uni-erlangen.de/

BRITAIN'S SECRET SERVICES

    http://www76.pair.com/spook/security/security.htm

NEWSPAPERS

    http://www.newo.com/

1. Where, given today's news, might the CIA want to send a spy well versed in specialized geographic and language skills?
2. What geographic skills will you need?
3. What cultural knowledge will you need of the place you are being sent?
4. How do you get a job like this? What and where do you study?
5. Given the places you picked for question #1, what might be the kind of information you would be seeking?
6. Locate, on a map, the countries you mentioned in #1.

Extensions. Also explore geography careers that involve city planning, and cross-reference with the lesson about when the gas runs out and the subway lesson.

Take a look at careers in geography that deal with the environment or hazardous waste. Have your students research the role of economics, cultures, mapping, and earth science in geography careers.

PART

SITES FOR
ALL YOU TEACH

My focus with these sites has been to provide you with Internet resources that directly relate to the existing curriculums in most states. As classroom teachers, most of us have state or provincially mandated curriculum guidelines. We can only work within that structure. For that reason, I looked for sites that would parallel those existing curriculums, giving you and your kids an opportunity to add to the lessons you've already prepared.

To begin with, you'll find TEACHER'S SITES with links to other teachers on the Net, their ideas, as well as curriculum sites not listed individually here.

Following that are PARENT'S SITES with information for parents with kids on the Net, and connections to parents who are beginning to use the Net for education.

Before you get into the curriculum areas, you will also find general KID'S SITES, primarily for those students in the elementary or middle grades. Here, you will also find illustrated story links, science and math sites for kids.

The URLs were taken directly off the Internet. If they do not work, try removing everything from the right side of the URL backward to the .com or the .edu and locate the actual site from its home page. Sites that have changed addresses since this book was published will probably reflect that change on their sites. Many will direct you to the new address for some time. Some of these sites may no longer exist, as that is the nature of the Net. Sites come and go. But rest assured: There are more than enough to help you and your kids.

Evaluating Sites

What makes one site more valuable or useful than another? Sites must be easy to maneuver through. The information must be accurate and well presented both in text and with graphics. With all the added effects on Web pages now, some information can get lost among all the bells and whistles. Frames are a new site addition and can either simplify your use of a site or confuse it, depending upon how well the Webmaster has used frames. Java or ActiveX enhanced script with moving messages (like those sign boards you see at banks and stadiums) can also add to the effect of the site if the script has a purpose. You will also see Java and other Internet languages being used to create special effects. Animations can be wonderful, but slow to load. Audio adds to a learning experience, but takes time. Judge as you would any materials for your classroom: Are these worth the time? Many are.

Creation of Web pages is a new and evolving art form. Web page designers will experiment with different effects, hoping that what they ultimately decide upon makes the information within the site easy to access and read. In the end, if your kids are confused by the layout or information, then the site is less than useful. A good site will have a logical, easy-to-use menu or map, will be well researched with accurate information, and will have graphics that enhance by illustrating or explaining with links to expand on one idea or take you to a logical extension.

Take the time to thoroughly check out a site you may want to use. Decide how you, given your equipment, will present this to your kids, and then begin expanding their frame of reference and their lives.

Tip: For more on evaluation of sites, go to

http://discoveryschool.com/schrockguide/

WEBRESULTS WEB SITE PLANNING

http://www.webresult.com/index.html

EFFECTIVE WEB PAGES

http://www.algonquinc.on.ca/pilot/test/eval.html

SITES FOR TEACHERS AND PARENTS

GENERAL SITES FOR TEACHERS

Are teachers using the Net? How? What is the future of the Net in our lives, in education? How are my colleagues teaching my subject? Here are some excellent starting points.

KATHY SCHROCK'S GUIDE FOR EDUCATORS

http://discoveryschool.com/schrockguide/

Some of the best links, training information, and teacher's sites around.

ACADEMIC INFO

http://www.academicinfo.net/index.html

Links for teachers and students.

PLUGGED-IN

http://www.pluggedin.org/pie/index.html

Check out *Plugged-In Enterprises,* run by teenagers who want to learn how their Net skills can earn them money. Then see how this site keeps its community informed.

More Sites

ACADEMIC NET

http://www.academic.com/

The online information and communication resource for technology-mediated instruction and learning in higher education.

BEST EDUCATION SOURCES

http://www.education-world.com/

An extensive list of resources for educators.

BUSY TEACHER'S WEB SITE

http://www.ceismc.gatech.edu/busyt/

Links to most every area we might teach.

CISCO EDUCATIONAL ARCHIVES

http://sunsite.unc.edu/cisco/

Educators helping educators — getting on the Web, using Web information, and links for administrators.

COOL SCHOOL TOOLS

http://www.bham.lib.al.us/cooltools/

Index to World Wide Web and other Internet resources for children and teenagers in grades K–12.

CYBER SCHOOLHOUSE

http://www.simonsays.com/kids/

From Simon and Schuster. Check out their teachers' room complete with activities.

DIGITAL EDUCATION NETWORK

http://www.actden.com/

In the "Dens," NewsDEN, MathDEN, and InternetDEN, you will find practice areas, information, and tips.

DIGITAL LIBRARIAN

http://www.servtech.com/~mvail/home.html

So many links to sites for all you teach and all the kids learn.

ED LINKS

http://webpages.marshall.edu/~jmullens/edlinks.html

Learn about who is creating curriculum online or find placement evaluation information for home-school children.

EDUCATIONAL CONNECTIONS

http://www.classroom.net/ Home Page
http://www.classroom.net/cgi/rofm/eduFind.html

This will get you started with links for all educators.

Educational Resource

http://www.ed.uiuc.edu/

Links to network-based educational activities.

Education Site Links

http://www.cpsr.org/program/education/educ.html

A long list of links for teachers, parents, and computer software developers.

Education Week

http://www.edweek.org/

An online news magazine to help teachers.

Education World

http://www.education-world.com/

This is an extensive site with information about educational issues, state resources, and links to colleges and vocational schools. It offers special education, student, parent, and teacher resources.

Educause

http://www.educause.edu/

Educom has now joined with CAUSE to create this educator's Web site.

Educom

http://www.educom.edu/

Presents a library of publications dealing with technology and education issues, legal issues, and national networking.

EDUNET

http://www.baxter.net/

A comprehensive set of links for educators plus travel information. Careers teachers, check out **Job Trek** in the Careers section — excellent site.

EdWeb Home Page

http://edweb.gsn.org/

Join in discussions on the role of the Web in education or learn how to make your own home page.

Electric Learning Web

http://www.chaos.com/learn/index.html

Created for teachers and students, globally, who are creating new learning communities based on communications, collaboration, and creativity.

Electronic School

http://www.electronic-school.com/

A site for the voice of school leaders who know technology as a means, not an end.

From Now On

http://www.fromnowon.org/

Keep up to date on Web issues as they affect school.

InfoList

http://www.cerfnet.com/~step44/ilist29jan6.html

Links to various sites for all teachers.

Internet Tools for Teachers

http://tdi.uregina.ca/~itt/

You'll find information about the Net itself, as well as how teachers are using the Net in their classrooms.

K-12 Educational Computing Projects

http://www.ed.uiuc.edu/Activity-Structures/web-activity-structures.html

A guide to projects already in progress using the Net.

K-12 Lesson Plans

http://execpc.com/%7Edboals/k-12.html

Links that can provide justification for a school district to launch a project to link all teachers to the Internet.

Online Educator

http://ole.net/ole/

A discussion forum for teachers, links to new sites, and a place to browse for information.

Reading

http://www.reading.org/

Check out the help and services from a national reading organization.

Role of the Web in Curricular Reform

http://edweb.gsn.org/web.effects.html

Read more about this critical issue here.

SCHOOL EXPRESS

http://www.schoolexpress.com/

Worksheets, message boards, links, and more resources for teachers and parents.

SUNSHINE ONLINE

http://www.sunshine.aust.com/

For elementary teachers and students, ideas and activities for incorporating the Internet into the classroom.

TEACHERS HELPING TEACHERS

http://www.pacificnet.net/~mandel/index.html

This site offers lesson ideas for using the Internet and links to other resources.

TEACHER'S INTERNET PAGES

http://www.iteachnet.com/index.html

Sources of information for international links in education.

TEACHER'S NET

http://teachers.net/

Informing teachers about what's on the Net, who's using it, and how.

TEACHNET

http://www.teachnet.com/

Online newsletter for teachers with links to lessons, ideas, and news.

USING TECHNOLOGY TO IMPROVE COLLABORATION

http://www-leland.stanford.edu/~ttorres/Education/home.html

A site dedicated to helping teachers and students work together.

WEB AS A LEARNING TOOL

http://www.cs.uidaho.edu/~connie/interests.html

An excellent set of links for most of the subjects we teach.

WEB 66

http://web66.coled.umn.edu/

A catalyst that will integrate the Internet into K–12 school curricula.

WORLD WIDE LECTURE HALL

http://www.utexas.edu/world/lecture/index.html

Links to pages created by faculty worldwide on a variety of subjects.

SPECIAL EDUCATION

Many resources exist on the Net for teachers of special needs students. These sites are excellent starting points.

BEHAVIOR PAGE

http://www.state.ky.us/agencies/behave/homepage.html

For information and effective practices when dealing with children with special needs.

BIG PAGE OF SPECIAL EDUCATION LINKS

http://www.mts.net/~jgreenco/special.html

Another excellent starting point to find what might help you.

BLIND LINKS

http://www.seidata.com/~marriage/rblind.html

Net links in areas such as employment, adaptive technology, and medicine.

BLINDSPOTS

http://www.vashti.net/blind/

Movie reviews for the blind, focusing on whether or not the film is easy to follow for the visually impaired.

CATALYST

http://home.earthlink.net/~thecatalyst/

An online resource for technology in special education.

OFFICE OF SPECIAL EDUCATION

http://curry.edschool.Virginia.EDU/go/specialed/

Another site for links to information about Special Ed.

SEM PROGRAM

http://www.asel.udel.edu/sem/

This site is dedicated to increasing the number of individuals with disabilities in SEM academic programs and professions.

SERI

http://www.hood.edu/seri/serihome.htm

Another vast collection of resources.

SPECIAL EDUCATION LINKS

http://members.aol.com/LCantlin/se_links.htm

An extensive set of links for teachers and parents.

SPECIAL EDUCATION SITES

http://libits.library.ualberta.ca/library_html/libraries/coutts/special.html

From Canada, another excellent list of resources.

SPECIAL NEEDS RESOURCES

http://www.bushnet.qld.edu.au/~sarah/spec_ed/

Arts and crafts resources for special needs students.

UNIVERSITY OF KANSAS SPECIAL EDUCATION ONLINE

http://www.sped.ukans.edu/

From the highly respected university, a set of links and information.

VOCATIONAL EDUCATION

JOURNAL OF TECHNOLOGY EDUCATION

http://borg.lib.vt.edu:80/ejournals/JTE/jte.html

A vocational/tech. prep journal online with several issues available.

NATIONAL CENTER FOR RESEARCH IN VOCATIONAL EDUC.

http://vocserve.berkeley.edu/

Begin here for links to information about school to work programs and other items of interest.

NATIONAL SCHOOL-TO-WORK INTERNET GATEWAY

http://www.stw.ed.gov/

Excellent resources about project-based learning, transitions, and other issues.

PETERSON'S GUIDE TO VOCATIONAL SCHOOLS IN THE U.S.

http://www.petersons.com/preview/votec.html

If your students are looking for a school, here is a good guide.

VOCATIONAL EDUCATION IN THE U.S.

http://nces.ed.gov/pubs/95024.html

Selected excerpts from a book on the history of vocational education.

Vocational Educational Links

http://webpages.marshall.edu/~jmullens/voc.html

Links to magazines and informational sources concerning all types of vocations.

Bilingual Education/ESL

Bilingual Education: Challenges for the Future

http://newlinks.tc.columbia.edu/pluribus/tricia.htm

An essay that discusses the problems ahead for bilingual education.

Bilingual Education Resources

http://www.edb.utexas.edu/coe/depts/ci/bilingue/resources.html

Links to bilingual network, a clearinghouse of information, and more.

Bilingual Education Institute

http://www.aetas.com/

History, services, language and culture training.

Bilingual Education Network

http://www.cde.ca.gov/cilbranch/bien/bien.htm

California Department of Education online information source.

EFLNet

http://www.eflnet.com/

Advice for people who write in the English language. Help with understanding the fundamentals, producing effective documents, and linking with other writers.

English Learner

http://www.englishlearner.com/

English tests and quizzes.

ESL Magazine

http://www.eslmag.com/

For English as a Second Language Professionals

ESL Page

http://home.sol.no/~andreasl/

Another set of links to Web sites.

ESL SITES ON THE WEB

http://www.alc.co.jp/kves/

Another set of links to Web sites.

FUN

http://thecity.sfsu.edu/~funweb/

Links to sites for ESL or EFL.

LANGUAGE EXPERIENCES

http://www.geocities.com/Athens/Academy/7726/

A site designed for English speakers wanting to learn another language. With exercises, resources, and projects.

LANGUAGE LEARNING

http://www.ozemail.com.au/~cdug/

Another site with excellent links to research, practice, theory, and more.

LANGUAGE LEARNING LINKS

http://www.comenius.com/

Some online practice with writing skills, vocabulary, and more links.

LEARNING ENGLISH ON THE WEB

http://www.lang.uiuc.edu/r-li5/esl/

With links to information about speaking, listening, and writing, plus other ESL links.

LINGUISTIC FUNLAND

http://linguistic-funland.com/

Overview of projects created by ESL students.

LONGMAN DICTIONARIES WEB SITE

http://www.awl-elt.com/dictionaries/home.html

For those learning the English language, this site offers games for practice from an elementary level up; there are several ways to practice your skills.

MODEL STRATEGIES

http://inet.ed.gov/pubs/ModStrat/

Lengthy discussion of the subject from the Department of Education.

NATIONAL MULTICULTURAL INSTITUTE

http://www.nmci.org/

More links to research, sites, and information.

ONLINE ESL ACTIVITIES
    http://www.owlnet.rice.edu/~ling417/

Only one activity for now with a QuickTime movie for actual language practice.

WINGS MAGAZINE
    http://weber.u.washington.edu/~wings/wings.html

Electronic magazine for ESL writing and art.

GRANT INFORMATION

If you have the time and energy, here are some resources for grant writing or sources of funding.

DISTANCE LEARNING FUNDING SOURCES
    http://www.technogrants.com/

A comprehensive list of sources for funding a telecommunications project.

GRANT GETTING PAGE
    http://www.uic.edu/depts/ovcr/

Another set of resources for private and public funds.

GRANT SOURCES FOR EDUCATORS
    http://lonestar.texas.net/~cawalt/grants.html

Links to information about who has the money and how to get it.

GRANTS AND OTHER PEOPLE'S MONEY
    http://quest.arc.nasa.gov/grants.html

Who has money and how do you get it?

GRANTSWEB
    http://web.fie.com/cws/sra/resource.htm

An extensive set of links will point you in the right direction for finding grant information on the Net.

NATIONAL ASSOCIATION OF GRANTWRITERS
    http://www.naogwanc.com/

Still more links to sources for funding.

RESEARCH FUNDING AGENCIES
http://www.cs.virginia.edu/research/sponsors.html

List of resources for scholarships and funding in science and technology.

SCHOOL GRANTS AND GRANT RESOURCES
http://www.morriscatholic.pvt.k12.nj.us/grants.html

Another site to help you find ways to pay for it all.

SITES FOR PARENTS

BABY AND CHILD PLACE
http://www.babyplace.com/

Online magazine for parents.

CHILD SAFETY ON THE INFORMATION HIGHWAY
http://www.4j.lane.edu/saftety/childtoc.html

An overview of the issues and concerns, plus guidelines and rules for safety.

DAILY PARENT
http://www.dailyparent.com/dailyfeatures.html

Issues for parents, including health, education, food, and money.

FAMILY EDUCATION
http://www.familyeducation.com/

Find information about parenting, education, special needs kids, and more.

FAMILY PC MAGAZINE
http://www.zdnet.com/familypc/

Read about some of the latest issues to concern families and computers.

FAMILY .COM
http://family.go.com/

Issues of importance to families, fun, and advice.

FATHERING MAGAZINE
http://www.fathermag.com/

An online magazine covering the needs of fathers.

Informed Parent

http://www.informedparent.com/

The magazine of pediatric medicine.

Parents & Children Together Online

http://www.indiana.edu/~eric_rec/fl/pcto/menu.html

A magazine for parents who are online with their kids. Including stories for grades K–6, articles on cats and dogs, and a story in Spanish.

Parents Place

http://www.parentsplace.com/

Advice for parents from doctors, teachers, and other professionals.

Teen World

http://www.teenworld.com.my/

An online magazine of news and opinion for teens. First register for this free area.

World Village

http://www.worldvillage.com/

A site for parents, educators, and kids, loaded with advice, safe software reviews, online games, and Internet guidance.

C H A P T E R

8

GENERAL SITES
FOR KIDS

KIDS SITES

Each of the sites listed below contains links to sites appropriate for elementary and middle school students. All of them are terrific, but some are more terrific than others.

These sites definitely answer the question "Where do you want to go today?"

In this chapter

- Kids Sites
- Science for Kids
- Stories and Magazines for Kids and Teens
- A Bit of Fun
- Book Sites for Kids
- Reference Materials

CYBERKIDS

http://www.cyberkids.com/

From coloring online to links for kids. Just click on the rocket once you enter the castle.

ENCHANTED LEARNING: LITTLE EXPLORERS

http://www.EnchantedLearning.com/

A terrific beginning site for younger elementary kids. Presented in dictionary format. It's extensive.

More Sites

ADVENTURE.COM

http://www.adventure.com/

Places for kids to learn and play.

AIR FORCE KIDS ONLINE

http://www.af.mil/aflinkjr/home.htm

Go here to read stories, make paper airplanes, and more.

Ask Jeeves for Kids
http://www.ajkids.com/

If you need an answer to any question, kids can safely find it here.

Berit's Best Sites
http://db.cochran.com/li_toc:theoPage.db

Serious stuff and fun stuff all rated for suitability — a good place to get caught up in the Net.

Children's Stomping Ground
http://www.oink.demon.co.uk/kids.htm

Learn to juggle, read stories, try tongue twisters, and more.

Education by Design
http://www.edbydesign.com/kidsact.html

Online activities for kids 5–12.

Homework Help
http://www.homeworkhelp.com/

Try this site for some help with those homework assignments.

Idea Box
http://www.theideabox.com/

Early childhood education and activities.

International Kids Space
http://www.kids-space.org/

Draw, write, make friends — nice site for the younger crowd.

Internet Youth Project
http://www.youth.org.uk/frame.htm

Wonderful sites for kids using the net — resources, advice, and more.

Jumpstart
http://www.jstart.org/

Helping to prepare kids with early education.

Just for Fun Page
http://www.teilhard.com/kids/index.html

For kids, games, art, galleries, and more just-for-fun stuff.

KIDDIE CAMPUS

http://www.kiddiecampus.com/

Early learning links and information.

KIDLINK

http://www.kidlink.org/

A site dedicated to getting kids 10–15 years old involved in a global dialogue. Check this one out.

KIDS CLICK

http://sunsite.berkeley.edu/KidsClick!/

Librarians put this site together for kids who want to search. Categories include current events, math, science, mysterious, sports, and more.

KIDS COM (FRENCH/SPANISH/ENGLISH)

http://www.kidscom.com/

A communications playground for 4–15 year olds in several languages.

KIDS FOOD CYBERCLUB

http://www.kidsfood.org/

Keep kids healthy with lesson plan ideas and activities.

KID'S STUFF

http://www.infostuff.com/kids/index.html

Learning fun from alphabet games to activities for kids.

KIDS WEB

http://www.npac.syr.edu:80/textbook/kidsweb/

Links for kids in the areas of science, literature, arts, social studies.

KIDSWORLD ONLINE

http://www.kidsworld-online.com/

A place for young writers to submit their writings, talk to other kids, enter contests and more.

KNOWLEDGE ADVENTURE

http://www.adventure.com/

3-D learning environment that integrates all the core components of elementary curricula in one location. For early elementary kids, too.

LOONEY BIN

http://www.geocities.com/Athens/3843/index.html

A place for kids to get help with their writing, tests, study skills, and job skills.

MAGIC BIT

http://www.magicbit.com/links/kids.htm

Presearched and previewed sites for kids. From the search engine Altavista.

NATURAL CHILD PROJECT

http://www.naturalchild.com/

Devoted to providing information, links, and exhibits that will help all children.

ROAD SAFETY

http://www.roadsafety.net/Kids/Menu/fs.html

Help kids learn how to be safe on the road. Includes a bike quiz.

SAFETY QUIZ

http://city.wheaton.lib.il.us/pd/kids.html

For kids, McGruff the Dog offers a chance to check your general safety IQ.

SURF MONKEY

http://www.surfmonkey.com/

A Web browser for kids.

TOMORROW'S MORNING

http://www.morning.com/

A newspaper for kids.

YAK'S CORNER

http://www.yakscorner.com/

A news magazine for kids.

WICKEDEST WEBSITE IN THE WORLD

http://www.wicked4kids.com/

Play games, make cookies, solve puzzles, and have fun.

ZOOM SCHOOL

http://www.enchantedlearning.com/school/

From the Enchanted Learning site. You can learn about different themes with games, quizzes, folk tales, and more.

SCIENCE FOR KIDS

5 TIGERS
http://www.5tigers.org/

Available in English and Bahasa (Indonesian); learn about an endangered species.

AUSTRALIAN ENVIRONMENT ONLINE
http://kaos.erin.gov.au/erin.html

Find out which plants and animals are endangered and what can be done to protect them.

BENNYGOODSPORT
http://www.bennygoodsport.com/

Fitness fun for kids.

CHEM4KIDS
http://www.chem4kids.com/

Help your younger kids understand chemistry with this site.

COLUMBIA VIRTUAL BODY
http://www.medtropolis.com/vbody/

Try this interactive presentation about how the body works.

COMIC BOOK PERIODIC TABLE
http://www.uky.edu/~holler/periodic/perodic.html

An interesting way to learn about the periodic table of elements.

CYBER JACQUES' CYBER SEAS TREASURE HUNT
http://www.cyberjacques.com/

Scavenger hunt lead by a crusty sea captain with prizes.

ELECTRICITY AND MAGNETISM
http://ippex.pppl.gov/ippex/PhysicsModules.html

Modules cover matter, energy, fusion, and more.

EXPLORESCIENCE
http://www.explorescience.com/

An animated science web online.

HOMEWORK HELP — MATH AND SCIENCE
http://www.trabuco.org/

E-mail your problems and get some help online.

INNER LEARNING ONLINE
http://www.innerbody.com/

Learn more about how your body or your car works.

INTERNATIONAL YEAR OF THE OCEAN
http://www.yoto98.noaa.gov/

Find out what this organization is doing to help the oceans.

KID CITY
http://www.azc.com/enn2/kidcity.htm

Some of the sites open are a zoo, computer lab, and science museum; more are in the works.

KIDS HEALTH
http://kidshealth.org/

Animations and information bring health issues to kids. Check in the Kids Closet for animations about how your body works.

LIVING THINGS
http://www.fi.edu/tfi/units/life/

Biology for kids with teacher tips, too.

NATIONAL AUDUBON SOCIETY
http://www.audubon.org/

Go here often to see what new photos and projects are online.

NATIONAL OCEANIC ATMOSPHERIC ASSOCIATION
http://www.noaa.gov

An extensive site with wonderful photos of ocean life and more.

QUESTACON
http://sunsite.anu.edu.au/Questacon/

From Australia comes a site with hands-on activities and several galleries exploring science.

RAINFOREST ACTION NETWORK
http://www.ran.org/

Learn more about how you can save the forests and what else is being done, as well as links to tribal information and more.

SAFARI TOUCH TANK

http://oberon.educ.sfu.ca:80/splash/tank.htm

Point, click, and get information about what type of sea creature is in the tank.

SAVING THE RAIN FOREST ORANGUTANS

http://www.redcube.nl/bos

Learn about the efforts to save this almost extinct species and its environment.

VISIT TO NASA

http://www.interlog.com/~mmarks/home.html

For the younger kids. An interactive story takes you on a tour of NASA.

ZOONET

http://www.mindspring.com/~zoonet/anilinks.html

A wide range of links to sites for animals, zoos, and information.

ZOO WEB

http://www.zooweb.net/

Links to zoos and aquariums online.

STORIES AND MAGAZINES FOR KIDS AND TEENS

AESOP'S FABLES

http://www.pacificnet.net/~johnr/aesop/

Find illustrated stories, as well as some you can hear with RealAudio.

AWESOME SITE FOR ALL AGES

http://www.marlo.com/allages.htm

After you send a postcard, make a card or an award, scroll down and find the wonderful online, illustrated stories for the younger kids.

BEDTIME STORY

http://the-office.com/bedtime-story/

Designed for the busy parent, this site offers previews of its illustrated stories.

BOOKGARDEN GALLERY

http://www.bookgarden.com/

Here you'll find art, fables, and links to rare books.

Candlelight Stories

http://www.CandlelightStories.com/

A delightful set of stories from writers and artists around the world and of all ages.

Children's Storybook Online

http://www.magickeys.com/books/index.html#books

Colorful illustrated stories like "Big Bird Can't Fly," presented in a read-along fashion.

Elves in Cyberspace

http://twig.res.cmu.edu/eic/

Online science fiction stories that can be downloaded for reading.

Fairy Tales

http://www.ika.com/stories/

In Spanish, German, or English, read some delightful illustrated stories.

Five Owls

http://www.hamline.edu/depts/gradprog/5owls/

This is an online journal for anyone interested, professionally or personally, in children's literature.

FreeZone

http://freezone.com/

Kids 8–14 can play games, post messages, find a pen pal, and explore.

Kid News

http://www.kidnews.com/

An online newspaper for kids with news, sports, profiles, and a place to submit writings.

KidPub

http://www.kidpub.org/kidpub/

A place for kids to publish their stories or read stories posted by other kids.

Kids Mysteries

http://www.thecase.com/kids/

Find mysteries to solve, contests, and magic for younger kids.

Kid's Stories on the WWW

http://home.earthlink.net/~merlin200/soap/kids.htm

Another place to look for illustrated stories for the younger kids.

Kid's World

http://www.kidsworld-online.com/

A news and artistic magazine for kids, with a place to submit your writings, too.

Lock the Rocket

http://www.msn.com.au/lock/

An online adventure written in episodes — it's a space adventure from Australia.

Making Hearts Sing

http://www.wildgear.com/stories/

International tales of traditional values, some of which are illustrated by kids.

MidLink Magazine

http://longwood.cs.ucf.edu/~MidLink/

A quarterly magazine for middle school kids with ongoing projects.

The Refrigerator

http://www.artcontest.com/

This site hosts an online art contest for kids of all ages (especially young ones). Check out "The Freezer" for a writing contest.

The Scoop

http://www.friend.ly.net/scoop/

Reviews of the latest in children's literature, plus some places to entertain and educate.

Spiderman in Amazing Adventures

http://www.ed.gov/inits/americareads/spidey

From the Department of Education, a fun way to practice reading.

Sports Illustrated for Kids

http://pathfinder.com/SIFK

Just the ticket to get kids interested in the Net.

Story Hour

http://www.ipl.org/youth.StoryHour/

More illustrated stories for younger and beginning readers.

Story Resources on the Web

http://www.enigmagraphics.com/stories/index.htm

Links to many story resources, including tales from other cultures and in other languages.

STORY BROOK LANE

`http://www.geocities.com/Athens/Parthenon/2087/`

With choices, kids can help determine the plot of these stories.

THEODORE TUGBOAT

`http://www.cochran.com/theodore/`

Interactive story for the young crowd.

TIME FOR KIDS

`http://www.timeforkids.com/`

For grades 4–6, *Time* Magazine online.

WEBKIDS

`http://www.hoofbeats.com/`

Online science fiction adventures for kids, written and illustrated by kids.

WILLY'S WEB OF BEDTIME TALES

`http://www.willysweb.com/`

Register to enter Willy's library and read wonderful stories online.

YES MAG

`http://www.yesmag.bc.ca/`

Our neighbors to the north have put together a magazine for kids for science.

YOUTH CENTRAL

`http://www.yc.apple.com/`

By kids and for kids; sports, news, contests, and more.

A BIT OF FUN

ADVENTURE ONLINE

`http://www.adventureonline.com/index.html`

Adventures in Central America and along the Nile.

BLACKBEARD LIVES

`http://www.blackbeardlives.com/`

Go on an adventure with the famous pirate.

Disney

http://www.disney.com/

Catch your kids up on the latest from Disney.

Dr. Toy

http://www.drtoy.com/drtoy/index.html

Offers advice about children's toys; the Top 100 and articles about toys.

Grossology

http://www.grossology.com/

Find out what kids all over the world think is gross!

History Channel

http://www.historychannel.com/

History classroom, this day in history, and more.

How to Love Your Dog

http://www.geocities.com/~kidsanddogs/

For kids of all ages wanting to know more about their canine companions.

Hundred Acre Woods

http://www.mindspring.com/~tyche/pooh.html

Take the Pooh Trivia Quiz, get answers to FAQs, play Pooh Sticks, and find other links.

Kidland

http://www.kidland.com/

Find educational links, games, books, magazines, activities, and more.

Kid's Cool Animation

http://www.kaleidoscapes.com/current.html

Samples from kids under the age of 12. The site also presents a tutorial on how to make an animated movie.

Kids Space

http://www.awl.com/www.cuisenaire.com/kids.html

Activities for all ages such as measuring, drawing, exploring the environment, and more.

KidsWorld

http://www.kidsworld.com/

An "interactive educational cartoon network" with lots of animation.

Matchbox Cars

http://www.matchboxtoys.com/

Now, create, color, and name your own car.

Four Faces of Pocahontas

http://www.co.henrico.va.us/manager/pokeypix.htm

Examines the many current depictions of this Native American.

Native Opinions about Pocahontas

http://indy4.fdl.cc.mn.us/~isk/poca/pocahont.html

Read some of the opinions of Native Americans about the Disney film.

Phoenix International Airport

http://www.phxskyharbor.com/skyharbr/kids/index.html

Kids can learn more about aviation and do some projects, too.

Pocahontas

http://www.apva.org/history/pocahont.html

Historical information can be found here.

Schoolhouse Rock

http://www.vbe.com/~spowell/shr/

Get the lyrics to Grammar, Multiplication, America and Science Rock.

Smithsonian Online

http://www.si.edu/

A great place to take a tour.

Toys R Us

http://www.toysrus.com/

Now you can browse without having to leave the house. Check out "Fun Stuff" for Concentration, a coloring book, and more.

What's It Like Where You Live?

http://www.mobot.org/MGBnet/

From the desert to the rain forest, pictures and text tell you what it's like to live in different places.

The Yuckiest Site on the Internet

http://www.yucky.com/yucky/

A humorous way to learn about bodily functions, creepy insects, and other yucky science stuff.

BOOK SITES FOR KIDS

CYBER SEUSS

http://www.afn.org/~afn15301/drseuss.html

Find 15 online stories and rare pieces from Dr. Seuss's college days.

DAYBREAK

http://daybreak.simplenet.com/

Book review magazine by and for kids.

GOLDEN BOOKS

http://www.goldenbooks.com/

At the Web site of the famous children's books, you can find jokes, riddles, and book reports.

KIDS BOOK

http://www.nhptv.org/kn/vs/bookrev.sht

Book reviews for kids by kids.

READING RAINBOW HOME PAGE

http://www.pbs.org:80/readingrainbow/rr.html

An impressive children's book list and activities to go with the titles.

SEUSSVILLE

http://www.seussville.com/

Look up old favorites and find a contest.

SEUSSVILLE

http://falcon.jmu.edu/~ramseyil/seuss.htm

Links to more resources on the Net for Dr. Seuss.

TEEFR

http://www.users.interport.net/~dinosaur/teefr.html

An online fantasy adventure for all ages.

WORLD OF READING

http://worldreading.org/

Your kids can add their book reviews to this collection from around the world.

REFERENCE MATERIALS

If your classroom lacks certain valuable resources from dictionaries to encyclopedias, you'll be able to supplement with Net resources. New trends on the Net include dictionaries and glossaries for everyone and everything. Take a look at the list of dictionaries available at this site:

http://www.onelook.com/

Here are samples of some of the available on-line dictionaries.

For a General Dictionary

http://www.dictionary.com/

Special Dictionaries

AMERICAN SIGN LANGUAGE DICTIONARY
http://www.deafworldweb.org/asl

AQUARIUM GLOSSARY
http://www.actwin.com/fish/glossary.html

BUSINESS GLOSSARY
http://www.washingtonpost.com/wp-srv/business/longterm/glossary/

ELECTRONICS DICTIONARY
http://www.twysted-pair.com/

ENERGY GLOSSARY
http://www.energy.ca.gov/glossary/

ENVIRONMENT DICTIONARY
http://www.netcore.ca/~gibsonjs/dict3g.htm

FASHION DICTIONARY
http://www.netcore.ca/~gibsonjs/dict1f.htm

GEOGRAPHY DICTIONARY
http://www.netcore.ca/~gibsonjs/dict1g.htm

LIFE SCIENCE DICTIONARY
http://www.biotech.chem.indiana.edu/pages/dictionary.html

LITTLE EXPLORERS DICTIONARY (FOR KIDS)
http://www.littleexplorers.com/

MONEY WORDS
http://www.moneywords.com/

POLITICAL DICTIONARY
http://www.fast-times.com/political/political.html

SPORTS GLOSSARIES
http://www.firstbasesports.com/glossaries/gloshome.htm

WORDS OF ART
http://www.arts.ouc.bc.ca/fiar/glossary/gloshome.html

Reference Sites

BARTLETT'S FAMILIAR QUOTATIONS
http://www.columbia.edu/acis/bartleby/bartlett/

For those who can't afford one, now you can have one at your fingertips.

CATALOG OF INTERNET RESOURCES
http://www.oclc.org/

Searchable database contains bibliographic records of worldwide resources.

CHARLIE FINK'S QUOTE OF THE WEEK
http://www.quoteoftheweek.com/

Complete with archives and a subscription service to keep you updated. It's geared toward helping kids find an appropriate quote to enhance their work.

CITING THE WORLD WIDE WEB
http://www.geocities.com/ResearchTriangle/1221/citation.htm

When you have to mention a site in your bibliography or footnotes, this site tells you how to write it out.

COLLEGES AND UNIVERSITIES ON THE NET
http://www.mit.edu:8001/people/cdemello/univ.html

A geographical listing of colleges is available here, as well as a search tool.

COOL STUDENT RESOURCES
http://www.teleport.com/~burrell/

Links for music, writing, economics, languages, etc.

DICTIONARY.COM

`http://www.dictionary.com/`

A dictionary at your fingertips and other resources

ELECTRONIC LIBRARY RESOURCES

`http://www.ntu.ac.uk/lis/elr.htm`

This United Kingdom site offers links to resources for business and marketing, art, computers, education, social science, law, science, and math.

ENCYCLOPEDIA.COM

`http://www.encyclopedia.com/`

What could be better than an online encyclopedia?

ENCYCLOPEDIA BRITANNICA

`http://www.britannica.com/`

Your school librarian might have to subscribe, but it's worth it to have an ever-changing encyclopedia at your fingertips.

FUNK AND WAGNALLS KNOWLEDGE CENTER

`http://www.funkandwagnalls.com/`

A great new site from an old educational partner with art exhibits and an encyclopedia.

INFORMATION PLEASE

`http://www.infoplease.com/`

Search almanacs, encyclopedias, and dictionaries for the answer you seek.

INTERNET SLEUTH

`http://www.isleuth.com/`

Another search engine you might try.

LIBRARYSPOT

`http://www.libraryspot.com/`

Another place to find information.

LISZT

`http://www.liszt.com/`

A mailing list directory for those looking for e-mail discussion groups.

LOOKSMART

`http://www.looksmart.com/`

Reader's Digest has put a search tool online that searches through over 100,000 previewed sites.

MARTINDALE'S REFERENCE DESK
http://www-sci.lib.uci.edu/HSG/Ref.html

Extensive links to online reference materials - very comprehensive

OXFORD ENGLISH DICTIONARY
http://www.oed.com/

Coming soon in '97. Look for their fee schedule for access.

PURDUE REFERENCE DESK
http://thorplus.lib.purdue.edu/reference/index.html

A reference desk at your fingertips — dictionaries, maps, science tools.

REFERENCE FROM GALE
http://www.gale.com/

History, biographies of women, poetry, and more.

RESEARCH TOOLS IN ONE PLACE
http://www.iTools.com/research-it/research-it.html

Language, geographical, and financial search tools all in one place.

ROGET'S THESAURUS
gopher://odie.niaid.nih.gov/77/.thesaurus/index

Add this to your classroom along with your dictionary.

VIRTUAL RELOCATION
http://www.virtualrelocation.com/

Before you move, try out the cost-of-living calculator, links to employment and housing, and the guide for kids.

WEBSTER'S DICTIONARY
http://c.gp.cs.cmu.edu:5103/prog/webster

Lack classroom sets? No need to buy.

WRITERS, READERS, SPEAKERS AND MORE:

THE LANGUAGE ARTS CLASSROOM ONLINE

LITERATURE ONLINE

There's more to English than just literature. Teaching English is teaching communication skills. The Net is the place to enhance those skills and see them in action. Bring works of literature to your kids, or let their work be published. Learn more about the times, places, people, and events behind the stories you read. Take your kids to the lands of literature.

In this chapter

- Kids Sites
- Science for Kids
- Stories and Magazines for Kids and Teens
- A Bit of Fun
- Book Sites for Kids
- Reference Materials

A Great Site

VOICE OF THE SHUTTLE

http://humanitas.ucsb.edu/shuttle/english.html

Presents links to other literature sources including minority literature, literature by genre, and other literature sources.

More Sites

AMERICAN LITERATURE

http://www.cwrl.utexas.edu/~daniel/

Secondary teachers, look here for stories, poetry, and links to lessons for selected texts.

AMERICAN LITERATURE ONLINE

http://www.missouri.edu/~engmo/amlit.html

Connections to some great sites, including general links and links to specific authors such as Whitman, Hawthorne, and Longfellow.

281

LESSON

13 SAMPLE LESSONS FOR LITERATURE

EO   ## Grade Level: 3rd and Up

Play and Search

SEPARATED AT VERSE

http://www.chaparraltree.com/games/sepverse.shtml

Read a poem, decide who was the author. Great way to practice searching and read a little poetry along the way!

CHARLIE FINK'S QUOTE OF THE WEEK

http://www.quoteoftheweek.com/

Complete with archives and a subscription service to keep you updated. It's geared toward helping kids find an appropriate quote to enhance their work.

Browse

STORIES FOR EVERYONE

http://www.enigmagraphics.com/stories/index.htm
http://www.magickeys.com/books/index.html#books
http://www.adventure.com/

Link/Bookmark

MAGAZINES FOR TEENS

http://www.yc.apple.com/

Explore

GASLIGHT STORIES

http://www.mtroyal.ab.ca/programs/arts/english/gaslight/gaslight.htm

From the Victorian era and on, there are some wonderful stories here.

AUTHOR'S PEN

http://www.books.com/scripts/authors.exe

Alphabetical links to authors.

BRITISH AND IRISH AUTHORS ON THE WEB

http://lang.nagoya-u.ac.jp/~matsuoka/UK-authors.html

For a chronological list of authors and links, check here.

CANTERBURY TOUR

http://www.hillside.co.uk/tour/tour.html

Start with a history of the town, then take a walking tour.

CAPA — CONTEMPORARY AMERICAN POETRY ARCHIVE

http://camel.conncoll.edu/ccother/wjbat/CAPApage

Bringing out-of-print poetry to the Net.

CARNEGIE/MELLON ENGLISH SERVER

http://english-www.hss.cmu.edu/

Humanities links to architecture, eighteenth century, drama, and fiction.

CELEBRATION OF WOMEN WRITERS

http://www.cs.cmu.edu/Web/People/mmbt/women/writers.html

Links to Net sites for a long and impressive list of women writers.

CHILDREN'S LITERATURE

http://www.ucalgary.ca/~dkbrown/

More places to find literature links for younger kids.

ELECTRONIC ARCHIVES FOR TEACHING AMERICAN LITERATURE

http://www.georgetown.edu/tamlit/tamlit-home.html

Essays, syllabi, bibliographies, and other resources for teaching the multiple literatures of the United States.

ELEMENTS OF LITERATURE

http://www2.rscc.cc.tn.us/~jordan_jj/OWL/ElementsLit.html

Definitions of basic literature terms; categorized.

EMILY DICKINSON

http://www.planet.net/pkrisxle/emily/dickinson.html

Not only links to 350 poems, but also biographic information and more.

ENCYCLOPEDIA MYTHICA

http://www.pantheon.org/myth/

An encyclopedia of mythology, folklore, and mysticism.

ENGLISH LITERATURE

http://www.thinkquest.org/library/3648.html

Created by students, this site arranges literature by historical period and offers background information about each period, information about the popular works or authors, and links to more resources.

ENGLISH LITERATURE

http://englishlit.miningco.com/

Links for those interested in literature.

FAERIES

http://faeryland.tamu-commerce.edu/~earendil/faerie/faerie.html

Links to worldwide literature about faeries; poems, stories, and legends.

FAULKNER'S PAGE

http://www.asahi-net.or.jp/~BB8S-SOY/cont/faulkner/faulkm.html

Information about the author — specifically, where he lived.

GREEK MYTHOLOGY

http://hyperion.advanced.org/23057/

Many of the stories and other links for the Greeks.

LITERARY RESOURCES ON THE NET

http://www.english.upenn.edu/~jlynch/Lit/

Links to literature sites organized by era and genre, including women's and ethnic literature.

THE LITERARY TRAVELER

http://www.literarytraveler.com/

Focusing on a new author, usually from New England, this site will show you where they lived and wrote.

LUMINARIUM

http://www.luminarium.org/

Medieval, Renaissance, and 17th-century literature beautifully presented.

MEDIEVAL AND CLASSIC LIBRARY
http://sunsite.berkeley.edu/OMACL/

Links to resources for Chaucer, Homer, and other classic literatures.

MYSTERIES AND CRIME FICTION
http://www.webfic.com/mysthome/

Links to Web sites for texts, magazines, Sherlock, and more.

NINETEENTH CENTURY AMERICAN WOMEN WRITERS WEB
http://clever.net/19cwww/

A collection of works and information.

OXFORD BOOK OF ENGLISH VERSE
http://www.columbia.edu/acis/bartleby/obev/

Extensive collection from 1250 to 1900, all online.

SCIENCE FICTION RESOURCE GUIDE
http://sflovers.rutgers.edu/Web/SFRG

Comprehensive guide to books, films, authors, reviews and more.

SHAKESPEARE'S SONNETS
http://www.wtirocks.com/books/shakespeare.html

This site offers read online.

TALES TO TELL
http://www.thekids.com/

Illustrated stories from around the world are among the offerings for young kids. Stories are categorized as fables, heroes and adventure, and stories from everywhere.

UNIVERSITY OF ALBERTA LITERATURE SITE
http://www.ualberta.ca/~amactavi/litlinks.htm

Links to a variety of literary areas, including authors' pages, texts online, gender issues, and theory.

VIRTUAL ENGLISH
http://tqd.advanced.org/2847/

Put together by high school students, this site offers more than 90 essays about novels, plays, short stories, poetry, and nonfiction books.

WOMEN WRITERS OF THE MIDDLE AGES

http://www.millersv.edu/~english/homepage/duncan/medfem/medfem.html

A long list of links to writers, their works, information, and materials.

WORLDWIDE GUIDE TO LITERATURE

http://www.worldwidenews.net/HUMANITI/LITERATU/SUBJECT.HTM

An extensive set of links to works from all over the world.

WWW VIRTUAL LIBRARY — AUTHORS' LINKS

http://sunsite.unc.edu/ibic/IBIC-Authors.html

An impressive list of links to authors represented on the Net.

A Few Publishers Online

There are many more.

AVON BOOKS

http://www.AvonBooks.com/

They provide writing advice for young writers from Beverly Cleary.

CHARLES RIVER MEDIA

http://www.charlesriver.com/

For some terrific books, go here!

HARPERCOLLINS

http://www.harpercollins.com/

Find information about their authors, schedules, and more.

PENGUIN

http://www.penguin.com/

Listen to authors, hear selections from books, find educational resources.

PUBLISHERS' CATALOGUES HOME PAGE

http://www.lights.com/publisher/

Links, by country, to publishers around the world.

RANDOM HOUSE

http://www.randomhouse.com/

Aside from standard information, find a spooky online serial called "The Lurker."

Samples of Sites Used to Enhance One Author or Work

Although this list is limited to a few authors, with very little searching it is possible to find information about most of the authors and their works found in most standard curriculums.

BROWN UNIVERSITY VICTORIAN WEB

```
http://twine.stg.brown.edu/projects/hypertext/landow/victorian/victov.html
```

Links to information about authors, their works, and the times in which they wrote.

DICKENS' KENT

```
http://lang.nagoya-u.ac.jp/~matsuoka/CD-Kent.html
```

Take a visual tour of the buildings and places that found their way into his works.

EDGAR ALLEN POE PAGES

```
http://www.poedecoder.com/Qrisse/
```

Information and links about this author.

GREAT EXPECTATIONS REVIEW

```
http://www.theatlantic.com/atlantic/atlweb/classrev/greatexp.htm
```

Written in 1861, just after the final installment of the novel was published, this review offers an interesting perspective on the man and his work.

HUCK FINN

```
http://etext.lib.virginia.edu/twain/huckfinn.html
```

Illustrations from the original and other sources, full text, and early reviews are at this site.

MARK TWAIN FORUM'S WEB PAGE

```
http://web.mit.edu/linguistics/www/forum/twainweb.html
```

Along with more resources, this site has book reviews, a photo gallery, and a section called "Mark Twain, then and now."

MARK TWAIN IN HARTFORD

```
http://www.courant.com/special/twain/index.htm
```

Learn more about the man and his works.

MARK TWAIN IN HIS TIMES

```
http://etext.virginia.edu/railton/
```

Twain on stage, references to specific works, and marketing Twain are some of the links on this page.

MARK TWAIN LIBRARY

http://cadsweb.colorado.edu/twain/

The creator of this page is putting together links to Twain resources. Good links to essays and short stories and other Web sites.

MARK TWAIN ON THE NET

http://www.lm.com/~joseph/mtwain.html

Biographical information, links to stories and discussions.

MARK TWAIN RESOURCES ON THE WEB

http://marktwain.miningco.com/

Another site for links; exhibits, biography and criticism, works, teaching resources.

MARK TWAIN'S HOME

http://webster.commnet.edu/corr/oct_95/jo.htm

From someone who lived nearby, this mostly text description of Twain's home offers some insights into his life and times.

SHAKESPEARE CLASSROOM

http://www.jetlink.net/~massij/shakes/

A good place to begin looking for all things Bard.

SHAKESPEARE ON THE WEB

http://daphne.palomar.edu/shakespeare/

Here you'll find some literary criticism and use of plays in education.

STEPHEN CRANE

http://www.cwrl.utexas.edu/~mmaynard/Crane/crane.html

Here you'll find some literary criticism and use of plays in education.

VERONA: A ROMEO AND JULIET ITINERARY

http://www.intesys.it/Tour/

Build a frame of reference for your students with this walking tour.

VIRTUAL VERONA TOUR

http://www.cosi.it/verona/eng/tour.html

Another site to help students understand what Verona was like.

WATERSHIP DOWN PAGE

http://www.inil.com/users/edamoth/water.html

After you read the novel, come here and compare your views or just read more about the novel.

WORKS OF SHAKESPEARE
http://the-tech.mit.edu/Shakespeare/works.html

Complete works and links to other sites.

Book Reviews

AMAZON
http://www.amazon.com/

Called "The Earth's Biggest Bookstore," they offer *New York Times* reviews and searchable titles.

AUTHORS LINKS AND INFO
http://www2.db.dk/jbs/mysthome/specaut.htm

An index to writers and their links on the Web — extensive.

BARNES & NOBLE
http://www.barnesandnoble.com/

Find more books online. Search for specific authors or titles. Shop online.

BOOKWIRE
http://www.bookwire.com/

Read the critics from *The Boston Book Review* and *Publishers Weekly*.

GBN BOOK CLUB
http://www.gbn.org/BookClub/

Search for reviews by author, title, or year.

HUNDRED HIGHLIGHTS — THE KONINKLIJKE BIBLIOTHEEK
http://python.konbib.nl/100hoogte/hh-en.html

From Holland's National Library, you'll see manuscripts and specimens from the paper history collection, plus a searchable exhibit.

Literary Variety

FOLKLORE, MYTH AND LEGENDS
http://www.ucalgary.ca/~dkbrown/storfolk.html

Take your students around the world with literature.

HYPERIZONS
http://www.duke.edu/~mshumate/hyperfic.html

Links to dozens of interactive stories.

Mythology on the Net

http://lead.csustan.edu/anthro/mythology.html

Links to mythology sources all over the world.

Pulitzer Prize Winners

http://www.pulitzer.org/winners/

List of and links to winners for the past two years.

Writing Black USA

http://www.keele.ac.uk/depts/as/Literature/amlit.black.html

Links to resources for African-American authors.

Read Some of the Great Works Online

Bartleby Library

http://www.columbia.edu/acis/bartleby/

Books online from Yeats and Frost to DuBois and Melville.

E-text Archives

http://www.etext.org/

Texts available on the Net. One such site; others are Bartleby and Gutenburg.

Modern English Collection

http://etext.lib.virginia.edu/modeng.browse.html

Links to full text versions by many authors.

Online Books Page

http://www.cs.cmu.edu/Web/books.html

Listings for 1100 books available online, and banned books information.

WRITING RESOURCES

There are numerous online writing labs (OWL) available for assisting with the writing process as well as with skill development. Purdue's site is well respected, and one of my favorites is the University of Victoria. Also worth looking into is the site from St. Cloud University.

A Great Site

UNIVERSITY OF VICTORIA WRITERS GUIDE

    http://webserver.maclab.comp.uvic.ca/writersguide/welcome.html

Excellent step-by-step instruction in the writing process.

More Sites

GUIDE TO GRAMMAR AND WRITING

    http://webster.commnet.edu/HP/pages/darling/original.htm

More writing help.

INKSPOT

    http://www.interlog.com/~ohi/inkspot/

Online magazine devoted to writing, publishing and help for young writers.

MLA-STYLE CITATIONS OF ELECTRONIC SOURCES

    http://www.cas.usf.edu/english/walker/mla.html

If your students use electronic sources, this will help them document them.

ONLINE RESOURCES FOR WRITERS

    http://www.ume.maine.edu/~wcenter/resource.html

Foreign language dictionaries, writing links, citation guides, ESL resources.

PURDUE WRITING RESOURCES

    http://owl.english.purdue.edu/

General writing concerns addressed step by step, including practice in paraphrasing.

RESEARCH PAPER.COM

    http://www.researchpaper.com/

This site boasts the "largest collection of topics, ideas, and assistance for school related research projects." Their step-by-step writing guide is excellent.

ST. CLOUD UNIVERSITY LITERACY ONLINE

    http://leo.stcloud.msus.edu/

Help with what's bothering you about your writing — very specific help for problems such as "My writing doesn't flow. It's choppy."

UNIVERSITY OF MISSOURI WRITING RESOURCES

    http://www.missouri.edu/~wleric/writehelp.html

Writing links with an aim toward publishing.

WRITE PLACE

http://www.rio.com/~wplace/

Check out writing lessons for actual practice and find other writing links.

WRITING ACROSS THE CURRICULUM

http://ewu66649.ewu.edu/WAC.html

Links to resources for writing across the curriculum.

WRITING RESEARCH PAPERS

http://owl.trc.purdue.edu/Files/94.html

Writing research papers — a step-by-step procedure.

THEATER AND DRAMA

A Great Site

THEATER CENTRAL

http://www.theatre-central.com/

The hub of Internet activity for links to all things related to theater.

More Sites

DRAMATIC EXCHANGE

http://www.dramex.org/

A site devoted to archiving and sharing scripts of plays.

ELAC ONLINE THEATER LIBRARY

http://websites.earthlink.net/~omniverse/elactheatre/library/library.htm

A wonderful set of links to theater arts, theater study, and a career center for thespians.

ENGLISH SERVER

http://english-www.hss.cmu.edu/drama/

Carnegie-Mellon University offers not only literature and humanities links, but also plays, scripts, discussions, and more.

ENGLISH VERSE DRAMA

http://etext.lib.virginia.edu/evd.html

This site is compiling links to texts of drama online plus a reference guide to data elements and their tags.

ONLINE SCRIPTS

http://www.yahoo.com/text/Arts/Drama/Plays/Web_Published/Works/

Links to scripts published online.

RESOURCES FOR SCREENWRITERS AND PLAYWRIGHTS

http://www.teleport.com/~cdeemer/scrwriter.html

Online scripts, advice for those interested in theater, and more links.

SCRIPTS-O-RAMA

http://home.cdsnet.net/~nikkoll/scripts.htm

The Webmaster at this site promises over 500 TV and movie scripts available online.

SELECTED RESOURCES

http://www.gettysburg.edu/response/ref/langdrama.html

Just a few links to theater resources.

THEATER RELATED RESOURCES

http://falcon.jmu.edu~ramseyil/drama.htm

A starting point for education resources, stagecraft, people in theater, and more.

WRITER'S GUILD OF AMERICA

http://www.wga.org/

This extensive site provides interviews with writers, research tools, helpful suggestions for writing, a newsletter, and more.

YAHOO DRAMA SEARCH

http://www.yahoo.com/Arts/Drama/

From categories from acting to directing to performance arts, find links here.

SPEECH AND DEBATE

ARCHIVES OF AMERICAN PUBLIC ADDRESS

http://douglass.speech.nwu.edu/

An archive of speeches which can be previewed by title, speaker, movement, or chronologically.

COMMUNICATING EFFECTIVELY

http://www.presentingsolutions.com/effectivepresentations.html

Information about structuring and presenting information.

GIFTS OF SPEECH

http://gos.sbc.edu/

Important women's speeches from around the world.

HISTORICAL SPEECHES

http://userwww.sfsu.edu/~sthoemke/speeches/speeches.html

Text of speeches by King, Malcolm X, and Marcus Garvey.

KEY STEPS TO EFFECTIVE PRESENTATION

http://www.access.digex.net/~nuance/keystep1.html

Another good site to help public speakers.

PRESIDENTIAL SPEECHES ARRANGED BY TOPIC

http://www.vote-smart.org/executive/sptopics.htm

Text of speeches on topics such as crime, economy, education, and affirmative action.

PUBLIC ADDRESS RESOURCES

http://douglass.speech.nwu.edu/comsrces.htm

An extensive set of links to rhetoric resources, translation tools, rhetorical terms, and more.

PUBLIC SPEAKING

http://www.sentex.net/~casaa/resources/sourcebook/acquiring-leadership-skills/public-speaking.html

Help organize yourself for a speech.

SPEECHES

http://phoenix.kent.edu/~dpowers/commdocs.html

Text of famous speeches.

SPEECHES BY WOMEN

http://www.feminist.com/art.htm

Text of speeches by Hilary Rodham Clinton, Bella Abzug, and others.

VIRTUAL PRESENTATION ASSISTANT

http://www.ukans.edu/cwis/units/coms2/vpa/vpa.htm

Help for those using their public speaking skills.

JOURNALISM

AMERICAN JOURNALISM REVIEW
http://www.ajr.org/

Articles, links to other magazines and newspapers plus job info.

CREATING A CLASS NEWSPAPER
http://interact.uoregon.edu/MediaLit/FA/MLCurriculum/LessonPaper1

Step-by-step instructions for grades 5–6.

CREATING A NEWSPAPER
http://voyager.snc.edu/lesson2web/week3/day1/newspaper.html

A lesson plan that walks you through the steps of creating a newspaper.

CREATING A NEWSPAPER ARTICLE
http://www.screen.com/mnet/eng/med/class/teamedia/newshan1.htm

Another step-by-step instruction site.

EDITOR & PUBLISHER
http://www.mediainfo.com/ephome/news/newshtm/news.htm

This site presents commentary on the Web as a communications tool.

HIGH SCHOOL JOURNALISM HOME PAGE
http://www.journalism.indiana.edu/HSJI/webpage.html

Check out their program, see their newsletter, and find other links.

JOURNALISM AND NEWS
http://www.mediahistory.com/

Links to photo galleries, archives, personalities, and historical documents.

LAUNCHPAD FOR JOURNALISTS
http://www.tribnet.com/journ.htm

An extensive list of links to news sources on the Net.

MEDIA LINK
http://www.medialinkvideonews.com/

The working journalist's source for info with daily satellite news feeds.

NATIONAL PRESS CLUB
http://town.hall.org/places/npc/

Links and information for reporters.

NEWSLETTERS, ELECTRONIC JOURNALS
http://www.nigel.msen.com/

Not personally explored, but sounds excellent.

NEWSPAPER WIZARD
http://www.ramat-negev.org.il/~ofek/english/lessons/newswiz/newswiz.htm

How to create a newspaper using a helpful wizard program found in MSWord.

QUILL MAGAZINE FOR JOURNALISTS
http://town.hall.org/places/spj/quill.html

A magazine that surveys and interprets today's journalism.

SEARCHABLE INDEX TO JOURNALISM PERIODICALS
http://dewey.lib.ncsu.edu/

A searchable list of library resources from North Carolina.

TEACHING IDEAS FOR JOURNALISM
http://www.indiana.edu/~eric_rec/ieo/journal/jourmenu.html

A few ideas for educators who teach journalism.

WWW VIRTUAL LIBRARY — JOURNALISM SECTION
http://www.cais.com/makulow/vlj.html

Links just for journalists and those in communications or media.

It's in the News

Want all the news from a variety of perspectives? Need to search for articles? Have kids who don't read newspapers and magazines? Find a place online to meet your needs.

New Trends
Keeping track of all the news!

NEWSTRACKER
http://nt.excite.com/

Search over 300 online news services for information on your topic

A Great Site
PATHFINDER

http://www.pathfinder.com/

Not only links to great magazines. Spend time searching their menus for some other terrific offerings.

Try These Sites
ALL TYPES OF MAGAZINES

http://www.enews.com/monster/

A huge site BUT has links to adult and alternative lifestyle magazines as well. Locate the magazine you want and give the students *that* address.

CNN WEB SITE

http://www.cnn.com/

Excellent news source; as good as watching on TV

CRAYON (CREATE YOUR OWN NEWSPAPER)

http://www.crayon.net/

If you could piece together your own newspaper, which sources would you use? Requires an e-mail address.

CYBERMART ONLINE

http://www.cybermart.net/

Links to online magazines listed by state and worldwide newspapers.

NATIONAL GEOGRAPHIC

http://www.nationalgeographic.com/

The well-known magazine goes online with maps, explorations, and more.

NATIONAL PUBLIC RADIO

http://www.npr.org/

The home page for this distinguished organization.

NETGUIDE MAGAZINE

http://techweb.cmp.com/techweb/ng/current/

Always a good source of Net information; sites are rated, and the articles are relevant to emerging technologies.

THE NEWSROOM

http://www.auburn.edu/~vestmon/news.html

Current affairs links and news links.

New York Times
http://www.nytimes.com/

Strong news coverage from a respected source.

Point Cast
http://www.pointcast.com/

Customized news feed — like having CNN on your computer.

Popular Mechanics
http://popularmechanics.com/

The famous magazine online; updated regularly.

Positive Press
http://www.positivepress.com/

An online newspaper delivering good news only!

San Francisco Chronicle
http://www.sfgate.com/

Contains a searchable archive for the past two years.

Smithsonian Magazine
http://www.smithsonianmag.si.edu/

Not only is the Institute online, but their well-presented magazine has a site, too. From here, you can get to the Institution site and to *Air and Space* magazine.

U.S. Newspapers Online
http://www.newslink.org/statnews.html

Find the state and then find which newspapers are online.

USA Today
http://www.usatoday.com/

Adds to your body of news sources.

Web Magazines
http://www.meer.net/~johnl/e-zine-list/index.html

A comprehensive list of e-zines; more than 1000 links.

Worldwide List of Online Newspapers
http://www.intercom.com.au/

Find what you're looking for with this major list of online newspapers.

ZIFF-DAVIS COMPUTER MAGAZINES
http://www.zdnet.com/

Extensive links to computer magazines online technology news.

Well-Known News Sites

ASSOCIATED PRESS
http://www.trib.com/NEWS/APwire.html

BBC
http://www.bbc.co.uk/

BUSINESS WIRE
http://www.businesswire.com/

THE ECONOMIST
http://www.economist.com/

FORTUNE
http://www.fortune.com/

MONEY MAGAZINE
http://www.money.com/

PC COMPUTING + OTHERS
http://www.zdnet.com/~pccomp

PEOPLE MAGAZINE
http://www.people.com/

REUTERS NEWMEDIA
http://www.yahoo.com/headlines/current/news

SAN JOSE MERCURY NEWS
http://www.sjmercury.com/

WALL STREET JOURNAL
http://wsj.com/

WASHINGTON TELECOM NEWSWIRE
wtn.com/wtn/wtn.html

News from Around the World

Find just the one you want.

http://www.newo.com/

ATHENS NEWS

http://www.dolnet.gr/Athnews/Athnews.htm

English language daily with economic news, arts, sports, back issues.

JERUSALEM POST

http://www.jpost.com/

National news and special sections including health and science.

THE KOREA HERALD

http://zec.three.co.kr/koreaherald/

A daily that prints sports and business news as well as opinion pieces.

MAXIMOV'S

http://www.maximov.com/

A Russian Web-based news service with news from MIR plus reliable, authoritative, and up-to-date political information.

THE POST

http://www.zamnet.zm/zamnet/post/post.html

A daily from Zambia.

THE STAR AND SA TIMES

http://www.satimes.press.net

From London's SA Times and South Africa, you'll find a bit of their best.

THE STAR

http://www.jaring.my/~star./

Malaysian paper offers news, technology updates, and job-seeking service.

THE SYDNEY MORNING HERALD

http://www.smh.com.au

Daily news with editorials and a place to send in your views.

MATH AND SCIENCES ONLINE

MATH SITES

Algebra and Geometry were our initial needs and are represented here more often than other areas of the field but several of these sites and those in the kid's section offer other aspects of mathematics study.

A Great Site
STREET CENTS

        http://www.halifax.cbc.ca/streetcents/

A terrific magazine for kids all about spending wisely. Articles they can relate to. For ages 10 and up.

General Math Sites

101% MATHEMATICS

        http://www.101percent.com/education/mathematics.html

Practice for algebra, geometry, calculus, and arithmetic.

APPETIZERS FOR MATH AND REASON

        http://www.cam.org/~aselby/index.html

Online problems for math and reasoning skills including algebra.

ARITHMETIC

        http://www.useekufind.com/learningquest/tmarithm.htm

Links to activities for the younger kids.

LESSON

14   SAMPLE LESSONS FOR MATH

EO   ## Grade Level: 3rd and Up

Browse

DR. MATH

http://forum.swarthmore.edu.dr.math/dr-math.html

MEGA MATHEMATICS

http://www.c3.lanl.gov/mega-math/

CORNELL MATH

http://www.tc.cornell.edu:80/Edu/MathSciGateway/math.html

Links and Bookmarks

STREET CENTS

http://www.screen.com/streetsite/topics.html

CALCULATORS

http://www-sci.lib.uci.edu/HSG/RefCalculators.html

Search Forward and Back

Computer development.
E Herman Hollerith's Punchcard reader F

Search and Cross-Reference

Fractals & Fabrics (at end of book).

ASK DR. MATH

http://forum.swarthmore.edu/dr.math/

More math help for younger students.

BASKETMATH INTERACTIVE

http://www.scienceacademy.com/BI/index.html

Very extensive online practice including map reading as well as division, decimals, and more.

BIG DADDY'S FREEWARE

http://www.dicarlolaw.com/shareware.html

Download some practice software for your kids' math skills.

CALCULATORS ONLINE

http://www-sci.lib.uci.edu/HSG/RefCalculators.html

Not just your basic calculator; too many types to mention — worth seeing.

CLEVER GAMES FOR CLEVER PEOPLE

http://www.cs.uidaho.edu/~casey931/conway/games.html

Games online, for people who like numbers.

CLICK ON BRICKS

http://tqjunior.advanced.org/3896/index2.htm

Learn to multiply with this student-created site.

CORNELL DIGITAL LIBRARY

http://moa.cit.cornell.edu/

Along with many math books and writings, you'll find the *Making of America* collection and more.

CORNELL MATH/SCIENCE GATEWAY

http://www.tc.cornell.edu:80/Edu/MathSciGateway/math.html

Wonderful set of links to general math, fractals, geometry, and more.

ELEMENTARY MATH

http://www.bottco.com/MATH.html

Links to problems, definitions, history, and more.

EXERCISES IN MATH READINESS

http://math.usask.ca/readin/menu.html

Practice algebra I and II, geometry, and trigonometry.

FRACTION TO DECIMAL CONVERSION

http://www.sisweb.com/math/general/arithmetic/fradec.htm

A table to help you learn how to convert.

GOOD NEWS BEARS STOCK MARKET PROJECT

http://www.ncsa.uiuc.edu/edu/rse/RSEyellow/gnb.html

For middle school students who want to know more about the stock market.

HOTLIST, MATH LINKS

http://sln.fi.edu//tfi/hotlists/math.html

A long list of links for math.

HUB RESOURCE FOR MATH AND SCIENCE

http://ra.terc.edu/HubHome.html

Excellent site for continuing your search for sites.

INTERACTIVE MATHEMATICS ONLINE

http://tqd.advanced.org/2647/index.html

Covering algebra, geometry, trigonometry, and an advanced math field called "chaos."

MATH

http://www.netrover.com/~kingskid/108b.html#math

Practice early concepts online, and read some stories, too.

MATH BASEBALL

http://www.funbrain.com/math/

Another fun place to practice your skills.

MATH COUNTS

http://thechalkboard.com/MC/

Practice your skills with a variety of online activities and find contests and links.

MATH DEN

http://www.actden.com/Math_Den/

Math problems online, a contest, and more links.

MATH TABLES

http://scnc.mcps.k12.mi.us/mathch.html

Addition and multiplication practice online.

MATH MANIA

http://csr.uvic.ca/~mmania/

Explore topics in higher mathematics.

MATH PRACTICE

http://www.exit109.com/~learn/mathdrill.htm

Online practice.

MATH RESOURCES

http://www.eiu.edu/~math/interest.html#fun

A list of links to math sites as well as projects and organizations.

MATH RESOURCES ON THE INTERNET

http://www.forum.swarthmore.edu/math.topics.html

Swathmore provides links for K–12 math and upper-level courses, too. Find lesson plans, software, and online help.

MATHEMATICAL ANIMATION GALLERY

http://mathserv.math.sfu.ca/Animations/animations.html

An interesting way to learn more about math.

MEGA MATHEMATICS

http://www.c3.lanl.gov/mega-math/

General help for various levels.

MIDDLE SCHOOL PROBLEM OF THE WEEK

http://tqd.advanced.org/2691/

So far there are only a few word problems here, but it's worth the visit to practice.

MONEYCENTS

http://www.kidsmoneycents.com/

Help kids learn more about handling money from knowing its history to learning about the economy.

MORE MATH LINKS

http://www.mathsoft.com/studyworks/prodinfo/swlist.htm

Links here to the Inverse Symbolic Calculator, KnotPlot, and other unusual math sites.

ONLINE EXERCISES

http://math.uc.edu/onex/demo.html

The beginnings of an idea of how to place quizzes online. A math sample is provided as well as information on how anyone can put an exercise online.

ONLINE MATH APPLICATIONS

`http://tqjunior.advanced.org/4116`

This site provides insight into real-life applications of math; and there's a stock market simulation.

STANLEY PARK CHASE

`http://schoolcentral.com/willoughby5/default.htm`

Use multiplication skills to help find the hidden gold.

VICTORIA SEARCH

`http://schoolcentral.com/necklace/vic1.htm`

Help the rabbit, answer the problem, and learn more about Victoria, British Columbia, too.

WEBMATH

`http://www.webmath.com/`

Solve some problems online. Includes everyday math, graphs, word problems, and more.

WORLD INTERNET DIRECTORY

`http://www.tradenet.it:80/links/arsocu/science_education.html`

An extensive set of links to many sites for math and science.

WOMEN MATHEMATICIANS

`http://www.scottlan.edu/lriddle/women/`

Biographies found chronologically or alphabetically.

Algebra

ALGEBRA AND COMPUTING

`http://www.comlab.ox.ac.uk/oucl/users/jonathan.bowen/algebra/`

A brief history of algebra.

ALGEBRA AND MATH RESOURCES

`http://www-atdp.berkeley.edu/1996/math/1526.Foundations/foundations5.html`

Links for teachers and students.

ALGEBRA ONLINE

`http://www.algebra-online.com/`

A place to communicate about algebra.

ALGEBRA PROJECT

http://www.algebra.org/

An online project for kids and teachers.

GIRLS TO THE FOURTH POWER

http://www-leland.stanford.edu/~meehan/xyz/girls4.html

A tutorial program for middle grade and high school girls in algebra.

HAWAII ALGEBRA LEARNING PROJECT

http://www.ed.hawaii.edu/Info/Algebra/home.html

A beginning algebra program that stimulates students to think.

INTERNET RESOURCES FOR MODERN ALGEBRA

http://www.forum.swarthmore.edu/advanced/modern.alg.html

An extensive set of links for those interested in modern algebra.

LANGUAGE OF ALGEBRA

http://www.bose.valencia.cc.fl.us/math/robinson/mat0020/ch3_20.htm

Definitions and examples of terms.

MATH FORUM

http://forum.swarthmore.edu/

Wonderful site with links for teachers, students, key issues, and math education.

SHORT COURSE IN ALGEBRA

http://www.hsu.edu/faculty/worthf/algebra.html

Just like it sounds.

Geometry

BUG'S FRACTAL ART PARADE

http://www.itsnet.com/~bug/fractals.html

Hundreds of examples of organic math (busy site — may take time to access).

FRACTAL EXPLORER

http://www.vis.colostate.edu/~user1209/fractals/index.html

More work with fractal concepts — one of several sites devoted to fractals.

FRACTAL MICROSCOPE

http://www.ncsa.uiuc.edu/Edu/Fractal/Fractal_Home.html

Interactive tool for exploring fractal patterns.

FRACTORY

http://tqd.advanced.org/3288/

For creating and exploring fractals, some students have created this interactive Web site.

GEOMETRY CENTER

http://www.geom.umn.edu/

From the University of Minnesota come links to downloadable software and other resources.

GEOMETRY IN ACTION

http://www.ics.uci.edu/~eppstein/geom.html

A good start at explaining where those concepts are really used — worth a look.

GEOMETRY PROBLEMS

http://tqd.advanced.org/2918/

Students have posted some geometry problems in Spanish and English.

GEOMETRY THROUGH ART

http://forum.swarthmore.edu/~sarah/shapiro/shapiro.drawing.diameters.html

Another unusual way to practice this subject.

INTERACTIVE GEOMETRY

http://www.geom.umn.edu/apps/gallery.html

Offering ways to make the subject interactive, from the University of Minnesota.

INTRODUCTION TO GEOMETRY

http://tqd.advanced.org/2609/

From students, problems, explanations and a final exam to help learn geometry.

LESSONS IN GEOMETRY

http://jwilson.coe.uga.edu/emt669/Student.Folders/Godfrey.Paul/work/euclid/start.html

History, explanations, and more.

STORYBOOK OF GEOMETRY

http://tqd.advanced.org/3654/

Here are just a few problems relating geometry to real-world situations.

VRML GEOMETRY TEACHER

http://www.voicenet.com/~techno/geom.html

Presents geometric images in 3D.

Calculus

Calculus, an Overview
http://home1.gte.net/paulp/calculus/practice.htm

Find integration practice problems here.

Calculus @ Internet
http://www.calculus.net/labs

Resources for students and instructors investigating calculus on the Net.

Calculus Lesson Plans
http://forum.swarthmore.edu/calculus/calculus.units.html

Some help from teachers; especially for AP Calculus.

Calculus Online
http://www.seresc.k12.nh.us/www/alvirne.html

Match your skills with the kids at Alvirne High and kids around the world as you solve any of the problems online. More than 28 problems are there.

Calculus Practice Exam
http://www.shu.edu/~wachsmut/Teaching/MATH1401/

Exactly what it sounds like; practice online with four tests.

Cybercalc
http://www.npac.syr.edu:80/REU/reu94/williams/calc-index.html

An interactive learning environment for calculus from Syracuse University.

Karl's Calculus Tutor
http://www.netsrq.com/~hahn/calculus.html

Some online instruction and practice in a site that is just beginning to grow.

Math Archive
http://archives.math.utk.edu/calculus/crol.html

Links to more calculus resources online.

Writing Assignments in Calculus
http://www.stolaf.edu/people/ratliff/writing.html

Samples of writing assignments used at St. Olaf College, complete with checklist for grading.

Science Sites

As you might expect, the Net is filled with valuable sites for science. Some of the most beneficial interactive sites have been developed for this area.

New Trends
Animations and tutorials.

Learning Matters of Chemistry
http://www.knowledgebydesign.com/tlmc/tlmc.html

Wonderful use of animation and images to teach chemistry.

G.Tek Cyber School
http://www.gtekil.com/distance

Sound, 3D diagrams, and music are part of the tutorials on static electricity and more.

Great Sites
ExploraNet
http://www.exploratorium.edu/

Just a wonderful site of hands-on science exhibits and information.

Weird Science
http://www.southern.edu/people/jrkorson/kidhumor.html

Kids answers for those really tough science questions. A fun read.

General Science

African Americans in Science
http://www.lib.lsu.edu/lib/chem/display/faces.html

Profiled here are African-American men and women who have contributed to the advancement of science and engineering.

Almanac of Disasters
http://disasterium.com/

Click on a date and find out where and when disasters happened.

Anatomy Modules
http://www.rad.washington.edu/AnatomyModuleList.html

Information and pictures to help in the study of anatomy.

LESSON

15

SAMPLE SCIENCE LESSONS

EO **Grade Level: 3rd and Up**

Browse

PATHFINDER — KIDS' STUFF

> http://www.pathfinder.com/

DISCOVERY CHANNEL

> http://www.discovery.com/

Links and Bookmarks

FROG DISSECTION

> http://curry.edschool.Virginia.EDU/go/frog/menu.html
> http://george.lbl.gov/ITG.hm.pg.docs/dissect/info.html

Search Forward and Back

MEDICAL BREAKTHROUGHS: PENICILLIN

> http://spin.lhsc.on.ca/about/medical.htm
> http://www.ivanhoe.com/

SEARCH AND CROSS-REFERENCE

> Wagons lesson
> The scavenger hunt

BEAKMAN AND JAX

> http://www.youcan.com/

Not only can you learn why your feet smell, but you can find more from the strange science guys.

BIOMES

> http://www.cotf.edu/ete/modules/msese/earthsys.html

Find interesting information about biomes.

BUGS IN THE NEWS

http://falcon.cc.ukans.edu/~jbrown/bugs.html

A series of short papers designed to get students interested in science.

DISCOVERY CHANNEL

http://www.discovery.com/

Just as terrific as the cable channel — worth a visit.

ELECTRONIC ONLINE SCIENCE JOURNALS

http://www.unix5.nysed.gov

New York State Education Department provides links to many educational areas.

ENVIRONMENTAL ORGANIZATION WEB DIRECTORY

http://www.webdirectory.com/

Agriculture, energy, wildlife, and more areas are available to search for environmental information.

FRANKLIN INSTITUTE SCIENCE MUSEUM

http://sln.fi.edu/

Visit several online exhibitions here, including one on the heart and links to other resources.

FISHER SCIENTIFIC

http://www.fisheredu.com/

Another great effort at bringing science to the Net.

HELPING YOUR CHILD LEARN SCIENCE

http://www.ed.gov/pubs/parents/Science/

An online book for parents and teachers with activities you can try.

MAD SCIENTIST NETWORK

http://medinfo.wustl.edu/~ysp/MSN/

Get answers to some science questions here.

MATH/SCIENCE GATEWAY

http://www.tc.cornell.edu:80/Edu/MathSciGateway/math.html

Excellent site from Cornell with excellent links.

MUSEUM OF SCIENCE AND INDUSTRY

http://www.msichicago.org/

Wonderful online exhibits from this Chicago museum.

NATIONAL AUDUBON SOCIETY

http://www.audubon.org/

Spend some time learning more about this organization and its work.

NATIONAL OCEANIC ATMOSPHERIC ASSOCIATION

http://www.noaa.gov/

They offer photos of submersibles and ocean creatures, plus environmental data.

NATIONAL SCIENCE FOUNDATION

http://stis.nsf.gov

Information about programs, grants, and the foundation itself.

NEW SCIENTIST

http://www.newscientist.com/

Science and technology news — worldwide.

ONLINE INTERACTIVE PROJECTS

http://quest.arc.nasa.gov:80./interactive.html

One site devoted to keeping track of interactive sites.

OREGON MUSEUM OF SCIENCE AND INDUSTRY

http://www.omsi.edu/

Make a paper helicopter, learn about the physics of fountains, and get more links.

SCIENCE FRIDAY KIDS' CONNECTION

http://www.npr.org/sfkids/index.html

At this site, aimed at the elementary crowd, kids can perform experiments about gravity, inertia, the brain, and more.

SCIENCE ONLINE

http://science-mag.aaas.org/science/

Distinguished magazine brings its expertise online.

SCIENCE QUEST

http://tqd.advanced.org/3542/

Offering science experiments in biology, chemistry, and physics at various levels of difficulty, this site includes audio explanations and education links.

SCIENCE SEARCH TOOL

http://www.fisheredu.com/v1/constr.html

An amazing search tool to locate sites for specific scientific areas. Will search more than 5000 already previewed sites.

SCIENTIFIC AMERICAN

http://www.sciam.com/

The venerable magazine is online with all the latest information and the monthly features it's so famous for.

THOMAS EDISON'S INVENTION WEB

http://home.earthlink.net/~zummos/edison/index.htm

A page dedicated to learning more about this amazing inventor.

VIRTUAL BODY

http://www.columbia.net/vobdy

A wonderful site for those who need pictures and information about the human body.

VIRTUAL CAVE

http://www.goodearth.com/virtcave.html

Images from around the world of what's inside the wonders of caves.

WEBLIOGOLOGY FOR SCIENCE

http://www.lib.lsu.edu/weblio.html#Science

Internet subject guides, including science, business, humanities, and social science.

WHY FILES

http://whyfiles.news.wisc.edu/

Explains the science behind the news.

WIND

http://sln.fi.edu/tfi/units/energy/wind.html

Facts and pictures about wind and its power from The Franklin Institute.

WIND ORGANIZATION LINKS

http://www.bwea.com/wlinks.htm

Learn more about the power behind the wind.

WOMEN IN NATURAL SCIENCES

http://www.ets.uidaho.edu/winr/

A journal aimed at women in forestry, fisheries, wildlife, and other natural science areas. The journal presents articles written by and for women, job information, and a place to advertise.

WRITING IDEAS USING IMAGINARY PLANETS
http://sln.fi.edu/planets/

Aimed at the younger student, a springboard for writing across the curriculum.

ZOO WEB
http://www.zooweb.net/

Links to zoos and aquariums online.

Science Magazines and Journals

DISCOVER MAGAZINE
http://www.discover.com/

A monthly magazine of science and technology.

NEW SCIENTIST
http://www.newscientist.com/

Another online magazine about science and technology.

POPULAR SCIENCE
http://www.popsci.com/

More science news online.

SCIENTIFIC AMERICAN
http://www.sciam.com/

Another wonderful science magazine online.

SCIENCE DAILY
http://www.sciencedaily.com/

Links to research news.

TECHNOLOGY REVIEW
http://www.techreview.com/

From MIT, an online magazine of technology and science.

Agriculture Science

AGLINKS
http://www.agpr.com/consulting/aglinks.html

A good place to start if you want more information about agriculture today.

AGRICULTURE, FARM AND RURAL

http://www.vrms.com/agri/

A North American resource guide.

AGRICULTURE, INTERNET RESOURCES

http://www.nal.usda.gov/acq/intscsel.htm

Just links and lots of them, by category.

AGRIGATOR

http://gnv.ifas.ufl.edu/WWW/AGATOR/HTM/AG.HTM

Links and resources for agriculture.

CALIFORNIA HEARTLAND

http://www.navgate.com/caheart/index.html

For more about California's agriculture and farming.

FARMNET

http://www.betabase.com/farmnet/

Another wonderful site to links for farming and agriculture.

NOT JUST COWS

http://www.snymor.edu/~drewwe/njc/

A directory of agriculture resources.

Biology

ACCESS EXCELLENCE

http://www.gene.com/ae/

For biological sciences: lesson plans as well as Probeware, which offers experiments and activities. Click on 21st century and you'll find Probeware.

BIOLOGIST'S GUIDE TO INTERNET RESOURCES, CENTER FOR SCIENTIFIC COMPUTING

finsun.csc.fi http://www.csc.fi/english/netnews.html

This site offers several links for anyone interested in biology studies.

BIOLOGY PLACE

http://www.biology.com/

You'll have to pay $10 for 6 months to use the learning activities and access their articles or join a discussion group.

BIOLOGY TOPICS AT HARVARD

http://huh.harvard.edu/

Links to resources for biology.

BIOLOGY WORKSHOP

http://www.thinkquest.org/library/2848.html

Students created this site for an exploration of some of the concepts of biology.

BOCK LABORATORIES

http://www.bocklabs.wisc.edu/

Articles about infectious diseases and other aspects of biology.

CABI ANIMAL CLONING

http://www.cabi.org/whatsnew/cloneani.htm

News about the cloning of the sheep Dolly.

CELL

http://www.thinkquest.org/library/3564.html

All of the sections of this extensive site aim at teaching about cells. Informative pages, a glossary, a search tool, and a quiz are all here.

CELLS ALIVE

http://www.comet.chv.va.us/QUILL/Index1.htm

Video clips and 3D animation of cells — a good study of cells.

CLONING, SPECIAL REPORT

http://www.newscientist.com/nsplus/insight/clone/clone.html

From *New Scientist*, a special report about the status of cloning.

FUN SCIENCE

http://www.best.com/~funsci/

A variety of presentations about cells, microscopes, and other topics.

GAME OF LIFE

http://www.research.digital.com/nsl/projects/life/life.html

Grow a colony of cells — find it by clicking "Our Work."

HUMAN CLONING PLANS

http://www.npr.org/news/health/980106.cloning.html

With RealAudio, hear what one American scientist says about human cloning.

INTERACTIVE FROG DISSECTION

http://curry.edschool.virginia.edu:80/~insttech/frog

One of two such sites on the Net where you actually go through the steps.

PREVIEW THE HEART

http://sln2.fi.edu/biosci/preview/heartpreview.html

Very colorful presentation of the heart — great graphics.

SURF SITES FOR CYBERBIOLOGISTS

http://pillo.unipv.it/~marcora/surf.htm

An extensive set of links for various aspects of biology.

VIRTUAL FROG DISSECTION KIT

george.lbl.gov/vfrog/

The second of the two sites for hands-on practice.

VIRTUAL MICROSCOPE

http://www.aber.ac.uk/~dcswww/CV/scope.html

This site is just beginning to develop its promise of incorporating Internet capabilities into the teaching of microscope technology.

VISIBLE HUMAN PROJECT

http://www.nlm.nih.gov/research/visible/visible_human.html

A project designed to bring anatomically detailed, three-dimensional representations of the male and female human body online.

Chemistry

AMERICAN CHEMICAL SOCIETY

http://www.acs.org/

This organization's home page offers career information and education updates.

CATALYST

http://www.thecatalyst.org/

A resource for high school teachers to find relevant information for teaching chemistry.

CHEM 101

http://tqd.advanced.org/3310/

Students created this site to help others learn this subject.

CHEM CENTRAL

http://www.prenhall.com/~chem/

Instructor's resources for biochemistry, general and organic, and more.

CHEMISTRY EDUCATION RESOURCES

http://www-hpcc.astro.washington.edu/scied/chemistry.html

Links to sites dealing with history, software, organizations, and more.

CHEMISTRY RESOURCES

http://www.rpi.edu/dept/chem/cheminfo/chemres.html

More links for educators and students.

CHEMISTRY TEACHERS' RESOURCES

http://www.rampages.onramp.net/~jaldr/chemtchr.html

Excellent set of resources designed specifically for those who teach.

CHEMISTRY WEB

http://www.nie.ac.sg:8000/~wwwchem/l-chres.htmlx

This site has been set up as a resource for lessons, journals, conferences, and reference materials.

CHEMIST'S ART GALLERY

http://www.csc.fi/lul/chem/graphics.html

"Visualization and animations in chemistry."

CHEMIST'S WEB

http://www.lookup.com/homepages/87500/html/chem.html

American and European links for chemists.

HIGH SCHOOL CHEMISTRY TEACHING

http://chemed.chem.purdue.edu/~sreed/chemteach.html

Resources for teachers and students.

PERIODIC TABLE OF THE ELEMENTS

http://www.cs.ubc.ca/elements/periodic-table

Available whenever you need it.

UNDERSTANDING OUR PLANET THROUGH CHEMISTRY

http://helios.cr.usgs.gov/gips/aii-home.htm

Shows how chemists and geologists use analytical chemistry to determine the age of the Earth, predict volcanic eruptions, document damage from pollution, etc.

Physics

AMERICAN INSTITUTE OF PHYSICS
http://www.aip.org/

Spend time and browse their large data base of articles and information.

AMERICAN PHYSICAL SOCIETY
http://aps.org/

A good place for students to read what this organization is all about.

BANG, BOING, POP
http://tqd.advanced.org/3042/

An interactive physics tutorial created by students for students.

CONTEMPORARY PHYSICS EDUCATION PROJECT
http://pdg.lbl.gov/cpep.html

A site devoted to understanding the fundamental nature of matter and energy.

EINSTEIN REVEALED
http://www.pbs.org/wgbh/nova/einstein/

A teacher's guide helps you navigate this site devoted to the man's genius.

EXPERIMENTS ONLINE
http://www.slac.stanford.edu/FIND/explist.html

A guide to high-energy physics experiments.

FERMI NATIONAL ACCELERATOR
http://www.fnal.gov/

Go where you will find the world's most powerful particle accelerator.

FUN @ LEARNING PHYSICS
http://medb.physics.utoronto.ca/Web/website/fun.html

This site presents an on-line course on dynamics, the study of motion.

HOW THINGS WORK: PHYSICS IN EVERYDAY LIFE
http://landau1.phys.virginia.edu/Education/Teaching/HowThingsWork/

Ask questions and see answers posted here.

INTERNET PILOT TO PHYSICS
http://www.tp.umu.se/TIPTOP/

A wonderful starting point for a virtual lab, online resources, a physics forum, and more.

INTERACTIVE PHYSICS PROBLEM SET
http://info.itp.berkeley.edu/Vol1/Contents.html

This site will take you step by step through an interactive problem.

PHYSICS IN THE AMUSEMENT PARK
http://tqd.advanced.org/2745/data/openpark.htm

Students created a site exploring the physics behind amusement park rides.

PHYSICS OF PROJECTILE MOTION
http://tqd.advanced.org/2779/

In response to a contest, this site was created bringing a short history of projectile motion plus some samples.

PHYSICS RESOURCES
http://marie.surrey.ac.uk/cti/extlinks.html

Lots of information and links from the U.K.

UNIVERSITY OF CALIFORNIA AT BERKELEY PHYSICS DEMO LAB
http://www.mip.berkeley.edu/physics/physics.html

An effort to bring demonstration online.

Sociology

AGNES SCOTT COLLEGE, SOCIOLOGY RESOURCES
http://www.scottlan.edu/fac_adv/soc.htm

Links focusing on opinion polls and data collection as they pertain to sociology.

CULTURE, POWER AND SOCIAL ACTION ON THE INTERNET
http://robotweb.ri.cmu.edu/~ppan/Essays/Maddox_essay.html

An essay concerning the Internet and sociology.

HARVARD UNIVERSITY SOCIOLOGY DEPARTMENT
http://wjh-www.harvard.edu/~mcdermot/Sociology.html

From Harvard, links to specific areas of study of interest to sociologists such as aging, children, culture, and mental health.

LINKS TO RESOURCES
http://147.26.186.101/areas.htm

Another set of links to Internet resources for sociology.

SOCIOLOGY

http://www.mcli.dist.maricopa.edu/~long/source/sociology.html

Other sources to try for information including census data and links to other Net sites.

SOCIOLOGY LIST OF HYPERLINKS

http://edie.cprost.sfu.ca/~rhlogan/raj.html

A short list of links to Web resources.

SOCIOLOGY RELATED LINKS

http://www.nvg.unit.no/~rowan/sociology.html

Sociology links to European and North American sites

SOCIOLOGY RESOURCES

http://blair.library.rhodes.edu/anthhtmls/socnet.html

An extensive set of links to Net sites, journals, references, and more.

Astronomy/Space

ASTRONOMY AND SPACE LINKS

http://www.servtech.com/~mvail/astronomy.html

The Digital Librarian provides numerous links.

ASTRONOMY ON THE WEB

http://www.stsci.edu/astroweb/astronomy.html

An extensive set of links for telescopes, people, data, organizations, and the research surrounding astronomy.

ASTRONOMY MAGAZINE

http://www.kalmbach.com/astro/astronomy.html

A magazine just for the astronomy enthusiast.

ASTRO WEB

http://www.stsci.edu/science/net-resources.html

Links for anyone interested in astronomy.

AWESTRUCK BY THE MAJESTY OF THE HEAVENS

http://www.adler.uchicago.edu/awestruck/

View some beautiful artistic illustrations of the heavens.

CASSINI MISSION

http://www.jpl.nasa.gov/Cassini/

Find out about the international venture to explore Saturn and its moon Titan.

EDMONTON SPACE AND SCIENCE CENTRE

http://www.ee.ualberta.ca/essc/

Take a tour of the Centre and find links to other science centers.

KENNEDY SPACE CENTER

http://www.ksc.nasa.gov/ksc.html

Shuttle information, viewing launches, archives about other flights, and more.

NASA HOME PAGE

http://www.gsfc.nasa.gov/NASA_homepage.html

Well-respected home page full of information and links.

NASA'S ONLINE RESOURCES

http://quest.arc.nasa.gov/OER/EDRC25.html

An extensive set of links from one of the best.

NINE PLANETS

http://www.npr.org/sfkids/

National Public Radio's previously broadcast programs with audio.

VIEWS OF THE UNIVERSE

http://www.geocities.com/CapeCanaveral/Hangar/2671/

Explore the solar system, learn some space terms, check on satellites, and more.

VOYAGER HOME PAGE

http://vraptor.jpl.nasa.gov/voyager/voyager.html

Be part of the exploration with pictures, data, a tour, descriptions, and more.

WINDOWS TO THE UNIVERSE

http://www.windows.umich.edu/

This site includes "images, movies, animations, and data sets, that explore the Earth and Space sciences and the historical and cultural ties between science, exploration, and the human experience."

Environmental/Earth

AMAZON INTERACTIVE
http://www.eduweb.com/amazon.html

You'll find an "Ecotourism Simulation" and other interactive activities, all designed to help students learn about the rainforest. Suitable for middle school on up.

AMERICAN FORESTS
http://www.amfor.org/

Find out what this organization is doing to save our forests, and plant a tree online.

AUSTRALIAN NATIONAL BOTANIC GARDENS
http://155.187.10.12/anbg/index.html

Just one of several gardens online that you can tour with.

CONSERVATION INTERNATIONAL
http://www.conservation.org/

Spend some time browsing through their articles and offerings.

CORAL REEFS AND MANGROVES
http://ibm590.aims.gov.au/

Wonderful colorful exploration that takes you under the ocean to view the beauty of some reefs.

EARTH SCIENCE RESOURCES
http://www.unige.ch/sciences/terre/esr/

Find some great links here.

EARTH SCIENCES DIRECTORY
http://sdcd.gsfc.nasa.gov/ESD/

From NASA, a place for information and links.

EARTHQUAKE AND WEATHER STATION
http://www.geocities.com/SiliconValley/3452/weather1.html

Up-to-date information for weather watchers.

EARTHQUAKES WORLDWIDE
http://www.civeng.carleton.ca/cgi-bin/quakes

Extensive information for those interested in earthquakes.

Envirolink

http://www.envirolink.org/

One of the largest resources for environmental education on the Net. Beautiful, colorful pictures.

Environmental Education Network

http://www.envirolink.org/enviroed/

A great resource for students and teachers of earth sciences.

Environmental News Network

http://www.enn.com/

Searching major newspapers daily for environmental news and putting it all in one place.

Geo Site

http://www.acc.umu.se/~widmark/wgeolog.html

For geologists — a good site.

Global Show and Tell Museum

http://www.telenaut.com/gst

A museum created by and for kids 2–17 with exhibits about endangered species.

Indonesian Tropical Rain Forest

http://www.geocities.com/RainForest/3678/

A virtural tour of the endangered forest and species that live there.

International Weather

http://www.weather.com/weather/int/regions.htm#europe

How's the weather in Europe, Asia or other places? Find out here.

Library of Environmental Writing

http://www.people.virginia.edu/~djp2n/library.html

Online texts that "address aspects of human interaction with the environment." Makes for a wonderful reading list.

Living Together in Harmony with Nature

http://www.stratosphere.org/projects/fpage008.html

From future cities and ecology in housing, this site teaches how to live in harmony with nature.

MEER

http://www.meer.org/

Marine and environmental education information and links.

NATIONAL WILDLIFE FEDERATION

http://www.nwf.org/

Check out the kids page with Ranger Rick and find environmental lessons and activities.

NATURE

http://www.nature.com/

The wonderful magazine online.

NAVIGATING THE WORLD

http://www.goals.com/

Several voyages are documented here in first-person accounts and photos.

NETSPEDITION AMAZON

http://sunsite.doc.ic.ac.uk/netspedition/

A site devoted to showing how a scientific expedition can be carried out using the Internet.

OCEAN PLANET

http://seawifs.gsfc.nasa.gov/ocean_planet.html

Environmental area, very well done. Designed to make us think about what we can do to conserve the ocean.

SCORECARD

http://www.scorecard.org/

Go here to see if your area is polluted and by what.

U.S. GEOLOGICAL SURVEY MAPS

http://www-nmd.usgs.gov/

Interesting materials to add to the study of the Earth.

VOLCANO WORLD

http://volcano.und.nodak.edu/

Pictures, updates on volcanic activity, and access to experts.

WEATHER CHANNEL

http://www.weather.com/

Check out the local weather or weather in another part of the world.

WEATHER UNDERGROUND
http://groundhog.sprl.umich.edu/

Resources and images and downloadable software for viewing weather imagery.

WOODS HOLE OCEANOGRAPHIC INSTITUTE
http://www.whoi.edu/

Information for such areas as ocean physics, biology, and chemistry, as well as a search engine.

WORLD ANIMAL NET
http://worldanimal.net/

Links to societies interested in the care of animals.

Psychology

METHODS IN BEHAVIORAL RESEARCH
http://methods.fullerton.edu/

The author of this text has posted chapters on scientific understanding of behavior, research methods, studying behavior, and Web links.

PSYCHCRAWLER
http://www.psychcrawler.com/

This is simply a searchable database helping to locate sites for those interested in psychology. Links to other sites are also provided.

PSYCHOLOGY LINKS
http://sacam.oren.ortn.edu/~jabutt/psych.html

Another set of links — as extensive and somewhat broader in coverage.

PSYCHOLOGY LINKS FROM LYCOS
http://a2z.lycos.com/Science_and_Technology/Psychology/

Connections to many aspects of psychology, including organizations, archives, research, theories, and more.

PSYCHOLOGY RESOURCES
http://s.psych.uiuc.edu/

From the University of Illinois, extensive links for psychology.

PSYCHOLOGY SITES IN BRITISH ISLES
http://online.anu.edu.au/psychology/PiP/bipsych.htm

An amazing set of links to sites from Aberdeen to York.

SCHOOL PSYCHOLOGY RESOURCES ONLINE

http://mail.bcpl.lib.md.us/~sandyste/school_psych.html

Links to sites about ADD, autism, learning disabilities, and more.

TESTS, TESTS, TESTS

http://www.queendom.com/index1.html

Samples of personality, IQ, attitude, and lifestyle tests.

SOCIAL STUDIES, LANGUAGES, COLLEGE, AND CAREERS

HISTORY AND GOVERNMENT SITES

Historical information is abundant on the Net and shows a major focus of Net activity for many universities.

New Trends

So many wonderful sites exist for history and historians. I placed a special file on the CD-ROM with some of the best that I've found. Enjoy!

A Good place to Begin

AMERICAN MEMORY

http://rs6.loc.gov/amhome.html

Trace America's cultural history with photos, documents, film, and recordings.

Civil War

ANDERSONVILLE TRIAL

http://www.law.umkc.edu/faculty/projects/ftrials/wirz/wirz.htm

Excerpts and impact of this civil war trial

BLUE AND GRAY MAGAZINE

http://www.bluegraymagazine.com/

A bi-monthly online magazine featuring the works of Civil War historians

LESSON

16

SAMPLE LESSONS FOR HISTORY

EO   **Grade Level: 3rd and Up**

Browse

TRAINS AROUND THE WORLD

    http://tqd.advanced.org/3253/

TOUR THE WHITE HOUSE

    http://www.whitehouse.gov/

HISTORY CHANNEL

    http://www.historychannel.com/

Links and Bookmarks

PICTURE TOURS OF ANCIENT CIVILIZATIONS

    http://www.ancientsites.com/
    http://www.raingod.com/angus/Misc/SiteMap.html

TOURS OF U.S. CAPITOL WITH LINKS TO MONTICELLO, VALLEY FORGE, AND THE WHITE HOUSE

    http://www.monticello.org/index.html
    http://www.libertynet.org:80/mmp/vr/

Search

SITES FOR TEACHERS: CROSSROADS

    http://ericir.syr.edu/Virtual/Lessons/crossroads/

FORWARD AND BACK — TRANSPORTATION: FREEWAYS AND THEIR VEHICLES

    http://db.photovault.com/
    http://www.nhm.org/petersen/index1.htm
    http://hfm.umd.umich.edu/index.html
    http://virtualroadtrip.com/

Search and Cross-Reference

    Civil War letters lesson

CIVIL WAR CYBER FIELD TRIP

http://tqd.advanced.org/2678/

Battle by battle, this site takes you, chronologically, through the events of the Civil War with descriptions and pictures.

CIVIL WAR DIARIES AND LETTERS

http://genealogy.org:80/~jmorris/cw/cwletter.htm

Additional historical perspectives.

CIVIL WAR HOME PAGE

http://sunsite.utk.edu/civil-war/

One of the most complete collections of information.

CIVIL WAR PHOTOGRAPHS

http://rs6.loc.gov/cwphome.html

From some of the noted photographers of the time, this site offers an amazing view of the war.

CIVIL WAR MEDICINE

http://www.powerweb.net/bbock/war/

Information about Civil War medical technology.

CIVIL WAR TIMELINE

http://www.historyplace.com/civilwar/index.html

Keep the names, dates and places straight.

LETTERS FROM A SOLDIER

http://www.ucsc.edu/civil-war-letters/home.html

What was the experience like from one in the battle? Read one soldier's letters.

LIBRARY OF CONGRESS CIVIL WAR HOME PAGE

http://rs6.loc.gov/cwphome.html

Extensive links to prints and photographs as well as a timeline; presented by year, with photographs, too.

LOVE LETTERS OF THE CIVIL WAR

http://scholar2.lib.vt.edu/spec/cwlove/cwlove.html

Copies of letters written to and from soldiers of the Civil War.

VALLEY OF THE SHADOW

http://jefferson.village.virginia.edu/vshadow/vshadow.html

Two towns were on either side of the Mason–Dixon Line; this is their well-documented story.

Historical Documents

ELECTRONIC TEXTS

http://www.hum.port.ac.uk/Text/

A site offering links to the Gettysburg Address and the Magna Carta, plus other public domain texts.

HISTORICAL DOCUMENTS EXHIBITS U.S.

http://chico.rice.edu/

A good source of historical documents.

HISTORICAL TEXT ARCHIVE

http://www.msstate.edu/Archives/History/index.html

Interesting site for locating historical documents.

HISTORICAL TEXTS 1700–PRESENT

gopher://gopher.lib.ncsu.edu:70/hftp%3Aftp.msstate.edu@/docs/history/index.html

Resources at this site include links to regional, topical, and national history, and more general resources such as archives, photos, and maps.

LINKS TO HISTORICAL MAPS WORLDWIDE

http://www.carto.com/links.htm

Not only maps of Jerusalem, Canada, and the United States, but pirate maps, too!

PENNY MAGAZINE

http://www.history.rochester.edu/pennymag/

This 19th-century magazine was for the working class in England.

RARE MAP COLLECTION

http://scarlett.libs.uga.edu/darchive/hargrett/maps/maps.html

American colonial, Revolutionary War, Civil War, and maps of cities and rivers.

VOICES, VESSELS, AND VELLUM

http://ultratext.hil.unb.ca/Texts/NBHistory/VVV/

One hundred 18th-century documents online.

Ancient History

ABZU

http://www-oi.uchicago.edu/OI/DEPT/RA/ABZU/ABZU.HTML

Guide to the study of the ancient Near East.

ALEXANDER THE GREAT

http://www.1stmuse.com/frames/index.html

Information about this great leader can be found here.

ALEXANDRIE

http://www.smartweb.fr/alexandrie/

A wonderful visual tour of Alexander's palace.

ANCIENT CIVILIZATIONS OF THE MIDDLE EAST

http://tqd.advanced.org/2840/

Take an interactive tour of ancient times, places, and cultures. You pick a character to be as you travel, and you'll find your journey is different, depending on who you choose to be.

ANCIENT HISTORY

http://rome.classics.lsa.umich.edu/

Links to many aspects of ancient history.

ANCIENT HISTORY AP COLLEGE LEVEL

http://www.ucsc.edu/index.html

Help with that course of study.

ANCIENT ROME

http://www.ghgcorp.com/shetler/rome/

Links to images and other ancient civilizations.

ANCIENT WORLD WEB

http://www.julen.net/aw/

African Studies, Alexander the Great, archaeology, and links to more history.

ARCHAEOLOGICAL ADVENTURE

http://tqd.advanced.org/3011/indexge.htm

This site explores the past, the present, and the future, with an emphasis on the technlology used in explorationsm

ARCHNET

http://archnet.uconn.edu/

Archaeologists have a well-done page available in several languages.

CAMELOT PROJECT

http://www.lib.rochester.edu/camelot/cphome.stm

Pictures, Arthurian texts, and bibliographies for this era.

CHIVALRY

http://www.chronique.com/

Learn about knighthood, chivalry, and tournaments of the 14th century.

CLASSICS AND MEDITERRANEAN ARCHAEOLOGY

http://classics.lsa.umich.edu/

A large set of links to resources for the study of classical civilization.

DIOTIMA

http://www.uky.edu/ArtsSciences/Classics/gender.html

Resources for the study of women and gender in the ancient world. Excellent site with images and information. Constantly being updated.

EIGHTEENTH-CENTURY STUDIES

http://english-www.hss.cmu.edu/18th.html

From the 18th century, you'll find novels, plays, memoirs, treatises, and poems.

EUROPE'S CULTURAL ROOTS

http://ottes.got.kth.se

This site, a work in progress, promises to trace the route of cultural and economic exchange that created modern Europe.

EXPLORING ANCIENT CULTURES

http://www.evansville.edu/~wcweb/

This site includes essays, maps, quizzes, and information about Ancient Egypt, India, China, Greece, Rome, and other cultures.

GREEK CIVILIZATION HOME PAGE

http://www-adm.pdx.edu/user/sinq/greekciv/carr.html

Among topics covered here are social classes, sports, philosophers, environment, and science. Very well done page.

HELLENIC CULTURE

http://www.culture.gr/

With links to information about Ulysses and Greek culture.

HISTORY OF COSTUME

http://www.siue.edu/COSTUMES/history.html

With some wonderfully colorful pictures, this site explores costumes and clothing through the ages.

HISTORY OF MONEY

http://www.ex.ac.uk/~RDavies/arian/llyfr.html

Using excerpts from a book, learn about the origins of money and banking, the trail of war and money, plus a chronology of money.

KINGS AND QUEENS OF EGYPT

http://eyelid.ukonline.co.uk/ancient/k-q-menu.htm

Information and pictures of the great kings and queens.

LABYRINTH

http://www.georgetown.edu/labyrinth/

Links to sites for medieval studies.

MAYAS

http://www.indians.org/welker/mayamenu.htm

Stories, art, languages, Mayan life and legends are all available here.

MEDIEVAL AND RENAISSANCE HISTORY

http://www.nyu.edu/gsas/dept/history/internet/geograph/europe/medieval/

This site provides extensive links to literature, history, music, art, and other aspects of this historical period.

MEDIEVAL STUDIES WEB SITES

http://kuhttp.cc.ukans.edu/kansas/orb/websites.html

A long list of links to history, literature and art, museums

ONLINE REFERENCE BOOK FOR MEDIEVAL STUDIES

http://orb.rhodes.edu/sponsors.html

The University of Kansas has begun a project of posting essays dealing with a wide variety of topics concerning some aspect of the medieval era.

ORIGINS OF HUMANKIND

http://www.dealsonline.com/origins/

Resources and links for those studying evolution.

THE PERSEUS PROJECT

http://www.perseus.tufts.edu/

An entire project about Ancient Greece and Rome, with clickable maps and classics in Greek.

PETRA

http://www.raingod.com/angus/Gallery/Photos/MiddleEast/Jordan/Petra/index.html

Take a walking tour of Petra, a 3rd-century city in Jordan, complete with photos and commentary.

QIN DYNASTY SOURCE BOOK

http://www.geocities.com/Athens/Academy/7547/

Learn more about this Chinese dynasty.

ROME PROJECT

http://www.nltl.columbia.edu/groups/rome/

Information about the political, military, philosophical, and general life in ancient Rome.

TRIP IN TIME

http://www.escape.com/~farras/ancient.html

Some views of ancient history organized by topic or geographically.

WORLD OF THE VIKINGS

http://www.demon.co.uk/past/vikings/

A starting point for those interested in links to Viking information.

World History

ALEXANDER PALACE TIME MACHINE

http://www.alexanderpalace.org/palace/

A tour with photos, floor plans, and personal stories of the last home of the Czar.

CYBRARY OF THE HOLOCAUST

http://remember.org/

This extensive site offers images of the Holocaust, books by survivors, information about the children of survivors, and links to other resources.

EMPIRES BEYOND THE GREAT WALL

http://vvv.com/khan/

Extensive historical collection about the heritage of Genghis Khan.

THE INCA TRAIL

http://www.raingod.com/angus/Gallery/Photos/SouthAmerica/Peru/IncaTrail.html

Take a walking tour to Machu Picchu with text and photos. Nice tour.

LA SALLE PROJECT

http://www.thc.state.tx.us/belle/

An extensive site detailing the exploration of a wrecked ship belonging to the explorer.

THE MATTHEW

http://www.matthew.co.uk/

Learn more about John Cabot and the ship he sailed on.

MAYA QUEST

http://www.mecc.com/mayaquest.html

Wonderful site exploring the Mayan civilization.

NAPOLEON SERIES

http://www.ping.be/~ping5895/

Find information about this ruler here.

ROYAL PALACE

http://www.camelotintl.com/royal/index.html

Information about current and historical royals.

ROYAL RUSSIA

http://www.angelfire.com/pa/ImperialRussian/index.html

A site maintained by the Imperial Russian Historical Society which provides excellent information about the Russian Royals

SEARCHING FOR CHINA — A WEB QUEST

http://www.kn.pacbell.com/wired/China/ChinaQuest.html

A model of how Internet resources can be pulled together to create a wide-ranging virtual exploration and experience.

SIGNIFICANT EVENTS

http://weber.u.washington.edu/~eckman/timeline.html

A compilation of literary and historical events from 1890 to 1940.

VICTORIAN LADY

http://www.dstylus.com/victorianlady/index.html

What was the role of women in the Civil War? Find out here.

WINSTON CHURCHILL HOME PAGE

http://www.winstonchurchill.org/

Excellent site for information about this leader.

WOMEN IN WORLD HISTORY

http://home.earthlink.net/~womenwhist/

Information and links.

WOMEN'S HISTORY

http://www.gale.com/gale/cwh/cwhbio.html

Biographies of important women, starting with Adams, Albright, and Anthony.

WOMEN'S HISTORY SOURCEBOOK

http://www.fordham.edu/halsall/women/womensbook.html

From human origins to modern times, this site offers links just about women in history.

WORLD HISTORY ACCORDING TO STUDENT BLOOPERS

http://www.nyu.edu/gsas/dept/history/internet/worldhis.html

A new address for this site, which relates history according to students — fun read!

WORLD WAR I MEMORIES

http://www.geocities.com/Athens/Acropolis/4144/mom/momentry.html

First-person perspective of the people who fought this war.

WORLD WAR II — GROLIER ONLINE

http://www.grolier.com/wwii/wwii_mainpage.html

Very extensive set of links and information, plus a quiz you can e-mail.

WW II MEMORIES

http://www.culturalbridge.com/phwwii6.htm

Site contains personal memories of the war, speeches, and other documents.

WORLD WAR II PHOTOS

http://www.geocities.com/Pentagon/Quarters/6171/

Helpful for building a visual frame of reference.

United States History

20TH-CENTURY AMERICAN HISTORY

http://www.liberty.edu/resources/library/research/subject/artsci/history/
american/american.htm

Links to major events including the Roaring 20s, the Depression, and Watergate.

AFRICAN-AMERICAN HOLOCAUST

http://www.tnp.com/holocaust/

This site will warn you of its explicit images before you access the photos. Each photo has a brief caption, and the site adds to the commentary with quotations.

AMERICA

http://www.partal.com/ciemen/america.html

Links to sites about native cultures.

AMERICAN HISTORY LINKS

http://mac94.ralphbunche.rbs.edu/history/demo.html

Starting with a tour of Philadelphia and then offering government locations, this site has extensive links.

AMERICAN STUDIES

http://tqd.advanced.org/3050/

For each unit of study in history, corresponding literary selections are suggested. Historical background information is given, along with a discussion of how the literature projected the times.

ARCHIVING EARLY AMERICA

http://earlyamerica.com/index.html

Original newspapers, maps, and writings from 18th-century America.

BLACK HISTORY

http://www.kn.pacbell.com/wired/BHM/AfroAm.html

By using Internet activities like a treasure hunt, this site explores Black History.

CALIFORNIA INDIAN LIBRARY COLLECTIONS

http://www.mip.berkeley.edu/cilc/brochure/brochure.html

Extensive information about native culture.

COLONIAL WILLIAMSBURG

http://www.wmbg.org/

A virtual tour of the historical site with pictures and information.

CONCORD REVIEW

http://www.tcr.org/

Read some essays about history.

DISPUTES IN AMERICAN HISTORY

http://tqd.advanced.org/3613/

This site is presented as a forum for students to post their opinions on the issues facing America from its formation to today.

EARLY AMERICAN REVIEW

http://earlyamerica.com/review/

A journal of fact and opinion on the people, issues, and events of 18th-century America.

ELLIS ISLAND

http://members.aol.com/EllisIsNJ/private/station.htm

An online tour of the historical gateway with pictures, quotes, and audio clips.

FAMOUS AMERICAN TRIALS

http://www.law.umkc.edu/ftrials/ftrials.htm

Interesting site with trial documents and background for Amistad, Scopes, the Rosenbergs, and more.

FAMOUS AMERICAN WOMEN

http://www.wp.com/Hirsane/women.html

Pictures and brief biographies.

FROM REVOLUTION TO RECONSTRUCTION

http://odur.let.rug.nl/~usa/

American history from Colonial period to Modern times presented in text.

GODEY'S LADIES BOOK

http://www.history.rochester.edu/godeys/

Read about and see what it was like to live in America in the 1850s, from a lady's point of view!

GUIDE TO THE U.S. CONGRESS

http://policy.net/capweb/congress.html

Find out what your Congressperson's position is on the latest issues, read speeches, and take tours.

HISTORY OF THE CHEROKEE

http://pages.tca.net/martikw/

History, images and maps, books, and newspapers.

LIFE HISTORY MANUSCRIPTS

http://lcweb2.loc.gov/wpaintro/wpahome.html

Check out "Voices from the 30s" to learn more about personal accounts of this era.

LIFE ON THE PRAIRIE

http://www.geocities.com/Athens/Olympus/4850/ZContent.htm

The pioneer's perspective with a photo essay, diary, and exhibit.

MARTIN LUTHER KING DIRECTORY

http://www-leland.stanford.edu/group/King/

Along with a biography, this site has speeches and articles.

MOUNT VERNON

http://www.mountvernon.org/

Home, background information, and more.

NATIVE AMERICAN RESOURCES

http://www.partal.com/ciemen/america.html

Wonderful site of links to resources, including tribal and government information, essays, and postings by Native Americans.

OLD STURBRIDGE VILLAGE

http://www.osv.org/

Take a walking tour through a place of history.

ONGOING VOYAGE, 1492

http://metalab.unc.edu/expo/1492.exhibit/Intro.html

An exhibition that examines the contact of early explorers with the native Americans.

PRESIDENTS

http://www.ipl.org/ref/POTUS/

Biographies, election results, notable events and more.

REMEMBERING NAGASAKI

http://www.exploratorium.edu/nagasaki/

Another unique historical perspective.

RESPONSES TO THE HOLOCAUST

http://jefferson.village.virginia.edu/holocaust/response.html

A source for researching, teaching, and learning about the Holocaust. Includes, but is not limited to, literature, philosophy, literary criticism, and theory, along with links to many other sites.

SHOAH VISUAL HISTORY FOUNDATION

http://www.vhf.org/

Videotaped testimony from Holocaust survivors, produced by Steven Spielberg.

THE SIXTIES

http://www.slip.net/~scmetro/sixties.htm

From rock 'n' roll to Kennedy and King, this site looks back at the decade.

TRAIL OF TEARS

http://www.ngeorgia.com/history/nghisttt.html

Documentation of the displacement of the Cherokees in North Georgia in 1838.

U.S. FOREIGN POLICY

http://www.mtholyoke.edu/acad/intrel/pre1898.htm

A long list of links to sites concerning U.S. foreign policy.

VIETNAM WAR HISTORY PAGE

http://www.bev.net/computer/htmlhelp/vietnam.html

This page is a starting point for links to sites pertaining to the war.

WPA LIFE HISTORIES

http://rs6.loc.gov/wpaintro/ctcat.html

First-person accounts from people who lived in Connecticut during the Great Depression.

WWII PROPAGANDA POSTERS

http://www.openstore.com/posters

An extensive collection of the posters that fired up Americans.

General History

BASIC DEMOGRAPHIC TRENDS 1980–1990

http://theuse.esd.scarolina.edu/

Something useful to add to research.

BIOGRAPHY

http://www.biography.com/

The *Biography* show from cable TV is online, with lots of information parallelling their shows.

BRITAIN AT WAR EXPERIENCE

http://www.britain-at-war.co.uk/second.html

Information and some pictures of their experience.

CENSUS

http://chico.rice.edu/

Just a bit of demographic information you might need.

DISTINGUISHED WOMEN OF THE PAST AND PRESENT

http://www.netsrq.com:80/~dbois/

Biographies of women who contributed to our culture in many ways.

EXPO — WWW EXHIBIT ORGANIZATION

http://metalab.unc.edu/expo/expo/busstation.html

From here you can visit the following: Vatican, Soviet Archive, 1492 Project, Dead Sea Scrolls, and more.

FAMOUS WOMEN

http://mustang.coled.umn.edu/exploration/Women.html

More extensive biographies of women to the present.

GOVERNMENT LINKS

http://gaia.sci-ed.fit.edu/InfoTechSys/resources/#government

A few different links, including the Army and the Marines.

HISTORY LINKS

http://history.cc.ukans.edu/history/index.html

This is a site that takes a while to load, from the sheer volume of links to every aspect of history imaginable.

HISTORY NET

http://www.thehistorynet.com/

Historical information from the National Historical Society.

HISTORY TRAVEL

http://www.historytravel.com/

If you like to include historic sites in your travels, or just want your kids to know where history happened, try this site.

HYPERHISTORY

http://www.hyperhistory.com/

A new project designed to bring historical information online — including a color-coded chart of scientific, cultural and political events. Very extensive.

INTERDISCIPLINARY 19TH-CENTURY STUDIES

http://www.nd.edu/~incshp/

Calls for papers for their conference are here.

NOTABLE CITIZENS OF PLANET EARTH

http://www.tiac.net/users/parallax/

More than 18,000 people who have influenced history can be located in a searchable data base. Also offered is a Master Biographer Challenge game to test your knowledge.

RECENT HISTORY, UP CLOSE AND PERSONAL

http://tqd.advanced.org/3483/

This student-created site presents personal remembrances of events such as the Depression, World War II, the Holocaust, and more.

RESOURCES FOR MILITARY HISTORY

http://www.army.mil/cmh-pg/

Links to many sources about military history,

RETRO

http://www.retroactive.com/

This site collects classic 20th-century American cultural items such as postcards and holiday items; also has articles of information about pop culture.

RULERS

http://www.geocities.com/Athens/1058/rulers.html

Past and present political leaders.

SOCIAL STUDIES LESSON PLANS

http://bvsd.k12.co.us

Help from other educators.

STATUE OF LIBERTY

http://www.nps.gov/stli/prod02.htm

Learn more about the famous statue from their official Web site.

TENEMENT MUSEUM

http://www.wnet.org/tenement/eagle.html

First-person accounts of life in New York in the 1930s and 1940s.

Geography

ALEXANDRIA DIGITAL LIBRARY

http://alexandria.sdc.ucsb.edu/

International map, gazetteer, and statistical information.

ALTAPEDIA

http://www.atlapedia.com/

Maps and statistics for most countries of the world.

BUBL LINK

http://link.bubl.ac.uk/geography/

Geography information for the world, as well as historical geography.

CENTER FOR WORLD INDIGENOUS STUDIES

http://www.halcyon.com/FWDP/

Learn about other peoples and places with cooperation as the goal.

COUNTRY STUDY

http://lcweb2.loc.gov/frd/cs/cshome.html

From the Library of Congress, studies of 85 countries, including history, geography, and current statistics.

GLOBAL HISTORY CONSORTIUM

http://www.stockton.edu/~gilmorew/consorti/index.html

Presenting history information for all continents.

GLOBAL STATS

http://home.worldonline.nl/~quark/index.html

Statistics and profiles of the countries of the world.

HISTORICAL ATLAS OF EUROPE AND THE MIDDLE EAST

http://maps.linex.com/map.html

Combining colorful historical maps with text, this site explores history from 3000 BC to the present.

INFONATION

http://www.un.org/Pubs/CyberSchoolBus/infonation/e_infonation.htm

Compare statistics for the countries of the United Nations.

INTERNET RESOURCES FOR PHYSICAL GEOGRAPHY

http://www.uwsp.edu/acaddept/geog/physgeo.htm

Another set of links — very extensive.

MAPBLAST

http://www.mapblast.com/

Another way to find your way around . . . interactive atlas.

MAPQUEST

http://www.mapquest.com/

An interactive atlas that pinpoints a street address you type in. United States available now.

MAPS ON US

http://www.mapsonus.com/

An interactive way to plan your trip with directions, zoom-in maps, and driving time.

NATIONAL ATLAS

http://www-atlas.usgs.gov/

U.S. maps and more to help promote geographic awareness.

UNITED STATES HISTORICAL CENSUS BROWSER

http://icg.fas.harvard.edu/~census/

From 1790 to 1970, learn more about the United States.

U.S. DEPARTMENT OF ED. — HELPING YOUR CHILD LEARN GEOGRAPHY

http://www.ed.gov/pubs/parents/Geography/index.html

A mostly text site offering ideas to help your child learn some of the principles of geography.

U.S. CULTURAL MAPS

http://xroads.virginia.edu/~MAP/map_hp.html

Along with maps from 1775 to 1920 showing U.S. expansion, this site offers links to more historical maps.

WHERE?

http://www.standard.net.au/~garyradley/WhereMenu.htm

Games, tutorials, and fun with geography — by country.

WHERE WOULD YOU LIKE TO GO?

http://www.ehnr.state.nc.us/EHNR/files/usa.htm

A clickable map takes you to all of the United States.

WORLDTIME

http://www.worldtime.com/

An interactive atlas with world times and a database of world holidays.

WWW VIRTUAL LIBRARY — GEOGRAPHY

http://www.icomos.org/WWW_VL_Geography.html

Find links here for those interested in geography.

United States Government

BIOGRAPHICAL DICTIONARY

http://www.s9.com/biography/

Brief information about thousands of historical figures.

CENTERS FOR DISEASE CONTROL

http://www.cdc.gov/

CENTRAL INTELLIGENCE AGENCY

http://www.odci.gov/cia

CONSUMER INFORMATION. CATALOG

http://www.gsa.gov/staff/pa/cic/cic.htm

DEPARTMENT OF AGRICULTURE

http://www.usda.gov/

DEPARTMENT OF EDUCATION

http://www.ed.gov/

DEPARTMENT OF ENERGY

http://www.apollo.osti.gov/home.html

DEPARTMENT OF HEALTH AND HUMAN SERVICES

http://www.os.dhhs.gov/

DEPARTMENT OF STATE

http://www.state.gov/

A terrific source of international news, policies, and travel advisories.

FBI

http://www.fbi.gov/

FEDERAL JUDICIARY

http://www.uscourts.gov/

News and updates about the federal court system.

FEDERAL WEB LOCATOR

http://www.law.vill.edu/fed-agency/fedwebloc.html

FEDWORLD INFORMATION NETWORK

http://www.fedworld.gov/

FOOD AND DRUG ADMINISTRATION

http://www.fda.gov/

A search feature, plus information ranging from animal testing in cosmetics to a seafood encyclopedia.

GOVERNMENT PRINTING OFFICE

http://www.access.loc.gov/

HOUSE OF REPRESENTATIVES

http://www.house.gov/

LIBRARY OF CONGRESS LEGISLATIVE INFORMATION.

http://www loc.gov/

NATIONAL PARK SERVICE

http://www.nps.gov/

Get information on specific parks with photos and directions.

NOTABLE CITIZENS OF PLANET EARTH

http://www.s9.com/biography/

Over 18,000 people who have influenced history can be located in a searchable database. Also offered is a Master Biographer Challenge game to test your knowledge.

SENATE GOPHER SERVICE

gopher://gopher.senate.gov/11/

SUPREME COURT DECISIONS

www.law.cornell.edu/supct/supct.table.html

TOUR OF U.S. GOVERNMENT

http://www.electricpencil.com/enter/archive/4.html

This site offers links to tours of most areas of the U.S. government.

UNITED NATIONS

http://www.pbs.org/tal/un/

This is a very extensive tour with comprehensive background and historical information.

UNITED NATIONS

http://www.un.org/

U.S. CENSUS BUREAU

http://www.census.gov/

U.S. DEPARTMENT OF JUSTICE

http://www.usdoj.gov/

U.S. FISH AND WILDLIFE SERVICE

http://www.fws.gov/

Take your kids here to learn about land, lakes, fish, fowl, and more.

U.S. INFORMATION SERVICE

http://www.usia.gov/usis.html

Guide to services, issues, initiatives, etc.

UNITED STATES SENATE

http://www.senate.gov/

WHITE HOUSE

http://www.whitehouse.gov/

Government in Action

CAPWEB

http://www.voxpop.org/

Find the Jefferson Project here and find government information.

CENTER FOR DEMOCRACY AND TECHNOLOGY

http://www.cdt.org/

Interesting information and views.

FUTURE OF DEMOCRACY

http://tqd.advanced.org/3154/

A student-created site explaining the history of democracy, voting issues, and educational issues facing a democracy.

GOVBOT

http://cobar.cs.umass.edu/ciirdemo/Govbot/

A searchable data base of government Web sites.

GPO GATE

http://www.gpo.ucop.edu/

A site designed to help citizens access the laws, regulations, data, and other government sources they need.

INTERNATIONAL RELATIONS RESEARCH ARCHIVE

http://www.irra.org/

Search by topic or author for articles, dissertations, and other research materials pertaining to international relations.

OYEZ, OYEZ, OYEZ

http://oyez.nwu.edu/

With RealAudio, hear the arguments of many important Supreme Court cases.

POLICY.COM

http://www.policy.com/

Policy news, briefings, and a range of viewpoints. A new issue is discussed daily.

POLITICS NOW

http://www.politicsnow.com/

A joint effort from ABC News, *Newsweek*, and others to cover the political scene.

PRESIDENTIAL DECISIONS

http://www.theAtlantic.com/atlantic/election/connection/decision/decision.htm

From *The Atlantic Monthly*, discussions about the election issues.

REINVENTING AMERICA

http://pathfinder.com/@@jKhLWmPdHAMAQEi*/reinventing/

Be part of the political process in the works.

Titanic Virtual Trial

http://www.andersonkill.com/titanic/

A mock trial, based on the events surrounding the sinking of the *Titanic*, provides a lesson in the U.S. judicial system.

U.S. Capitol Tour

http://tqd.advanced.org/2813/

Mixing text and graphics, historical information and current events, this tour offers an overview of Washington and its history.

Washington Weekly

http://dolphin.gulf.net/

An electronic political newsmagazine.

Multicultural

ABC Flash

http://www.abcflash.com/

An online magazine for the Asian community with articles of relevance, classified ads, extensive searchable links to other sites, and a calendar of events.

Africa Online

http://www.africaonline.com/

News, classifieds, stock markets, safaris, and more.

All the Scripts in the World

http://idris.com/scripts/Scripts.html

Presents a sample of every script used in any of the 6000 languages in the world.

Asian Community Online Network

http://www.igc.apc.org/acon/

Information and resources for Asian Americans.

Asian Enterprise

http://members.aol.com/asianent/index.html

Online magazine for Asian Pacific Americans.

Asian Voices

http://www.nyu.edu/pubs/asian.voices/

This magazine is published once a year by students at New York University and expresses their ideas, poems, writings, and opinions on issues of importance to the Asian community.

Black Enterprise Online

http://www.blackenterprise.com/

A magazine with financial strategies, business news, and information.

Channel A

http://www.channela.com/

Community information, health and wellness news, business information, and arts and entertainment coverage for the Asian community.

Cultural Studies Central

http://home.earthlink.net/~rmarkowitz/

You'll find links to African-American culture, 1990s culture, Spanish culture, postmodern culture, and more.

Gondwana Art Gallery

http://www.gondwana.com/contents.html

Beautiful photos of African masks, sculptures, and other objects.

Kwanzaa

http://www.melanet.com/kwanzaa/

The African cultural experience explored.

Multilingual Web

http://www.nyu.edu/acf/multilingual/index.html

Links to multilingual technology resources — learn about technology issues worldwide.

Museum of Tolerance

http://www.wiesenthal.com/mot/

This site explores the dynamics of racism and prejudice in America, and the history of the Holocaust.

NativeWeb

http://www.maxwell.syr.edu/nativeweb/

More from the UNIVERSITY of Kansas — this about Native Peoples

OPEN MEDIA RESEARCH INST.

http://www.omir.cz/

A site devoted to analyzing media in former Sov. Union and Eastern Europe

REAL SAIGON

http://www.realsaigon.com/

An e-zine published in Southern California to meet the needs and concerns of the Vietnamese community.

RELIVE THE SIXTIES

http://www.slip.net/~scmetro/sixties.htm

Pictures, sounds, information all about that decade.

RESOURCES FOR WOMEN'S STUDIES ON THE WEB

http://www.library.ucsb.edu/subj/women.html

Access to online journals and magazines, women's history and literature, and links to women online — very extensive

WORLD HERITAGE LIST

http://www.unesco.org/whc/heritage.htm

UNESCO's list of cultural and natural heritage.

WORLD RIGHT NOW

http://www.cam-orl.co.uk/world.html

Live camera shots of more than 140 places in the world.

African Americans on the Net

Tariq Mohammad, Techwatch editor of *Black Enterprise Magazine*, feels that the Net will be the great equalizer for African Americans, affording them equal opportunities to become part of this new medium. Many Net sites display their already impressive presence.

AFRICAN-AMERICANS IN MATH AND SCIENCE

http://tqd.advanced.org/2907/

A student-created site provides biographies of some past, present, and future scientists and mathematicians.

AFRICAN AMERICAN MOSAIC

http://lcweb.loc.gov/exhibits/african/intro.html

A resource guide for the study of Black History and Culture.

AFRICAN AMERICAN RESOURCES

http://www.rain.org:80/~kmw/aa.html

Links and a search tool for locating other resources.

BLACK ENTERPRISE MAGAZINE

http://www.blackenterprise.com/

This magazine presents business news, strategies, and resources for professionals.

BLACK FILM CENTER ARCHIVE

http://www.indiana.edu/~bfca/index.html

An archive of films by and about African Americans.

BLACK WORLD TODAY

http://www.tbwt.com/

A magazine designed for people the world over to exchange ideas, read the latest news, and do business.

CONDUIT

http://www.imhotech.com/conduit

A newsletter educating African Americans about technology.

FACES OF SCIENCE

http://www.lib.lsu.edu/lib/chem/display/faces.html

African Americans in the sciences.

NETNOIR

http://www.netnoir.com/index.html

A site for cultural, business, and entertainment news.

UNIVERSAL BLACK PAGES

http://www.gatech.edu/bgsa/blackpages.html

An extensive set of links to businesses, educational resources, the written word, history, art, and more.

WILSON BROWN GALLERY

http://www.wbgallery.com/

Presenting original works by African American artists.

WORLD AFRICAN NETWORK

http://www.worldafricannet.com/

Explore the history and culture of people of African descent. Also has articles on politics, education, and other issues.

YOUR ASSIGNMENT TODAY

http://www.studiolink.com/yatoday

An educational tool for high school students.

Law-Related Sites

Listed here are sites for anyone interested in law, legal careers, or government.

COURT TV

http://www.courttv.com/

Excellent site. Includes matching wits with the Supreme Court, and how to know if you'd make a good prosecutor.

TEEN COURT

http://tqd.advanced.org/2640/

A student-created site tells how to set up a teen court, explains the role of the participants, and even provides mock trials.

More Law-Related Sites

1000 LAW LINKS

http://seamless.com/road.html

Amazing set of references for all things legal.

ACLU

http://www.aclu.org/

Search their library for landmark cases, check congressional voting records.

ANATOMY OF A MURDER

http://tqd.advanced.org/2760/homep.htm

Follow a legally accurate murder investigation from the beginning. See court documents and learn more about the justice system.

CIVIL LIBERTIES ISSUES RELATING TO TECHNOLOGY

http://www.cdt.org/

Another site, exactly what it sounds like.

CIVNET

http://www.civnet.org/

Civics education online.

CONGRESSIONAL E-MAIL AND WEB SITES

http://wwwlib.umich.edu/libhome/Documents.center/federal.html

Want to e-mail someone in government? Start here.

CONSTITUTION OF THE UNITED STATES

http://www.law.cornell.edu/constitution/constitution.overview.html

Full text broken into its parts.

COUNSEL CONNECT

http://www.counsel.com/

Find articles on contemporary legal issues — in particular, an explanation of our court system for kids.

CRIME LABORATORY DIRECTORS HOME PAGE

http://www.ascld.org/

Information from this organization about policies, newsletters, and links to other forensics sites.

CRIMINAL JUSTICE LINKS

http://www.mitretek.org/business_areas/justice/cjlinks/index.html

Terrific site with links to areas concerning criminal justice.

CRIMINAL JUSTICE STATISTICS

http://www.ojp.usdoj.gov/bjs/

Helpful statistics on a variety of areas.

DOCUMENTS IN THE NEWS

http://www.lib.umich.edu/libhome/Documents.center/docnews.html

News headlines about subjects such as affirmative action, chemical weapons, flat tax, the marriage defense act, and others are discussed by presenting the full text of legislation, news articles, and analysis.

ELECTRONIC FRONTIER FOUNDATION

http://www.eff.org/

A non-profit, civil liberties organization, working to protect privacy, free expression, access to public resources, and information online, as well as to promote responsibility in new media.

ELECTRONIC TOWNHALL

http://www.electronic-townhall.com/

Provides a place for the user to respond to political surveys on topics such as race, environment, politics, the next generation of Americans, and others.

FEDWORLD

http://www.fedworld.gov/supcourt/index.htm#jump

This site contains a searchable data base of Supreme Court Decisions from 1930 to 1975.

FOREIGN AND INTERNATIONAL LAW

http://lawlib.wuacc.edu/washlaw/forint/forintmain.html

Information and links for those interested in these aspects of law.

FORENSICS

http://haven.ios.com/~nyrc/homepage.html

A set of links for the study of forensics.

FORENSICS REFERENCES

http://users.bart.nl/~geradts/forensic.html

Extensive set of links for this area of science and law.

FOUNDING FATHERS

http://www.clark.net/pub/thomjeff/

For a discussion of the issues facing America today, check out this site. But check out its tone and point of view before you send the students.

HOW OUR LAWS ARE MADE

http://thomas.loc.gov/home/lawsmade.toc.html

This site takes you, step by step, through the process by which an American bill becomes a law.

HUNGER WEB

http://www.brown.edu/Departments/World_Hunger_Program/

Research, advocacy and policy, education and training as they relate to world hunger are all discussed with the hope that informed people will help solve the problem.

INTERNATIONAL LAW PAGE

http://www.noord.bart.nl/~bethlehem/law.html

Education information, discussion groups, links, and more.

LAW.COM

http://www.laws.com/

A compendium of law resources on the Net.

LAW ISSUES AND THE NET

http://www.ionet.net/~mdyer/front.shtml

Exploration of the legal issues facing this vast new resource.

LAW JOBS

http://www.lawjobs.com/

Who does what, and what does it take to do it?

LAW JOURNAL EXTRA

http://www.ljx.com/indexhigh.html

Good source for reading up on latest issues.

LAW LIBRARY

http://www.io.org/~jgcom/librlaw.htm

Excellent source of references.

LAW LIBRARIES

ftp://ftp.netcom.com/pub/lo/loftus/buddies/home.html

An extensive set of links.

LAW TALK

http://www.law.indiana.edu:80/law/lawtalk.html

Segments deal with some aspect of law or legal studies.

LAWYER'S WEEKLY

http://www.lweekly.com/wm/lw/form/lw/mainmenu

A journal with both American and Canadian versions.

LEGAL EDUCATION ONLINE

http://www.lawinfo.com/

Excellent source of information.

LEGAL RESOURCES (IN ENGLISH, SPANISH, FRENCH)

http://www.hg.org/

Practice languages and law.

MOJO400

http://www.mojones.com/coinop_congress/mojo_400/mojo_400.html

List of the top 400 campaign contributors with biographies and photos.

NATIONAL BUDGET SIMULATION

http://garnet.berkeley.edu:3333/budget/budget.html

This simulation asks you to cut the 1995 fiscal deficit in order to achieve a balanced budget.

NATIONAL LAW ENFORCEMENT OFFICERS RIGHTS CENTER

http://dns.sas.ab.ca/pdhome/napo/leorc.html

Review the rights of the people who protect you.

PATENT LAW

http://www.patents.com/

Whatever you need to know, find it here.

POLRISK

http://www.polrisk.com/

This site provides a large data base of information for most major countries and includes data on history, geography, economic conditions, social climate, political people, and political climate.

PRACTICING ATTORNEYS HOME PAGE

http://www.legalethics.com/pa/main.html

Just what it sounds like.

PRESIDENTIAL DECISIONS

http://www.theAtlantic.com/atlantic/election/connection/

Interesting site for an election year.

SELF HELP LAW CENTER

http://www.nolo.com/

Information from Nolo Press for the layman.

SUPREME COURT DECISIONS

http://www.law.cornell.edu/supct/supct.table.html

Just what you think.

TOUR OF U.S. GOVERNMENT(LINKS TO ORGANIZATIONS)

http://www.electricpencil.com/enter/archive/4.html

A virtual tour and how all the parts work.

UNIFORM CRIME REPORTS

http://www.magicnet.net/advantor/crime.html

Statistics about U.S. crime.

VIRTUAL LIBRARY: LAW SCHOOLS AND LIBRARIES

http://www.law.indiana.edu/law/lawschools.html

Links to law schools and libraries.

VIRTUAL TOUR OF U.S. CAPITOL

http://gopher.senate.gov/capitol/virtour.html

Exactly what it says.

VOTE SMART

http://www.vote-smart.org/

Government procedures, proposed amendments, and links.

WOMEN'S LAW JOURNAL

http://www.lightlink.com/wlj/

Legal issues concerning women presented with humor, seriousness of thought, and even some poems.

WORLD CRIME SURVEY DATA

http://www.ifs.univie.ac.at/uncjin/mosaic/wcs.html

Links to information about crime from the United Nations.

WORLD LIST

http://www.law.osaka-u.ac.jp/legal-info/worldlist/worldlst.htm

Information related to the laws and governments of over 70 countries.

WORLD'S MOST WANTED

http://www.MostWanted.com/

Information about some of the world's most wanted criminals.

FRENCH SITES

As my school only teaches three languages, French, Spanish, and German, these are the ones we researched. Others are represented equally well on the Net.

One interesting site you might try:

http://www.babelfish.altavista.digital.com/

This site can crudely translate your English into other languages. It can also be interesting when you ask the phrase to complete a full circle and come back to you in English!

Software that really will translate Web sites does exist but can cost about $200.00. For more on those, check Yahoo in the category

business and economy/companies/computers/software/localization

ONLINE FILM DICTIONARY

http://userpage.fu-berlin.de/~oheiabbd/moviedict_e.html

Available in German, English, or Spanish, this site will help you understand movie terms.

More French Sites

FRENCH CULTURAL EXPLORER

http://ottawa.ambafrance.org/

Using the Eiffel Tower as a guide, this site offers a variety of cultural and language experiences and information.

LESSON

17

SAMPLE LESSONS FOR FOREIGN LANGUAGES

EO

Grade Level: 4th and Up

Browse

LANGUAGES FOR TRAVELERS

    http://www.travlang.com/languages/index.html

KLINGON

    http://www.kli.org/

RUSSIAN

    http://solar.rtd.utk.edu/oldfriends/language/course/school.html

Links and Bookmarks

A COUNTRY TOUR IN TWO LANGUAGES

    http://ottawa.ambafrance.org/index_eng.html
    http://www.paris.org/
    http://www.hol.edu/main/frn_lang.htm
    http://www.udg.mx/

Search

Plan a vacation to a country where your language is not the native language.

    http://lonelyplanet.org/
    http://www.expedia.msn.com/

Search and Cross-Reference

Language Exploration Lesson (in back of book) or The Language Scavenger Hunt

LANGUAGES FOR TRAVELERS

http://www.travlang.com/languages/index.html

Come here to learn some of those phrases you might need, complete with quizzes.

ALL ABOUT FRANCE

http://www.geocities.com/CollegePark/Union/7230/

Study some basic French. Try out some grammar and practice the language.

BONJOUR

http://tqd.advanced.org/3399/

Students have created this interactive practice site for beginners.

CAUSERIE — TO CHAT IN FRENCH

(e-mail) listserv@uquebec.ca

Set up pen pals for your students.

FRENCH CULTURE FAQ

http://gaia.sci-ed.fit.edu/

Interesting information about many aspects of French culture.

FRENCH CULTURE ONLINE

http://www.france.net.nz/

Wonderful links for learning more about the people and culture.

FRENCH-ENGLISH DICTIONARY

http://humanities.uchicago.edu/forms_unrest/FR-ENG.html

Practice here.

FRENCH EMBASSY IN WASHINGTON

http://www.info-france.org/

Find information about studies and travel in France, links to other sites, trade and technical information.

FRENCH HISTORY AND CULTURE

http://philae.sas.upenn.edu/French/caroly.html

Listen, see pictures, and read about the history and culture of France.

FRENCH LANGUAGE PRESS

gopher.msu.edu/

An interesting way to practice the language and learn more about the land and people.

FRENCH NEWSPAPERS ONLINE

http://newo.com:80/news/france.html

An interesting way to practice the language.

FRENCH POEMS

http://www.sura.org/~patois/poesie/

Text, in French, of poems by Baudelaire, Brassens, and others.

HISTORICAL MAPS OF PARIS

gopher://gutentag.cc.columbia.edu/11/fun/pictures/art-history

Incredibly detailed maps from 1721 to 1870, reproduced online.

L'ATELIER D'ECRITURE

http://horslimites.gulliver.fr/souris/

A site in French, dedicated to writing and posting writings.

LE VILLAGE

http://www.webconcept.fr/levillage/

This site takes you to a Paris sidewalk cafe where you can chat.

MAPS OF PARIS

http://paris.org/Musees/

Provides an interesting frame of reference.

PARIS

http://www.paris.org/

Add to your students' frame of reference with a tour.

THE PARIS METRO

gopher.jussieu.gov/

Take a tour of the famous Metro system.

TABLE OF FRENCH RESOURCES

http://www.acs.appstate.edu/~griffinw/website/freplaces.html

This location provides links to many other French resources on the Net.

TENNESSEE BOB'S AMAZING FRENCH LINKS

http://unix1.utm.edu/departments/french/french.html

An amazing list of links to hours and hours of French exploration.

TREASURE OF FRENCH LANGUAGE

`http://humanities.uchicago.edu/ARTFL/ARTFL.html`

Research into the French language.

VIRTUAL BAGUETTE

`http://www.mmania.com/`

French Magazine online — very nicely done!

VIRTUAL CHAMPS ELYSEES

`http://www.iway.fr/champs_elysees/`

Take an actual walking tour of the famous street.

VIRTUAL FRANCOPHONE VOYAGE

`http://depts.vassar.edu/~french/DJH/projet.html`

An interactive voyage of discovery in French or English.

VIRTUAL TOUR PARIS

`http://www.virtualtourism.com/Pariscope/welcome.F.html`

In French, take a tour of the city with movies, pictures, and descriptions.

SPANISH SITES

Just as French and other languages have sites on the Net, so does Spanish.

A Good Starting Point

LA OPINION

`http://www.opinion.com.mx/`

Spanish national, international, finance news and more -well done

More Spanish Sites

COMPENDIUM

`http://www.frontiernet.com/~ho2943/`

Language resources for students of the Spanish language.

CULTURE QUEST

`http://www.geocities.com/Athens/Oracle/6676/`

This site is developing quests to explore Hispanic culture, music, art and dance.

DISCOVER SPAIN

http://www.ozemail.com.au/~spain/overview.htm

Tour Madrid, learn about Spain's parks, currency, weather, and culture.

FOREIGN LANGUAGE RESOURCES ON THE WEB

http://www.itp.berkeley.edu/~thorne/HumanResources.html

From Berkeley, an extensive set of links.

HISPANIC ONLINE

http://www.hisp.com/

A monthly magazine filled with articles pertinent to the Hispanic culture.

HISPANIC/LATINO TELARANA

http://www.latela.com/

Links to Spain, famous Hispanics, Spanish-speaking countries, and more.

HUMAN LANGUAGES PAGE

http://www.hardlink.com/~chambers/HLP/

A comprehensive catalog of language-related Internet resources. Look here for links to other languages.

LANGUAGES FOR TRAVELERS

http://www.travlang.com/languages/index.html

Come here to learn some of those phrases you might need — complete with quizzes.

LATINO LINK

http://www.latinolink.com/

Latino news, business, commentary, lifestyles, entertainment, and more.

LATINONET

http://www.latino.net.co

A site dedicated to providing information about technology and increasing the use of telecommunications technology among the Latino community.

LATINOWEB

http://www.catalog.com/favision/latnoweb.htm

This site provides links to Latino art, history, newspapers, and more with an aim toward empowerment of Latinos on the Net.

MEXICAN EMBASSY KIDS' PAGE

`http://www.embamexcan.com/KidsPage/k-index.html`

A site where kids can learn more about Mexico.

MUNDO 21

`http://humanities.byu.edu/spanish/mundo/mundo.html`

A tour of Spanish-speaking countries.

MUSEUM OF PRE-HISPANIC CULTURE

`http://mexplaza.udg.mx/Museo/`

A site all in Spanish that explores the ancient cultures. Make sure you click on the pictures and exhibits for enlargements and comments.

PAGINAS AMARILLAS

`http://www.amarillas.com/`

Lots of links to Hispanic sites, including Yellow Pages to find sites online.

SPANISH LANGUAGE RESOURCES

`http://funnelweb.utcc.utk.edu/~hoyal/spanish/spanish3.htm`

More fantastic links to online resources.

SPANISH LESSONS

`http://www.drtomorrow.com/drtomorrow/spanish/`

Another place to practice.

SPANISH LESSONS ONLINE

`http://www.june29.com/Spanish/`

Practice already set up online, plus links to dictionaries and more.

SPANISH MAGAZINE ONLINE

`http://www.elperiodico.es/`

Great way to practice the language and learn about Spain.

SPANISH RESOURCES

`http://members.aol.com/Jsnipesabc/index.html`

Links to many resources.

TIEMPO INTERNET, HONDURAS

`http://www.tiempo.hn`

Excellent server from Central America. News in Spanish too!

TOUR OF SPAIN

http://www.tourspain.es/

Take a tour of the cites, the countryside, and more.

WEB SITES

http://www-lib.usc.edu/Info/Boeck/websites.html

Simply link after link to resources for Spanish on the Net: literature, culture, business.

WEBSPANOL

http://www.cyberramp.net/~mdbutler/

A guide for beginners in the Spanish language — lessons for students and travelers and information about books, too, plus a dictionary and free software to download.

GERMAN

AMERICAN ASSOCIATION OF TEACHERS OF GERMAN

http://www.aatg.org/

See what conferences are coming up, read about scholarships, and more.

CASTLE ON THE RHEIN

http://www.caltim.com/reichenstein/

Victor Hugo stayed here, and the site is a wonderful tour with history.

CHAMPS-ELYSEE

http://schau-ins-land.com/

Teachers can connect here to others who teach German, French, Spanish, or Italian.

DEUTSCHES HISTORISCHES MUSEUM

http://www.dhm.de/

Collections concerning German history.

DEUTSCHES MUSEUM

http://www.deutsches-museum.de/e_index.htm

The largest technical museum in Germany. Learn about their programs here.

GERMAN CHANGELING LEGENDS

`http://www.pitt.edu/~dash/gerchange.html`

These legends are in English, but provide insight into the literary history of Germany.

GERMAN–ENGLISH ONLINE DICTIONARY

`http://dictionaries.travlang.com/GermanEnglish/`

With more than 130,000 entries, this will help add to your class.

GERMAN LANGUAGE PAGE

`http://www.globalserve.net/~ihayes/lang/german/index.html`

Stories and articles with links to English translations, plus other ways to practice.

GERMAN TEXT TO SPEECH SYNTHESIZER

`http://www.bell-labs.com/project/tts/german.html`

You can type and hear your words online.

GERMANIC MYTHS, LEGENDS, AND SAGAS

`http://www.pitt.edu/~dash/mythlinks.html`

Links to online texts and other sites about Germany.

GERMANIC WORLD

`http://www.pitt.edu/~dash/northlinks.html`

Learn more about the countries where German is spoken.

INTERNET RESOURCES FOR GERMANISTS

`http://polyglot.lss.wisc.edu/german/links.html`

A wonderful resource for teachers the world over.

PICTORIAL GERMAN HOME PAGE

`http://ibis.ups.edu/homepage/Richards/RICHARDS.HTM`

Frau Richardson brings you a pictorial tour in German or English.

RHEINLAND PFALZ CASTLES

`http://www.caltim.com/rheinland/`

Take a tour of some of the beautiful castles of Germany.

TEXTHAUS

`http://www.texthaus.com/`

Try this interactive online learning service.

WEB TRANS DICTIONARY

http://search.tu-clausthal.de/WebTrans/

Another place to go for translations.

WEBMUSEEN

http://webmuseen.de/

In German, a guide to German museums and exhibits.

COLLEGE, CAREERS, AND GUIDANCE

For college planning, scholarships, test preparation, or financial aid, these are some of the best sites around.

New trends include help for everything from homework, SAT preparation, finding funding for school, or a job from an online data base.

STUDENT CENTER

http://www.studentcenter.com/

Find ways to improve your résumé, a test to help you determine what career is right for you, and help with interviewing. Try "The Virtual Interview."

More College Sites

ABOUT WORK

http://www.aboutwork.com/

If you are new to the job, changing careers, or working from home, or if you are an entrepreneur, this site offers information and advice.

AMERICAN EXPRESS UNIVERSITY

http://www.americanexpress.com/student/

Check out the Money Pit for résumé templates, interview tips, and assess your strengths

A–Z SCHOLARNET

http://tqd.advanced.org/2925/

A student-created site that offers a searchable data base of college scholarships.

BIRCHWOOD SCHOLARSHIP SERVICES

http://www.birchwood.com/

One more source for funding that you pay for.

CALIFORNIA SCHOOL COUNSELOR ASSOCIATION

http://www.serve.com/CSCA/

Resources for counselors, professional links, and student information.

CATAPULT

http://www.jobweb.org/catapult/catapult.htm

A site dedicated to offering information and links for those seeking a career or learning about careers.

CLIFF'S HOME PAGE

http://www.cliffs.com/

Cliff's Notes, the students best friend — information online.

COLLEGE MONEY MATTERS

http://jerome.signet.com/collegemoney/

Funding sources, money management, college planning, and budgeting.

COLLEGE POWERPREP

http://www.powerprep.com/

More help for the SAT.

FINANCIAL AID INFORMATION

http://www.finaid.org/

Helpful for the college-bound.

HISTORICALLY BLACK COLLEGES AND UNIVERSITIES

http://www.edonline.com/cq/hbcu/

Links and information plus a geographical search.

INTERNET COLLEGE EXCHANGE

http://www.usmall.com/college

Any questions about picking the right college and paying for it? Look here.

KAPLAN TEST PREP

http://www.kaplan.com/

Prepare for the GRE and other tests online.

KIDS AND JOBS

http://www.pbs.org/jobs/

Check out the Teen Career Center and see what's online for teachers and parents.

JOB CORPS

http://www.jobcorps.org/

Find out what they have to offer students.

JUNIOR ACHIEVEMENT

http://www.ja.org/index.asp

Learn more about their programs, send a postcard, and more.

LINK: DIGITAL CAMPUS

http://www.linkmag.com/

Almost like being there, with articles about issues, experiences, and things to know.

MAIN QUAD

http://www.mainquad.com/

Access to more than 150 companies, a résumé template, and job-hunting tips.

MY FUTURE

http://www.myfuture.com/

Here is help with your career direction, résumé, and money for college.

NATIONAL EMPLOYER LEADERSHIP COUNCIL

http://www.nelc.org/

They are working to enhance the quality of the workforce. Find out how.

PERPETUAL STUDENT

http://www2.web-hyogo.or.jp/~ps/psw/

Learn how to study efficiently with study tips presented here.

PETERSON'S EDUCATION CENTER

http://www.petersons.com/

Wonderful site for picking a college, distance learning, career planning.

RÉSUMÉ ONLINE

http://www.ypn.com/jobs/

Post your résumé online free for a year, or find other job information.

SCHOLARSHIP BOOK

http://www.scholarshipbook.com/

Lists of scholarships online, free for 30 days.

SCHOOL-TO-CAREER RESOURCES

http://www.stcresource.org/

Learn what this organization is doing to help people in their work transition.

SCHOOL-TO-CAREERS WEB GUIDE

http://www.thomson.com/rcenters/stc/default.html

Curriculum guides, state links, sites of interest, and a glossary.

SCHOOL-TO-WORK NEWS

http://www.stwnews.org/

For parents and educators who are getting someone ready for work — and for the students, too.

STANFORD STUDY GUIDE

http://www.testprep.com/wwlist.html

Test preparation materials.

STUDENT SERVICES

http://www.fastweb.com/fastweb/index.cgi/index.html?refer=studentservices

Searchable data base of funding sources.

THE STUDENT SURVIVAL GUIDE

http://www.luminet.net/~jackp/survive.html

Helpful hints for kids going to college include writing tips, note-taking, and how to make the most of your college experience.

STUDY PLACE

http://www.ilt.columbia.edu/academic

A place for scholars to find information.

STUDY WEB

http://www.studyweb.com/

Access to articles for research and other types of research help.

TEST PREP

http://www.testprep.com/

Help for those preparing for the SAT.

TESTER ONLINE

http://tester.review.com/

From Princeton, a place to review. Register and practice for tests.

Getting a Job

Many sites online will not only connect you to people who are hiring, but also help with job preparation skills and résumés. See what your kids can do with the skills they are mastering.

AMERICA'S JOB BANK

http://www.ajb.dni.us/index.html

Many listings of career openings,

FUTURESCAN MAGAZINE

http://www.futurescan.com/

An interactive career guide for teenagers, helping them learn about specific careers. Featuring articles such as "The World of Experience."

CAREER COMPANION

http://www.careercompanion.com/

Information about improving career skills, jobs, industry trends, and several personality/career assessment tests.

CAREER MAGAZINE

http://www.careermag.com/careermag/

Wonderful tips on getting a job and other career-related materials.

CAREER MOSAIC

http://www.careermosaic.com/

Well-presented information about who is hiring, résumés, etc.

CAREERPATH

http://www.careerpath.com/

More information for the career seekers.

CAREER RESOURCES HOME PAGE

http://www.rpi.edu/dept/cdc/homepage.html

Links to other sites containing career information.

CAREER RESOURCE LINKS

http://199.94.216.72:80/jobseek/center/cclinks.htm

Excellent resource on the processes of preparing for a career.

CAREER SITE

http://www.careersite.com/

Employment search and recruiting site.

CAREER TOOLBOX

http://www.careertoolbox.com/splash.html

Contains downloadable résumé samples, as well as other tips for careers.

CAREERWEB

http://www.cweb.com/

Links to information about careers.

HITECH CAREERS

http://www.hitechcareer.com/hitech

What are they, and where are they?

JOB HUNT

http://www.job-hunt.org/

Links to jobs openings and other job-hunting information.

MONSTER BOARD (EMPLOYMENT RESOURCES) 🔗

http://www.monster.com/home.html

Excellent source for career information.

OCCUPATIONAL RESEARCH GROUP

http://www.coe.uga.edu/~jcoker/

Provides educational research and curriculum development services.

ONLINE CAREER CENTER

http://www.occ.com/

Search tool for locating careers.

VIRTUAL RÉSUMÉ

http://www.virtualresume.com/

Site offers résumé help, tools for job seekers and employers, and a place to post your portfolio.

ALL THINGS COMPUTER-RELATED

12

There are too many sites to list relating to computers, because the term is too general. Here are sites about a few particular aspects of computing.

Two good general sites:

InterNIC

    http://rs.internic.net./cgi-bin/whois

Names for Web sites are in great demand. What Web site names are available? Find out here.

Web Reference

    http://webreference.com/

For those who want to know more about the Web. From creating your own Web page, to the stress of over-mousing, to the future of the Net, this is a good place to start.

In this chapter

- Virtual Reality
- MIS
- Internet Help and Languages
- Web Page Design
- Tech Support
- Computer News
- Additional Computer Sites
- Art and Computer Graphics
- Lesson 18. Sample Art Lessons
- Business and Finance

VIRTUAL REALITY

Emerging on the Internet, long a staple of video games, this medium offers great promise for educators and students. One of my favorite samples of 3D is a tour of one of the ancient cities at http://www.ancientsites.com/. Try some of these, too.

3D WORLDS
http://www.kahunanui.com/vrreview.htm

See some wonderful samples of 3D modeling.

DOCKING BAY
http://www.csd.uu.se/~johnn/

See a wonderful example of what can be created in 3D.

HOT AIR BALLOON SIMULATOR
http://www-vrl.umich.edu/People/saha/HAB.html

Almost a step-by-step tutorial on how this is being created.

MINDWAVE
http://www.mindwave.com/

Not all uses of virtual reality are for games of violence. Find out more here.

NOWWWHERE
http://imagiware.com/nowhere/

Animation, sound, and puzzle-solving in 3D.

PLANET9
http://www.planet9.com/

This is an amazing site with 3D representations of major U.S. cities. Take a virtual tour after you load the plug-in and enjoy.

UNIVERSITY OF OREGON, VIRTUAL TOUR
http://darkwing.uoregon.edu/~admit/visit/qtvr/

Walk around, enjoy yourself.

VIRTEX
http://www.virtex.co.uk/

Over 40 virtual exhibits you can browse once you download the plug-in.

VIRTUAL EARTH
http://www.virtualearth.com/

Amazing panoramic movies like the one of Big Sur are a hint of what's to come on the Net.

VIRTUAL REALITY HOME PAGE
http://www.ncsa.uiuc.edu:80/Viz/VR/VRHomePage.html

Another great source of information.

VIRTUAL REALITY RESOURCES
http://www.hitl.washington.edu/

Good place to learn more about the concept. From the Home Page, click on projects, then click on knowledge, then find on the Net.

VIRTUAL STONEHENGE
http://www.intel.com/cpc/explore/stonehenge/

Download the software and take a virtual tour.

WEB DEVELOPER'S VIRTUAL LIBRARY
http://www.stars.com/Vlib/Providers/VR.html

More information and links.

MIS

Someone has to manage all the information that is generated in business and over the Internet. Here are sites about and for those who manage information and develop the systems to do the job.

INFOSERVER
http://www.infoserver.com/

A journal for those wanting more information about outsourcing.

JOURNAL OF MANAGEMENT INFORMATION SYSTEMS
http://rmm-java.stern.nyu.edu/jmis/

Articles and information for the professional.

MIS
http://mis.commerce.ubc.ca/interest/interest.html

Information for anyone interested in MIS.

MIS ENGLAND
http://www.open.mis.surrey.ac.uk/

A good source of information from across the waters.

MIS FORUM
http://cism.bus.utexas.edu/issues/iindex.html

Issues and information.

MIS RESEARCH AND REFERENCE.
http://www.brint.com/ISResearch.htm

Great set of links and information about MIS.

YAHOO MIS INFO PAGE
http://www.yahoo.com/Business_and_Economy/Management_Information_Systems/

Another good set of links.

INTERNET HELP AND LANGUAGES

Learn about the new languages evolving to create those astounding Web pages.

A BEGINNER'S GUIDE TO HTML
http://www.ncsa.uiuc.edu/General/Internet/WWW/HTMLPrimer.html

Learn how to make your own home page.

BARE BONES GUIDE TO HTML
http://werbach.com/barebones/

A tutorial that has been translated in many languages and is downloadable.

BROWSER WATCH PLUG-IN PLAZA
http://www.browserwatch.com/plug-in.html

Plug-ins for your Net browser are described and sampled for testing here.

HTML CRASH COURSE
http://www.w3-tech.com/crash/

Step-by-step instructions from basic to advanced. Some Java instruction, too.

HTML FOR THE COMPLETE IDIOT
http://www.geocities.com/SiliconValley/Campus/1924/index.html

Web page help when you need it in clear language and an easy-to-manage site.

HTML GRINDER
http://www.matterform.com/grinder/index.html

A downloadable Web site maintenance tool.

INTERNET TUTORIALS

http://www.albany.edu/library/internet/

Overview of a training course plus a glossary of Internet terms and more.

LINKS TO PROGRAMMING LANGUAGES

http://www.hypernews.org/HyperNews/get/computing/lang-list.html

Need info about computer languages? Start here.

LINGUA CENTER

http://deil.lang.uiuc.edu/web.pages/www.scavengerhunt.html

A teaching tool to help with searching the Web.

MORE HELP WITH HOME PAGES

http://www.cwru.edu/help/introHTML/toc.html

Case Western Reserve University gives some help with Web site creation.

NET LINGO

http://www.netlingo.com/

Look up those new Internet and technology terms that no dictionary has even heard of, or go right to the Web sites of many computer companies.

NETSCAPE NAVIGATOR

http://home.netscape.com/

Find not only the famous browser, but a built-in HTML editor.

OUR DOMAIN GALLERY

http://www.ourdomain.com/gallery

Some terrific graphics for your Web pages.

POINTCAST

http://www.pointcast.com/index.html

Download software that will bring you a personalized news service.

STAY TOONED

http://www.staytooned.com/

Information for the worldwide animation community.

VISUAL BASIC ONLINE

http://www.vbonline.com/vb-mag/

Information for those learning this computer language.

YOUNG BASIC PROGRAMMERS CLUB

http://ybpc.eclipse.net/

A site for those into programming, complete with FAQs and new ideas.

WEB PAGE DESIGN

An emerging field for educators and students. How long before we're all online?

ABC GRAPHICS

http://web.online-graphics.net/

Balls, bullets, backgrounds, buttons, and more to use on your Web page.

DICK'S WEB DESIGN WORKSHOP

http://www.geocities.com/SiliconValley/Way/1036/

A tutorial and some wonderful samples to help with your Web page design.

DZINE

http://www.lcc.gatech.edu/gallery/dzine/

An online guide to help you make good Web pages.

FONTSITE

http://www.fintsite.com/

Offers guidelines about choosing fonts and laying out your page.

LAURIE'S FREE WEB GRAPHICS

http://www.geocities.com/SiliconValley/Horizon/1501/

Bullets, animated GIFS, themed pages, and a lot more.

MEDIABUILDER VIDEO

http://www.mediabuilder.com/videosearch.html

If you're searching for movies online or pictures, this search engine will help.

RESOURCES AND ASSISTANTS FOR WEBMASTERS

http://www.akula.com/~aphelion/raw/

Tools, tips, graphics, and much more.

WEB GRAPHICS

http://members.xoom.com/SSWebGraphics/

Another site with lots to share for your home page.

WEB SITE DESIGN

http://www.shire.net/learnwebdesign/index.html

An online course to teach Web page design.

WEB PUBLISHING

http://www.thegiim.org/

Help with that home page creation.

WEBBERY AND NETTERY

http://www.strum.co.uk/webbery/

Hints and advice for those making their own Web pages.

WEBMASTER

http://www-scf.usc.edu/~bako/webmaster/index2.htm

Some beautiful backgrounds, icons, and Java examples are here.

YALE WEB STYLE GUIDE

http://info.med.yale.edu/caim/manual/

Help with design, layout, and covering all the aspects of creating a Web page.

TECH SUPPORT

Don't be left hanging with a hardware or software problem. Get help.

24-HOUR TECH SUPPORT

http://www.nowonder.com/

When your software or hardware is driving you crazy, they're ready to help.

APPLE SOLUTION PRO NETWORK

http://www.apple.com/support/

Technical support for Mac users.

COMPUTER VIRUS DATABASE

http://www.datafellows.fi/vir-desc.htm

Extensive list of viruses out there.

MAC MANAGERS HOME PAGE

http://www.mac-mgrs.org/mac-mgrs.html

Questions and answers about Macs.

MORE MAC TECH SUPPORT

http://macexpert.com/

Support directly from Apple.

NETWORKING AND MACS

http://oak.forest.net/anma/anma.html

Information and FAQs about networking Macs.

NO WONDER

http://www.nowonder.com/

Tech answers with a 24-hour turnaround.

OS/2 HOME PAGE

http://www.mit.edu:8001/activities/os2/os2world.html

Operating system help.

PC HELP ONLINE

http://www.pchelponline.com/

Resources all in one place to save you time.

PC LUBE & TUNE

http://pclt.cis.yale.edu/pclt/default.htm

Another site to help you fix what's wrong with your PC.

QUILL SERVICES CONFLICT COMPENDIUM

http://www.quillserv.com/www/c3/c3.html

Lists Mac conflicts by platform and product.

SUPPORT HELP

http://www.supporthelp.com/

Search through a directory and find the help you need.

SYSTEM OPTIMIZATION

http://www.sysopt.com/

Plagued with computer problems? This site may help.

TECH SUPPORT

http://www.xmission.com/~trevin/help/trevhelp.html

Need a technician at odd hours? Here's one.

TIPWORLD

http://www.tipworld.com/

Tips for everything from Windows 95 to MS Office.

COMPUTER NEWS

With so many changes, so quickly, it's important for educators to keep up.

BROADCASTING INFORMATION

http://www.well.com/user/rld/vidpage.html

Information about broadcasting, the National Association of Broadcasters, and research.

BYTE MAGAZINE

http://www.byte.com/

One of the best magazines, online.

CNN TECHNOLOGY NEWS

http://cnn.com/TECH/index.html

Excellent information from a great source; constantly updated.

COMPUTER LIFE

http://www.zdnet.com/complife/

The user-friendly magazine online.

HEADCOUNT

http://www.headcount.com/

Who's online and where.

INFORMATION WEEK

http://www.informationweek.com/

Computer industry news.

NEW PRODUCTS NEWS
http://www.hotproductnews.com/

For the latest news on hardware and software, check here.

PUBLISH MAGAZINE
http://www.publish.com/

This is an online magazine for desktop publishers and includes tips, techniques, topics of importance, utilities, and more tools of the trade.

STREET TECH
http://www.streettech.com/

Technology news.

TECH WEB
http://www.techweb.com/

Magazines such as *Interactive Age, Electronic Buyer, Communications Week,* and *Tech Web* are here.

VIRTUAL VOICE
http://www.virtual-voice.com/

If you are keeping up with the latest technology involving telephony, this site attempts to update you on all the latest news and technological developments.

ADDITIONAL COMPUTER SITES

BOBBY
http://www.cast.org/bobby/

Find out how friendly your site is for people with disabilities. This site will examine your site.

BOSTON COMPUTER MUSEUM
http://www.tcm.org/

Learn about computers and have fun doing it.

BUILDER.COM
http://www.builder.com/

Find information and tools to help with your Web needs.

DIGITAL VIDEO

http://www.videomaker.com/

If you're a videomaker, this site offers an informative classroom with glossary.

DOWNLOAD.COM

http://www.download.com/

Find games, utilities, browsers, and other software to download here.

ENTERTAINMENT TECHNOLOGY CENTER

http://www.usc.edu/dept/etc/

USC collaborates with the entertainment world to advance technology.

FREEPROFIT

http://www.freeprofit.com/

A guide to who is making money on the Net, how, and why.

HAPPY PUPPY

http://www.happypuppy.com/

Another place to find software to download.

HISTORICAL COMPUTER SOCIETY

http://www.cyberstreet.com/hcs/hcs.htm

A walk through the history of the PC.

HISTORY OF TECHNOLOGY

http://www.ahandyguide.com/cat1/h/h318.htm

Links to sites dealing with the history of the Internet, technological advances, aerospace, telecommunications, and some of the big names in the industry.

HITCHHICKERS.NET

http://www.hitchhikers.net/

Make an electronic postcard here and send it, or learn more about Net resources.

INQUIRY

http://www.inquiry.com/

Information on software products, development techniques, and emerging technologies.

JUMBO (SHAREWARE AND FREEWARE)

http://www.jumbo.com/

Maybe that piece of software you're looking for is here.

LucasArts

http://www.lucasarts.com/

Industrial Light and Magic: find news, views, jobs, and more.

Multimedia

http://www.crs4.it/HTML/LUIGI/MPEG/mpegfaq.html

Compilation of data about multimedia.

Past Notable Women of Computing

http://www.cs.yale.edu/homes/tap/past-women.html

Biographies of women in math and early computing, plus links.

PBS Triumph of the Nerds

http://www.pbs.org/nerds/

Find out about the people behind the technology and more.

PrivNet

http://www.privnet.com/

Free software that identifies and takes out ads as you browse.

Virtual Museum of Computing

http://www.comlab.ox.ac.uk/archive/other/museums/computing.html#local

If you need any information about where it all started, here's a good place to go.

Art and Computer Graphics

3D Images

http://www.3dvisions.com/

Among other things, you'll find 150 samples of 3D art.

AGFA

http://www.agfaphoto.com/

Lessons in photography and more from this photographic and imaging company.

Animation

http://www.deltanet.com/animalu/

Samples of animation by one artist.

LESSON

18

SAMPLE ART LESSONS

EO   **Grade Level: 4th and Up**

Browse

Tour some museums

```
http://www.lam.mus.ca.us/webmuseums/
http://www.artscenecal.com/Listings/Indexes/MsmIndex.html
http://sunsite.unc.edu/louvre/
```

Links and Bookmarks

An animation tour

```
http://www.awn.com/index.html
http://jollyroger.com./animation.html
```

Search Forward and Back

Film legend James Dean.

```
http://192.189.45.3/ac/rs/aed/flm/flm.htm
http://www.gen.umn.edu/faculty_staff/yahnke/film/cinema1.htm
http://www.ex.ac.uk/bill.douglas/contents.html
```

Search and Cross-Reference

When Rembrandt was painting (where, by the way?), who was composing at the same time? Designing buildings? Inventing? Writing? Where?

ARCHITECTURE LINKS

```
http://www.architecturelinks.com/
```

Too many links to mention for things related to architecture.

ARCHITECTURE LINKS

```
http://www.arch.buffalo.edu/pairc/
```

More links to related sites.

ART DEADLINES LIST

http://custwww.xensei.com/adl/

A list of competitions, contests, call for entries/papers, grants, scholarships, fellowships, jobs, internships, etc., in the arts.

ARTLEX

http://www.artlex.com/

A dictionary of visual art.

ART STAND

http://www.hukilau.com/art/

Exhibits, news, art magazines, and more.

ARTS EDGE

http://artsedge.kennedy-center.org/

Linking art and education with technology. Learn about art education and links.

ARTS EDNET

http://www.artsednet.getty.edu/

A place to exchange ideas for art education grades K–12.

BUILDING CONNECTIONS — ARCHITECTURE FOR KIDS

http://burgoyne.com/pages/bldgconn/a.htm

Online activities and exhibits to teach kids about architecture.

CITYSPACE

http://www.cityspace.org/

A collaboratively built virtual environment. Your kids can explore, read, or build.

COMMUNICATION ARTS

http://www.commarts.com/

Professional print journal for graphic designers and others in the visual arts or related areas.

COMPUTER ANIMATION

http://www.bergen.org/AAST/ComputerAnimation/

A student-created site to teach about computer graphics and animation.

COMPUTER ART LINKS

http://www.nerdworld.com/nw1177.html

Links to all things related to computer art.

COMPUTER GRAPHICS

http://mambo.ucsc.edu/psl/cg.html

Links to graphics sites for 3D, raytracing, animation, and more.

COMPUTER GRAPHICS WORLD MAGAZINE

http://www.cgw.com/

Samples and information for graphic designers.

COREL ONLINE

http://www.corelnet.com/

The drawing software company has some interesting information online.

CYBURBIA

http://www.arch.buffalo.edu/pairc/

Internet resources for architecture.

DESIGNSPHERE ONLINE

http://www.dsphere.net/

A site devoted to building an electronic community for the communications arts, graphic arts, prepress, and printing industry.

DESIGN TECH

http://www.angelfire.com/biz/DesignTech/index.html

Web design help with free downloads.

DESKTOP PUBLISHING

http://www.teleport.com/~eidos/dtpij/dtpij.html

Internet jumpstart for desktop publishing.

DIGITAL IMAGE FINDER

http://sunsite.berkeley.edu/ImageFinder/

Looking for a specific type of picture? This may help you find it.

GARGOYLE HOME PAGE

http://ils.unc.edu/garg/

Find pictures and information about these interesting sculptors.

GEORGE EASTMAN HOUSE

http://www.eastman.org/

Find a timeline of photography here, plus more about photography.

GLOBAL CHILDREN'S ART GALLERY

http://www.naturalchild.com/gallery/page11.html

Art from children around the world is exhibited. Your kids can post theirs too.

GRAFFITI ONLINE

http://www.graffiti.org/

Amazing worldwide drawings showing the art form graffiti has become.

GRAPHICS AND PHOTOSHOP

http://the-tech.mit.edu/KPT/

Tips and tricks with Adobe Photoshop.

GUIDE TO MUSEUMS AND CULTURAL RESOURCES

http://www.lam.mus.ca.us/webmuseums/

Worldwide guide and links.

HOLOGRAPHY

http://www.holoworld.com/

See holograms of the Titanic and movies in a multimedia theater, plus games and a kids' page.

INCREDIBLE ART DEPARTMENT

http://www.artswire.org/kenroar/

Links to artists, periods, magazines, lessons, and more.

INTARTDATA

http://www.kulturbox.de/univers/e_intart.htm

Art directories worldwide.

LION LINK MUSEUM LIST

http://www.ilovelongisland.com/museums/

Direct links to specific museums around the world.

LOTHLORIEN

http://www.elfwood.com/

Fantasy art works, more than 140, from amateur artists. Each artist is profiled and explains some of the technique or thought behind the work.

MUSEUM GUIDE

http://www.museumguide.com/

Find museums from all over the world.

MUSEUM OF ART AND ARCHITECTURE
http://www.research.missouri.edu/musuem/index.htm

Find some online previews of exhibits.

MUSEUM SHOP
http://www.museumshop.com/

If you want to introduce your students to objets d'art, try this site.

NATIVE AMERICAN ART
http://www.heard.org/

Exhibits and activities from the Heard Museum.

OLDIES AND GOODIES
http://fromnowon.org/museum/oldies&goodies.html

Links to articles about building virtual museums and some samples of school virtual museums.

ONEWORLD
http://oneworld.org/

Check out the OneWorld Gallery for animation, art, videos, and more.

PHOTOSHOP PICTURES
http://www.fns.net/~almateus/photo.htm

A collection of works created with Photoshop.

RAYTRACED IMAGES
http://www.mclink.it/personal/MC0693/

More samples of an art form.

SLIDE SHOW OF VARIOUS PERIODS OF ART
http://www.mip.berkeley.edu/query_forms/browse_spiro_form.html

Build a frame of reference for your students with wonderful images.

STONE CARVER
http://www.mcs.net/~sculptor/

Find some information and samples of the work of a sculptor and stone carver.

TEST FRACTAL GENERATOR
http://www.pangloss.com/seidel/Frac/

Put in some numbers and let the computer generate the art.

WEB GALLERY OF ART

http://sunserv.kfki.hu/~arthp/index.html

Digital reproductions of 3500 images and tours.

WORLD ART TREASURES

http://sgwww.epfl.ch/BERGER/

Find links to many of the finest art works the world has to offer.

WORLD WIDE ARTS RESOURCES

http://wwar.com/index.html

Extensive set of links to galleries, artists, performance arts, and more.

WORLD WIDE COMPUTER ART

http://WWW.UC.EDU/~kidart/kidart.html

Just what it sounds like.

BUSINESS AND FINANCE

Doing business on the Web is becoming big business and many companies, Fortune 500 as well as smaller companies, now not only have Web pages, but offer information or services, too. Other business sites offer advice, news, and simulations.

New Trends

Appealing to the small entrepreneur or business with services and help and sites that offer more than just an ad for the company.

SMALL BUSINESS FOCUS

http://www.sbfocus.com/

A search engine that will focus on helping find useful statistics, contacts, or information.

FORD MOTOR COMPANY

http://www.ford.com/

Ford lets you build a Mustang online. Other companies offer other services.

MAILBANK
http://www.mailbank.com/

Lets you register your own name as a domain name.

BROADCAST.COM
http://www.broadcast.com/business/investorrelations.stm/

Real-time audio lets you sit in on the annual meeting or other events of some companies.

AMERICAN STOCK EXCHANGE
http://www.internetbroadcast.com/amex

From the floor, see live video of trading.

A Great Site

SIERRA ONLINE STOCK MARKET SIMULATION
http://smc.sierra.com/

Actually challenge the market online — excellent practice.

Young Investors' Web Sites

For those introducing students to money matters or economics, these sites might help.

EDUCATIONAL EMPOWERMENT
http://www.digiserve.com/nlp/articles.html

Read several articles on kids and economics.

EDUCATIONAL TIPS
http://www.e-analytics.com/

For the teacher working with kids and money.

LAVAMIND
http://www.lavamind.com/

Makers of business simulation games such as, *Gazillionaire*, *Zapitalism*, and *Profitania*.

MONEYHUNTER
http://www.moneyhunter.com/

Investors can be found here. Last year, $17 million was awarded to applicants through this site.

MONEY MANAGEMENT

http://www.moneymanagement.com/

Search this site for money management articles.

TEACHER'S RESOURCE PAGE

http://www.finitycorp.com/

More help for educators.

TEEN BIZ

http://www.teenbiz.com/

Another excellent site for kids learning about how to handle money.

YOUNG INVESTOR

http://www.younginvestor.com/

Information for young people investing their money.

YOUNG INVESTORS GUIDE

http://www.adtechpro.com/investing

Another place to look for information about investing.

WORKSMART

http://pbs.org/jobs/worksmart.html

Learn how to "work smart."

Business Sites

A-1 EXPOSURE

http://uran.net/pq/global/ads.html

An online newsletter for those interested in Internet advertising, marketing, commerce, and working at home.

ACCUTRADE

http://www.accutrade.com/

Internet trading simulation — see if you can make money.

ADVERTISING WORLD

http://advertising.utexas.edu/world/

Massive amounts of information and links to resources for advertising.

AMERICAN DEMOGRAPHICS
    http://www.marketingtools.com/

Demographic info and consumer trends.

AT&T BUSINESS NETWORK (INFORMATION)
    http://www.att.com/

Areas of interest from this established company.

BETTER BUSINESS BUREAU
    http://www.bbb.org/

Issues covered by this well-regarded organization.

BUSINESS WIRE
    http://www.businesswire.com/

International press releases and business news.

CNN FINANCIAL NEWS
    http://cnnfn.com/index.html

Excellent site from an excellent source.

CONSUMER WORLD
    http://www.consumerworld.org/

A guide to consumer resources on the Net.

EXPERIMENTAL STOCK MARKET CHARTS
    http://www.stockmaster.com/

Quotes and charts on U.S. stocks and mutual funds.

FAVORITE ELECTRONIC COMMERCE WWW RESOURCES
    http://e-comm.iworld.com/

Extensive list of links for anyone thinking of doing business on the Web.

FINANCIAL AND DEMOGRAPHIC DATA/DUN & BRADSTREET
    http://dbisna.com/

Valuable information from an excellent source.

FINANCIAL LINKS
    http://www.catalog.com/intersof/commerce/entrepre.html

Another site for resources to those interested in financial areas.

FINANCIAL WEB

http://www.finweb.com/

Issues and information about various finance-related topics.

FOREIGN TRADE

http://www.census.gov/ftp/pub/foreign-trade/www/

Interesting information and statistics.

HOOVERS ONLINE

http://www.hoovers.com/

10,000 company profiles, Web site links, contact information, and stock quotes.

iBANKER INDEX

http://www.ddsi.com/banking/

Locates banks on the Internet.

INC ONLINE

http://www.inc.com/

An online magazine for small businesses.

LEAD STORY

http://www.bnet.att.com/leadstory/

AT&T Business Network explores a major story in depth.

NASDAQ FINANCIAL EXECUTIVE JOURNAL

http://www.law.cornell.edu/nasdaq/nasdtoc.html

Stocks and other information.

NEWS PAGE

http://www.newspage.com/

An excellent source of news about industries; listed by category

OHIO STOCK MARKET GAME

http://ucunix.san.uc.edu/~derenslb/

An online simulation from the Cincinnati Center for Economic Education.

ONLINE BANKING DEMO

http://www.edify.com/

Interesting demonstration of what some believe to be banking of the future.

RESOURCES FOR ECONOMISTS
http://econwpa.wustl.edu/EconFAQ/EconFAQ.html

Links and resources for statistics, forecasts, journals, and more.

SEC EDGAR DATABASE
http://town.hall.org/edgar/edgar.html

Another interesting source of financial statistics.

SMALL BUSINESS ADMINISTRATION
http://www.sbaonline.sba.gov/

Home page from the SBA with information and issues of concern.

SMART BUSINESS SUPERSITE
http://www.smartbiz.com/

Business news, career, and how-to information.

STAT USA
http://www.stat-usa.gov/stat-usa.html

Another good site for statistics.

STOCKPLAYER
http://207.102.139.3/

Stock information and list of quotes readily available.

STOCK QUOTES
http://cnnfn.com/markets/us_markets.html

When you need to know how your portfolio is doing, go here.

US BUDGET
http://sunny.stat_usa.gov/

Where does the money go?

WEB 100
http://Fox.NSTN.Ca:80/~at_info/

A directory of the largest U.S. and international corporations on the Web.

WELLS FARGO PERSONAL FINANCE
http://wellsfargo.com/per

Information and links from a well-respected company.

WORLDCLASS

http://web.idirect.com/~tiger/

This extensive site brings daily updated financial and business news, profiles of major companies worldwide using the Net, a virtual tour of the Chicago Board Options Exchange, newspapers and business magazines listed by country, and more.

SPORTS, ENTERTAINMENT, AND TRAVEL ONLINE

HEALTH, SPORTS AND FITNESS SITES

Sites for those interested not only in PE, but also in fitness and health.

Good General Sites

HEALTHFINDER

    http://www.healthfinder.gov/

A site with articles about current medical topics

SPORTSLINE

    http://www.sportsline.com/

Game summaries, box scores, and a searchable archive of players

Health and Fitness

ACHOO — INTERNET HEALTHCARE DIRECTORY

    http://www.achoo.com/

A complete medical directory with search capabilities.

AMERICA'S HOUSECALL NETWORK

    http://www.housecall.com/

A source for health information and a search tool as well.

LESSON

19

SAMPLE HEALTH/PE LESSONS

EO

Grade Level: 3rd and Up

Browse

SPORTS ILLUSTRATED FOR KIDS

    http://www.siforkids.com/

ROLLER HOCKEY

    http://www.rhockey.com/

or

VISIT THE OLYMPICS SITES

    http://www.olympic.org/
    http://www.sydney.olympic.org/

or

SNOWBOARDING

    http://www.twsnow.com/

or

GIRLS IN SPORTS

    http://www.gogirlmag.com/

Links and Bookmarks

Track one sport with Sportsline, ESPN NFL, soccer.

    http://espnet.sportszone.com/
    http://www.sportsline.com/

Search

Games people play—track a sport around the world. I found basketball team schedules for Europe. What can you find?

    http://espnet.sportszone.com/

Search and Cross-Reference

Plan a sports vacation with a budget of $5000.

    http://travel.org/

AMERICAN GIRL

http://www.americangirl.com/ag/ag.cgi

A site just for girls with advice, places to comment, articles, and more.

AMERICAN HEART ASSOCIATION

http://www.americanheart.org/

Excellent information from this organization.

BALANCE MAGAZINE

http://www.turq.com/balance/index.html

Excellent fitness magazine online.

BODY ATLAS

http://bluecares.com/good/body/

Blue Cross offers a wonderful tour of the human body with diagrams and definitions.

CENTERS FOR DISEASE CONTROL

http://www.cdc.gov/

An excellent organization's home page.

COLUMBIA NET

http://www.columbia.net/

Health care information and links.

CONSUMER PRODUCT SAFETY COMMISSION

http://www.cpsc.gov/

Find information about various products here — download Adobe Acrobat to read some of the files.

DUKE UNIVERSITY MEDICAL CENTER

http://www.mc.duke.edu/healthcr/index.html

Health care information from Duke and other links.

EYENET

http://www.eyenet.org/

Learn more about eye anatomy, and eye health, and ask a doctor questions.

FITNESS FOR KIDS

http://www.fitnesslink.com/changes/kids.htm

Articles and information for parents and for kids.

Food, Nutrition, and Health

http://www.hoptechno.com/bookidx.htm

Links to pamphlets about health, nutrition, and food.

Global Health Network

http://www.pitt.edu/HOME/GHNet/GHNet.html

Excellent information from this organization.

Global Medic

http://www2.cgocable.ca/

Online health and wellness in French and English.

Go, girl! Magazine

http://www.gogirlmag.com/

Girl power finds a place on the net with sports and fitness news for women.

Good Health Web

http://www.social.com/health/index.html

Information on eating well and staying fit.

Health and Fitness Worldwide

http://www.worldguide.com/Fitness/hf.html

Good coverage of the issue from a more global perspective.

Health and Human Services

http://www.os.dhhs.gov/

Health information from the government.

Health Care Information Resources.

http://www-hsl.mcmaster.ca/tomflem/top.html

Links for help in health-related matters.

Health Resources on the Net

http://www.xnet.com/~hret/statind.htm

This site is just links to federal, state, hospital, and educational sites dealing with health matters.

Healthy Refrigerator

http://www.healthyfridge.org/

Teach kids to eat right and stay fit. There are contests.

HYPERDOC: THE NATIONAL LIBRARY OF MEDICINE

http://www.nlm.nih.gov/

Home page and links from the National Library of Medicine.

IFIC FOUNDATION

http://ificinto.health.org/homepage.htm

A good jumping-off point for information about food and nutrition.

INSTITUTE FOR WORK AND HEALTH

http://www.iwh.on.ca/home.htm

Canadian Institute for Work and Health Home Page. Dedicated to improving understanding of the factors that determine workplace health.

INTERNATIONAL FOOD INFORMATION COUNCIL

http://ificinfo.health.org/

More about eating well.

KIDS HEALTH

http://www.4kidshealth.com/

Links to resources, magazines, organizations, and topics of interest.

LOW FAT VEGETARIAN ARCHIVES

http://www.fatfree.com/

More information on eating well.

MAYO CLINIC

http://www.mayo.edu/

Prestigious medical facility with information online.

MEDWEB

http://www.cc.emory.edu/WHSCL/medweb.html#toc

Good source of medical information.

MEDICAL AND HEALTH CAREERS

http://www.furman.edu/~snyder/careers/medical.html

Links to descriptions about medical and health careers.

NORTH AMERICAN VEGETARIAN SOCIETY

http://www.cyberveg.org/navs/

This site offers information about eating well and staying fit.

ONLINE HEALTH NETWORK

http://healthnet.ivi.com/

From the Mayo Clinic, good information and advice with search capabilities

SPORTS MEDICINE

http://www.sports-miedcine.com/

A page for basic information on all kinds of sport injuries.

STRETCHING AND FLEXIBILITY

http://www.enteract.com/~bradapp/docs/rec/stretching/stretching_toc.html

Site devoted to helping you get ready to exercise and carry on once you start.

UNIVERSITY OF PITTSBURGH ALTERNATIVE MEDICINE

http://www.pitt.edu/~cbw/altm.html

Sources of information on unconventional, unorthodox, unproven, or alternative, complementary, innovative, integrative therapies.

VA IMAGE BROWSER

http://www.vis.colostate.edu/cgi-bin/gva/gvaview

Pictures of parts of the body.

VEGETARIAN SOCIETY OF UK

http://www.veg.org/veg/Orgs

Promoting a healthy diet.

VIRTUAL HOSPITAL

http://indy.radiology.uiowa.edu/

Take a tour and see how a hospital is organized.

VIRTUAL MEDICAL CENTER

http://www-sci.lib.uci.edu/HSG/Medical.html

A complete medical reference.

WELLNESS ONLINE

http://www.wellnesscenter.com/

Another place to find information and links for staying healthy and fit.

WELLNESS WEB

http://www.wellweb.com/

A resource whose mission is to help people discover the best and most appropriate medical information available.

WHOLE FOODS MARKET

http://www.wholefoods.com/wf.html

An informative guide on sports nutrition and the healing power of food.

WORLD HEALTH NET

http://www.who.ch/

Information with a global perspective.

YSN

http://www.ysn.com/health/

Health and fitness information for kids.

General Sports

ADVENTURE SPORTS ONLINE

http://www.adventuresports.com/

For the more adventurous sportsperson.

BECKET MAGAZINE

http://www.beckett.com/

The sports magazine online — for trading card aficionados.

BICYCLING MAGAZINE

http://www.bicyclingmagazine.com/

Information, news, articles, and links for bicyclists.

BICYCLE TRANSIT AUTHORITY

http://www.bikeinfo.com/

Visit the repair shop, find bikes for sale, check out bike clothing, and more.

CHEER ONLINE

http://www.cheeronline.com/cheeronline/index.html

Online magazine for cheerleading.

CYBER-STADIUM

http://www.interlog.com/~mvanhoek/cyber-stadium/cybrstad.html

A wonderful site maintained by a Canadian with links to all sports.

Disabled Sports USA

http://www.dsusa.org/~dsusa/

Links, information, history, and profiles.

Femina Web Search

http://femina.cybergrrl.com/

Links to sites on women in sports, especially college.

Field and Stream

http://www.fieldandstream.com/

If you can't go fishing, this is almost the next best thing.

Footbag WorldWide Information

http://www.footbag.org/

Hacky Sack or FootBag, it's played all over the world. Here's where to learn more.

International Snowboard Federation

http://www.isf.ch/

For snowboarders the world over, this is your place with a monthly magazine.

Jump into Snowboarding

http://tqjunior.advanced.org/3885/

Kids created this site for others who are interested in some information and tips.

Locker Room Sports for Kids

http://members.aol.com/msdaizy/sports/locker.html

Helpful tips, information about your favorite sports stars, and more

Motorsports Hall of Fame

http://www.mshf.com/

Racing fans can go here to the Hall of Fame and a museum.

Nando Sports Server

http://www2.nando.net/SportServer/

Latest news, pictures, columns, and archives for all sports.

National Sports Center for the Disabled

http://www.nscd.org/nscd/

A great place to find information, links, and education resources.

PERSONAL TENNIS COACH

http://tennisserver.com/coach/

Try this site for help with that serve.

ROLLER HOCKEY ONLINE

http://www.rhockey.com/

A magazine for kids and adults with online skates on their feet.

SHORTER REPORTER

http://www.sikids.com/shorter/index.html

Sports articles for kids from *Sports Illustrated for Kids.*

SPORTING NEWS

http://www.sportingnews.com/

Check their archives for sports history information or just read the latest sports news.

SPORTSQUEST

http://www.sportsquest.com/

Another new site for those into all kinds of sports. Check out the coaching tips and sports science sections.

SYDNEY 2000 GAMES

http://www.sydney.olympic.org/

What will the sites look like? What preparations are they making?

WEIGHTLIFTING PAGE — PUMPING STATION

http://www.geocities.com/HotSprings/Spa/580/

For those into this sport — lots of information.

WINTER SPORTS FOUNDATION

http://www.wintersports.org/

If winter sports are for you, so is this site.

WOMEN IN SPORTS

http://www.arcade.uiowa.edu/proj/ge/

Just what you think.

YAHOOLIGANS SPORTS PAGE

http://www.yahooligans.com/content/spa/

Scores, news, standings, and links.

Baseball

Two Great Sites

J. SKILTON'S BASEBALL LINKS

http://www.baseball-links.com/

More than 1642 links to information about baseball from pros to Little League.

SPORTSZONE

http://www.sportszone.com/

Up-to-the-minute sports news with audio, video, commentary, and more for all sports.

More Sites

BALLPARKS

http://www.ballparks.com/

If you want more on the history and statistics of some of America's most famous playing fields, just check here.

FANLINK

http://www.fanlink.com/

The home page for U.S. minor league teams

KIDS ONLY BASEBALL PAGE

http://www.cubs.com/fanfare/kids/kidson.htm

Learn how to pitch a fastball, manage a team, hit, and catch.

LEARN2 UNDERSTAND BASEBALL

http://learn2.com/05/0542/0542.html

Step by step, how to play the game.

LEGENDARY LADIES OF BASEBALL

http://members.aol.com/legendlady/index.html

History, pictures, and biographies of the players.

NATIONAL BASEBALL HALL OF FAME

http://www.baseball/halloffame.org/

Take a tour — not to be missed by baseball fans.

NEGRO LEAGUE ARCHIVES

http://www.infi.net/~moxie/nlb/nlb.html

The history of the athletes who played in the Negro Leagues.

NEGRO LEAGUES BASEBALL ONLINE

http://www.nc5.infi.net/~moxie/nlb/nlb.html

Information covering 75 years of baseball.

NEW YORK YANKEES HOME PLATE

http://www.yankees.com//

Baseball fans must report here — even if you live in Atlanta!

Basketball

ALLEYOOP

http://www.alleyoop.com/

Another site for fans of pro and college round ball.

BASKETBALL MANIA

http://tqjunior.advanced.org/3952/

Kids created this site so you could learn more about the game.

COLLEGE BASKETBALL PAGE

http://www.onlysports.com/bball/

Up-to-date information for college basketball fans.

HOOP DREAMS — NBA

http://www.nba.com/

The site for the fan who wants scores, updates on teams, and more.

JUST HOOPS

http://www.justwomen.com/justhoops.html

Basketball information about women players.

LEARN2 PLAY BASKETBALL

http://learn2.com/05/0543/0543.html

Step by step, learn the game, its history, and how to play.

NATIONAL WHEELCHAIR BASKETBALL ASSOCIATION

http://www.nwba.org/

A sport played around the world is profiled here.

PROFESSIONAL BASKETBALL SERVER

http://www.netgen.com/sis/NBA/NBA.html

More information for the fan.

WOMEN'S NATIONAL BASKETBALL ASSOCIATION

http://www.wnba.com/

Follow this new pro sport here.

Football

AMERICAN FOOTBALL QUARTERLY

http://www.afqmag.com/

A journal for professional coaches.

FOOTBALL SERVER

http://www.nando.net/SportServer/football/

A great site for the fan.

NETSPORT NFT MAGAZINE

http://www.netsportmag.com/

Online magazine for football fans with links and a place to chat.

NFL HOME PAGE

http://www.nfl.com/

Of course they have a home page.

NFL INFO WEB

http://www.cs.cmu.edu/afs/cs/user/vernon/www/nfl.html

More for the fan.

PRO FOOTBALL HALL OF FAME

http://www.canton-ohio.com/hof/

Read about the history and the great players of this sport.

Golf

CYBER GOLF

http://www.cybergolf.com/lessons/lessons.html

Online golf lessons.

GOLF WEB

http://www.golfweb.com/

Professional golf — everything you need to know.

GOLF ONLINE

http://www.golfonline.com/

News, instruction, equipment, resorts, and the latest coverage.

MASTERS

http://www.augustagolf.com/

History of the tournament, news about the players, and photos.

TAYLOR MADE KIDS

http://www.taylormadekids.com/

A game, bulletin board, and news.

UNITED STATES GOLF ASSOCIATION

http://www.usga.org/

Complete golf coverage.

Hockey

AWESOME HOCKEY LINKS

http://www.lgcy.com/skyway/links/AAEZhock.htm

For the ice and inline enthusiast, the links here cover the world of hockey.

COVERING THE NHL

http://www2.nando.net/SportServer/hockey/nhl.html

Nando Sports provides all the inside info, schedules, and scores.

HOCKEY LINKS

http://galaxy.einet.net/galaxy/Leisure-and-Recreation/Sports/Hockey.html

Another set of links for hockey, including underwater hockey and Stanley Cup trivia.

Hockey News

http://www.thn.com/

Wonderful coverage online of this worldwide sport.

Hockey Player Magazine

http://www.hockeyplayer.com/

Get an online issue of *Hockey Player* or *Women's Hockey.*

In the Crease

http://www.westol.com/~bluliner

For the hockey fan, this site is just what the coach ordered. IHL and NHL info and links.

NHL Home Page

http://www.nhl.com/

This is a very comprehensive site for NHL fans with scores, schedules, cool shots, news, and notes.

Science of Hockey

http://www.exploratorium.edu/hockey/

Find out what's going on when you hit a slapshot, check a player, and hit the ice.

WWW Hockey Guide

http://www.hockeyguide.com/

More than 1100 links to hockey worldwide.

Soccer

Awesome Soccer Links

http://www.lgcy.com/skyway/links/AAHQsocc.htm

A long list of links for those interested in soccer around the world.

Planet Soccer

http://www.planet-soccer.com/

This site covers soccer: U.S.A., youth, international, camps, and more.

SoccerAmerica

http://www.socceramerica.com/SA/

News stories and information about college, national, and pro teams.

SOCCER NEWS ONLINE INFO

http://www.intermark.com/soccer/index.html

Covers U.S. and world news in soccer.

U.S. SOCCER WEB PAGES

http://www.cs.cmu.edu/~mdwheel/us-soccer/

Information about professional, amateur, and youth soccer, with links for coaching and refereeing as well.

USA Today SOCCER NEWS

http://www.usatoday.com/sports/soccer/sos.htm

From the daily newspaper comes great coverage.

INTERESTING SITES

A variety pack of sites that might prove fun. Provided to give you some idea of the scope of what you'll find online and perhaps some ways to broaden your students' horizons.

New Trends

Live events: Almost like a TV Guide, listings will tell you when shows like these samples from recent chats are live:

Mystery Place; Writer's Workshop

Spanish Chat Game

Homefront (home improvement)

Tennis Chat

Godzilla Movie Premiere live from Madison Square Garden

One place you can find updates of live events is at http://www.ylive.com/

Two Great Sites

HOMETIME

http://www.hometime.com/

Quite a few sites are online for home improvement. This is just one of them.

PROJECT CENTRAL AMERICA

`http://www.adventureonline.com/pca/`

Teachers created a real-time learning experience with journals, pictures, geographical information and more.

More Sites

7 WONDERS OF THE WORLD

`http://pharos.bu.edu/Egypt/Wonders/`

What could be better for building a frame of reference.

ANGUS' ON THE NET

`http://www.raingod.com/angus/Misc/SiteMap.html`

A young man from the UK has posted not only tours of ancient lands, but some wonderful photos, computer graphics, HTML help, and recipes.

AVALON

`http://www.avalon.co.uk/avalon/`

Avalon is a role-playing world, a mythological place where you can develop your own character and interact with other real-life and imaginary beings.

BIGBOOK

`http://www.bigbook.com/`

Among their offerings are a search facility for locating types of businesses. But check out their map (bottom of home page) and type in your address. It will zoom right to your neighborhood!

CASTLES ON THE WEB

`http://www.castlesontheweb.com/`

Information, pictures, and a tour of some famous castles.

CHICAGO MUSEUM OF SCIENCE AND INDUSTRY

`http://www.msichicago.org/`

Find some wonderful interactive adventures here, movies, sounds, and great science.

CHINA THE BEAUTIFUL

`http://www.chinapage.com/`

Wonderful site with art, stories, history, and more.

CHINA EXPERIENCE

http://zinnia.umfacad.maine.edu/~mshea/China/china.html

An informative and pictorial tour of China.

CITY GUIDE

http://cityguide.lycos.com/

Once you click on a U.S. state, you can get extensive information about major cities in that state. Weather, educational facilities, hometown sports and news, a bit of local flavor, and pictures are added.

CITYNET

http://www.city.net/

Another place to find information about cities.

DANSWORLD SKATEBOARDING

http://web.cps.msu.edu/~dunhamda/dw/dansworld.html

Even the kids on these wheels have a page. Find out what they're into.

FIND YOUR TRUE HOME

http://pathfinder.com/money/best-cities/searchopener.html

Plug in your preferences and get matched with the city for you.

FLAGS OF THE WORLD

http://www.imagesoft.net/flags/flags.html

A large searchable data base. Do those in your text need updating?

GENEALOGY

http://www.firstct.com/fv/tmapmenu.html

This online tutor will help you understand public documents or other records as you begin to track family history.

GEOCITIES

http://www.geocities.com/

Find some of the best pages posted by individuals. Searchable by category.

GORP

http://www.gorp.com/

Great Outdoor Recreation Pages — the name says it all. Guides and a library.

HOMEFAIR

http://www.homefair.com/

Find mortgage information here, but also check out the salary calculator: allows you to determine the salary you would need to make in a new city, based on cost-of-living differences. The moving calculator tells the cost of a move.

HOTWIRED MAGAZINE

http://www.hotwired.com/frontdoor/

News and commentary about American society.

HOUSENET

http://www.housenet.com/

For the home improvement and do-it-yourself crowd, this site offers sage advice and more.

IMPACT ONLINE

http://www.impactonline.org/

Find out how your kids can get involved in helping their community.

INTERACTIVE MAPS

http://wxp.atms.purdue.edu/interact.html

Makes the use of maps come alive.

J-TRACK SATELLITE TRACKING

http://liftoff.msfc.nasa.gov/RealTime/JTrack/

Amazing site that links you to real satellites like those for search and rescue, spacecraft, or weather.

JEOPARDY

http://www.jeopardy.com/

Play online, learn, and take a challenge.

KING ARTHUR

http://www.bretagne.com/english/doc/histoire/arthur.htm

A site for the history behind the legend.

LONELY PLANET

http://www.lonelyplanet.com/

Travel information for travel routes beyond the ordinary.

MapBlast

http://www.proximus.com/

Find any address in the United States, zoom in and see what's around there. Also see European city maps in the future.

National Genealogical Society

http://www.ngsgenealogy.org/

Documents here help you conduct oral history interviews, preserve family photos, and more.

National Scenic Byways

http://www.byways.org./

For some wonderful views of breathtaking scenery, go here.

The Nobel Foundation

http://nobel.sdsc.edu/

Official site of the foundation. Find here information about the winners and the work of the foundation

Park Search

http://www.llbean.com/parksearch/

L.L. Bean offers a place to explore nearly 900 outdoor locations.

PBS

http://www.pbs.org/

Check out their array of offerings from the photo essay on the Pursuit of Happiness to lemurs.

Pen Pals Online

http://www.shadetree.com/~rplogman/

If you're looking for online pen pals for your kids, start here.

Pirates, Privateers, Buccaneers

http://www.columbia.edu/~tg66/piratepage.htm

History of pirates, facts and folklore, and places of pirate lore.

Roadside America

http://www.roadsideamerica.com/

If offbeat attractions are just what you're looking for, try this page before you travel.

SECOND HARVEST

http://www.secondharvest.org/

Find out what you can do to help the hunger problem in America.

SEND A POSTCARD

http://postcards.www.media.mit.edu/Postcards/

Go online, make a postcard, and send it to a friend.

SERVENET

http://www.servenet.org/

Type in your zip code and find organizations that can use your volunteer help.

SITES THAT DO STUFF

http://www.amused.com/sites.html

Check them out before using — but lots of fun stuff here.

SUBWAY NAVIGATOR

http://metro.ratp.fr:10001/bin/cities/english

Pick one of many cities worldwide, check the map of the subway, and plot your route (available in French, too!).

TRAVEL EXCHANGE ONLINE

http://www.travelx.com/

Another place to plan a vacation or learn more about a country.

UNICA ISLAND

http://library.advanced.org/10005/

A student-created site that explores communication, its history, and technology.

USA CITY LINK

http://www.neosoft.com/citylink/

Need to know something about a city? It might be here.

VACATIONS

http://www.vacations.com/

Take a break and go! Or see how you can plan your vacation online.

WHEEL OF FORTUNE

http://www.wheeloffortune.com/

Play the famous game online.

FOR PEOPLE INTO PUZZLES

ACROSS PUZZLE GALLERY

http://www.litsoft.com/across/gallery.htm

Play online.

ONLINE CROSSWORDS

http://www.clearlight.com/~vivi/xw/big.html

Another site for playing online.

PUZZLE DEPOT

http://www.puzzledepot.com/

Crossword puzzles, games, and trivia to play online.

PUZZLES BY FRED

http://www.macnamarasband.com/

Download the software and try some of these puzzles.

FOR KIDS OF ALL AGES INTO CARS

One way of getting to high school kids is through their love of cars, music, TV, and movies. Check out some of these sites for them and with them.

ALLDATA

http://www.alldata.tsb.com/

Information for servicing and repairing your car.

AUTO CHANNEL

http://www.theautochannel.com/

News about cars and the industry; very up-to-the-minute.

AUTOSITE

http://www.autosite.com/

News and links for the car enthusiast.

AUTO WEEK

http://www.autoweek.com/

Another place for car info for you and your driving kids.

AUTOMOBILE SAFETY FOUNDATION

http://www.cyber.net/asf

This organization is involved in automobile safety.

CAR AND DRIVER

http://www.caranddriver.com/

Car fans' favorite magazine is now online.

CARPOINT

http://www.carpoint.msn.com/

Microsoft offers links to car information.

CAR TALK

http://www.cartalk.com/

National Public Radio's popular call-in show with tons of information.

EDMOND'S

http://www.edmonds.com/

More online car infomation.

FRANK'S LAND YACHT MARINA

http://www.voicenet.com/~perches/landycht.html

Site for info about long-ago behemoths that ruled our roads.

HARRIS MOUNTAINTOP

http://www.semi.harris.com/automotive/

A page with dozens of links to automotive sites.

HEMMINGS MOTOR NEWS

http://www.hmn.com/

Old car buffs have this site online.

INTELLICHOICE

http://www.intellichoice.com/

Advice about what it really costs to own an auto.

KELLEY BLUE BOOK

http://www.kbb.com/

Want to know what that old car is worth or whether you're paying too much for a new one? Check out the experts.

NATIONAL HIGHWAY SAFETY TRANSPORTATION ASSOCIATION

http://www.nhsta.dot.gov/

How safe is your car? How do they test them? Look here for answers.

ROAD TRIP USA

http://www.moon.om/rt.usa/rdtrip/rdtrip.html

The author has logged 25,000 miles in search of vanishing ways of U.S. life. Find some of America's oddities here.

TURBOZINE

http://www.magicnet.net/~joeg/turbo-mag/

A fast car magazine with tell-it-like-it-is commentary.

Car Manufacturers' Home Pages

BMW

http://www.bmwusa.com/

CHRYSLER

http://www.chryslercars.com/

FERRARI'S HOME PAGE

http://www.ferrari.it

FORD

http://www.ford.com/

GENERAL MOTORS

http://www.gm.com/

MERCEDES

http://www.mercedes.com/

TOYOTA

http://www.toyota.com/

MUSIC

Most of the more famous bands have Web sites. Some of these, plus other music sites, can be other than mainstream. Check them out before you turn the kids loose.

New Trend
Before you try out some of the music sites, download the best software for streaming audio. It will sound almost like CD quality. Try one of these sites.

LIQUID AUDIO

    http://www.liquidaudio.com/

A2B MUSIC

    http://www.a2bmusic.com/

REAL AUDIO

    http://www.real.com/

A Great Site
MUSIC BOULEVARD

    http://www.musicblvd.com/

A comprehensive site with audio for those interested in jazz, classical, rock, and more.

More Sites
ADDICTED TO NOISE

    http://www.addict.com/

Online music magazine.

ALLSTAR

    http://www2.rocktropolis.com/main/allstar/home.asp

News, reviews, information, and interviews.

AMERICAN MUSIC CENTER

    http://www.ingress.com/amc/

Classical music links as well as scores are available here.

LESSON

20

SAMPLE LESSONS FOR MUSIC

EO   ## Grade Level: 4th and Up

Browse

MUSIC AROUND THE WORLD

```
http://www.rootsworld.com/rw/
http://www-scf.usc.edu/~jrush/music/
http://www.music.indiana.edu/misc/music_resources.html
```

Links and Bookmarks

WHAT'S POPULAR AROUND THE WORLD?

```
http://www.billboard-online.com/
http://www.musicblvd.com/
```

Search Forward and Back

SWING BANDS OF THE 1940S.

```
http://pastperfect.com/
```

Search and Cross-Reference

Theater scavenger hunt.

BILLBOARD ONLINE

```
http://www.billboard-online.com/
```

The famous chart plus a quiz and reviews.

CLASSICS WORLD

```
http://www.classicalmus.com/bmgclassics/index.html
```

Artists, composers, opera, and news.

Eardrum — World Music Radio

http://www.eardrum.com/eardrum_home.html

Hear the music of the world.

The Hitlist

http://www.hitsworld.com/

Not only offers links to hit lists, but will recommend music just for you.

Jazz Online

http://www.jazzonln.com/

You'll find lots to learn about jazz here.

Johns Hopkins Sheet Music Collection

http://musicbox.mse.jhu.edu/

The Lester S. Levy Sheet Music Collection is available here to study.

Library of Musical Links

http://www-scf.usc.edu/~jrush/music/

Connect to concerts, artists, pop, classical, and worldwide sites

MTV

http://www.mtv.com/

Go here to find out what the kids are listening to.

Music Central

http://musiccentral.msn.com/Default/Home

Concert reviews, daily news, and music information.

Music Education Online

http://www.geocities.com/Athens/2405/index.html

Resources for music teachers.

Music Resources on the Internet

http://www.music.indiana.edu/music_resources/

Here you'll find links to performers, orchestras, bands, and more.

Music Theory Online

http://smt.ucsb.edu/mto/mtohome.html

An online journal covering topics of interest.

NATIONAL ENDOWMENT FOR THE ARTS

    `http://arts.endow.gov/`

Resources, news, and links for all the arts.

PASTPERFECT

    `http://pastperfect.com/`

Remastered versions of some of the great music of the 1920s,'30s, and '40s.

REAL MUSIC FOR THE REAL WORLD

    `http://www.rootsworld.com/rw/`

Samples of music from around the world.

ROLLING STONE MAGAZINE

    `http://www.rollingstone.com/Splash.phtml`

The well-known music magazine is online now.

SONICNET

    `http://www.sonicnet.com/`

Live events, video premieres, debuts of new music.

SOUND MARKET

    `http://soundmarket.net/`

Country music covered in depth.

THE ULTIMATE BAND LIST

    `http://www.ubl.com/`

Music links you can search by genre, letter, or resource.

VIBE

    `http://www.vibe.com/site/index.html`

Rhythm and blues, rap, soul, and traditional African-American entertainment are covered.

MOVIES

Sites exist these days for almost every major film released. Better yet are sites that discuss films and provide previews, like this one:

PREMIERE MAGAZINE

```
http://www.premieremag.com/
```

Find interviews, previews, reviews, and more.

More Sites

BOXOFFICE ONLINE

```
http://boxoff.com/
```

Reviews, previews, and in-depth articles about movies and the people who make them.

CYBER FILM SCHOOL

```
http://www.cyberfilmschool.com/
```

A collection of film-related material plus a curriculum on making movies.

CINEMA 1

```
http://www.cinema1.com/
```

In Spanish or English, follow the latest news on film.

CINEMANIA

```
http://www.msn.com/cinemania/
```

Film reviews, commentary, and news articles.

CINEMEDIA

```
http://www.afionline.org/CineMedia/welcomes/you.html
```

A searchable data base to help you find more about your favorite film.

DIRECTORS GUILD

```
http://dga.org/dga/
```

You'll find interviews, information on various programs, and links to other sites.

FILM.COM

```
http://www.film.com/
```

Site provides a critical perspective and reviews of films.

FILM SCOUTS

```
http://www.filmscouts.com/
```

Previews, interviews, and coverage of film festivals.

FOOTAGE.NET

```
http://www.footage.net:2900/
```

Film clips available from several sources.

HOLLYWOOD CREATIVE DIRECTORY

http://www.hollyvision.com/

Entertainment address book of hundreds of companies, agents, and executives.

HOLLYWOOD INTERNET ENTERTAINMENT INDEX

http://www.hollywoodnetwork.com/

Interviews and chats with those in front of and behind the camera. Also has industry news.

HOLLYWOOD ONLINE

http://www.hollywood.com/

Movie and video guide, showtimes, movie talk, and movie music.

INTERNET MOVIE DATA BASE

http://us.imdb.com/

Well-indexed database of movie information.

MOTION PICTURE INDUSTRY

http://library.advanced.org/10015/

If you didn't know how the industry works, after viewing this site you will.

MOVIELINK

http://www.movielink.com/

Type in your zip code and get the local listing for movies — places, times, ratings, and previews of coming attractions.

VARIETY MAGAZINE

http://www.variety.com/

The magazine all about Hollywood is now online.

TELEVISION

As with film, almost every popular show and channel has a Web site. This list is more general.

ENTERTAINMENT WEEKLY

http://cgi.pathfinder.com/ew/

Covers all aspects of media. You can certainly find current information here.

FRONTLINE ONLINE

http://www2.pbs.org/wgbh/pages/frontline/

The esteemed news show brings its ideals to the Net with well-researched and cross-referenced stories.

MEDIA UNPLUGGED

http://library.advanced.org/11360/

Learn how the industry works, program an evening of entertainment, or create a show

MEGA MEDIA LINKS

http://www.rtvf.nwu.edu/links/links.html

Over 700 links for TV, radio, film, video, new media, and more.

MR. SHOWBIZ

http://www.mrshowbiz.com/

News, reviews, gossip, and a plastic surgery lab; match the faces with the names.

MZTV MUSEUM OF TELEVISION

http://www.mztv.com/mztv/mztvhome.html

Good writing and excellent graphics make this site an interesting TV find.

TOTALLY TV MAGAZINE

http://www.tottv.com/index.html

Articles on shows, TV news, and Totally Teen TV.

TV ARCHIVES

http://tvnews.vanderbilt.edu/

What was on the TV news: full coverage going back several decades.

TV PLEX

http://directnet.com/wow/tv/

Interviews with the stars along with photos and biographies.

TV SCHEDULES AROUND THE WORLD

http://www.buttle.com/tv/schedule.htm

A collection of guides that tell you what's on where and when.

TV TONIGHT

http://www.tvtonight.com/

Episode summaries, schedules, and links to individual show sites.

SHOPPING ON THE NET

As the Net gets more commercial and using credit cards online becomes more secure, many people will take advantage of the convenience of shopping online.

New Trends

Shopping around the world. Prepare before you shop:

MONEYMINDED

http://www.moneyminded.com/

Useful articles for women who are in charge of the finances.

More Sites

Here, as a sample, are some places already online for you to shop.

21ST CENTURY PLAZA

http://www.21stcenturyplaza.com/

Not only can you find Bubba Gump Shrimp here, but you will also find Pit Stop for NASCAR fans, a sports shop, and more.

ALL INTERNET SHOPPING DIRECTORY

http://www.all-internet.com/

Find what you need online with this searchable site.

AMAZON BOOKS

http://www.amazon.com/

They have more than 1 million books for the whole family to browse through.

B & G

http://www.bggolf.com/

For golf, bowling and racket sports, this is a good place to start.

BIGDEAL

http://www.bigdeal.com/

For the skateboarders, wakeboarders, and snowboarders in your family. Let them check this site out!

BIGTOE SPORTS

http://www.bigtoesports.com/

Clothing, footwear, and equipment for cheerleading, soccer, football, basketball, track and field, and wrestling.

CD NOW

http://www.cdnow.com/

Looking for music? Looking for movies? This may be the place to find it all.

CYBERTOWN

http://www.cybertown.com/

For more than just shopping, take a tour here. You'll find a library, a mall, an education center and much more.

ECOMALL

http://www.ecomall.com/

This site contains links for those who want to know more about shopping for all your needs with the ecology in mind.

GOOD GUYS

http://www.thegoodguys.com/

For your electronic needs, computer needs, or for just browsing the latest technology, start here.

I MALL

http://www.imall.com/

This site lists itself as the largest retailer on the Web with more than 750 stores. You could spend some time here!

L.L. BEAN

http://www.llbean.com/

For people who love the outdoors, here is your clothing store. Order online or request a free catalog.

LANDS' END

http://www.landsend.com/

Another store online where you can order clothes for the entire family.

MADE IN TUSCANY

http://www.madeintuscany.com/

What could we buy if we went to Italy?

PRODUCT ZOO

http://www.productzoo.com/

Famous brands of clothing, computers, household items, sports, education, and entertainment items can be found here.

SHOP AUSTRALIA

http://shopaustralia.com.au/

From an Aboriginal artist marketplace to gourmet bush food, this is the place to shop.

SHOP IRELAND

http://www.shopireland.com/

You don't have to travel there to shop for Irish crafts and fine goods.

TORONTO MALLS

http://www.torontomalls.com/

See what Canada has to offer the world.

TOYTROPOLIS

http://www.toytropolis.com/

From around the world, for any kid, any age, you'll find great toys here.

U.K. SHOPPING CITY

http://www.ukshops.co.uk/

Shop for goods from the United Kingdom

WEEKEND A FIRENZE

http://www.weekendafirenze.com/waf00.htm

Shop Italy.

WWW SPORTS GOODS

http://www.sportsgoods.com/

Baseball, basketball, hockey, football, softball, and soccer equipment and clothing are all available here.

VIAMALL

http://www.ishops.com/

A long list of links to places to shop is here — more than 25,000 items.

PLAZATOWN

http://internet-plaza.net/plazatown/

You can use their search engine to help you find what you need, or you can go window shopping through a long list of sites.

TRAVEL THE WORLD

Listed below are a sampling of sites that will let you and your students visit a foreign country.

New Trends

More wonderful and picturesque sites from people all over the world who want to showcase their city, country, home town, etc.

THE VIRTUAL TOURIST

`http://www.vtourist.com/`

Plan to take your kids anywhere and see the sites. This is a great place to start your worldwide travels.

LONELY PLANET

`http://www.lonelyplanet.com/`

A wonderful site for sightseeing all over the world.

Africa

AFRICA.COM

`http://africa.com/content.html`

News, business, travel, and more information.

AFRICAN CONNECTIONS

`http://www.melanet.com/melanet/connections`

AFRICAN TRAVEL GATEWAY

`http://www.africantravel.com/index.html`

Find getaways, accommodations, sites to see, and more.

ARAB NET

`http://www.arab.net/`

Covering history, business, travel, culture, and geography in an extensive site.

IVORY COAST

`http://www.webperfect.com/afrinet/ivory/ivory.html`

ON SAFARI

http://www.onsafari.com/Default1.asp

Plan one or just pretend and visit the wonders of this continent.

TOURS AND SAFARI IN ZAMBIA

http://www.zamnet.zm/zamnet/zntb.html

Asia

ASIA ONLINE

http://www.asia-online.com/index.html

Business, industry, and regional news.

ASIA TRAVEL

http://asiatravel.com/

Plan your tour or vacation from this site.

INFO HUB — ASIA

http://www.infohub.com/TRAVEL/TRAVELLER/asia.html

Extensive site with tour information.

JAPANESE NATIONAL TOURIST ORGANIZATION

http://www.ntt.jp/japan/TCJ/TC.html

SINGAPORE ONLINE GUIDE

http://www.ncb.gov.sg/

TOUR IN CHINA

http://www.ihep.ac.cn/tour/china_tour.html

TRAVEL ASIA

http://www.asia-online.com/travel/index.html

Travel essentials and resources.

TRAVELING IN THE MIDDLE EAST

http://travelers.israel.net/middle-east/

A comprehensive guide to help you with your trip.

VIETNAM TRAVEL

    `http://maingate.net:80/vn/`

WESTERN CHINA

    `http://www.public.iastate.edu/~qzourb/homepage.html`

Australia and South Pacific

AUSTRALIA TOURISM NET

    `http://www.atn.com.au/`

Tours, adventures, national parks, and recreation are covered.

HIDEAWAY HOLIDAYS

    `http://www.magna.com.au/~hideaway/`

If an island vacation is what you want, this might be the place to start.

ORBIT OVER THE PACIFIC ISLANDS

    `http://public-www.pi.se/~orbit/pac.html`

Choose your island, choose your vacation spot.

PACIFIC ISLANDS INTERNET RESOURCES

    `http://www2.hawaii.edu/~ogden/piir/index.html`

For travel or other information, check this site.

SYDNEY

    `http://www.ozemail.com.au/~eau/sydbest.html`

Tour the city Down Under.

TELSTRA

    `http://springboard.telstra.com.au/australia/index.htm`

A springboard to everything you need to know about Australia.

UNIVERSAL TRAVEL MAGAZINE

    `http://www.travel.taanz.org.nz/`

From New Zealand, information you can use before you travel.

Canada

ALBERTA ADVENTURE TOURS

http://www.discoveralberta.com/AATours/welcome.html

Take a look at one of Canada's western provinces.

BRITISH COLUMBIA

http://www.gov.bc.ca/tourism/tourism.html

Visit this beautiful province online.

CALGARY EXPLORER

http://www.calexplorer.com/

Take a look at one of Canada's beautiful cities.

CTC — QUEBEC

http://206.191.33.50/tourism/Canada/quebec.html

Prepare for your tour of this province by going here first.

MONTREAL

http://www.montreal-live.com/

What to do, where to stay, and what to see.

IT'S ONTARIO

http://www.gov.on.ca/MBS/english/its_ontario/

A guide for all visitors with history, government, and places to see.

NOVA SCOTIA

http://TTG.SBA.Dal.Ca/nstour/

Take a tour.

OTTAWA

http://www.scs.carleton.ca/ottawa/ottawa.html

Canada's capital is clean, friendly, and online.

RECREATIONAL TRAVEL LIBRARY

http://www.solutions.net/rec-travel/north_america/canada/

TELEGRAPHE DE QUEBEC

http://www.telegraphe.com/

Online guide to this remarkable city.

TORONTO'S INFORMATION GUIDE

http://www.torinfo.com/

Search and learn about this beautiful city before you travel.

TOUR MONTREAL

http://www.cam.org/~fishon1/montrea.html

Montreal architecture, the churches of the city, and other interesting sites.

TOURISM TORONTO

http://www.tourism-toronto.com/

Where should you stay? What should you see? It's all here.

Europe

AMSTERDAM VIRTUAL TOUR

http://www.channels.nl/

Visual tour that's almost like being there. Be careful, though — you can visit their red light district. It's avoidable, though, and the other information is terrific.

AUSTRIA

http://austria-info.at/index.html

DISCOVER FRENCH CHATEAUX

http://www.chateaux-france.com/

We went here to find the Count of Monte Cristo's house.

FRANCE

http://www.france.com/

Start your tour here and see some of the sites.

FRANCE, CULTURE, LANGUAGE, AND TRAVEL

http://cyberzone.net/wharton/France/

Another way to learn more about the country.

HOLLAND

http://www.xxlink.nl/nbt/

ICELAND

http://www.rfisk.is/english/iceland/rest_of_iceland.html

INTERNET WAY (VIRTUAL TOUR FRANCE)

http://www.iway.fr/internet-way/uk/

LATVIA ONLINE

http://www.vernet.lv

THE RUSSIAN CHRONICLE (TRAVELING THROUGH RUSSIA)

http://www.worldmedia.fr/

SPANISH MAPS

http://edb518ea.edb.utexas.edu/html/spanishmaps.html#Chile

UNITED KINGDOM GUIDE

http://www.cs.ucl.ac.uk/misc/uk/intro.html

VIRTUAL LONDON

http://www.a-london-guide.co.uk

Tour this wonderful city.

THE VIRTUAL ROME

http://www.pathfinder.com/@@PhaM2uHPFgAAQJ18/twep/rome/

South America and Mexico

AMAZON EXPLORERS

http://www.travelsource.com/ecotours/amazon.html

BOLIVIA, PERCHED IN THE CLOUDS

http://www.taponline.com/tap/travel/features/bolivia/

View the wonderful land that once was the home of the Incas.

BRASIL WEB

http://www.escape.com/~jvgkny/Brasil.Web.html

BRASILIA

http://www.civila.com/brasilia/

Tourist sites, history, and more about this famous city.

COLUMBIA

http://www.uniandes.edu.co/Columbia/IndiceColumbia.html

DESTINATION ARGENTINA

http://www.lonelyplanet.com:80/sam/argie.htm

Another beautiful country explored.

GALAPAGOS

http://www.discovergalapagos.com/mainmenu.html

MAGRI TURISMO

http://www.bolivianet.com/magri/index.htm

Travel to Bolivia — adventure and the Amazon await.

MEX GUIDE

http://rtn.net.mx/mexguide/

A colorful guide to help you plan your visit.

MEXICO CONNECT

http://www.mexconnect.com/

Extensive site to visit to learn about the country before you visit.

MEXICO TRAVEL GUIDE

http://www.go2mexico.com/

With the Spanish helper and travel tips, this is a good place to start a tour.

REPUBLICA ARGENTINA

http://www.sectur.gov.ar/

Travel tips, what to wear, and what to see.

WELCOME TO CHILE

http://sunsite.dcc.uchile.cl/chile/chile.html

A Few Other Places

ATHENS, PHOTOGRAPHIC TOUR

http://www.medievolic.com/viajes/athens/

This site provides an extensive slide show of this ancient city.

CALIFORNIA HOME PAGE

http://www.ca.gov/s/

For information about the state of California.

COSTA RICA

http://www.gorp.com/crexpert/

Visit this beautiful country online.

ISRAEL

http://www.israel-mfa.gov.il/mfa/israel50/posters.html

Take a tour of Israel here.

LANDSCAPE AND NATURE PHOTOGRAPHY OF HAWAII

http://hoth.ou.edu/~bgibson/gallery/gallery.htm

Some beautiful scenes, especially of Kilauea Volcano.

MASSACHUSETTS

http://www.state.ma.us/

A great overview of this state from their site.

NEW JERSEY ONLINE

http://www.state.nj.us/

Visit this Eastern state.

NEW YORK SKYSCRAPERS

http://www.geocities.com/CapeCanaveral/3366/nyc.html

Pictures and information.

VIRGINIA

http://www.state.va.us/

Visit this state online.

LOOKING FOR BED AND BREAKFASTS

Another segment of the travel industry is online.

BED AND BREAKFAST DIRECTORY

http://www.bbdirectory.com/

Find a bed and breakfast by city or state.

Bed and Breakfast Encyclopedia Online

http://homearts.com/affil/ahi/main/ahihome.htm

Find a place to stay in the United States or Canada.

Bed and Breakfast — The Ultimate Directory

http://innformation.com/

Find a place to stay in the United States or the rest of the world.

Bed Breakfast Net

http://www.bnbnet.com/

Pictures and information about inns in many countries.

Border to Border

http://www.moriah.com/inns/

Bed and Breakfasts of Oregon, Washington, and California.

Inns and Outs

http://www.innsandouts.com/

Bed-and-breakfast information online.

Travel Assist

http://travelassist.com/

A directory of bed-and-breakfast inns and other small hotels.

Search Engines

As the Net grows, competition is fierce for those wanting to help you find what you are looking for. New search engines crop up every day and the old ones must provide you with a wider search if they are to remain competitive.

Altavista

http://www.altavista.digital.com/

One of the best search tools — searches by keyword.

Dogpile

http://www.dogpile.com/

This one searches several of the most common engines for you.

EXCITE

```
http://www.excite.com/
```

Another search by concept or keyword tool.

INFOSEEK

```
http://www.infoseek.com/
```

Yet another excellent search tool.

INTERNET SLEUTH

```
http://www.isleuth.com/
```

Search by category or keyword.

JUMPCITY

```
http://www.jumpcity.com/list-page.html
```

Links you only to sites they have reviewed — broken into categories.

KIDSCLICK

```
http://sunsite.berkeley.edu/KidsClick!/
```

A kids' search engine from the University at Berkeley.

LOOKSMART

```
http://www.looksmart.com/
```

Reader's Digest's excellent site is growing every time we check in. Safe sites only are listed here.

LYCOS

```
http://www.lycos.com/
```

One of the best search engines — searches by keyword.

SEARCH.COM

```
http://www.search.com/
```

Excellent. Several search engines in one place — try **Infoseek.**

SNAP

```
http://home.snap.com/
```

Similar to Yahoo in format. Another place to cross-reference.

STARTING POINT

```
http://www.stpt.com/
```

Still another comprehensive search engine.

YAHOO

`http://www.yahoo.com/`

The famous search engine — search by category.

YAHOOLIGANS FOR KIDS

`http://www.yahooligans.com/`

Search for the younger kids here.

P A R T

III

LIVING WITH THE NET

445

THE INTERNET AT HOME AND OTHER USEFUL TIPS

I n my training classes with parents, I am often asked what kinds of activities can be done at home for those with an Internet connection. Here are some suggestions for keeping your kids involved in the learning process and bringing the whole family to the online experience.

> **In this Chapter**
>
> - Sites for Browsing at Home
> - Ideas for Practicing Searching at Home
> - Ways to Practice Using Hyperlinks at Home
> - Plug-Ins
> - Copying and Pasting from the Internet
> - Copyright Laws

New Trends

Doing some preparation at home. Whether you're car shopping, looking for an apartment, thinking of a vacation, or just want more information, the Internet is becoming the tool many people turn to. We've researched some of the following:

- Hotel accommodations for Judy in Palm Springs for the week of computer training she would attend.
- Plane fares for Lana for a trip in November.
- Jobs for Jason
- Apartments for Ashley
- Cars for me
- Health aids for Mom
- *Blue Book* value of his car for Jon
- Laptops for Larry

What we are finding is that the Internet is becoming an invaluable tool, the tool we turn to more often for more reasons.

The Digital Generation at Work

My favorite use of online time lately was the day Jim was lost in L.A. and late for a meeting. He used his cell phone to call Jon, who logged on to the Net with his laptop. He went to MapBlast (http://www.mapblast.com), and while Jim relayed his present location and the address of where he was supposed to be, Jon typed them into this map generator site.

In a matter of seconds, Jon had a map on his screen with driving directions from point A to point B. While Jon read the directions, Jim drove. Jon would tell him what streets would be coming up, how far he had to go, where and when to turn. Electronically connected to his personal guide, Jim followed Jon's directions and arrived just a bit late.

That is how this generation works. Connectivity on many different levels is essential for them. They are the generation who uses pagers, cell phones, fax machines, e-mail, and the Internet as easily as they use their remote controls.

Help prepare them at home for the tools they will use at school and work tomorrow.

BROWSING

Send your family to any one of these sites, just for fun:

THE DISCOVERY CHANNEL

http://www.discovery.com/

Spend some time exploring, and don't forget to bookmark.

PBS

http://www.pbs.org/

This site has some wonderful explorations.

PATHFINDER

http://www.pathfinder.com/

After you're done reading your favorite magazine — *Time, People, Fortune,* etc. — check out the games section and look for a game called S.P.Q.R., which takes you on a tour of Ancient Rome.

THINK QUEST

http://www.thinkquest.org/

Explore this site and see what kids are capable of creating. For the past two years this site has held a contest, and the top prizes are excellent. The sites that are created are truly wonderful. See what kids can do . . . your kids, too!

MATCHBOX TOYS

http://www.matchboxtoys.com/

Go through the garage door (the big flashing one at the bottom of the screen), click on "vehicles," and then go to "Custom Auto Body." Now, create, paint, and name your own truck.

ANGUS

http://www.raingod.com/angus/index.html

This site is one example of how people the world over are using the Net to share. Created and maintained by a young man in Paris, he shares his paintings, recipes, photographs, and wonderful tours of two ancient cities, Petra and the Inca Trail. Enjoy!

THE SMITHSONIAN INSTITUTE

http://www.si.edu/

Take your family on a tour of this wonderful museum and be prepared to book-mark and spend time.

NATIONAL GEOGRAPHIC

http://www.nationalgeographic.com/

See what wonderful projects they have online.

KIDS CLICK!

http://sunsite.berkeley.edu/KidsClick!/

For school or fun, search for sites here.

DIGITAL LIBRARIAN

http://www.servtech.com/public/mvail/home.html

A wonderful librarian has posted links for everyone and everything.

SEARCHING

1. *Some searches to try*: You can add to this list from your family's interests or start checking out one of these topics.

Art museums
Lighthouses
Zoos
Gardens
Aquariums
Science museums
Monuments
Festivals
Castles
Seven Wonders of the World (ancient and modern)
National parks

Get topics from your family, put them in a hat, pick one, and search.

2. *Homework Topic of the Week:* Which student has a project looming? Prioritize the kids' homework, and whoever has online time can do some searching and bookmarking of that topic. Here is where you need to make bookmark folders for each topic.

3. *Site of the Week:* Have family members submit their nominations for site of the week. As a group, check out the nominations and vote for the one you want to spend more time at. Bookmark it too.

4. *Shopping online for the next family birthday:* Each family member can search for just the right item for that next birthday person. Can the items found be purchased online? Locally?

5. *Bookmark Surprise:* Have each family member set up a bookmark folder for their favorite sites. It's nice when someone else adds a site they know you'll like to your folder.

6. *If you could redo your room:* What would you change? Start at one of the virtual malls for furnishings. If the family is thinking of buying some new household item, you can research online first, and everyone can be part of the looking and deciding.

```
http://www.virtumall.com/
http://www.cybertown.com/
http://www.ecomall.com/
http://www.ishops.com/
```

7. *Home improvement:* Plan your next home improvement using online resources. Everyone can search and bookmark sites to create a folder of useful information.

8. *Sports nuts:* Bookmark the best sites for scores, interviews, schedules, playing tips, magazines, audio, video, and players' home pages.

9. *Magazines for everyone:* Bookmark and put in folders, magazines for every member of your family. Don't forget to look for appropriate e-zines they might like, as well as the more popular magazines that are now online.

10. *Hobbies:* Bookmark sites for your hobby or for someone else in the family. Surprise someone with a new site. E-mail for catalogues, information, and help, and to connect with others who like your hobby.

11. *Your favorite school subject:* Bookmark sites that let you explore more about a subject you really like.

12. *Your worst subject:* Bookmark sites that help you conquer the class or classes that are posing problems in your schedule. Look for and bookmark homework help sites. There are many out there.

USING LINKS

1. *Plan a family vacation:* If you can't travel there in reality, it's fun to bookmark some sites that take the family on a virtual vacation. Put together a folder of sites that show you your special dream place or places. Escape any time you want with just a few clicks of your mouse button.

   Don't forget to follow links to hotels, side trips, weather, restaurants, museums, etc.

2. *Try Crayon:* Create your own newspaper. Follow the directions at http://crayon.net to create your family's personalized newspaper. Link to all the things you want to read. (Requires an e-mail address.)

MULTIMEDIA AND PLUG-INS

Plug-ins (Helper Applications)

You can add many new applications to your browser to take advantage of all the wonders of the Net. Shockwave will make it possible to view animations. Real Audio lets you hear a variety of things, and QuickTime lets you see movies created for the Net.

These additions are called "plug-ins" and are available online for free if they are not already loaded with the new version of your browser. Most of the common plug-ins are preloaded on MSIE and Netscape Communicator. If they are not already part of your browser (and you'll know when you go to a site that uses a plug-in and you are instructed to download it), then you'll have to download it.

There are two basic types of plug-ins: for audio and for video or animation. Audio, also called "Streaming Audio," lets you hear music, sounds, and voices. Video gives you the ability to watch *avi, mov,* and *mpg* files. Which plug-in you download depends on what you have already, what you need, which type of computer platform you are using, and where you live.

For most downloads, you'll need an additional piece of software which you can also download. For the Mac, you'll need Stuffit Expander. (Check your hard drive to see if it's there, or download it.) For the PCs, you'll need PKZip, which you can also download.

Some Names to Watch for

- Real Audio http://www.realaudio.com/ — for sound
- VDOLive, StreamWorks — for sound and movies
- VivoActive, Shockwave — for movies and animation
- Java, ActiveX — for animation and other effects
- VRML — for 3D graphics

MSIE comes with Active Movie for watching movies online. VRML is already built into Communicator and Explorer.

Places to Go to Get Them

```
http://w3.ag.uiuc.edu/AIM/2.0/plugins.html
http://browserwatch.internet.com/plug-in.html
http://www.clubvdo.net/download/Home.asp
http://www.plugins.com/
```

Sites to Hear RealAudio

INTERNATIONAL INTERNET RADIO STATIONS

```
http://goan.com/radio.html
```

RADIO NEWS AND SITCOM VIDEO CLIPS

```
http://www.abc.com/
```

LIVE NEWS, BUSINESS, BPORTS, JUKEBOX

http://www.audionet.com/

RACES AROUND THE WORLD

http://www.autochannel.com/

THE GROOVE SITE

http://www.groovesite.com/

Music from all over the world.

NEWS, PARENTING, WOMEN'S MEDICINE, SPACE PROGRAM

http://www.cbsnews.com/

YOU PICK THE MUSIC

http://www.the dj.com/

Video Sites

3D VISUALIZATION OF THE HUMAN HEART

http://www-leland.stanford.edu/~dmiller/dmdesign1.html

HOUSTON CHRONICLE

http://www.chron.com/voyager/

See how their Voyager site uses audio and video.

LISTEN TO SOME JAZZ

http://www3.jazzcentralstation.com/newjcs/main/splome.asp

MURDER MYSTERIES ONLINE (NEEDS VDOLIVE)

http://www.nowtv.com/mystery

BILL NYE, THE SCIENCE GUY

http://nyelabs.kcts.org/

THE SCI-FI CHANNEL (NEEDS QUICKTIME)

http://www.scifi.com/

THE SHOCKER LIST

http://www.shocker.com/shocker/cool.html

For a list of sites that use Shockwave, go here.

Shockrave

    http://www.shockrave.com/

Aside from shocked sites, you can test your plug-ins here

The Rock and Roll Hall of Fame

    http://www.rockhall.com/

USA Sports

    http://www.sportsline.com/

Tales from the Crypt

    http://www.cryptnet.com/

Voyage to Galapagos

    http://www.terraquest.com/

Scan the Airwaves

    http://www.timecast.com/

Copy and Paste

Copy and paste from the Net, to your word processor, to your kids. One of the ways many teachers start with Internet use in their classroom is to copy materials either directly from the Net by printing or from a word processor. Here is an overview of how to copy and paste text and graphics from the Net into a word processor. But first . . .

Copyright and the Internet

It is important that everyone understand how copyright laws pertain to Internet information. U.S. copyright law is relatively clear concerning what can be copyrighted and what cannot. Specifically, "ideas, procedures, methods, systems, processes, concepts, principles, discoveries, or devices" are not subject to copyright. Descriptions, explanations, and illustrations are. For additional information, go to

    http://www.gasou.edu/psychweb/tipsheet/apacrib.htm

This means that every time your students use Internet information — text, graphics, illustrations, etc. — they need to cite their sources.

For a discussion of copyright laws, go to:

```
http://www.benedict.com/
http://fatty.law.cornell.edu/uscode/
```

For additional sites to help with citing references taken from the Net:

```
http://www.lib.usm.edu/userguides/apa.html
http://www.geocities.com/ResearchTriangle/1221/citation.htm
http://www.english.uiuc.edu/cws/wworkshop/bibliostyles.htm
```

How to Copy

Mac: Copying pictures

Have your word processor open at the same time you have your Internet browser running. If you are on an older Mac and cannot run both, go to your Control Panel and see how your memory is set. We found this worked well: Modern Memory Manager off; Virtual Memory on. And if there is one more memory, turn it off.

From the Internet

- Point your mouse at the picture you want to copy.
- While pointing at the picture, hold down your mouse button and wait for a menu to appear.
- Automatically chosen from the menu should be "Copy this picture."
- Let go of your mouse button. The picture is now copied.
- Switch to your word processor — do not close your browser.
- Locate the icon for paste or go to the Edit menu and highlight "paste." You should immediately see your picture. If not, repeat the process. If a picture still does not appear, try another picture. Some of them will not copy.

IBM (PCs) Copying Pictures — Save Then Insert

- Create a folder on your hard drive for Internet graphics and text
- When on the Net, point to the picture you want and click your *right* mouse button.
- The menu will appear with several items. Select "Save Picture As."
- Your internal hard drive (C) will show up wanting to know where you want the item.
- Find the folder you created and click "Save."

Putting Those Pictures into Your Word Processor

- Go to pulldown menu item "Insert."

- Select "Object."

- Click on "Create from File."

- Click "Browse."

- Locate the folder where you saved your graphic.

- Locate the name of the file you saved in that folder.

- Highlight the file name you want and click "OK."

- Your picture should show up.

To avoid any copyright infringement, Advanced Technologies Academy developed an authorization slip for using others' graphics. My students e-mailed (check for e-mail address of Webmaster) a copy of the authorization to any site with graphics they wanted to use in a project. They e-mailed those sites that did not specifically state that the graphics were shareware or free to be used.

Find a copy of the authorization here:

```
http://www.atech.org/room805/projects/lessons/authorization.html
```

Copying Text: Mac and PC

Again, your word processor should be open and available.

- Locate the text you want to copy.

- Carefully highlight the text you want by dragging your mouse over the text with the mouse button held down. Be careful — if you stay in one place too long before you start the copying process, you'll get the message "Back or Forward." You have to highlight by dragging the mouse quickly over the text without staying in one place too long.

- Once the selected text is highlighted, go to your pulldown menu item "Edit." Highlight "Copy."

- Transfer to your word processor and click on the "Paste" icon or go to the "Edit" menu and click on "Paste." Your text should be copied.

Sometimes the text does not appear in neat rows as if you had typed it. This is because of the embedded language coding. Try this (if you are using MS Word):

- Select "Edit."
- Highlight "Select All."
- Go to Format and click "Auto format" and see if this makes it neater.

A LITTLE BIT ABOUT OUTPUT

We began the year doing paper and pencil, word processing, and other types of output. We progressed to creating Web pages with just one group of kids doing the actual creating of pages with input from the others. We ended the year with all of the kids using Netscape Communicator to create their own pages to add to our collective site.

We found that we needed maps in our room even though we were in an English room. We had to know where our literature took place. We also found a need for timelines to place the things we had learned in perspective.

Output can take many forms. We did not start with Web pages. Let the assignment, the type of information gathered, and your kids' skills help determine which form works best for any given exploration.

NOTES FROM THE HIGHWAY

Net use is exploding. Jeopardy.com gets over 40 million hits a week. Time spent watching TV, in homes with the Internet, is down. That means kids are scanning more information. They may not be reading *The Old Man and the Sea,* but they are being exposed to more graphics and textual information since baby boomers read *Nancy Drew* and *Hardy Boys.* Their reading habits are different because the medium is different. We have to understand the differences not only in what kids are exposed to, but how.

We also have to deal with the implications of the new technologies. We brought computers into our classrooms, but there never was too much dialogue on campus about how this was affecting kids. We just let it happen. With the introduction of the Internet over an ever-widening area, in and out of schools, the impact of technology will be felt similarly. We will have to talk about its uses, its impact, its values, etc.

There will be a day when reading and writing teachers grapple with the same issue math teachers face when discussing the use of calculators. Kids don't memorize the times tables any more, teachers complain, because they use calculators and the issues are not yet resolved as to how and when students should use them. By now, calculators are such an integral part of many people's math process that a person's life usually dictates how much they use a calculator. Perhaps the same will be true of the new reading and writing computers.

What is going to happen when technology lets kids talk and their computer will write for them, or when they listen while the computer speaks? Do we let the machine do the work, or do we tell them what they are missing if the machine does the work? What argument do we use to get kids to memorize times tables?

What this means, is that we have to begin to more clearly define what skills and pieces of knowledge are essential given the new technologies and their ever-widening spread.

In this new age, for what purpose will people still need the skills of reading and writing? Are we fighting a losing battle if we insist on improving all types of writing skills? Will the essay give way to the Web page? Will reading give way to listening and video watching with just a bit of scanning done by the "real" readers, humans?

And, once they have those skills, what do they do with them? I believe we want all people to be learners. Learning is good. But for some reason, many kids in today's schools look at teachers as if we are trying to give them something bad. "No, don't give my that biology book to read. It might hurt me," seems to be a common attitude. But we all know that knowing things is good. "Duh, I dunno," I told my kids, "is not an acceptable answer."

But with so much information out there and so many potential questions, what is a kid to learn if he wants to avoid the above answer? What is he to learn in your class? And because of the infusion of the Internet and so much more information and because teachers always say they "can't cover it all," how are you going to determine *what are* the important pieces of information in your class?

And then, spend some time focusing on skills. What skills does this class/subject offer that will help students continue to be lifelong learners, as well as people who use and adapt to new technologies?

So all of us will have to decide what the essential pieces of knowledge are and what the most valuable and necessary skills are that need to be amassed given our curriculum, skills, interests, technology, and other available tools.

In my school district, we are getting many computers into classrooms. However, in elementary schools especially, these tools are being placed into one big (20+ computers) lab. In my opinion, it would be better to get 20 classrooms started with one computer each and let the teachers and students work that tool into their ever-expanding toolchest. The computer and the Internet should be integrated into students' lives and their studies just as books, pencils, and films have been traditionally. Teachers should receive hands-on training in these tools to a level of comfort so complete that, after training, using the Net is as familiar to them as using the library, which is covered in more detail in the next chapter.

If the computer is down the hall, in a lab, waiting for your class' next "lab day," but your kids thought of an extension to their studies they'd like to research on the Net today that computer is wasted as a useful tool. Bring the machine to the teachers first, so they can bring it to their kids.

We must present our curriculum with these new technologies in order to bring the main communication tool of this era to the kids who are going to need to know how to use it. If your students hope to own businesses one day, chances are they will do business online. Artists post online. Writers create magazines with the artists who are also online. The big difference is that anyone can publish on the Net. Wide-open prairie spaces are available. No one is getting the best spaces in an Internet land grab, because all are given equal tools to get started. Promote equal access in your school.

What kind of changes in routine can you expect as you become an Internet classroom? Your kids will gain, for one thing, a much broader frame of reference and, carefully guided by you, the teacher, they will have a broader vocabulary, discernment skills constantly being honed, and growing confidence and curiosity — potentially boundless.

Skills for the New Millennium

In the real world, jobs will be created and jobs will be lost (read about General Motors' struggles). New media will be created (streaming audio and video) while old media will shift (online newspapers). Technologies will develop and expand, and if your students practice new skills, the Net can be a source of jobs for them. Web site design is a great place for your artists, writers, filmmakers, and musicians. Your scholars and thinkers, along with your code makers and breakers, will find a place on the Net too. There will be jobs right out of high school, and for some, jobs while they are still in the classroom.

Down the Line?

As Net use grows and the amount of information grows with it, tools will be developed (some are in their infancy now) that will help you manage all that information. People will specialize and centralize their Internet needs and skills, and the focus for students will be information attainment, management, and use.

The problem now is that there are so many tools to choose from. If you check http://www.download.com/ or any other site with downloadable software, you'll find long lists of tools available to help you manage your online and offline time. Push technology, which lets you customize your favorite search tool, your e-mail and news, is certainly direction many sites are moving.

New Issues on the Net Horizon

Net access is on the increase in schools, and the technology is changing as quickly as it's implemented. If your school suddenly gets connected, what are some of the hot topics you might run into?

Curriculum changes, assessment, training and access are the main issues that need to be addressed. Detailed information on these is included in the next chapter.

Browser Wars

The most commonly used browser (the software that gets you connected and exploring) is Netscape recently purchased by AOL. Microsoft is also in the market with Explorer, a direct challenger to Netscape. Articles can be found in most Internet magazines comparing the two. Which one should you use? That will depend on several factors. New IBM computers and some compatibles will come to you loaded with MS Explorer, making the choice issue moot.

If you are in a position to choose, is one better than the other? Actually, both must have similar capabilities just to run what comes over the Net. One reviewer of both platforms felt that Microsoft will go after the commercial market and will be able to do that successfully. Other reviewers felt that Netscape will maintain its dominance, for a while at least. For your needs, either browser will do. Both are user-friendly and kid-friendly.

Look for updates from each of the browsers. Netscape offers Netscape Communicator, which requires one of the newer computers with a great deal of memory to use effectively. For business, these added tools may be helpful, but they are not as necessary for education, where some of us are still struggling with computers with puny memory.

The war of the browsers rages on, with each company trying to offer one more service or link that will draw more users than the other. In school, we need to look at which browser does the job best in our setting, but we should also expose the kids to both. Most schools tend to use one or the other, but try to stay away from having a mix on the kids' computers. Check the chapter on browsers (Chapter 2) for more on which we preferred.

Connectivity

Connecting through your local cable provider is limited currently but will expand more in the near future. An ISDN terminal adapter that connects your computer at 128kbps is a fast means of connection and another possibility is smart phones. They offer a reduced level of connectivity but do offer e-mail and some access to the Net. T1 and T3 lines are also very fast and dedicated to just providing online access, but these are costly. Our first year online was paid for by our local Rotary Club. Perhaps you have some organization in your city that will pay for your connection.

CU See Me

This is the device that lets you see the person you are connecting with online as you talk. Systems range in price, with one from Intel running around $400. This is one of those items that we, in schools, probably will put towards the end of our wish lists; but it has great potential with kids. Can you imagine the impact on your kids if they can see the person, perhaps thousands of miles away, they are talking to?

Tools for Knowledge Management

Many of the experts believe that browsing is not always productive. Therefore, products like Freeloader (http://www.freeloader.com/) will be used for knowledge management. These products, referred to as "smart agents," help delegate the use of the Net. For example, if you "tell" the software which sites you use most often, the software can be programmed to let you know whenever the site is updated or the URL has changed, or if the site has gone off line.

Audio/Video Streaming

For business, this means talking with someone without having to physically fly around the world; expensive and time consuming. For consumers, this means concerts, sports, and shows online. For your kids, it means hearing and seeing demonstrations from sites that post hands-on demonstrations, as well as listening to news and other transmissions.

This is one part of Net technology that grew the most in sophistication this past year. Many sites now make use of audio and video, and the reception is much smoother.

Encryption

To protect the safety of online financial transactions, encryption will become more necessary and sophisticated. Legislation is expected in this area.

With so many people shopping online, security of sites seems to be meeting the needs of most Net users. I have heard many success stories from buyer's and seller's, so it seems to be a safe bet.

HTML

The language of the Internet, Hypertext Markup Language, is a simple but powerful programming language. You can find HTML starting points listed in this book for those of you who want to start creating your own Web pages without the benefit of ready-made programs.

Watch for DHTML (Dynamic Hypertext Markup Language) as well as Java to become must-know languages to create on the Net.

USENET AND BBS

Although most of the information that my students and I access is on the World Wide Web or other parts of the Internet, there are still more computers storing information in newsgroups and on bulletin board services.

The number and use of BBS and Usenet user groups is growing and offering people other ways to communicate online.

Usenet

You must make sure that your Internet Service Provider offers you access to Usenet newsgroups. Most providers offer access, but it is wise to check.

One site on the Internet for a listing of educational Newsgroups can be found at

```
http://www.pierian.com/oasis/news/news2.html
```

Here you will find newsgroups for every subject taught, K–12.

At a Usenet site, you can discuss a wide variety of subjects with others. You read what they wrote, post your own response, and check back again for more input. Prefixes identify the type of newsgroups:

alt   Alternative groups that contain unusual topics. Check these out before you let your kids explore.

bionet   Biology research.

bit   Newsgroups that started as mailing lists.

comp   Computer-related groups.

misc   Groups that fit in no other category.

rec   Recreational groups. Look here for sports, music, games, etc.

sci   Scientific groups other than biology.

soc   Social groups; these are often organized by ethnicity.

An excellent online source for newsgroups is DejaNews:

    http://www.dejanews.com/

Here, you can search for newsgroups, post information, or find just the one discussion group that meets your kids' needs.

Bulletin Boards

Posting and reading information, questions, ideas, and thoughts is also done on bulletin board services. Many educational institutions manage bulletin boards for teachers and students. A quick search using Lycos, Altavista, or another search engine will bring you a list of bulletin boards you might find useful. I searched for teacher BBS sites and found a very nice list of links at

    http://www.digicity.com/maincomm.htm

The Education Station offers links to several places where you can leave and read messages from other teachers. You will also find links to Usenet groups and chat areas.

Also check the Teacher's Net Chat Board (http://www.digicity.com/maincomm.htm) for a place to read and respond to existing postings on a variety of subjects. This will show you a typical BBS setup.

ACCEPTABLE USE POLICY

As you prepare to bring your kids online, it is smart to prepare an acceptable use policy for each student and parent/guardian to sign. We researched similar policies online and developed the following:

Advanced Technologies Academy's policy is to make Internet access available to students in the library and classrooms as a learning tool to reach educational goals and objectives. Students are expected to research only areas directly related to the classroom. However, students may find ways to access materials which may be inappropriate. Methods to regulate student Internet access may not guarantee full compliance with A-TECH's policy. Students who use Internet inappropriately will be denied access by A-TECH. Ultimately, parents and guardians of minors are responsible for setting and conveying the standards their children should follow when using media and information sources. Advanced Technologies Academy, staff, and/or the Clark County School District is not legally liable for student inappropriate use of Internet.

Student access to Internet is based on parent/guardian permission for the student to use Internet. A standard parent/student signature form can be attached to the Acceptable Use Policy.

Additional information about acceptable use policies can be found online at

```
http://access.k12.wv.us/~pjustice/aup.htm
http://teams.lacoe.edu/documentation/classrooms/belinda/teacher/aup.html
```

Don't forget to add e-mail and Web page creation policies to your acceptable use policy.

A Bit about HTML and Web Pages

When you and your kids finally get comfortable using the Internet, you may want to start creating your own Web page. At my school, we have a team of students who are creating our home page, to which teachers, with the help of students, can post their projects, information, writings, etc. We also have many students who are creating Web pages on their own.

To provide a tutorial in HTML (the language of Web page creation) is beyond the scope of this book and the expertise of this educator. (I have many students who know HTML and have a school-based Web team ready to post my work, so I have had no need to learn the code.)

What I can do is point you to Internet HTML tutorials, books and magazine articles, and software packages that will help get you started. Also explore the capabilities of Netscape Communicator, if that is your browser. We created our Renaissance Literature project with Communicator.

Online resources (tutorials and primers):

```
http://www.ncsa.uiuc.edu/General/Internet/WWW/HTMLPrimer.html
http://www.flash.net/surf/tutor.html
http://werbach.com/web/wwwhelp.html
http://www.hwg.org/resources/html/
http://werbach.com/web/wwwhelp.html
```

A search of Amazon books (`http://www.amazon.com/`) turned up a long list of books. Search by subject: HTML or Web design.

Web page publication software is also available.

- *Powerpoint Assistant:* For those of you with Powerpoint, this add-on allows you to convert your slides and templates into HTML pages. For more on this, go to

    `http://www.microsoft.com/office/mspowerpoint/internet/ia/`

- *Microsoft Web Publishing Wizard*: A beta version is available online to download. This software transfers your already-created pages to the Internet through your service provider. For more, go to

    `http://www.microsoft.com/windows/software/webpost/`

- *HyperStudio* is another software package that lets you create Web pages and post them online. For more information, go to

    `http://www.hyperstudio.com/`

Some of the tools available for Web publishing require that the creator of the page know HTML, while other tools assume no such knowledge. For information about both types of software, go to

```
http://www.webcom.com/html/tools.shtml
```

With all of the books and online tools available, it is easy to get even the youngest student online. Once you are comfortable with the basic tools of the Net, move on — and perhaps, soon, we'll see your kids on the Net.

ONLINE PROJECTS

One of the most exciting aspects of using the Internet is the opportunity to get your students involved in projects with other kids and other schools. Some of the existing projects involve geography, environmental issues, multiculturalism, math, and more. At my school, we are just beginning to use the Internet in our classrooms, create Web pages, and devise curriculum projects. At this time, we are not involved in any online projects with other schools. Therefore, I cannot speak to their effectiveness or strategies that might be useful in joining an existing project. I can, however, point you in the direction of several helpful sites.

Check here for a list of current projects:

```
http://www.yahoo.com/Education/Instructional_Technology/
    On_line_Teaching_and_Learning/Projects/
```

NASA projects can be found at

```
http://quest.arc.nasa.gov/interactive/index.html
```

K–12 education projects, indexed by category, can be found at

```
http://www.eduplace.com/hmco/school/projects/index.html
```

For helpful hints on posting your online project, check out

```
http://www.eduplace.com/hmco/school/projects/how2.html
```

NickNacks is another site filled with suggestions for getting started with online projects. Find NickNacks at

```
http://www1.minn.net:80/~schubert/NickNacks.html
```

DEVELOPING
A VISION

N ow that you have learned *how* to integrate the Internet into your classroom, you need to consider all of the issues involved in making technology a part of your teaching and your school's vision.

Most schools have developed mission statements that briefly articulate the goals they set for their students. However, unless this statement has been updated within the past few years, it probably makes no reference to technology. Given the rapid change and implementation of technology in the marketplace and in schools, it's essential that schools develop a vision that articulates their understanding of several technology issues and places in the forefront essential goals for student technology use.

> **In this chapter**
>
> - Training
> - Changing Classrooms/Changing Curriculum
> - Our Medieval Project as a Sample of Changing Curriculum and Assessment
> - Assessment
> - Into the Classroom

Bellingham, Washington, has developed a technology rationale that begins by stating, "Washington State's education system must prepare students for their futures, not this generation's past." This is an extremely important point because it calls on us to examine our educational system and its reliance on "what has always been done," and to find a balance between the old and the new. Avoid any attempt to throw out the old ways in favor of the new, simply because they are old. Merge new technologies with old structures until new structures emerge. Don't reinvent the wheel — just modify it.

The Bellingham Rationale also indicates an understanding that there is "tension between an education system for the industrial age and the reality of an information age." It is this understanding that must drive your vision as you bring your school or classroom online.

What are the skills that today's students need to take with them into the marketplace? What are the essential pieces of knowledge students must arm themselves with to be competitive? And, since we're a knowledge-based curriculum faced with a skills-based workplace, how do we adapt?

According to Bellingham, "Technology is the key to learners' achievement of world class standards." This has also become an issue — world class standards. Given the changing nature of our world and the feeling that we're not isolated from anyone anymore, what tools do we give kids so they are globally competitive?

Finally, if accessing information, manipulating data, synthesizing concepts, and creatively expressing ideas are essential for success in today's marketplace, how do we achieve that goal and also produce lifelong learners who have taken responsibility for their own learning?

As you bring technology into your school and as you start to make it an integral part of students' learning, gather together staff, students, parents, and community members and articulate your goals — your vision for your students. Read about the issues you will face and discuss them. Study the available research about marketplace skills in a global economy and the effect of the Internet on student learning.

Talk about what skills you as a school want for your students, and then ask your teachers to define what skills they want to impart from their classes. Discuss everything as it relates to emerging technologies: how best to use them, assess student achievement with them, and plan for the future.

A remarkable change is happening in education. It will not happen overnight, and it will not happen easily. The Internet is not a quick, easy fix for educational problems, but it is a tool that opens the door to lifelong learning. Without some guidance, some vision, from the leaders of a school, it will not happen at all.

Bellingham's Technology Rationale can be found at

```
http://www.bham.wednet.edu/tech/techplan.htm
```

Read up on the issues you might face:

```
http://www.rmcres.com/improve/tech.html
```

Training

Having spent the past 15 years training teachers to use technology and the past two years helping teachers prepare for Internet use in the classroom, I've made some observations:

Assume nothing. Many teachers will come to your training session with no computer background, much less Internet background. Many are afraid they'll mess things up. Once you get them comfortable with the mouse — and learning the browser is a very productive way to learn the mouse — they get braver.

Some teachers are not willing to adopt new technologies and will resist all efforts to bring them into the digital age.

Many teachers will claim they have no time in their curriculum to incorporate technology.

Some teachers are anxious to bring technology into their classrooms, but have no idea of the best way to proceed. These are the ones most likely to come to training sessions.

Before you bring the technology into your school and start your training, think about these:

Budget

One necessary part of your planning will be to budget for staff training. Too often, hardware is purchased and installed, but no money has been allocated to train the staff.

Goals

Just because a computer and the Internet show up in a classroom does not mean that the teacher is prepared to use both effectively. Teachers are given technology with no direction for use, no guidelines for implementation, and no hints as to how best to merge the technologies into their curriculum.

Notice that I do not say "merge the technologies into their *classroom*." Because teachers, in most areas, are working from a set of curriculum guidelines, the technologies need to be correlated to these standards and guidelines until those guidelines change to reflect new ways of thinking.

Starting Points

I begin training teachers by matching the technologies' capabilities to their curriculum and their students. What are you teaching, and how can the technology available to you help your kids?

I encourage teachers to rethink the use of drill and practice software and move more toward practical applications of the knowledge and skills they are teaching.

It takes time and a decent facility to train your staff and students. Schools with large staffs might not have one lab that will accommodate everyone at once, and multiple sessions will have to be held. Training by departments works well to begin with; they'll help each other out. Eventually, mix your departments up to foster cross-curriculum collaboration.

Setting up lessons by your staff for use in the classroom also takes time. Give your staff the time and the equipment to accomplish this. Release time for departments or individuals to set up lessons is time well spent.

Before Training

Think about how you can help teachers who will only step so far away from what they have to "cover" to truly incorporate these new tools. Which brings up the question, exactly what are we dealing with here? Just what are these machines good for?

If I have a Mac G3 or Pentium II PC in my English classroom, what are its practical and effective uses? Which software and hardware do I use, and how often? What if that machine is in a fourth-grade class? A junior high math class?

Certainly, uses vary by subject and grade level, and therefore the needs of the teacher and the students are not all the same. It's for each of you and your schools to determine the most practical and effective uses of these machines for your students. Do they all need to type, use e-mail, search the Net, use a data base? Are any of those negative skills or nonmarketable skills? They all look good on a résumé, and they'll help your kids get hired. Which ones, therefore, do you teach? Who teaches the skills? Where do they practice them? How? How much?

Teaching Troubleshooting

It is crucial that districts and school sites spend money and time training teachers. If the teacher doesn't use the computer, the students are less likely to do so. What training does your staff need? Make sure they are comfortable with word processing, especially copy and paste and formatting documents. Also, train all staff in the use of at least one browser. In addition, troubleshooting hardware and software is very helpful. I can't tell you how many times teachers have let computers sit because they thought they were broken when some simple adjustment was needed.

Those of you who use Macs, take the time to learn how to adjust the memory, reinstall system software, empty the Internet cache, set up an alias in the Apple Menu, and generally stop problems before they develop. Learn to handle common problems without having to wait for a tech.

IBM-compatible users, in my experience, will have less troubleshooting to do. If you're one of these, you should still understand how to configure the machine for optimum use. If you have multiple users, and most of you will, teach your students to respect the machines and ask them to leave well enough alone. I once had a student who wanted to try out the tools in the control panel and wondered what would happen if he adjusted the colors on his screen. He wondered what white letters on a white background would look like! That took quite a while to reset without reinstalling the system.

I set all my machines to optimum settings, teach the kids what and why those are, and then tell them to leave them alone. Even the youngest children can be taught the basics of setting up a machine and how to leave well enough alone. If kids want green text on a purple background, I tell them to enjoy the experience on their home computer, but in the classroom, they need to stay as uniform as possible for multiple users.

On-Site Techs

Establish on-site techs who can fix most hardware and software problems. Usually, teachers who are constant users become techs, whether they want to or not! Give them time to help, if you can schedule it. Clark County Schools is also setting up a core of student techs called "CyberCorps." They are trained during the summer and given the responsibility of helping out their school and others. Use the talent you have and create opportunities for other staff members and students to help out as well.

Training

Teach your students as many tools and technologies as you can. Start them early with the keyboard so they don't have to play catch-up. If you have older computers, make them keyboard learning stations or word processors. I don't want a Mac G3 or Pentium PC used only as a type-writer. As kids progress through your schools, they should be using the skills they've learned and adding more that are appropriate. Math and science classes will probably find more practical uses for data bases than English classes will, but all students need to know how a data base works and how they can use one effectively.

Use simulation software to enhance your curriculum. Evaluate the money you spend on software. See what's available online for downloading.

Teach your staff and students the basics of word processing, data bases, spreadsheets, presentation software, and the Internet. Then add in as many more uses and technologies as you can.

Rethinking

Yes, using technology, and especially the Internet, will take time. It takes time not only to prepare a lesson, but also to complete that lesson. How does a teacher who has no time in the curriculum bring new technologies to students? What do you do with the teacher who's hidden a usable computer behind a pile of books for years, or the teacher who refuses all technology, from manipulatives to calculators to PCs?

Go one on one with reluctant teachers and amaze them. Find out enough about what they teach to truly locate something wonderful and helpful for them, using technology. I prepared a lesson to help a teacher switch from physical newspapers to electronic ones, since the classes had greater Internet access and the librarian preferred electronic to expand his limited budget. Her initial reluctance gave way to modifications, and her students broadened their newspaper horizons.

Some teachers who type out their worksheets on a word processor or allow the typing of final drafts feel that this is a powerful use of technology. Some see broader use as overuse. When is technology use too much?

I've talked with other teachers who are using the Internet to some degree or other, and many find the same reaction. Caution, they are told — don't overuse.

As my kids and I progressed through the year, we felt we were learning an amazing amount of "stuff," all of it from our starting point, our curriculum. But since I didn't assess them in the traditional manner, the attitude of some who assessed me and my students was, "Let's wait and see what the test results are." If my kids don't do well on achievement tests, we'll all look as if, on some level, we've failed. But if you test my kids on their ability to enhance their reading by broadening their own frame of reference, collaborate with others, work in teams, use many technologies, demonstrate analysis skills, etc., I know they'll do well.

Are those the skills they'll be tested on, or will they be asked to remember lines from *Romeo and Juliet*? Read the section on assessment and spend some time online reading what others say about the changes technology brings to your curriculum. Then get in on the debate. I suspect that if you have this book, you're in the debate! Welcome, and join those of us who sometimes feel we're out in cyberspace on a cyberlimb and someone might be ready with a chainsaw!

I can only tell you what my kids told me when it came to Internet use in our classroom. JM e-mailed me after the year was over and wrote, "I wanted to tell you how much that class helped me learn about the Internet and through the Internet, the many things and places around the world I saw in your class." He signed it "Your Russian student" because he was the one who rose to a leadership position on his team — the "Russian gang." Along with his team, he turned in, promptly, some of the best sections of our Medieval Project.

We used our computers to type, research, communicate, read, calculate, organize, demonstrate, and create. We also used novels, a textbook, a thesaurus, maps, dictionaries, pencils, rulers, glue, and staples.

Did we overuse? Or do some teachers underuse? Time and the kids will tell.

Sites for Online Training Help

INTERNET 101

http://www2.famvid.com/i101/

THE INTERNET FOR BEGINNERS

http://discoveryschool.com/schrockguide/

LEARN THE NET

http://www.learnthenet.com/

CHANGING CURRICULUMS/CHANGING CLASSROOMS

From *Educom Review*, 1995

EDUCAUSE

http://www.educause.edu/

> *"Our educational system is, believe it or not, teacher-focused, not learner-focused.*
>
> *"By giving the learner the tools and the flexibility of actually learning on their own, we re-define the focus of the teacher, and by nature, the educational system.*
>
> *"For educational planners the real point of thinking about the future is not prediction but self-examination. The real point is to allow the future to inform the present and shape today's decisions — to prompt us to ask, 'Well, if that's where we will be in 25 years, what should we be doing now?'"*
>
> —ROBERT C. HETERICK, JR. AND JOHN GEHL, *EDUCOM REVIEW*, 1995

From *Plugging In*

"Today's workplaces and communities — and tomorrow's — have tougher requirements than ever before. They need citizens who can think critically and strategically to solve problems. These individuals must learn in a rapidly changing environment, and build knowledge from numerous sources and different perspectives. They must understand systems in diverse contexts, and collaborate locally and around the globe.

"These attributes contrast sharply with the discrete, low-level skills, content, and assessment methods that traditional ways of learning favor. The new workplace requirements for learning are incompatible with instruction that assumes the teacher is the information giver and the student a passive recipient. The new requirements are at odds with testing programs that assess skills that are useful only in school."

Our Medieval Project as a Sample of Changing Curriculum and Assessment

When we began our study of the literature of the Middle Ages, the first thing we did was look in our textbook for information and samples of the literature. Finding little other than isolated stories, and no background information, we headed out to search the Net. What else could we learn about the literature, the times, the people, and the places?

On the first day of our search, we learned that oral storytelling was the norm in the Middle Ages. Not too many books were printed, and not too many people read. We also began to read some of the tales and found one interesting fact that helped focus the remainder of our research and discussion.

Reading about the stories of the Middle Ages, we learned that in the original version, Little Red Riding Hood drank Grandma's blood. We also found out that in addition to Knights of the Round Table, this was the time period that gave voice to trolls, wizards, witches, and not-so-nice mermaids.

"What's up with that?" the kids asked.

What we found online lead us to wonder what conditions would give rise to such dark and sinister images.

This, then, became the focus of our research and our goal. What, we wondered, were the most recognizable stories of the Middle Ages, and why would storytellers tell such frightening tales? With this goal in mind, we began the first of our in-depth Web journeys.

Six classes of students, sophomores and freshmen, were divided for the sake of convenience into groups representing the following countries: Italy, France, Spain, Germany, Russia, the Scandinavian countries, Ireland, Scotland, Wales, and England. The freshmen concentrated on Great Britain, while the sophomores divided up the other countries. Students were given the opportunity to join the country group of their choice and to determine, within that group, which area of research they would concentrate on.

The areas of research were determined by class discussion. What do we need to know about a country to understand its literature? The areas of research were the stories, the main events of the time, and the people. We also felt we needed to "see" more of the country and the life style of medieval peoples. Therefore, architecture, the countryside, clothing, music, and art were additional categories.

Students began researching one area for one country with the idea of learning more about the people and the times that created such enduring stories with such dark images.

Along the way, our research lead us to add additional categories: inventors, scientists, explorers, and mathematicians. Students wanted to know more about the people who believed that bloodletting was good medicine and that the earth was flat.

Information was gathered. Each student reported his or her findings to a group leader who, in turn, reported to me. I also asked to be kept informed of any areas where information was unavailable or limited to see if we could collectively help out the research. Group leaders compiled information, illustrations, and Web addresses. An additional team went to work — the HTML team. This group was made up of students who knew enough HTML code to help create the ultimate Web site we were amassing.

Collectively, we read the stories in our text and others from online that were recommended by students. Additionally, we researched and shared our information about the major events of the times.

Ultimately, we learned about the Crusades, the Black Plague, the Spanish Inquisition, the Hundred Years War, and other events that influenced the storytelling of the time. Students began to see how the people lived and where, what their lives were like and why. Finally, they decided that the times dictated the stories.

My job throughout the project was to orchestrate. I kept track of the research by e-mailing group leaders. I suggested areas to research and sites to read through, and I helped organize the visual and text output of our findings.

Creating a Web page was, in itself, an interesting step in our project. If we wanted to share our findings, how could we best present our information, our findings, our understanding so that others would find it logical, easily understood, and coherent? For us, this was a new step in the process. We had never created for such a potentially wide and diverse audience and had never had as much information to pull together.

All of our work — the planning, research, and output — was developed as we learned more. The information we gathered influenced our output and made it necessary for us to think in different ways. For one thing, we had to think visually. Our output was not only going to be written; it would also be visual and, in the case of those researching music, auditory. How best to present this was a question all the students put their minds to. Those with suggestions e-mailed group leaders and the HTML team.

For example, after researching the architecture, it was suggested that a castle was representative of the times and might make an interesting visual menu. As that was being prepared by one team, another was finding coats of arms for each country, and still another was locating tapestries that told stories to add to our visual effect.

As research progressed, interesting stories about the people of the times came to light. We learned about Juana the Mad and Ivan the Terrible, among others. This led each country team to pick what seemed to be the defining moment of the Middle Ages for their country and to put together a first-person narrative account of each event. We now had, to add to our Web site, a story about Juana the Mad and her strange journey with her dead husband, another about Ivan the Terrible and his habit of drinking blood, still another about the Spanish Inquisition, and more.

The information base grew. The potential of the Web site expanded.

All of this work reached its final stages. Students began to see which parts of their research helped answer our questions and reach our goal. They began putting their understanding into visual forms with text added to explain or demonstrate.

The Web site grew, but to this day, our project remains unfinished. When I transferred to another school before the end of the year, our group leaders were not allowed the online time needed to complete their sections.

Even though we never saw all our work collected in a Web site, the kids felt that our original goal had been achieved. We understood, better than we had expected, why the Middle Ages handed down to us such strange tales to be told late at night.

The question still remains: By going in this direction, did our curriculum change?

Had we confined ourselves to our textbook's treatment of the literature of the Middle Ages, we would have focused more on the style and content of two or three stories and would not have seen a broader picture of the people, places, and events. We would have learned less, and that was not OK with the kids.

Did our classroom assessment change?

With so many diverse pieces of knowledge being collected, in order for me to prepare a more traditional test, I would have had to take more time with the students just to finalize important facts they should memorize. I chose, instead, to have students share broader understandings and concentrate on broader issues that are not as easily assessed by multiple-choice tests. Because I did this, the students took with them to the next era we researched these questions: What was the literature like, and from what people, places, and events did it spring? We also developed an interest in the language and style of each era and added to our quests a desire to understand where those had come from.

Can those students think critically? Learn in a rapidly changing environment? Strategically solve problems? Build knowledge from numerous sources and different perspectives? Collaborate locally?

And will a standardized test assess that?

If not, how should I assess the kids?

ASSESSMENT

A funny thing happened when a long-term sub took over my classes . . . tests were given. In the entire 8 months we were together, I had yet to give my kids a test — a multiple choice, fill-the-blank, true/false, memorize-the-facts test. Instead, I'd had to learn new ways to assess their proficiency, as most of our work consisted of research, writing, visual projects, Web page creations, discussions, conversations online, and more.

Even when we read novels together, I refrained — deliberately, I must admit — from giving them tests. I doubted that the standard type of tests would assess what they had been learning. Standardized tests reflect what you remember, not what you do to get the information or what you can do with it once you have it.

In a time when what you can do is far more marketable than what you know, it's important to develop new ways of assessing not only the knowledge students have, but the skills they acquired along the way. The skills are the hardest to assess with standard tests, but they are the most important.

When I graduated from college with a Language Arts major and entered the job market, I was asked by an employment counselor, "What can you do?" Not much that the business world wanted, I found. Many graduating seniors from American high schools and colleges cannot *do*. They can, perhaps, be trained to do, but so many of them cannot walk into a place of business and list the skills they have to offer the work place. If they've never used a computer, they cannot list that skill. Word processing, faxing, e-mail, complex phone systems, electronic accounting, manipulation of data, locating data — these are the skills the business world uses. Collaboration and critical thinking are skills students need.

How does one measure a student's ability to carry on a conversation? To communicate effectively with e-mail? To collaborate? To think critically? To plan a project, organize its structure, and create a final, visual output? To manage time and meet deadlines?

How does a teacher decide which pieces of knowledge within the subject are essential and which skills are also worth time and effort?

It's incumbent on those of us who are using the Net in different and exciting ways to share our methods of assessment of skills.

Educator Marion Brady has developed an evaluation tool that rates your school's current curriculum. On a scale of 1–10, Brady asks a school to look at some of the following:

My school's curriculum:

1. Relates to students' immediate experience
2. Involves students in a full range of thought processes
3. Makes clear the importance of knowledge
4. Emphasizes direct contact with the real world
5. Is comprehensive and reveals the futility of "covering the material"
6. Prefers active to passive

For the full text of Brady's criteria, go to http://ddi.digital.net/~mbrady/survey.htm

If your school is moving toward being digital, with many of your students' assignments relying on digital technology for preparation, participation, and feedback, then new ways of assessment will be in order.

Some of the methods being used include portfolios, summary reports, guidelines, checklists, rubrics, and observations. It is with observation that I made many of my assessments as students were working on projects, and it was with rubrics that I was able to evaluate their final output.

Dialogues about alternative forms of assessment can be found online, and it's imperative that your staff become part of those dialogues.

Keep in mind, too, that how we assess students comes after we've decided what we're assessing. This means rethinking the curriculum. According to Marion Brady, "We still have a curriculum which tells us nothing about the relative importance of various kinds of knowledge." Brady goes on to state, "Given the sorry state of education, it's surely time to move the curriculum in a different, logically defensible direction. Behind the soft-focus memories of how much better it was when we were young, behind the never-ending administrative mixing and matching of the same old stuff, behind the view that everything will be OK when everybody has a PC and it's plugged into the Ultimate Data Base, lies the assumption that the disciplines are what educating is all about. That assumption is moving us steadily toward educational bankruptcy. If we don't dump it, and dump it soon, we're our of business." (http://ddi.digital.net/~mbrady/repackag.htm)

One more thought on this subject comes from Dr. Jamie McKenzie (http://www.fromnowon.org/), who states, "While schooling in the 19th and 20th centuries was primarily about students mastering processed information — the core curriculum — it is likely that schooling and learning during the next century will be characterized by far more prospecting — the purposeful, skilled, but somewhat haphazard search for insight and truth across a complicated information landscape."

FOR MORE ON ASSESSMENT

```
http://www.fromnowon.org/
http://www.ncrel.org/sdrs/areas/issues/methods/assment/
http://www.cua.edu/www/eric_ae/
http://www.asu.edu/aff/aera/home.html
http://www.eduplace.com/rdg/res/litass/index.html
http://www.research.apple.com/go/acot/full/acotRpt07full.html
```

RUBRICS FOR ASSESSMENT

```
http://www.npes.nn.k12.va.us/public/techrub.html#4-5
```

EVALUATION RUBRICS FOR WEB SITES

```
http://www.siec.k12.in.us/~west/online/eval.htm
```

BLUE WEB'N WEB SITE EVALUATION

```
http://www.kn.pacbell.com/wired/bluewebn/rubric.html
```

ELECTRONIC PORTFOLIOS

```
http://www.essdack.org/port/index.html
```

WEB PAGE EVALUATION RUBRIC

```
http://fs04.ael5.ocps.k12.fl.us/tips/hs/Rubrics/HS_General_Rubrics.htm
```

CREATING RUBRICS

```
http://mailer.fsu.edu/~jflake/rubrics.html
```

RUBRICS AND CHECKLISTS

```
http://www.cyber.crwash.k12.ia.us/compcomp/templates/Assessments.html
```

MANKATO INTERNET SKILLS RUBRIC

```
http://www.isd77.k12.mn.us/resources/dougwri/internet.rub.html
```

BUILDING RUBRICS

```
http://www.sover.net/~mttop/arts/rubrics.html
```

WRITING RUBRICS FOR ONLINE PORTFOLIOS
    http://204.98.1.1/dist_ed/eng/rubrics.html

RUBRICS
    http://www.ebe.on.ca/DEPART/RESEAR/RUBRIC.HTM

ASSESSMENT RUBRICS
    http://129.7.160.115/COURSE/INST_5931A/Rubric.html#Class

INTO THE CLASSROOM

A decade ago, I was teaching computer literacy in a room 35 feet long and no more than 15 feet wide. At one end, I had one lone Apple IIE, with a 13-inch green monitor. It was this machine I used to explain and demonstrate, to my 40 kids, those tools and concepts they would practice in the lab the next day when they and their partners were in front of their Apple IIE.

I know that as I demonstrated, I lost a few kids at the back of the room, so I moved them around and learned to quickly restate the new concepts at the beginning of lab time. I also know that many of you are still using that one lone computer. I just hope it's Internet capable.

What can you do when one shiny new Internet-ready computer gets placed in your classroom? Let's assume you have only one with a colorful 13-inch monitor just like you have at home. What do you do to bring the Net experience to all your kids?

Bring your kids as close as possible to your monitor. Rearrange your room if necessary. Locate Web pages with graphics that can be seen from a distance. Read text you can see or print class sets of pages you need.

For example, if I were doing the Wizard of Oz lesson, I would look for sites with text I can read off the screen and additional text to print. Graphics will add to seeing the people and places in both the story and the American Midwest. I would evaluate each site for classroom use with my computer setup in mind.

Tools to teach:

- The basic tools of your browser.
- How and where to type in a URL.
- How and what to bookmark (branch out later into folders).

- How to search by keyword and demonstrate what each major engine gives you as feedback. Discuss which tools seem to work best for your class needs and bookmark them.
- How to scan sites for the information you need — teaches the kids to focus on the task at hand. Even if the site was terrific and had lots of graphics, that didn't mean it helped us in our search.
- Create projects that use the Net as just one more resource. Gather up additional materials: CD-ROMS, encyclopedias, almanacs, *National Geographics*, magazines (I have some from the 1920s through the 1950s that I've used since the 1970s, when I bought them.) Set some kids to searching through alternative materials while others are on the Net.
- Use sites to improve skills. There are tests online, quizzes, tutorials, simulations, practice sites, etc. Find the ones that the whole class can view or print what you need.
- Evaluate sites as you use them so the kids see what works and what doesn't. When they are ready to make their own pages, this will help guide them.
- Create your class home page offline if necessary. Then post it when possible, or, if necessary, one of your kids will post it. My first page for my classes was posted by one of my students using his home connection.
- Use e-mail with your kids and encourage them to e-mail experts, each other, you. Respond to surveys, get a pen pal, ask for homework help, etc. Have your kids think about, prepare in advance, and show you appropriate communications, then e-mail for them.

One Easy Way to Start

Here's a way to build vocabulary and writing skills and to add to their frame of reference.

When we were studying Greek mythology and, in conjunction, learning more about the setting, Greece, I provided my kids with sentences like these:

The ship is on the shore.

The woman wore a garment.

The man worked with tools.

They did the following:

For sentence #1:

1. Search for information and pictures about Greek ships.
2. Search for pictures and descriptions of Greek shores.
3. Rewrite the sentence with appropriate embellishments.
   Sample from kids: The wooden ship was on the sandy shore.
   Could be better, I thought.
4. Be more descriptive. Use your thesaurus. I still can't picture that Greek wooden ship, and did that sandy shore have palm trees nearby, towering pines, or rocks?
5. Review and add to your visual frame of reference, online or off.
6. Rewrite.

Next sample from kids: The wooden galleon landed safely on the white sandy beach below a ledge of rocks.

Getting better, and now I offered extra credit for more refinements. Describe the ship a bit more. Try to describe what made it distinctive — and while you're at it, what kind of rocks are they? Craggy, towering?

Sentences 2 and 3 were approached in the same manner. I gave different kids, different sentences to broaden our collective frame of reference.

Time online:

With prepared bookmarks — 1 hour

Without prepared bookmarks — 2 to 3 hours

Other times, I asked for specific parts of speech to be used in the embellishment. Students also learned about overembellishment with some samples I provided.

You can easily use the Net to find information that helps set the scene or prepare kids for new lessons, new concepts. We spent 2 hours collectively researching and reading about Julius Caesar and his Rome before we read the play. We also learned more about Cassius and Brutus, the times they lived in, their treatment of women, etc.

Our research taught us more about the man than our text provided, and this information made it possible for the kids to place Caesar in our China Dam Lesson.

Start out simply, embellishing your curriculum and your vocabulary, and grow from there.

Online Discussion Groups

Once all my students had obtained e-mail accounts, I found out just how much they enjoyed communicating. I realized early on that answering e-mail from each of them on any given discussion topic, was not feasible. But I hated to limit their enthusiasm for discussion and discuss they did. They talked to me about assignments and class topics. They talked to each other about social things as well as class issues. They talked and talked until the amount of e-mail became overwhelming. E-mail, for these kids, became their favorite way to communicate, and it became very conversational. It also became too much to handle.

In order to manage 125 kids and their discussions, I chose to try online discussion groups. I started by selecting group leaders — those with Internet access at home or with more connect time at school. I looked for kids with good typing skills to help with the time management problem, but I also selected some kids to lead who I felt would be responsive to the leadership position. In all cases, all the group leaders rose to the occasion.

For the first set of discussions dealing with the novel *Herland*, I placed kids with leaders in their own class period. I started the conversation by e-mailing a topic for discussion to the group leaders who, in turn, e-mailed the topic to their group members.

Over the next two days, the students e-mailed their thoughts to their leaders, who compiled the responses and e-mailed me with a general consensus. I then summarized the responses and brought the information to the classes in the old-fashioned way — out loud. From there, we refined our ideas, added more thoughts to be discussed, and continued our conversation.

Before we started discussion groups, many students were reluctant to offer their observations or opinions in a class discussion setting. Once they'd been given the chance to speak out less publicly, by e-mail, classroom discussions were much more lively. They were less reticent to answer if called on, and some were more eager to offer their thoughts. They became brave.

Eventually, kids e-mailed me with homework, classwork, ideas, Web sites, jokes, thoughts on our reading, questions, or reading suggestions. They e-mailed each other to offer help, to carry on class discussions, and to be social. E-mail, after a short time, became just another tool we used to communicate and help each other, and it became indispensable for all of us.

We continued using e-mail and discussion groups as the year progressed. After discussing their way electronically through two novels, the kids began to see what we would focus on, needed less input from me to guide them, and became much more vocal in class. They also carried on rousing discussions electronically, like the time Steve B. threw out the thought that Hazel, a rabbit character in *Watership Down*, just might not be a manly rabbit and a fit leader. Thoughts on that ranged from "You don't have to be manly to lead (haven't you read *Herland*?" to "What's in a name?"

E-mail got them started conversing, freed them from embarrassment, and empowered them in a way no regular class discussion ever had.

A word about chat rooms: We set up, on our Web site, a chat room, but never found time to use it. We wanted to make sure the chatting was supervised, and the logistics of getting everyone online at the same time was just not realistic.

A word about IRC (Internet Relay Chat): We also set this up on our computers but, as with the chat room, we found it a less effective way for all of us to talk together.

I liked using e-mail as opposed to other electronic discussion methods because it gave the kids time to think and a way to practice writing well-phrased communications, and it didn't penalize those with weaker typing skills.

Using e-mail can be time-consuming but, on balance, the benefits were worth it.

So get your students, classroom, and school connected, and enjoy the adventure.

ABOUT THE CD-ROM

A ll of the information on how to access the files and folders contained on the CD are included here. Please read it before using the CD and refer to it if you have questions. A copy is also located in the back of the book.

DESCRIPTION OF CD

The CD contains the following Folders:

Educating with the Internet

This folder contains a folder CD CONTENT. Within this folder are a Directory of Sites by Category, Additional Lesson Plans, and Additional Teacher Resources for the Internet.

To use the contents of these folders, simply click on the folder you would like to access and then select the items you would like to use. Please note that the URLs are highlighted in blue. If you are online, you can open these folders and directly link to the URL you select. But in order for the link to work, you must be online.

You may use these lessons in your courses or as handouts to your students.

Microsoft Internet Explorer Version 4.0

This folder contains Microsoft's Internet Explorer 4.0. If you don't already have a browser or if you would like to add this one, simply click on the Internet Explorer 4.0 folder and click on the IE4SETUP.EXE file or IE4SETUP. The installation will be automatic. If any conflicts arise with the setup, this will be a system issue that needs to be addressed to Microsoft. We are including Internet Explorer as a courtesy and cannot provide technical support for any installation or setup issues. You may also try to download it from their website if you are unable to install this version (www.microsoft.com).

Internet Glossary

This glossary has been included for your reference and convenience. It is an excellent resource for anyone new to the Internet, or if you need to look up a new technology term you are encountering for the first time. The file is in HTML format, which means you must have a browser resident on your computer (Internet Explorer 4.0 or Netscape Navigator). If you have a browser resident, simply click on the folder and select the letter or word you would like to look up. The file will automatically open your browser and an in-depth definition will be provided. This glossary is from THE INTERNET TRAINING CD-ROM, copyright 1998 Charles River Media.

WatchDog DEMO

This folder includes a 10 Day trial demo of an innovative monitoring tool that allows teachers or parents to monitor the activity of their students or child. This demo is only available for Windows 95/98 machines currently.

Unlike blocking devices, which must be updated regularly and cannot block all questionable information on the Internet, this program monitors the activity on the computer — on or off the Internet. By capturing screen shots, and logging applications accessed, teachers or parents can review the activity log for the computer. No blocking or continual updating is required.

To install and use the demo, select the WatchDog Folder, then select INSTALL folder, and click on the Install Icon. The program will take you step-by-step through the setup. If you have difficulty with the installation or with using the program, please refer to the Manual included in the WatchDog folder.

If you have difficulty installing this version, you may also access at www.charlesriver.com. Click on the Networking/Internet Boathouse and go to the Internet WatchDog product. Select the demo icon and all the necessary files and information will be downloaded.

System Requirements for this CD include the following:

- PC with Windows 95 or higher
- Macintosh with System 7.5 or higher
- A Browser (Internet Explorer 4.0 included on the CD or Netscape Navigator preferred).

INDEX

Note: All capitalized terms refer to Internet links mentioned in the text.